A

BOOK

The Philip E. Lilienthal imprint
honors special books
in commemoration of a man whose work
at the University of California Press
from 1954 to 1979
was marked by dedication to young authors
and to high standards in the field of Asian Studies.
Friends, family, authors, and foundations have together
endowed the Lilienthal Fund, which enables the Press
to publish under this imprint selected books
in a way that reflects the taste and judgment
of a great and beloved editor.

The costs of publishing this book have been defrayed in part by the Hiromi Arisawa Memorial Awards from the Books on Japan Fund. The awards are financed by The Japan Foundation from generous donations contributed by Japanese individuals and companies.

Japan in Print

ASIA: LOCAL STUDIES/GLOBAL THEMES

Jeffrey N. Wasserstrom, Kären Wigen, and Hue-Tam Ho Tai, Editors

Japan in Print

INFORMATION AND NATION
IN THE EARLY MODERN PERIOD

Mary Elizabeth Berry

UNIVERSITY OF CALIFORNIA PRESS
BERKELEY   LOS ANGELES   LONDON

University of California Press, one of the most distinguished university presses in the United States, enriches
lives around the world by advancing scholarship in the humanities, social sciences, and natural sciences. Its activities
are supported by the UC Press Foundation and by philan-
thropic contributions from individuals and institutions.
For more information, visit www.ucpress.edu.

University of California Press
Berkeley and Los Angeles, California

University of California Press, Ltd.
London, England

First paperback printing 2007
© 2006 by The Regents of the University of California

Library of Congress Cataloging-in-Publication Data

Berry, Mary Elizabeth, 1947–
   Japan in print : information and nation in the early
modern period / Mary Elizabeth Berry.
      p.   cm. — (Asia—local studies/global themes ; 12)
   Includes bibliographical references and index.
   ISBN 978-0-520-25417-6 (pbk : alk.)
   1. Printing—Japan—History—17th century.   I. Title.
II. Series.
   Z186.J3B47 2006
   686.2′0952′0909032—dc22

                                        2005016916

Manufactured in the United States of America

15   14   13   12   11   10   09   08   07
10   9   8   7   6   5   4   3   2   1

Again, and ever, for Anne and Kate

CONTENTS

FIGURES

ACKNOWLEDGMENTS

Elizabeth Huff came to Berkeley as founding curator and head of the East Asian Library in 1947, the year I was born. Then a recent Harvard Ph.D. in Chinese literature, she had spent most of the previous seven years in China, including thirty months of internment by the Japanese army in Shantung. Once in Berkeley, Miss Huff (as everyone remembers her) undertook a visionary plan of development that would double and then redouble the library's East Asian holdings by 1950. Her boldest decision, approved that year during extraordinary summertime consultations between President Robert Gordon Sproul and the Regents of the University of California, was to purchase 100,000 items offered by the Mitsui Bunko in Tokyo. Among those items were 736 sheet maps and almost 5,000 book titles (in over 16,000 volumes) that were printed in Japan during the Tokugawa period (1600–1868). This collection of early Japanese printed material is the largest outside Japan.[1] It forms the foundation of this book, just one of the many legacies of a woman I never met but routinely visit in spirit.

The second muse of this book is Donald Howard Shively, who came to Berkeley first in 1950 as an assistant professor of Oriental Languages and later in 1983 (after appointments at Stanford and Harvard) as head of the East Asian Library and professor of Oriental Languages (now East Asian Languages and Cultures). The return followed our marriage and the birth of our daughter, Anne. Don brought new life to the Mitsui collection, languishing in storage and inventoried mainly in manuscript notebooks, by initiating projects to conserve and provide full bibliographic records for both the maps and the books. Funded between 1985 and 1987 by the Department of Education and the National Endowment for the Humanities, the projects relied on exceptional contributions from the East Asian Library staff (led by Hisayuki Ishimatsu), the Conservation Department of the University of California Library (led by Barclay Ogden), and expert consultants from Japan (including Oka Masahiko, Yamori Kazuhiko, Kodama Fumiko, and Tozawa Ikuko).[2] Their work has lasting importance for scholars around the world. It had immediate impact at Berkeley, where many of us gathered for the first time to look widely at the Mitsui collection and chat with our Japanese colleagues about its many treasures— particularly during seminars concerning the maps that Don organized for faculty and students in 1986.

Professor Yamori, one of Japan's most eminent cartographic historians and the third muse of this book, presided over a number of our meetings. I find in my notes the dozens of canny remarks and fruitful leads that guided my own research. I find at the front of my memory an image of Professor Yamori flipping unceremoniously through perhaps thirty huge maps heaped on our seminar table. Not much reverence there. And certainly no sense that the maps were important because rare. He had seen most of them in many impressions and countless collections throughout Japan. So with practiced gestures he would not have thought to explain in words, Professor Yamori transformed the maps for me from forbiddingly precious goods into exhilaratingly mundane expressions of a print- and information-rich world. I was off.

Over succeeding years, as I planned a monograph on early modern cartography, many scholars helped me think about maps as complex cultural documents. I am especially indebted to Professors Kuroda Hideo and Sugimoto Fumiko of the Historiographical Institute at Tokyo University, whose work set a standard for my own. Their commitment to collaborative research led us to a three-year project, joined by an international team of colleagues and funded by Japan's Ministry of Education, which resulted in *Chizu to ezu no seiji bunka-shi* (University of Tokyo Press, 2001). I also received generous advice from Professors Henry Smith, Ronald Toby, Ugawa Kaoru, David Woodward, and Yoshida Toshihiro. For wonderful assistance during my frequent visits to the Map Room of the National Diet Library, I owe great gratitude to Ms. Suzuki Junko and Ms. Tozawa Ikuko.

The shift in my research from maps to the many related texts I came to call the "library of public information" was tentative at first; for the sheer scale of the material warned me against an enterprise too reckless for one lifetime. Still, my project expanded inexorably through conversations with the peerless Fujiki Hisashi and a year of reading with Tsuji Mayumi (then one of Professor Fujiki's graduate students at Rikkyō University). A masterful young historian who grasped the dimensions of this book before I did, Mayumi opened my path with unerring bibliographical prodding. I kept to it because of Thomas C. Smith and Marcia Yonemoto. Tom immediately saw the connections between my sources and many of his own (particularly agrarian manuals). And he made me work them out during the Athenian walks and Spartan lunches (always from the salad bar of the Berkeley Faculty Club) that continued until his final illness. Marcia, while completing the dissertation that became the splendid *Mapping Early Modern Japan* (University of California Press, 2003), was more mentor than student in a dialogue stretching limitlessly before us.

Once I began drafting and lecturing on a manuscript I considered well along, numerous colleagues stalled my progress. For marvelous remarks I was smart enough to heed but not often enough to rise to, I thank Susanna Barrows, James Bartholomew, Shmuel Eisenstadt, Anthony Grafton, Susan Hanley, Mack Horton, Lynn Hunt, Edward Kamens, William Kelly, Victor Lieberman, Kate Nakai, Peter Nosco, Geoffrey Parker, Peter Sahlins, John Treat, and Kozo Yamamura. Sheldon Garon should share the credit or blame for the concluding chapter, which emerged fitfully from a question he asked at Princeton about the differences between early modern and modern society. My sights had been trained on the revolution in knowledge that separated early modernity from medieval antecedents. Shel made me leap forward.

Anne Walthall and Kären Wigen improved this book mightily with the comments they offered while reading the manuscript for the University of California Press. Janice Kanemitsu, dauntless in research and fastidious in detail, provided invaluable assistance with notes and the bibliography. She also compiled the index. I received constant and openhearted help at Berkeley's East Asian Library from Hisayuki Ishimatsu, Bruce Williams, Tomoko Haneda, and the current director, Peter Zhou. Kathryn Kowalewski did a brilliant job digitizing most of the illustrations. The digitized images of the Mitsui maps come from the magnificent web site of David Rumsey, Cartography Associates (davidrumsey.com/japan). For generous support of my research, I am grateful to the Japan Foundation, the Social Science Research Council, the Office of the President of the University of California, the Center for Japanese Studies at the University of California, Berkeley, and Stanford University. For uncommonly fine copyediting, I am grateful to Peter Dreyer.

Don's inspiration runs throughout my life and work. Perfect joy streams from our daughters Anne and Kate.

ONE

A Traveling Clerk Goes
to the Bookstores

SUPPOSE YOU LIVED in Kyoto about three hundred years ago and were
facing your first trip to Edo, the Tokugawa shogun's capital, some five hundred kilometers away. To flesh out this fantasy, let's make you a senior clerk
in a firm that retails silk cloth. You are being sent on a temporary assignment from the main shop in Kyoto to a branch in Edo.

You might prepare for your journey, as novices have always prepared in
the past, by canvassing seasoned travelers and then trusting to advice along
the way. If fortunate and well connected, you might also scan travel diaries
in manuscript. But because you live around 1700, you have a further
choice—one barely available to your grandparents. You can prepare for
your journey by seriously hitting printed books. Since 1640 or so, remarkable numbers of commercially published texts have been converting private knowledge into public information. The mysteries of the road, and
many others besides, have been unlocked for both solitary readers and the
radiating circles of relations around them. You are one of the readers and,
for our purposes, quite a methodical and practiced one. To give you a good
budget for buying and borrowing material, which can be costly, we'll make
you the heir to that silk shop.

Being something of a bibliophile, you begin your research by consulting
recent booksellers' catalogues, rough equivalents of *Books in Print*, which
have been appearing in major cities since at least 1659. *Kōeki shojaku
mokuroku* (A Catalogue of Publications for Public Utility), published by a
consortium of Kyoto firms in 1692, contains entries on over 7,000 current
titles divided into 46 main categories (and numerous subcategories).[1] You
winnow leads from some obvious sections ("Geography," "Travel," "Famous Places") and from a few less obvious ones as well ("Erotica," "Military Affairs"), hoping to come across additional items—ephemera, pri-
vately printed matter, texts published outside Kyoto that may not have
made it into the catalogue—as you browse the shops. There are over 100 of

Fig. 1. "Bookseller," from *Jinrin kinmōzui* (An Illustrated Encyclopedia of Humanity, 1690). National Diet Library, Tokyo.

them. Some are small printing houses stocking their own titles. Others retail texts on specialized subjects such as Chinese learning or poetry or medicine or Zen Buddhism. Yet others, and the ones you frequent, distribute disparate material from disparate firms in both Kyoto and more distant publishing centers, principally Edo and Osaka. There you will gather a generous selection of texts, borrowing many of them for fixed but renewable terms at a fraction of the list prices.[2]

To orient yourself geographically, you start with maps. Although your choice is substantial, in both sheet and atlas form, you will probably settle on a current edition of Ishikawa Ryūsen's *Nihon kaisan chōrikuzu* (Map of the Seas, Mountains, and Lands of Japan)—a map so legible and packed with information that it has been revised and reissued annually since its first publication in 1689.[3] It charts the nation's provinces and castle towns, land and water routes, famous sites and scenic places. It labels every ferry crossing and every post station along the major highways, listing the distances between stops in an index. Thick with social and political geography, it also identifies all regional lords, or daimyo, with notes on the gross

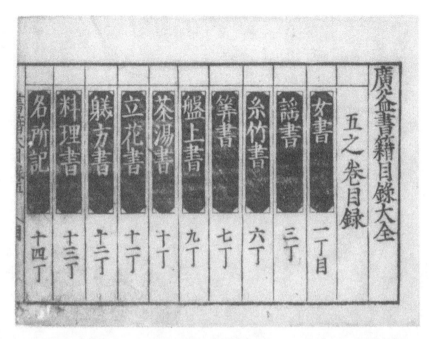

FIG. 2. *Kōeki shojaku mokuroku taizen* (A Catalogue of Publications for Public Utility, 1692), partial table of contents for fascicle 5, listing the following subject categories (and their beginning page numbers): women, noh chanting, musical instruments, calculation, board games, tea ceremony, flower arrangement, etiquette, cooking, and accounts of famous places. Courtesy of the East Asian Library, University of California, Berkeley.

productivity of their domains. The map is a large one (81 × 171 cm), made by pasting together numerous individual sheets and folding them for convenience. In a print market tailored to most imaginable needs, you could certainly find smaller, handier maps—single-sheet or accordion-pleated editions, for example, tuckable into a kimono sleeve. But the big maps attract you, and most consumers, because they offer space for exploding detail and many indexes. They also offer space itself, mimicking in their size the expanse of real terrain. You will spread out Ryūsen's map on the floor and crawl over and around it to capture the relationship between cartographic representation and the physical landscape. I suspect you may change your socks and walk across the map as well, perhaps pacing the main highways from Kyoto to Edo.[4] Reading it presents no particular problems. Your school primers (including *Nihon ōrai* [Japan Basics], published in 1688) have taught you the basic nomenclature, cultural land-

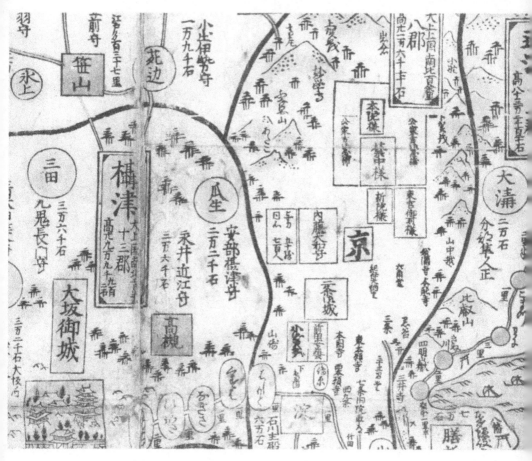

FIG. 3. Ishikawa Ryūsen, *Nihon kaisan chōrikuzu* (Map of the Seas, Mountains, and Lands of Japan, 1694), detail centered on Kyoto and showing the provinces of Ōmi, Yamashiro, and Settsu. Woodblock, 81 × 171 cm. Courtesy of the East Asian Library, University of California, Berkeley.

marks, and economic features of the national scene.[5] And to help with obscure names, you keep to hand both family encyclopedias and dictionaries.

Your geographical knowledge refreshed, but your route undecided, you turn next to *Shokoku annai tabi suzume* (The Traveling Sparrow's Guide to the Provinces, first published in seven fascicles in 1687).[6] A compendium of itineraries issued individually in previous years, the Sparrow takes you along the country's principal highways, noting not only post stations and distances but travel times, road conditions, fees for porters and pack horses, licensed accommodations, seasonal pleasures, and notable touring sites. It also moves outside the highway system to cover the secondary roads and paths that connect scores of popular destinations. Thus you will find itineraries not only from Kyoto to Edo (two principal routes with hints on detours and byways), but from Kyoto to Mount Kōya, the Arima hot springs, Yoshino, and other fabled locales. Finally, the Sparrow moves beyond roadways to describe sea routes. If you hanker for a sail, the Sparrow will guide you by land to the Inland Sea and then by water to Edo Bay.

Suppose, though, that comparison of the Sparrow's data persuades you to choose the fastest and best-maintained land course from Kyoto to Edo, the Tōkaidō, or Eastern Sea Highway. At this point, you may want a convincing visual image of the impending journey. So spend some time with *Tōkaidō bunken ezu* (The Pictorial Survey of the Tōkaidō, published in five fascicles in 1690).[7] Instead of individual pages, each fascicle consists of a long scroll of paper, formed of separate sheets pasted end to end, that folds every 12 centimeters to make an accordion-style book. Together the fascicles picture the mighty sweep of the Tōkaidō on a scale of 1:12,000, reproducing the 486 kilometers between Edo and Kyoto in just over 40 meters of drawing.

The Pictorial Survey, drafted by the cartographer Ochikochi Dōin and illustrated by the painter Hishikawa Moronobu, resembles a photographic record. It portrays the wide road (mostly about 5.5 meters across) packed with sand or stone, the abutting gutters and streams, the fifty-three post stations and their buildings, the transport and lodging facilities available along the way, the bridges and fords and ferries, the shade trees and Buddhist statues standing like sentries, the sanctuaries and villages located in the distance. Accurately depicting bends in the highway, the Survey also enters every distance marker (at intervals of one *ri*, or about four kilometers), every stone guidepost at the intersections, and every barrier where officials monitor travelers and check their papers. The cartographer adds compass points from span to span, indicating the gently changing orientations of a road that curves where a scroll cannot.

Juxtaposed on this businesslike log of the highway are myriad vignettes that invite all viewers "from the loftiest nobles to the lowliest women and children to see themselves as if in a brilliant mirror" (as the preface puts it). Hishikawa Moronobu's illustrations provide an ethnography in motion, depicting long military processions, travelers of all ages and stations, farmers and fishers at work, vendors and peddlers of tea and tobacco and souvenirs, sightseers exploring famous sites and viewing Mount Fuji from the optimal vantage points. Travel is thus transformed in the Survey from

Fig. 4. Ochikochi Dōin and Hishikawa Moronobu, *Tōkaidō bunken ezu* (Pictorial Survey of the Tōkaidō, 1690), opening page of fascicle 3, "From Fuchū to Yoshida," showing the post station and castle town of Fuchū and listing castle officials, transporters, and portage fees. National Diet Library, Tokyo.

tough and unpredictable work into a seeming occasion for pleasure and discovery, casual companionship and shopping for novelties.

Now that you know the way and what to expect, you are ready for background on the places you will pass. Again, you have some basic proficiency in historical and social geography, not only from school primers but the family encyclopedias (such as *Banmin chōhōki* [Everybody's Treasury], published in two fascicles in 1692) that assemble knowledge about past and present rulers, calendars and chronologies, the distribution of local lords, and the like.[8] But for denser accounts, you turn to a national gazetteer. You choose a recent one, *Kokka man'yōki* (The Ten-Thousand Leaf Record of the Provincial Flowers, published in 1697 in 21 fascicles and over 2,000 pages), which decants each of the provinces into conventional categories.[9] You concentrate on the fifteen provinces along the Tōkaidō, reencountering some material familiar from the Sparrow (the numbers of districts, geographical features, annual productivity totals, chief crops and manufactures, the names of castle holders, principal sanctuaries and famous places). Yet you also find capsule histories of each of the provinces, their ruling families, and their many monuments—not only temples and shrines but castle ruins, old battlegrounds, graves, and stone stellae. Entries include poems inspired by various sites, typically from classical and medieval anthologies, to improve your literary education. The Ten-Thousand Leaf Record contains a fair amount of administrative detail as well. Beyond providing the names and genealogical tables of daimyo, this gazetteer identifies an unusual number of local officeholders: domainal elders, regional intendants, municipal magistrates, and heads of the military guard.

If you plan to linger on the way for pleasure, spending perhaps twenty days on a trip normally requiring about twelve (unless the Ōi and Abe Rivers flood, stranding you indefinitely), you might use the Ten-Thousand Leaf Record for sightseeing information. But a better bet is a specialized guide to a single site or the sequential attractions on your route. *Tōkaidō meishoki* (An Account of Famous Places of the Tōkaidō, published in 1661 in six fascicles), a travelogue covering the Eastern Sea Highway, pairs a worldly priest with an insouciant commoner, whose adventures and dialogues construct a narrative of the road.[10] Between the theaters and brothels of Edo (where they start out) and the fashionable streets of Kyoto (where they end up), the companions barrel through dozens of noteworthy sites—all apparently open to the curious—while exchanging remarks on the lore and landmarks of temples, the histories of martial families and legendary men, the properties of the better hot springs. All such material is offered as ready information for the traveler rather than privileged insider learning.

Finally ready to concentrate on Edo itself, you might stagger under the weight of available intelligence were you not familiar with the even more voluminous, and prototypical, texts concerning Kyoto. Again, you start with maps. And, again, you have an enormous choice, since over 200 different maps of the military capital have been printed since the early part of the century, including the Great Map of Edo, a set of five sectional maps based on an exhaustive survey by the Tokugawa shogunate (first published section by section between 1670 and 1673). But you prefer a version by Ishikawa Ryūsen, which is less exact but more legible and vivid in detail.[11] It measures 100 by 160 centimeters. Like most of its counterparts, this map centers on the Tokugawa castle, fastidiously depicts the moats, canals, and rivers that thread the city, and extends to the bay on the east and the agrarian outreaches at the other cardinal points. It identifies all bridges and embankments and most fields for martial sport. It tracks every street (and most alleys), labeling every ward. It also locates dozens of temples and shrines, scores of warehouses, and hundreds of military mansions (with prodigious details about their occupants). To clarify social topography, Ryūsen's map uses family crests and regalia to mark daimyo residences, color-coding to distinguish the commoner and religious zones. The pleasure quarters are labeled too, if inconspicuously.

You can find a verbal equivalent of the map in another Sparrow—the Edo Sparrow, this time (*Edo suzume,* published in twelve fascicles in 1677).[12] Principally a heroic street index, it moves through the city section by section, noting the sites that front each step of the way. If you fail to keep count yourself, the author concludes with assurances that he has covered "over 520 mansions of great lords, 2,870 lesser military mansions, 850 temples, 120 shrines, 900 neighborhoods, and 2,880 *chō* of distance [roughly 300 kilometers]."

Classification is a contagion, you discover, as you turn to an urban directory, *Edo kanoko* (The Dappled Fabric of Edo, published in six fascicles in 1687 and regularly revised thereafter).[13] This encyclopedic source offers you many versions of many Edos as it organizes and reorganizes the city in a kaleidoscope of patterns. You will probably buy rather than borrow the Dappled Fabric, since its punishing catalogues defy any summary consultation, and you will probably select the celebrated edition of 1690. This directory includes a list in 26 categories of over 300 physical features (natural and manmade); the annual ritual calendars of both the commoners and the military houses; a list in 22 categories of almost 400 famous tea objects, with the names of owners; a list in 10 categories of major Buddhist and Shinto icons; a list of over 60 shrines with notes on history, administration, and income; a list of over 100 temples, organized by sect, with notes on history, administration, and income; a street-by-street survey of Edo with selective inventories of shops; a guide to the principal entertainment

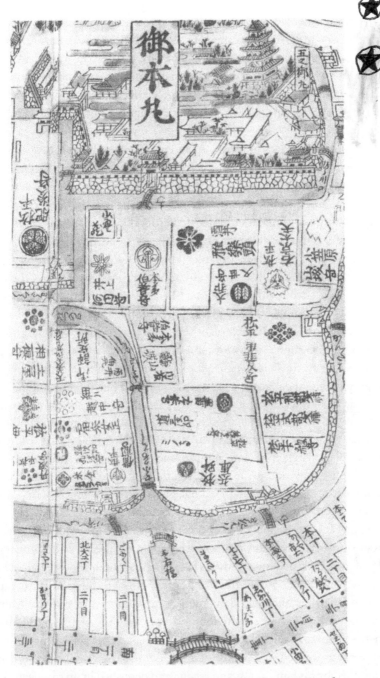

FIG. 5. Ishikawa Ryūsen, *Bundo Edo ōezu* (Great Survey Map of Edo, 1710), detail featuring Edo castle and the Bridge of Japan. Daimyo residences are marked by family names, titles, and crests. Commoner neighborhoods appear as white space. Woodblock, 100 × 160 cm. Courtesy of the East Asian Library, University of California, Berkeley.

quarters; a list of famous vistas; a list in 43 categories of roughly 300 prominent artists, teachers, and providers of services (doctors of various specialties, poets of different schools, removers of ear wax), most with addresses;
a list in 193 categories of almost 700 prominent craftspeople and merchants (the gold and silver guildsmen, textile dealers, incense blenders,
handlers of Buddhist goods), most with addresses; and a list of 21 licensed
wholesale firms.

Awesome in its lists but sparing in exposition, the Dappled Fabric leaves
you ready for fuller accounts of the Edo scene. Narrative tour guides help
close the breach. You have something of a choice, since the earliest dates
from 1621 and the most recent from 1694. The habit of recycling a substantial amount of old material under new titles may reduce the appeal of the
later work, but it is still best to stick with a current text, since sheer coverage improves. Edo's "places of fame," roughly a dozen according to a guide
of 1621, numbered 46 by 1643, 80 by 1662, and 100 by 1687. (By the nineteenth century they would total 1,043.)[14] The inflation results not so much
from new building as from greater inclusion: once-parochial sites have
been converted into public places in response to both competition between metropolitan centers for fame-studded landscapes and changing attitudes toward the landscape itself. A wide common gaze is invading, and
appropriating, the space of a putatively common history. Famous places do
include scenes of beauty and pleasure. But you will find most of them defined by notable pasts that seemingly bind countrymen together. The sort
of friendly raconteurs who led you along the Tōkaidō reappear in the Edo
guides to exchange more lore about miracles and battles, priests and generals, elite customs and great events. And they deliver their stories with the
same sort of casual knowingness that presumes popular access to a shared
historyscape.[15] NO

Game for more? Specialized books of all kinds beckon, if only you can
figure out what you want to know. Perhaps your interest in administrative
detail has been whetted rather than sated by ubiquitous references to
daimyo and their castles. You are headed, after all, for a political capital
where official arcana are a daily diet. So refer to a Mirror of the Military
Houses, or full personnel roster of the Tokugawa shogunate (first published
in 1643 and continually revised thereafter by competitive firms).[16] These
rosters start with current lists of all daimyo lords, roughly 250 of them, each
identified by his family crest and regalia and described in up to 44 categories
(family and personal name, courtly rank and title, age, location and gross
productivity of the local domain, addresses of all residences in Edo, names
of heirs and other family members and major retainers . . .). The rosters

also continue, if you buy an amplified edition, with lists of the principal of-ficeholders in the Tokugawa shogunate—almost two thousand of them, serving in Edo as well as the provincial centers of shogunal authority, all lined up under as many as 231 job titles. These entries, too, are long. They typically include (among other items) each official's name, address, stipend, crest, deputies, tenure in office, and previous appointments.

The Military Mirrors will probably seem familiar to you, perhaps be-cause you have seen equivalent treatments of the courtly aristocracy in var-ious family encyclopedias, gazetteers, and guides to Kyoto. The emperor and his household, the 200-some noble families, the princely abbots and abbesses—all appear in rosters that, like the Military Mirrors, specify name, rank, title, crest, income, residence, and major deputies.[17] But you are just as likely to recognize the style of the Mirrors because you have seen equivalent treatments of the demimonde.

Circulating since the 1650s, and now numbering in the hundreds, ros-ters of prostitutes and actors have long treated the universe of play as the Mirrors treat the universe of power. Texts like *Yoshiwara hito tabane* (A Bundle of Personages from the Yoshiwara, published in 1680) list courte-sans with their names, ranks, crests, professional houses, and residences.[18] Most include maps and illustrations as well, and some go so far as to state fees (which appear to parallel military stipends). Similarly, rosters of actors, like the *Yarōmushi* (Rogue Bugs, 1660),[19] note their names, troupes, man-agers, principal roles, and crests. But while mimicking the schemes of honor and identity characteristic of the Military Mirrors, the rosters of the demimonde depart from the model by offering critiques of performance. Love and entertainment are for sale. Best to buy prudently. So you are given appraisals of physical attributes and artistic skills, warned away from women who surrender too soon or actors who rely on bombast. If you are worried about your own performance in the quarters, you can find guides to etiquette that will take you from bath to table to bed. And, indeed, so popular is the coverage of the sex trade that storytellers are appropriating the style of the rosters for comic purposes. The current rage is Ejima Kiseki's *Keisei iro jamisen* (Sex Music), which covers over 1,750 women, in seven principal ranks, who work the great cities.[20]

—

Now you are tired, eager to quit a literature of lists and categories. Your brain swollen with numbers, you're ready for the comfort of fiction, where story will replace inventory. So you turn to the master, Ihara Saikaku. The book you select, *Kōshoku gonin onna* (Five Women Who Chose Love), worries you a bit with its arithmetical title. Still, you are soon distracted by the tale of Oman, a merchant's daughter who is as ravishing as she is rich. She loves Gengobei, who is nearly as ravishing (if somewhat worn) but no longer rich (since he has spent the family fortune on eight years of single-minded sex). Resolute before the obstacles that love requires, Oman manages to lure Gengobei from both the boys he prefers and the clerical vows he professes. Eventually, after some low-life misadventure, Oman brings the rake home. With a marriage in view, her oddly overjoyed parents welcome the prospective groom. And you welcome the end to a good story free of inventory.

But too soon. Closing his tale, Saikaku tells us that Oman's parents hand over to Gengobei

> the various keys of the house—three hundred and eighty-three in all. Then, an auspicious day having been determined, they set about a Storehouse Opening. First they inspected six hundred and fifty chests, each marked "Two Hundred Great Gold Pieces," and eight hundred others, each containing one thousand small gold pieces. The hundred-weight boxes of silver, which they next examined, were mildewed from disuse and a fearful groaning came from those underneath. . . . [C]opper coins lay scattered about like grains of sand. . . .
>
> Proceeding now to the outside storehouse, they found treasures galore: fabrics brought over from China in the olden days were piled to the rafters; next to them precious incense lay stacked like so much firewood; of flawless coral gems, from ninety grains to over one pound in weight, there were one thousand two hundred and thirty-five; there was an endless profusion of granulated shark skin and of the finest willow-green porcelain; all this, together with the Asukawa tea canister and such other precious ware, had been left there pell-mell. . . . Other wonders too were in that storehouse: a mermaid picked in salt, a pail wrought of pure agate. . . . [21]

As vigorously as any author of a gazetteer or urban directory, Saikaku, too, counts and calculates, lists and labels. He delights in things of wonder, and in things made wonderful by their names and variety and plenitude. If he does not unlock every single storehouse, Saikaku pushes toward the exhaustive tour. And if he classifies the goods more casually than not, he works down a rough catalogue of metal currency, bulk storage, and masterpieces. There is no escape for you. You live in a world of numeration and classification. You swoon. You sleep.

TWO

The Library of Public Information

SAIKAKU'S TOUR OF THE STOREHOUSES is a flaming piece of parody.
Loaded with lists and totals and taxonomic tricks, it takes immediate aim
at the bookkeeping culture of the tradespeople who made up the prime
audience for contemporary fiction. More broadly, the tour mimics a contemporary style of knowledge that dominated the sort of texts I assigned
my hypothetical clerk. As gazetteers and the like inventoried local crops
and manufactures, or Buddhist icons and celebrity graves, so Saikaku inventories the heaps of his merchant's stuff. Then he transposes inventory
into hilarity by bumping up numbers (383 keys, 130,000 large gold pieces,
1,235 flawless coral gems), imposing accounting routines on breathtaking
treasures (granulated shark skin, agate pails), and juxtaposing the merely
marvelous (willow green porcelain) with the fabulous (a mermaid pickled
in salt). The comedy responds to the surfeit of texts that organized things
all too relentlessly for readers like my clerk. And it presumes an audience so
sated by catalogues that parody is a tonic.

Such fictional fun was all but inevitable by the time Saikaku published
Oman's tale in 1686. From the beginning of the century, multiplying numbers of investigators had been taking stock of multiplying numbers of subjects. And from the middle of the century, they had been filling the market
with their findings—often enough, in the telegraphic style of the balance
book. The flood began with maps. In one of the most prodigious cartographic projects in the early modern world, surveyors mapped, and repeatedly remapped, the nation, its provinces and transport arteries, its major
cities and famous sites. They turned, too, to charts of power and privilege,
using exhaustive personnel rosters to expose the anatomy of the shogunal
administration and the courtly aristocracy. They went on to produce both
comprehensive dictionaries of work and workers (starting with courtiers,
ending with beggars) and catalogues of individual specialists—merchants,
craftspeople, masters of fine skills (from medicine to music), painters,

priests, actors, and prostitutes. Investigators also ordered the natural world, not only in massive encyclopedias of flora and fauna but in local lists of notable rocks, streams, trees, blossoms, hills, and the like. And with exceptional ardor, they identified thousands of marketable goods created by earth, water, and human fabrication. Much in the manner of early ethnologists, they examined cultural practice in accounts of diet and cookery, ritual and festival calendars, marriage and burial customs, and the distinctive vocabularies of different professions. Many used their observations to provide systematic instruction in both the great metiers, such as agronomy and sericulture, and the genteel avocations—including the arts of poetry, decorative gardening, healing, lovemaking, and spell casting. Because social geography tended to be the subject most compelling to writers and audiences, the market was especially thick with guidebooks, gazetteers, and urban directories that took immense quantities of data and put them in shape. Here the structural imagination of authors, who learned to organize such complex notions as citiness in a newly urbanized world, was as startling as their command of detail.

The ambition of these undertakings was hard to miss, for many of them vaunted their reach with splendid titles and demonstrated it at heroic length. The botanist and ethnologist Hitomi Hitsudai, for example, assembled thirty years of field notes on 492 types of edible flora and fauna in a book he called *Honchō shokkan* (The Culinary Mirror of the Realm).[1] Published in 1697 in twelve fascicles, it takes up over 1,800 pages in modern print (covering everything from animal habitats to cultivation practices, from local diets to local recipes). *Kokka man'yōki* (The Ten-Thousand Leaf Record of the Provincial Flowers), published the same year, exceeds 2,300 pages in the woodblock original.[2] If most texts were considerably shorter, their titles intimate a search for knowledge always big and mirror-bright. So we find The Complete Military Mirror, The Great Mirror of Sex, The Great Map of the Great Japan, The Festivals of the People, and The Compendium of the Famous Products of the Provinces.

But ambition rarely precluded clarity in material so neat that Saikaku found it an easy target. As they sorted out the human and natural worlds, investigators wrote overwhelmingly in a vernacular Japanese studded with both phonetic reading aids and the devices of textual order—tables of contents, headings and subheadings, numerical totals, extensive lists, and copious illustrations. Their work intersected, moreover, with an expanding literature of basic education. Hundreds (eventually thousands) of primers were schooling children in the vocabulary of geography, history, and individual crafts and callings.[3] And for continuing household reference, pictorial dictionaries glossed the nomenclature of employments and products, Buddhist sects and titles, the natural and man-made environments, and much else.[4] In effect, the strikingly detailed, seemingly challenging accounts of gazetteers and the like were backed up by texts that taught—and began to instill presumptions about—something emerging as a common social lexicon. Information was also distilled into handy digests, the rough equivalent of family almanacs or encyclopedias, that put together something emerging as a common social knowledge. *Banmin chōhōki* (Everybody's Treasury, 1692), for instance, provided lists of courtly and shogunal personnel, era names and annual rituals, the productivity totals and castle towns of the provinces, the tropes of vernacular poetry, the major roads of Kyoto, the highways of the nation, and a good deal more.

We sampled this rich batch of material in the reading list of my hypothetical clerk. Diverse in genre, it ranges across an enormous spectrum of maps, atlases, encyclopedias, dictionaries, calendars, almanacs, rural gazetteers, urban directories, travel accounts, personnel rosters, biographical compendia, manuals of work, manuals of play, guides to shopping and local products, and school primers. Certainly, this very variety discourages any inclusive treatment. Nowhere, tellingly, does the material appear together in either the catalogues of early modern booksellers or the scholarship of modern historians.[5] Here, however, I stash it all into what Saikaku might have called the "Storehouse of Worldly Reckonings,"[6] and I conceive as the "library of public information."

This library is no particular archive but a metaphorical place where we can array the many early modern sources that fit together because of their common purpose: to examine and order the verifiable facts of contemporary experience for an open audience of consumers. If the material is disparate, it is also linked in obvious and subtler ways. Some texts, like primers and dictionaries, prepared readers for the challenges of more advanced work. Others, like the family encyclopedias, synthesized the learning gathered more elaborately elsewhere. Many texts, moreover, overlapped in general content if not in detail. (Outright recapitulation was not, in fact, unusual.) Thus the gazetteers covered much the same ground as the urban directories and the tour guides; the shogunal personnel rosters began with data available in political cartography. Mimicry was also rife, as catalogues of actors and prostitutes derived from catalogues of daimyo. Broad affinities of interest and method connected the information texts as well. Dictionaries of work led to dictionaries of food. Attention to the ritual calendars of courtiers and military men generated interest in the ritual calendars of townspeople and individual farming communities. Systematic

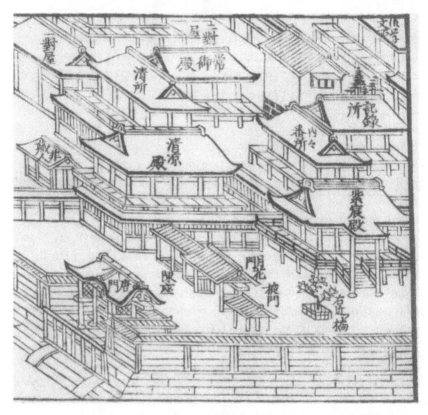

FIG. 6. Layout of the Imperial Palace Complex in Kyoto, from *Kokka man'yōki* (The Ten-Thousand Leaf Record of the Provincial Flowers, 1697), compiled by Kikumoto Gahō. The illustration labels all gates and major structures, including

surveys of crops and agrarian productivity inspired systematic research into improved cultivation practices. Analysis of martial culture was followed by cultural analyses of townspeople, farmers, and entertainers.

But the strongest link between the texts is attitude. And it is here that the merit of thinking about them collectively comes clear; for the information library discloses pervasive habits of mind. The texts affirm the knowability through observation of worldly phenomena. They presume the coherence of those phenomena through holistic and taxonomic modes of analysis. And they declare the entitlement of anonymous and ordinary readers to know what is known. Insofar as the texts rely for communication on a body of master conventions and build on a core of standard information, they also trace the lines of that fugitive source of collective

the *shishinden* (the main ceremonial building) and the *seiryōden* (the emperor's residence). Courtesy of the East Asian Library, University of California, Berkeley.

WHEN DOES THIS GET INTERESTING

identity we call common knowledge. Making society visible to itself, they conspired in the making of society.

Indeed, their facility with comprehensive social concepts—from the categories of national cartography to the categories of national labor (or ritual life or urban systems)—has real shock value for anyone accustomed to the fracture of medieval sources. The ceaseless inventories of roads and products and professionals that Saikaku could mock in the 1680s would have been unimaginable to anyone born much before 1600, not simply because of their exceptional detail, but because of the exceptional mentality that sought out and systematized so much data. Saikaku's humor would have been lost, in all but its surface nonsense, on his grandparents. Certainly no sixteenth-century traveler would have had in hand (or in mind) a national road map, a guidebook to all the famous places along the way, a methodical roster of administrative personnel, a gazetteer for each province, or a directory for each major city. However high born, that earlier traveler would have moved within the ancient webs of intelligence spun by scouts, informants, poets, painters, and diarists. The point is not that orderly information on worldly affairs did not circulate before the seventeenth century, but that it barely existed. In effect, the texts of the information library represent a quiet revolution in knowledge—one that divides the early modern period from all previous time. They invented for popular audiences a Japan.

There were, to be sure, crucial precedents for the information texts, particularly in the classical period, when an ambitious government produced a national map as well as a number of provincial gazetteers. Then, and in the medieval period, we also find dictionaries, encyclopedias, genealogies, calendars, lists of famous places and famous products, and educational primers.[7] The distance between these sources and the early modern material is nonetheless very great. And it resulted from three interrelated changes in the investigative style of seventeenth-century writers, their audience, and their conceptual armature. These changes depended, in turn, on two profound developments—commercial publishing on the one hand and state-making on the other—that created a "public" where there had been none.

Apart from the sheer volume and variety of the new information library, it departs most obviously from the precedents with an investigative style that is generally empirical in method and mundane in outlook. Many texts are certainly larded with lore, particularly in sections given over to the historical background of religious institutions or martial houses. Many, too, rely on hearsay and casually collected or recycled data. Most also invoke the authority of documents—family and temple records, the historical literature, and even other contemporary titles—in a bibliophilic culture that demanded acknowledgement of literary learning. But the new library broke with a tradition centered in documentary authority by grounding its truth claims in observation.

Thus in a characteristic statement of credentials, Miyazaki Yasusada prefaces *Nōgyō zensho* (The Complete Book of Farming) with remarks on forty years of travel through sixteen provinces to collect information on the cultivation of 145 crops. Then he punctuates his text with local conversations and field notes.[8] Similarly, Fujimoto Kizan opens *Shikidō ōkagami*

(The Great Mirror of Sex) with assurances that, from the age of twelve and for forty years thereafter, he has "cultivated the art of love unremittingly day and night, forgetting food and sleep, and mastered its supreme doctrines."[9] Street directories, travel guides, illustrated lists of martial regalia, botanical and culinary encyclopedias—all include guarantees of eyewitness accuracy. So strong appears the expectation of personal authentication that it is the rare author who neglects the interjection, "I saw this" or "I did that," whether the declaration bears testing or not. Even vicarious chroniclers represent themselves as observers, and even Saikaku renounces a glancing summary of Oman's wealth to push his readers past every box of gold and pile of cloth in those storehouses.

This emphasis on empirical fact-gathering derived in good part from a concern in the information texts with timeliness. If authors continued to make near-obligatory references to a deep past and thick culture, they concentrated on a "now" that required restless attention to change. A fair amount of material was forthrightly ephemeral. Dated exactly, described in their titles as "new" or "revised" or "expanded" (or, indeed, as "newly revised and expanded"), texts such as maps and personnel rosters came out at least annually (often more frequently) to keep users up with new buildings and new appointments and the like. Some publishers even offered to emend texts by hand, for a small fee, as a service to clients unable to wait for the next scheduled revision.[10] Currency also demanded the updating of urban directories, family almanacs, commodity catalogues, and school primers (since an obsession with novelty kept altering the lexicon of trade). Guidebooks, too, were superseded as authors added sites to their itineraries or improved data concerning the roads. Although some of the information texts became perennials (such as *Chōnin bukuro,* The Townsman's Satchel) and others (such as The Complete Book of Farming) achieved a kind of canonical status, most required correction. And hardly any went unchallenged by competition, for the rivalries between commercial printing houses remained a critical stimulant to new and better coverage.

Yet beyond the concern with timeliness, the concern with mundane experience—and its exacting details—drove the need for observation. Authors of the information texts trained a broad and level gaze on topics, and lives, largely absent from the scholarly literature. They also rejected portraits fixed on the familiar or the aggregate to explore variety. Glossing work and workers under 496 entries, the anonymous compiler of *Jinrin kinmōzui* (The Illustrated Encyclopedia of Humanity, 1690) dispatches nobles and warriors and priests in one volume, committing six others to the likes of ox tenders, rock peddlers, bath attendants, river rafters, ocean

whos working them?

divers, carvers of bone and horn, salt harvesters, and whalers (who went out, we are told, in flotillas of twelve boats, each manned by four sailors).[11] So, too, urban guides disaggregate the specialties of merchants, craftspeople, and masters of the various arts in exhaustive lists, complete with addresses, that range from Confucian tutors to eyebrow pluckers, from wholesale magnates to rag dealers. They itemize hundreds of distinctive goods (lapis, coral, mother of pearl, cypress, sandalwood, hawk tails, incense), dozens of distinctive services (including instruction in the vertical flute, the horizontal flute, the small drum, the large drum, the lute, and the samisen). In the Great Mirror of Sex, Fujimoto Kizan provides a classified lexicon of the argot of the prostitution quarter; the rules of conduct for both entertainers and their guests (with notes on the steadily higher levels of proficiency achieved by adepts); a guide to the high arts of music and letter writing; a survey of the quarters themselves (history, management, customs, maps); and accounts of their ranking women (with names, crests, artistic genealogies, and personal anecdotes). Virtually no aspect of brothel culture—from hair styles to bathing etiquette, from cuisine to pillow talk—goes unremarked in this masterwork.[12]

For ethnographers, of course, particularity ruled. In his Culinary Mirror of the Realm, Hitomi Hitsudai lingers not only over the grand staples of the diet but rare recipes for rat and snake, good sources of aphrodisiacs, and local hunting practices. Compilers of the Aizu gazetteer Aizu fudoki, fūzoku-chō tracked down the marriage and burial rituals of every individual village in the domain.[13] And even poets turned from stale tropes to celebrate the manifold images of daily life. Kefukigusa (Feather-Blown Grasses), a guide to an avant-garde style of haikai linked verse, names over 1,800 "famous products" of the nation, encouraging aspiring poets to lace their verse with references to corn, for example, and radish, plum dye, persimmon flowers, charcoal braziers, and mountain peaches.[14] As mundane experience captured the attention of investigators, mundane testimony began filling the market as well. A growing literature of biography and autobiography embraced common people such as the Kyoto pharmacist Iwagaki Mitsusada. In Akindo sugiwai kagami (Mirror of the Merchant's Calling), a memoir of commendable self-scrutiny (if not self-importance), Mitsusada reflects on fifty-five years in the trade to advise heirs and readers about inventory control, pricing, etiquette toward clients, the education of women and children, and the overarching importance of business-firstism.[15]

In short, the information texts focused on the world in its observable and mutable variety. They placed a high premium, consequently, on the labeling and counting that announced both the particularity of things and the punctiliousness of the witness. Writers named names and titles and offices and places and objects. They identified addresses and incomes and ages and wives. They measured distances and harvests. They quantified crustaceans (54 types) and emperors (114 by 1688) and famous products (1,823).[16] They ranked sumo wrestlers and Confucian teachers and turnips.[17] Dead accuracy, if often promised or implied, was not invariably delivered. Authors got things wrong, and their followers repeated the mistakes. They recirculated data—notably the agrarian productivity figures calculated by the regime—that was purely conventional. But they committed themselves to watchfulness. And thus the litany of nouns, more emphatically than the march of numbers, became the hallmark of their style. Small wonder, in an age of lists, that dictionaries covered over 30,000 words by 1680 or that primers for urban children distinguished fastidiously between brocade, satin, damask, gossamer, crepe, figured silk, velvet, Chinese twill, and gauze.[18] Worldliness fused with wordiness to keep the information texts tactile—seemingly literal in their accounts of concrete experience and material phenomena.

There is, in this capacious literature, an occasional taste of voyeurism or sensationalism. There is also the rampant virtuosity of authors who delighted in outdoing each other at the knowledge game. When Fujimoto Kizan introduced the Great Mirror of Sex with references to no fewer than thirty-five earlier books on the gay quarter, he was not so much acknowledging able predecessors as clearing the way for his own—bigger, better—encyclopedia of love. Yet no less than Saikaku's parody, the stretch for surprise or notoriety is itself a symptom of the penetration of the information culture.

The attention in the new library to the timely observation of a diversely mundane experience engages a second defining feature of the information texts: their new audience. The classical and medieval antecedents, all in manuscript and most in Chinese, addressed an elite, intimately connected, and culturally cohesive readership concentrated in Kyoto. The early modern texts, overwhelmingly printed in vernacular Japanese, addressed a mixed, impersonal, and socially stratified readership distributed across the country. The shorthand explanation for this revolution is "commercial publishing." But buried in the phrase is a welter of transformations that were neither inevitable nor inevitably interlocked.

One set of changes involved the emergence after 1600 of a publishing industry. Here a confluence of factors, some predictable but others not, came to bear: the spike in urban populations that enlarged and reorganized markets; the shift in entrepreneurial climate that encouraged new enterprise; the experiments with technology that broke the monastic hold on print; and the bookish formation of the samurai who, as core consumers in new cities, generated basic demand. Yet altered modes of book production and circulation do not, in themselves, alter the contents of books. If commercial publishers were to move in novel directions, rather than simply repackage the standard repertoire of a manuscript culture in printed form, they required a novel mentality.

Hence another set of changes involved the creation of a reading public for a different sort of reading. Critical here was a dynamic interplay. On the one hand, the spread of literacy and disposable wealth among segments of the commoner population expanded the potential market for books. On the other hand, ambition and competition moved the publishing fraternity to take risks—to gauge the needs and tastes of virgin customers in an innovative fashion. Titles responsive to the potential market were consequently "public" in a dual sense. Not only were they *accessible to* any anonymous buyer with means, they were also *produced for* an imagined audience—the "you" implicitly addressed by authors—that constituted a permeable reading community bound by both common interests and common frames of reference. The projection of this "you" was the enabling condition, and extraordinary achievement, of popular publishing.

Its genesis, though, is a devious matter that leads us beyond obvious changes in social context, whether the growth of publishing or the growth of literacy, to tectonic shifts in social identity. Particularly in their new fiction and their accounts of recent wartime history, early modern writers drew on collective experiences of upheaval to appeal to a nascent collectivity of readers, one defined not by station or education or place of residence but by shared crisis. This stretch in subject and audience required imagination. But the texts of the information library—the maps and gazetteers and urban directories and the like—also required definitions of structural order that belong more to statist invention than to authorial resource. Hence before resuming discussion of reading and publishing in the early modern period, a third feature of the new library requires introduction.

For all its attention to the manifold particularity of mundane experience, the most remarkable aspect of the new library is the holistic and taxonomic coverage of big subjects. The great subject became the place variously called Nihon, Dai Nihon, Honchō, and Yamato.[19] Again and again, writers made the whole country, conceived of integrally as a singular national space, the site of analysis. The myriad details of their topics—political administration, social geography, religious organization, work, food, festival life, transport arteries, famous places and products—were parsed within this unifying frame. So, too, these individual topics received thoroughgoing rather than perfunctory treatment. Transport guides, as my clerk discovered, moved from high roads to low and from land to water with attention to travel times, portage and ferry fees, accommodations, checkpoints, and the like. Lists of famous places spread copiously over Buddhist and Shinto sanctuaries, old battlegrounds, lost cities, castle ruins, graves and stupas, scenic wonders (from mountain vistas to solitary pine trees), legendary wells and bridges, and the sites of urban entertainment.

The scope of the information texts was clearly not always (or normally) national. Yet even discrete studies sought completeness within their compass. Individual urban directories accompanied readers through every street, across every bridge, and past every notable landmark of total cityscapes. The rosters of shogunal personnel provided a profile of every daimyo and the title and income of every bureaucrat.

The vehicle of this holistic coverage was classification—the breaking down of big subjects into manageable components. Classification could sometimes be messy and hectic, all but overtaken by thick description or jolting shifts of interest. Still, many of the worldly reckonings were finicky about categories and most were broadly systematic. The list, as we have seen, ruled. The paradigmatic example of classification in early modern Japan was mapmaking. The enterprise required, as a defining precondition, that cartographers abstract from limitless circumstances a set of generic attributes for a space and then plot all variations within these conventions. If other genres had less exacting demands for classification, all efforts at comprehensive coverage called for organizing principles—either to guide inquiry in the first place or sort findings in progress. Thus, compilers of national gazetteers started with a body of common descriptive categories (principal crops and manufactures, productivity totals, famous places, and the like) and proceeded to fill them in province by province. So, too, encyclopedists of work began by blocking out master typologies of workers (nobles, warriors, priests, specialists in professional learning and the arts, farmers, merchants, craftspeople, itinerants, and entertainers) before running through the ever-finer variations of individual employments. Alternatively, agronomists such as Miyazaki Yasusada seem to have begun with extensive observations that they gradually disciplined into order (in Yasusada's case by tracking cultivation practices crop by crop).

Classification emerged as something more, however, than a practical tool for disciplining data. A form of logic, lodged in philosophical premises about the world, taxonomy did not so much assist as enable inquiry by positing the intelligible connection of phenomena within comprehensive structures. Things were not, in effect, infinitely discrete or random aspects of a fragmented being. When investigators broke big subjects into components, they projected the existence of unifying wholes that linked, and became understandable through, their parts.

Integral models of power and society did exist before the early modern period, but they were few and discontinuous. Consider the case of cartography. Figure 7, a version of a national map first drafted under the auspices of the classical regime, quite precociously represents a holistic spatial politics.[20] Presumably using coastal and hilltop sightings, surveyors created a recognizable outline of the major islands and then imposed on it a state story: extending from the central capital, named and bounded provinces express an administrative union that is elaborated by a pervasive highway system. Although this figure was reproduced on occasion in the medieval era, there is no evidence after the ninth century of either resumed national surveying or efforts to revise the prototype (for all its precocity, a rudimentary one) in accord with the polities of successor regimes.[21] Instead, mapmakers concentrated on discrete parts of a fragmented landscape, producing small area maps that focused invariably on individual landholdings and depended remorselessly on local terms of reference. They left no large area maps—no district or province maps, not even maps of the capital, Kyoto—to orient the medieval viewer in a realm beyond the specific proprietary holding. The point, I believe, is that they had no body of conventions to subsume complex local practices within master categories. Conventions require classification of a whole. And this was a mode of thought uncommon to medieval politics and society. The capital itself was imagined less as an urban unit than as a patchwork of small dominions administered by individual temples, shrines, noble houses, and military officials. The first panoramic paintings of Kyoto—the first images of the entire city—date from the sixteenth century.[22]

If spatial representation focused on fragments, so, too, did representations of governing institutions. Again, we find in the early classical period magisterial compilations of administrative law that projected notions of orderly national rule through a carefully graded officialdom. But not until the seventeenth century would efforts to plot a comprehensive national bureaucracy occur again. Certainly, political structures are apparent in the vast body of medieval statutes, legal decisions, official appointments, land confirmations, and the like. These are the texts of everyday governance, however, and they thus chiefly expose (like all such texts) the

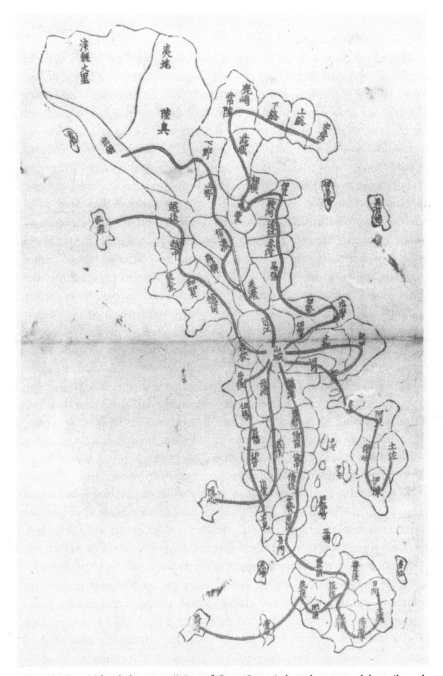

FIG. 7. *Dai Nihonkoku no zu* (Map of Great Japan), based on a model attributed to the monk Gyōki, which appears in an early seventeenth-century moveable-type edition of the medieval encyclopedia *Shūgaishō*. Courtesy of the Tenri Central Library of Tenri University, Nara.

dynamics of changing circumstances rather than the clean and stable lines of a normative superstructure.[23]

The issue here is only partly one of actual practice. The particularity of medieval texts and the holism of early modern texts do reflect different forms of political and social organization. Still, linkages between reality and representation are hardly tight. We might well imagine in medieval Japan a persisting tradition of national cartography and integral administrative law. Not only did hereditary elites and historians cultivate the idea of continuity with the classical past, the durable institutions of court and shogunate embodied coherent polities. Similarly, we might well imagine an early modern Japan, however centralized by medieval measures, without the comprehensive surveys of the information library. Centrifugal forces remained powerful (some would say paramount) in a federal polity[24] weighted toward the highly variable rule of local daimyo rather than the unifying dominion of the shogun. Complicated in form, the polity was also dynamic, frequently circumstantial, in operation—more like medieval politics at the level of everyday governance than the elegant maps and administrative charts that purported to represent it.

We might note, incidentally, that even if the Tokugawa shogunate had run a clockwork system, the holistic vision of the information library would remain arresting. National mapmaking was not universal in the early modern world. Nor was the sort of extensive data collection that produced provincial gazetteers and urban directories and the like. So where, then, did the new library come from? If it did not develop from customary medieval models, and bore no axiomatic relationship to the normal practices of early modernity, the library needs a creation story.

Writers and publishers conspired vigorously in its development. Its origins, though, belong to the state—a state, whatever we make of its unfolding course, that undertook visionary projects of definition well before survival was more than a phantom. During the convulsive transition from war to peace around 1600, the conquest regimes used programs of cadastral and cartographic surveying to collect data on natural and human resources. Then they labeled and classified both the resources and the jurisdictional units into which they fit, projecting a normative superstructure onto a war-torn landscape. In the process, they invented a new kind of public. This was not (yet) the public of anonymous consumers served by the market or the public of collective readerships imagined by publishers. This public was an object of official scrutiny and aggregate analysis. But the categories imposed on it would become the conceptual armature of the information library. And the style of comprehensive surveying that underlay its formation would become the model of information gathering.

Back, now, for a closer look at the publishing industry and the state that variously intersected and diverged to produce both new information and new publics.

—

What is surprising, really, about commercial publishing in Japan is that it developed so late. Printing itself was old, in continuous use in woodblock form from the eighth century. And movable type, if not employed domestically, was familiar from Chinese and Korean books imported during the Middle Ages. A culture of reading and writing also flourished within the aristocratic, monastic, and martial elite, which exchanged in manuscript thousands of titles ranging from Buddhist and Confucian philosophy to history, belles lettres, and lowbrow tales.[25] This elite was centered, moreover, in the enormous capital of Kyoto (with a population well over 100,000 in the medieval period), where a well-developed market catered to most imaginable forms of luxury demand.

But rather than suggesting some perverse lag in development, the absence of commercial publishing in a context seemingly so conducive to it serves as warning that the enterprise is not the inevitable outcome of some formulaic process. If we can begin to sort out the factors at work in the seventeenth-century transformation, their weight and interaction is harder to figure. A critical point of departure, though, is urbanization. During the latter half of the sixteenth century, not much more than 3 percent of Japan's population lived in cities. Toward the close of the seventeenth, the figure approached 15 percent. In the accompanying upheaval, no less than in the sheer volume of migration, the publishing industry took root.

This urban boom was an unintended consequence of two political decisions taken to curb civil violence (which had raged from the 1460s as strongmen began carving the country into petty dominions) and to preserve an uncertain peace (which came into view in the 1580s as Toyotomi Hideyoshi combined conciliation with conquest to unite surviving daimyo in a federal form of rule). The first decision, made by Hideyoshi in 1591, was to remove vast numbers of samurai fighters from the villages that had provided men and matériel for continuing rebellion. Over the course of the next generation, most samurai were relocated to the castle towns of the individual daimyo they served. There they lived on annual stipends, the equivalent of salaries, forfeiting the landholdings that had formerly accorded them a dangerous independence. The second decision was to tighten the leash on the daimyo—as grave a threat to the peace as errant samurai—by requiring their personal attendance on the hegemon. The policy was formulated, following Hideyoshi's death and lacerating battles over succession, by the early heads of the Tokugawa house, who ruled from 1603 until 1868 under the imperially granted title of shogun. First as a matter of custom but by 1642 as a matter of law, the shogun demanded that all daimyo spend half of each year in the Tokugawa capital of Edo.[26]

The removal to towns of the samurai, as well as the periodic residence in Edo of the daimyo, provoked the remorseless urban growth that influenced every facet of the early modern experience in Japan. At 6 to 8 percent of the total population of Japan in 1600 (variously estimated at twelve to eighteen million), samurai and their families constituted a formidable core of new city people. They also served as magnets for the multiplying numbers of migrants—merchants, craftspeople, providers of specialized services, servants, day laborers, and various hangers-on—who trailed them for profit. Transformed from landholding village notables into stipend-receiving urban consumers, the samurai generated, and depended on, dense market constellations. By the time they reached a mature stage of development, twenty castle towns in the larger domains had populations of over 70,000 and sixty had populations of over 10,000.[27]

Urban growth across the national scene was accompanied by the development of three monster cities. Edo neared one million around 1700 under the combined impact of bureaucratic gigantism and periodic residence by all the country's daimyo, with their formidable retinues. The port of Osaka also grew phenomenally, to about 400,000 in 1700, as the national center of the wholesale trade in rice, the principal medium for collecting taxes and paying samurai stipends during the Tokugawa period. Kyoto, Japan's leading producer of fine goods, grew from something over 100,000 people in 1600 to something over 350,000 around 1700—the result partially of military influx but primarily of expanded manufacturing to supply the growing urban network.

It was in this context of urban expansion that a publishing industry developed. The population figures alone suggest one stimulus, since cities delivered the big prospective readerships necessary for a viable trade. But numbers are not everything, as the case of medieval Kyoto suggests. More important immediately was a change in entrepreneurial climate. Commerce in wartime Kyoto had remained organized by medieval structures of patronage and thus insulated against both outsiders and innovation. It was also troubled by dislocation as the once wealthy consumers who had driven the economy disappeared—courtly aristocrats into penury, the large officialdom of the Muromachi shogunate into exile and provincial wars. Toyotomi Hideyoshi, who made Kyoto his headquarters, restored a basic prosperity to the city—quietly by stabilizing the incomes of the nobility and the Buddhist establishment, flamboyantly by bringing in his own martial retinues. More to the point, he opened up room for an altered economy by breaking the medieval guild system, eliminating urban taxes, dismantling toll barriers, and prohibiting market fees.[28]

While various forms of trade protection would emerge in the early modern cities of Japan, a certain freedom of opportunity was conspicuous in the formative years of the unification regimes. Hideyoshi's reforms in Kyoto belonged to a pattern of similar wartime innovations in market towns, and, after peace was established, most prevailed in the great castle centers, which urgently needed goods and services. In scores of new or newly transformed cities, hundreds of thousands of newcomers were inventing lives in an environment close to carte blanche. In the old but regenerated city of Kyoto, commoner wards expanded so greatly in number and density that neighborhood organizations doubled within three generations.[29]

One notable development accompanying the swell of immigrants was the emergence of mid-market enterprises. There had been two poles to Kyoto's medieval and wartime commerce: the trade in basic commodities (including the wholesale and processing of foodstuffs) and the trade in luxury goods. Early modern entrepreneurs moved aggressively into the domain between necessity and extravagance, offering both commoners and samurai a range of services and goods formerly provided only to affluent households by personal retainers. They worked as hairdressers, doctors, teachers, tailors, and entertainers. And they sold all kinds of ready-made furnishings, as well as used goods and novelties, from tobacco to spectacles. As city people broadened their habits of elective consumption, once rare enterprises became normal.

Publishing was one of these mid-market enterprises, insofar as it made available to samurai and commoner constituencies goods previously available to elite communities through the labor of copyists. The industry first stirred, though, with rarified experiments driven not by the market but a foreign technology. During two attempts to conquer Korea in the 1590s, Japanese troops plundered Korean monasteries and cities and returned home with substantial fonts of movable copper type, as well as books printed from them. Around the same time, Jesuit missionaries brought Roman type to Japan, establishing presses for devotional and instructional literature in Kyoto, Nagasaki, and other towns. Japanese artisans may actually have printed a number of Confucian texts from the Korean type. More significant, however, was a curiosity about the technique that inspired both the emperor Go-Yōzei and the shogun Tokugawa Ieyasu to have wooden fonts cut in Japan for themselves. Ieyasu, who was committed to developing a shogunal library, oversaw the printing from his font of Confucian classics and the *Azuma kagami,* a major Japanese historical work of the thirteenth century. A number of private ventures also arose at the turn of the seventeenth century, most spectacularly a collaborative effort by the calligrapher Hon'ami Kōetsu and the merchant Suminokura Sōan to put out lavish illustrated editions of Japanese literary classics.[30]

Small in scale and confined to elite circles, most early printing retained the character of an elegant hobby. But it quickened interest in an unfamiliar technology and, far more important, helped clear the way for commercial enterprise by breaking with two powerful conventions. For almost a millennium, printing had been associated with woodblock carvers in temples who turned out copies of Buddhist canonical literature (and occasionally Confucian texts and collections of Chinese poetry) for clerical and lay audiences. The printing initiatives of rulers and artists ended this monastic monopoly. In addition, the trailblazers expanded the scope of printing from chiefly Buddhist to secular works. Since secular Chinese material in Chinese printed editions (using both woodblock and movable type) had long been imported to Japan, the innovation that mattered most was the original printing of work written in Japanese.

This innovation had an essential aesthetic dimension. Apart from high demand and habitual practice, mechanical reproduction had focused on Buddhist material because woodblock copies could convey the highly formal, reasonably uniform Chinese characters of the sources. But handwriting appeared indispensable to vernacular texts that were savored for distinctive calligraphic styles. Hon'ami Kōetsu and his followers unsettled certainties by demonstrating that the native script could be transferred to type with the exceptional beauty formerly associated only with manuscripts.[31]

Overwhelmingly, indeed, commercial publishing operated, in its first stages, as an extension of the copyist's art. Following the lead of early innovators, small firms—all in Kyoto, most short-lived, many with a decidedly secondary interest in printing—converted to print standard titles of the Chinese and Japanese traditions: Confucian as well as Buddhist works, major histories, literary classics, and poetry collections. Their output was strong for a fledgling industry, though a bare taste of what was to come: at least 500 titles were printed in Japan from 1593 until 1625, 80 percent of them with movable type. But thereafter things changed fast. Kyoto, the forerunner of the early modern industry, had over one hundred publishers by the 1640s, booksellers' catalogues by 1659, and over 7,000 titles in print by 1692 (excluding ephemeral and pulp publications too unwieldy for bibliographic control).[32]

A symptom as well as a cause of growth was the gradual abandonment of movable type and the move (backward? forward?) to woodblock printing. Type proved costly because of the number of Chinese and Japanese characters required for all but the most elementary texts. Since even a single font had to include many thousands of pieces, a printer's basic investment was high and expansion into multiple fonts prohibitively expensive for most, at least in a nascent market. And because a printer's projects were necessarily confined to the number of fonts on hand, only the rare firm could work on more than one text at a time. The reissue of a popular title remained just as demanding as a new undertaking once the type had been broken down and diverted elsewhere. The problem of the character base was exacerbated, moreover, by a seemingly untamable taste for calligraphic variety—a taste that type could serve only if printers were able to keep and constantly redesign multiple fonts.

Block carving, on the other hand, suited the desire for distinctive styles and permitted the seamless integration of text and illustration. It also enabled printers to recover investments title by title, without a huge initial outlay, and assume as many projects as they had carvers. And once material had been cut and stored, it could be retrieved for profitable reprints or revisions, or, indeed, for sales to other firms.[33] These combined economic advantages opened up opportunities for increased book production by an increasing number of small enterprises. Insofar as they acted to improve their competitive advantage in a market now tested and deemed viable, the (re)turn to woodblocks also suggests growing book consumption.

The push and pull between producers and consumers, always a vexed issue in economic history, is particularly fraught in the case of publishing, which depended not only on money and taste but literacy and a culture of reading. Early on, the industry could appeal to established readerships with printed versions of manuscript texts. But growth depended on some combination of bigger audiences and new titles. Here urbanization came into the equation, partly because the size and number of cities created immense consumer pools for both local and interurban trade. More to the point, the core populations of cities were samurai friendly to the book. The tone was set by Tokugawa Ieyasu—an intrepid librarian, cultural curator, publisher of ethical and historical texts, archivist of his own administration, master of distant precedents, and founder of a Confucian academy in his capital.[34] He and his advisors, together with a number of intellectually ambitious daimyo, cultivated the notion that military rule was to emanate from learned men. The education of a now vast, city-based body of samurai was, in practice, pursued erratically and often on individual initiative. Very gradually, though, disparate forms of training—in everything from motley temple schools to the shogunal academy—brought the majority to literacy and a minority to scholarly distinction. For peacetime soldiers stripped of battleground activity and notoriously underemployed by the shogunal and daimyo bureaucracies, learning became both a rationale for privilege and an opportunity for work—as doctors, political advisors, tutors, teachers, and authors.[35]

Spread across numerous cities, and far larger than the noble and monastic elites, this constituency of samurai readers appears to have shaped most publishing decisions throughout the seventeenth century. Booksellers' catalogues remained thick with the Buddhist, Confucian, literary, and historical titles prominent from the inception of commercial printing. They also showed an increasing emphasis on subjects close to samurai interests: martial genealogy, family and military history, military science, military etiquette, medieval law, mathematics, medicine, noh drama, and the linked verse (*renga* and *haikai*) popular in martial circles.[36]

But we find, too, a breaking away from the literature of erudition and high culture. With accelerating velocity from the 1640s, and a major place in the market from the 1670s, new titles were appearing for a popular readership. This material, which was overwhelmingly original, may have appealed to an established readership even as it reached—with its simple vernacular language and phonetic glosses of less familiar characters—for more general, and first-time, book buyers. If they built their business on the sophisticated tastes of already literate audiences, publishers created opportunities and stimulated literacy with overtures to the middlebrow and lowbrow markets. Common samurai must have made up a fair share of these markets. But so, too, did the common townspeople who were constructing their own apprentice-based systems of education and purchasing titles clearly intended for them: primers of commercial vocabulary, manuals of household management, guides to bookkeeping and business practice, and basic dictionaries.[37]

Although this move toward a popular audience may seem all but inevitable, it required something more than a certain risk-taking spirit. Authors and publishers had to imagine what we call a "reading public"— *interest!* a body of general consumers connected by interest rather than any strict calculus of class, occupation, neighborhood, or education. They had to imagine that reading might be normal among different social strata. And they had to imagine that persons of disparate backgrounds might sufficiently share, or learn to share, the common frames of reference that made the words and images of a text intelligible. Certainly, many texts addressed particular audiences—of, say, merchants, flower arrangers, tea fanciers, theatergoers, or poets. Even here, however, the bonds between readers were variously loose (since "merchants" covered a sweeping spectrum) or purely elective (since tea practice, like all the gentler pursuits, transcended status). And most texts—from maps and travel guides to dictionaries and encyclopedias—addressed audiences without defining features.

The notion of permeable reading communities connected by interest and some collective orientation takes hold with the very process of popular publishing. But a readiness for such connection may have resulted from the collective experiences accompanying the early modern transition itself. Consider, for example, the unprecedented mobilizations that occurred in the final stages of civil war. During the two Japanese invasions of Korea in the 1590s, and during the climactic battles for domestic hegemony fought between Toyotomi and Tokugawa partisans in 1615 at Osaka, armies approaching 300,000 engaged in the first national campaigns ever known in Japan. To estimate the number of those immediately affected by each of these mobilizations (families and neighbors of the troops, suppliers and support personnel, locals responsible for barracking the soldiers, and even curious spectators), it is not unreasonable to multiply the number of combatants by ten, giving a total of 20 to 25 percent of the population.[38] Although a century of conflict had entangled most of the population in local contests, these last confrontations ranged vast numbers, from all locales, on just two sides, which was as close as the people of Japan had come to a common experience. Consider, alternatively, the urban migrations around 1600, which affected nearly everyone—not only the migrants themselves but the communities they left behind and the agrarian producers increasingly engaged in supplying cities.

Numerous policies of the early modern state—from the disarmament of civilians to the extirpation of Christianity through annual interrogations of village communities—would bind Japanese by corporate disciplines. But, however perversely, the mass upheavals of war and urban migration provided an exceptional commonality of experience that transcended place and station. And these were the events that constructed the original frames of reference for a "reading public" and inspired much of the material generated for popular consumption.

Publishers had to be careful about material that awakened official sensitivities, particularly battle tales touching on the honor and legitimacy of the Tokugawa victors. The power of wartime subjects is nonetheless clear from the wealth of titles, particularly concerning Toyotomi Hideyoshi, that emerged in the early seventeenth century and continued to circulate on the manuscript market throughout the early modern period. Japan's first broadsheets, ancestors of the newspaper, may also have appeared after the final encounter between Toyotomi and Tokugawa forces to announce details of the battle. Although caution kept the martial history of the Tokugawa underground, the print market handled an increasing number of texts concerning other wartime houses (the Oda, Asai, Miyoshi, Takeda, and Toyotomi), as well as puppet theater libretti that transposed recent wartime history into medieval settings and thus camouflaged potentially provocative stories as safely remote dramas.[39]

Meanwhile, vernacular fiction took as its first and most consuming subject the city scene. City life likewise became a core subject of the emerging kabuki and puppet theaters, the dominant forms of popular urban entertainment. Both fiction and drama were notable for their contemporaneity—their emphasis on the recognizable details of place, argot, and fashion—and their panoramic quality. In a "drifting world," city people crossed paths as newcomers, tourists, pilgrims, shoppers, and seekers. And they shared sufferings and pleasures: love, debt, swaggering superiors, ready entertainment, escape into anonymity. Literary style veered from the anecdotal pastiche and fabulous romance reminiscent of medieval tales to the shapely satire mastered by Ihara Saikaku toward the end of the seventeenth century. The contents of popular art, however, hewed close to the mundane experience of citiness that connected the lives of the reading majority.[40]

By drawing upon the collective experiences of war and urban transition, authors and printers significantly enlarged the compass of the publishing industry from old to new titles, from erudite to accessible material. Most important, they enlarged the industry's audience from learned to general readers. Here was a "public" imagined as open in boundaries, linked by certain broad interests, and receptive to entrepreneurial advances on its tastes. And here, too, was an indispensable context for the emergence of the information library. But because that library depended on an additional projection of the public—one that posited society not just as a market but as an object of analytical observation—we must extend discussion to the state that first conceived and classified it.

—

Whether they examined work or food, cities or provinces, the authors of the information texts reached outside themselves to unfamiliar worlds. They broke the confines of immediate knowledge and attachment—the confines of place, station, and household—to explore what they did not know and could not claim as intimate. Wandering in body and mind, they presumed the permeability of boundaries that outsiders could cross in search of data. The agronomist moved from village to village; the urban geographer from temple to brothel; the compiler of official personnel rosters from the shogun to his dentist. These writers also presumed the malleability of boundaries that an observer could draw to suit his purposes. Thus they lifted famous places outside the context of local piety and local history to array them together for tourists in great surveys of the cultural terrain. They ignored barriers of prestige to line up obstetricians with tatami makers in catalogues of city specialists. They took esoteric knowledge typically possessed by closed circles—of poets, tea practitioners, flower arrangers, masters of military etiquette, healers, and chess players—and arranged it in manuals of instruction available to anyone.

From the vantage of these writers, the public was something other than an audience. It was an arena of inquiry that they could enter with a certain freedom and observe with a certain detachment. To compile his Culinary Mirror, for example, Hitomi Hitsudai traveled as an anonymous ethnologist through the villages that he combed for evidence and then departed. This combing discloses another dimension of the observer's mind: the assumption that what was unfamiliar was neither unfathomably strange nor irreducibly particular. The human landscape could be known through the investigation of the outsider, not only the long local experience of the insider. And it could be sorted into patterns linking apparently discrete phenomena.

In this arrangement of evidence—in this holistic and taxonomic approach to evidence—the concept of the "public" mutates once more. The public is not only an arena of inquiry but also something made visible through systematic analysis. It is a collective body larger than the small and scattered parts whose various common attributes—from farming and religious practices to social and political organization—can be exposed (and then made known to itself). If commercial publishing helped create an

FIG. 8 (*above and opposite*). "Kabuki at the Shijō Riverbank," from Nakagawa Kiun, *Kyō warabe* (A Child of Kyoto, 1658), one of the earliest printed guidebooks in Japan. Courtesy of the East Asian Library, University of California, Berkeley.

open audience of book consumers, where did this investigative attitude come from?

There was much in the practical experience of the early modern polity

that must have disposed observers to look widely at the human landscape and find patterns of connection there. Again, war and mass urban migration surely mattered; for the upheaval that provided a disturbing unity of experience also made the unfamiliar commonplace and the boundary porous for people in motion. The wandering body and mind became normal. Motion also, perhaps paradoxically, threw into relief the outline of social organization: the divides among, as well as the interdependence of, salaried urban samurai, the city people who built a market on their wealth, and the agrarian producers who supplied that market. This social structure demanded an infrastructure—of land and sea transport, wholesale grain and commodity exchanges—that, even in rudimentary form, further exposed a relationship between functionally differentiated units. And in the domain of politics, the complex cohesion of parts found physical expression in the obligatory traffic between Edo, the central metropolis, and the castle towns of daimyo. The zoning of cities, where samurai and commoners occupied distinctive wards, offered another physical statement of political structure.

Nudged by practical experience to think systematically about society, writers faced practical incentives as well. The increasing number of customers of an increasingly diverse publishing trade needed—or could be persuaded to need—clear overviews of the new world they were navigating: road maps, city maps, travel itineraries, commercial directories, personnel rosters, and the like. While urban fiction and martial history bound them together in communities of feeling and memory, a good street map could put the daily realm quite usefully in order. Writers had precedents, however, for the fiction and the history. They had no precedents for the street map. Or the urban directory, the personnel roster, the comprehensive gazetteer, the popular travel guide.

Such material might have developed autonomously in the publishing market. Still, structural thinking is not easy. In this case, it required not just a consciousness of patterns and interactions in social conduct but the ability to block a competing consciousness of singularity and dissonance. It required not just some longing for order among individuals caught in the urban whirlpool but some confidence that order was more than the eccentric construction of an individual eye. Thus it required, above all, an apposite vocabulary to name and sort things out, as well as a master plot in which to arrange them. To take hold, the vocabulary and the plot had to appear to make sense; they had to win recognition as convincing conventions.

The work of distilling the Japanese social body into conventional order began, in a situation of numbing disorder, in the decades just before and after 1600. If the publishing market might eventually have put together a foundational story about a coherent society, it did not have to. A nascent state struggling for survival used two general programs of registration—the cadastral survey and the cartographic survey—to put on paper, and in the minds of participants, the tropes of union. Although authors and publishers would variously build on and bend these tropes, the library of public information was grounded in the worldview invented and projected by the unification regimes. A vision of the nation was the astonishing feat of overlords who foresaw an integrated state before it became a reality.

Cadastral surveying (to which we return in the next chapter) was, in brief, an effort to record the human and natural resources required for wartime mobilizations and peacetime governance. Long under way in individual daimyo domains, it changed radically when the Toyotomi and Tokugawa regimes attempted registration projects that were both national in scope and empirical in method. Instead of collecting extant documentation, registrars were meant to measure fields and harvests physically, according to (more or less) well-defined principles. Their work was guided, moreover, by two conceptual breakthroughs. First, the surveyors of the unification regimes took the tens of thousands of local communities spread across the countryside—all of them distinctive in topography and ecology, nomenclature, history, organization, proprietorship, and productive enterprises—and conceived of them uniformly as "villages." Then, after measuring their resources (more or very much less) systematically, the surveyors converted the totals, by formula, to a universal standard of value. Each "village" was registered with an "assessed yield" (or *kokudaka*) that expressed gross annual productivity in terms of a rice equivalent. Thus, for example, a village with an assessed yield of 3,000 *koku* produced annual harvests (whatever their kind) that surveyors had assigned a value equal to 15,000 bushels of rice (one *koku* = roughly five bushels). In effect, the cadastral surveys abstracted a physically intricate, politically riven landscape into integers.[41]

The surveys became indispensable to virtually all functions of early modern rule, from levying taxes and labor to assigning daimyo domains and samurai stipends. Just as critically, they provided a universal vocabulary of land—one that highlighted "village" and "assessed yield" but extended to broadly conventional terms for field types, measures, the subunits of the village, and the cultivators who were named in cadastral registries. In essence, these words defined the categories that made up the integral agrarian community. The cadastres also conveyed a master plot about land: the village was the foundational unit of social formation (a unit sufficiently stable to bear institutional examination) and the productive source of wealth. Although particular (and thus individually named, located, and described), the village took its place in a national constellation of villages, all of them conformable to a common lexicon. Although generated by diverse production, its wealth found expression in a common measure that accorded prestige to the (putatively) prime crop of rice.

The lexicon and master plot for land that derived from cadastral surveys extended to a lexicon and master plot for power that derived from cartographic surveys (again, a subject to which we return). The universalizing notions of "village" and "assessed yield" made possible a legible, consistent representation of the polity on the maps drafted by the Tokugawa regime, following no fewer than four comprehensive cartographic surveys, during the seventeenth century.[42] Within the armature of physical geography, cartographers prominently marked the castle towns of all daimyo, labeling each with the name of the town, the name and title of its daimyo ruler, and the total assessed yield of all villages within his jurisdiction. Because the productivity figures encoded both knowledge and control, mapmakers could elide the villages themselves (too numerous for inclusion) and the boundaries of the individual daimyo domains (too tortured for stable delineation). They created, in effect, a radiant image of power by visually conflating the castle node, the ruling lord, and the standardized figures that signified dominion over village producers and their methodically measured resources. Throughout the total space of the nation, the maps declared, authority flowed out from daimyo castles, while wealth flowed in. The systemic union of the polity was implicit in the uniform style of the cartographic entries and the slight exaggeration of the shogunal headquarters of Edo (and other cities under direct Tokugawa control). It was explicit in the elaborate representation of highways—each marked by distance indicators, post stations, barrier checkpoints, and the ports leading to marine transport—that conveyed not only physical connection but a formidable apparatus of information gathering and surveillance.

Official mapmakers conveyed union of another kind—a union of history and culture rather than power—by orienting the polity within seemingly timeless frames. Reviving an ancient conception of Dai Nihon, they centered their maps on the imperial capital and divided them internally into the provincial units established during the classical period. They punctuated the landscape, moreover, with the famous places of natural beauty, historical resonance, and sacred meaning that, embedded in the imagery of art, putatively animated "our country."

In both their national and small area maps, the Tokugawa regime expanded on the lexicon of the cadastres to define the conventions of social geography. The whole of Japan was parsed in the language of province, dis-

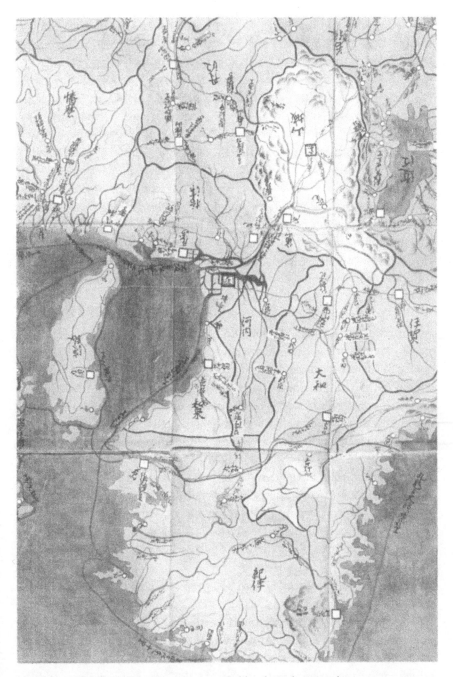

FIG. 9. *Nihonzu* (Map of Japan), compiled by the Tokugawa shogunate c. 1640, detail including Kyoto and the home provinces, the Kii Peninsula, Lake Biwa, and part of the Inland Sea. Manuscript, 370 × 433.7 cm. National Diet Library, Tokyo.

trict, village, castle town, city, port, famous place, circuit, highway, post station, barrier checkpoint, assessed yield, shogun, daimyo, daimyo domain, samurai, intendant, farmer, townsperson, urban ward, street. Although most of these words were old, they acquired a generic quality rare in the medieval world—when the meanings of terms like "samurai," "daimyo," "village," and "ward" depended entirely on the vantage of the user. The words functioned as labels in the clear visual order of maps, thus naming and disaggregating phenomena of apparent specificity and stability. And they folded the named parts of society into master plots bigger than those of the cadastres. In fact, Tokugawa mapmakers used elegantly simple symbol systems to tell many complex and overlapping stories about time, culture, power, class, and economic functions. But the basic message was straightforward enough. Within an ancient country founded on a sacred throne and marked pervasively by the sites of shared culture, a united company of shogun and daimyo ruled from great cities over the (rice-)rich villages of a fully measured and connected landscape.

The labeling and ideological construction of the polity went together with important forms of schooling; for both the cadastral and cartographic surveys taught the habits of investigating and being investigated. Over the course of (repeated) inspections, thousands of military deputies learned to enter unfamiliar communities as outsiders, to examine human and physical resources impersonally, and to record them categorically. They learned, in effect, how to see a public as the object of aggregate scrutiny. They learned, too, how to be public men—officeholders entitled to observe and assess social activity. The huge numbers of local informants who assisted the official surveyors learned similar lessons, although as insiders (ambivalently stretched in identity between the surveyors and the surveyed) rather than outsiders. In time, village headmen would be obliged to apply such lessons by generating local maps and conventionalized tax statements of their own.[43] As for the general population of villagers, they learned to live under the watchful eyes of registrars and see their resources registered by convention. They learned, in effect, how to be a public—an object of analysis and collective definition.

The cartographic enterprise, and the exceptional circumstances that led new conquerors to imagine in integral terms a polity still in formation, is the subject of the following chapter. Yet implicit in this overview is the powerful legacy of the surveys for the library of public information. Some of the information texts, preeminently the commercial maps, essentially reproduced official models. Many more of them depended on official data— concerning distances and productivity, say, or martial appointments and elite incomes. And virtually all of them relied on an official lexicon to organize their material. Thus urban directories built on the tropes of official urban cartography: castle compound, martial residence, commoner ward, temple zone, famous place, street, and physical landmark. So, too, provincial gazetteers used the categories of provincial cartography (as well as domainal reports on resources) to cover castle towns, districts, villages, transport, crops, manufactures, famous goods, famous places, temples and shrines, natural features, and ritual calendars. Wealth was always a matter of assessed yields; measures conformed to shogunal standards.

Behind the conventions, moreover, was the holistic vision of the official surveys. The writers who comprehensively explored the food of the realm (or the brothels, the sanctuaries, the festivals, the work) came in the wake of the surveyors who comprehensively plotted the fields of the realm (and the highways, the cities, the post stations, the distribution of the daimyo). They effectively emulated those predecessors in both mobility and synoptic thought. Indeed, many of the writers were direct successors to the surveyors; for they shared not only an attitude toward investigation but a common formation. Numerous authors of the early information texts were samurai themselves, and thus trained, like the cadastral and cartographic registrars, for careers of surveillance.[44] They also coped as samurai with the continuing dislocations that made them homeless observers of a wide world. The sons and grandsons of fief holders who had been decanted into castle towns, these demobilized soldiers were often kept in motion. Many followed their daimyo lords to new domains in the course of the periodic transfers that occurred well into the seventeenth century. Many accompanied their lords to and from Edo every year. And many lost their lords to the disciplinary attainders that converted vassals into masterless "men of the waves" (or *rōnin*). Even samurai in fairly stable situations faced the mental commotion of underemployment and unemployment, since pacification created redundant soldiers without any practical military function beyond policing. Administrative posts in the shogunal and daimyo bureaucracies also remained far fewer than the great numbers of candidates. Some samurai consequently hit the road in search of useful work; others hit the books in search of alternative careers.

The early modern polity produced a strange elite: one tied neither to land nor to necessarily fixed locations and one lacking, below the highest ranks, either sufficient purpose or comfortable remuneration. Samurai were paid and honored by the regime, but often paid poorly and honored rhetorically. Conducive to independence and skepticism, this tension encouraged the samurai to fashion roles for themselves. Some would increas-

ingly detach the notion of service from old values—from martial proficiency, submission to individual lords, even hereditary calling—and attach
it to new ones: to learning and learned criticism of the regime, and to work
in the popular domain. The option of scholarship came to loom large,
partly because of its traditional prestige and the professed association between learning and fit rule. Yet scholarship also met a pressing need for legitimating activity and real employment. The samurai who hit the books
would use variable doses of education to work as doctors, schoolmasters,
advisors to shogun and daimyo, natural scientists, agronomists, and writers. They would write fiction, history, philosophy, and poetry. They would
also write a large sample of the texts of public information—dictionaries,
encyclopedias, gazetteers, farming manuals, travel guides, and the like.

In sum, the influence of the state on the new information library was
profound in at least two respects. In the cadastral and cartographic surveys,
the state laid out the lexicon and the holistic framework for social examination. And in the formation of the samurai class, the state produced an
elite trained to leadership and privilege, and instilled with the values of education and service, which was nonetheless constrained severely in official
opportunity. Here were the ambitious but anxious men in motion who
took up the work of the surveyors in altered form. They, too, looked
widely, and as outsiders, at a public they scrutinized and sorted. Yet their
subjects steadily diverged from the surveys to take in a society bigger and
more complex than the symbols on maps. Their work further diverged
from the surveys insofar as these authors joined two types of public—the
public as analytical object and the public as consuming audience—by
writing for commercial publication. They put their findings *about* society
on the market *for* social consumption. Through their disparate books,
readers ate up information about themselves.

The authors of the information texts wrote for various purposes—to en-
tertain, to edify, to instruct, to discharge obligations to the social body, to
deepen self-knowledge, to make a living, to make a name. Like the agronomist Miyazaki Yasusada or the educator Kaibara Ekiken, some responded
to a perceived responsibility for popular service as well as a neo-Confucian
conviction that empirical investigation yielded philosophical understanding. Some were inspired by older and more recent Chinese texts, funneled
in expanding numbers through the port of Nagasaki, which served as
models for their own investigations. Many were enlivened by one another,
or a need for cash, or a devouring curiosity. Each writer, and each work,
came out of distinctive circumstances. To describe the general context for
the emergence of the information library is not to explain away the partic-

ular conditions surrounding individual texts. Yet just as this library required a publishing industry to make material publicly accessible, so it required an integral imagination to make society publicly visible. The preconditions for the imaginative leap lay in the conventional lexicon and master plots of the surveys and in the mentality of wandering observers.

In the following chapters, we look more closely at several major types of information texts—first at the maps undergirding the new library, then at shogunal personnel rosters, urban directories, tour guides, and family encyclopedias. All were synoptic accounts of contemporary politics and culture in the popular mainstream. And all, too, showed the strain implicit in their genesis. The conventions that facilitated information gathering led in one direction—toward conventionality. The restless minds that sought it out led in another—toward discovery and the shattering of stable worldviews. The texts of the information library are shot through with tension between these poles. Hewing to the lexicon and ideology of official cartography, the texts to a remarkable degree reiterated a standard knowledge about society. Incrementally, however, they also opened and recast the conventions.

Thus, on the one hand, the essential conservatism of the information library remains striking. Commercial mapmakers stayed so close to official prototypes that the popular cartography of the mid nineteenth century still recognizably derived from the original shogunal surveys. Consider the case of Edo. Roughly two hundred commercial editions of Edo maps had appeared by 1700, and roughly twelve hundred by 1860.[45] Successive mapmakers tracked the changes resulting from fire and earthquake, population influx and new building. They also inflected their work with varying artistic details and increasing emphases on famous places. Nonetheless, they reproduced a largely unchanged idea of the capital. Fully in the manner of the prototypes, later maps continued to focus on a dominant shogunal castle, exaggerated in size, which was surrounded by the elaborately marked residences of the martial elite (each labeled with the name, title, and domainal wealth of the occupant). Temples and shrines appeared prominently as well, in some cases with pictorial illustrations, whereas commoners' wards remained undifferentiated white space. Nowhere in the "new" and "revised" maps of commercial cartographers do we find subjects unexplored in the prototypes—the burgeoning shantytowns of day laborers, for example, or the pervasive houses of unlicensed prostitution. Absent, too, were efforts to reclassify or resignify urban phenomena. New maps did not decenter or diminish the castle to reorient the city around markets and financial institutions. None blanked out daimyo residences while labeling the firms and governing associations of commoners. None lavished pictorial illustration on the entertainment quarters instead of the temples. None, in short, reconceived Edo. The model held.

Fidelity to models is apparent not only in commercial mapmaking but in many other texts of the information library, particularly the rosters of shogunal personnel and the provincial gazetteers. There, a reliance on the basic tropes of social analysis reinforced the scaffold of conventional meaning. Provinces were places of castle towns, (rice-producing) villages, and religious sanctuaries—and hence not, at least very visibly, places of manufacture, mining and lumbering, migrant labor, and rich peasant landlords. Legitimate authority was a matter of courtly and martial pedigrees, official titles, and registered incomes—and hence not a phenomenon that extended at all explicitly to village councils, neighborhood elders, and mercantile associations. Calculations of wealth focused entirely on agrarian yields and hence left unexplored the income generated by industry, trade, and services. Religious life remained tied to lists of institutions and ritual calendars that left unmentioned the practices of diviners, magicians, hermits, and shamans.

The conformity to models and tropes is not so surprising. Official maps proved enormously influential because they did such hard work so convincingly. With meager precedents, surveyors carried out the daunting labor of measuring and plotting huge, bewildering landscapes. And then they isolated from those landscapes a fixed, seemingly cogent set of categories to define physical and human geography. Cartographers created an Edo, for example, of streets, waterways, wards, bridges, natural landmarks, military and civilian residential areas, major temples and shrines, and the official warehouse facilities at the port of Edo Bay. Here, certainly, were the critical components of a real and recognizable city. And they were arranged in a legible, seemingly judicious representation. A vast castle, military mansions occupying three-quarters of the cityscape, and substantial reli-

FIG. 10 (*opposite*). Mori Fusae, *Bunken Edo ōezu* (Great Survey Map of Edo, 1858), detail covering roughly the same space as figure 5. The Tokugawa crest, rather than an illustration of the grounds, marks the castle, and many of the ward names in commoner neighborhoods appear within the block rather than on the thoroughfares. The conception of the city is unchanged. Woodblock, 179 × 198 cm. Courtesy of the East Asian Library, University of California, Berkeley.

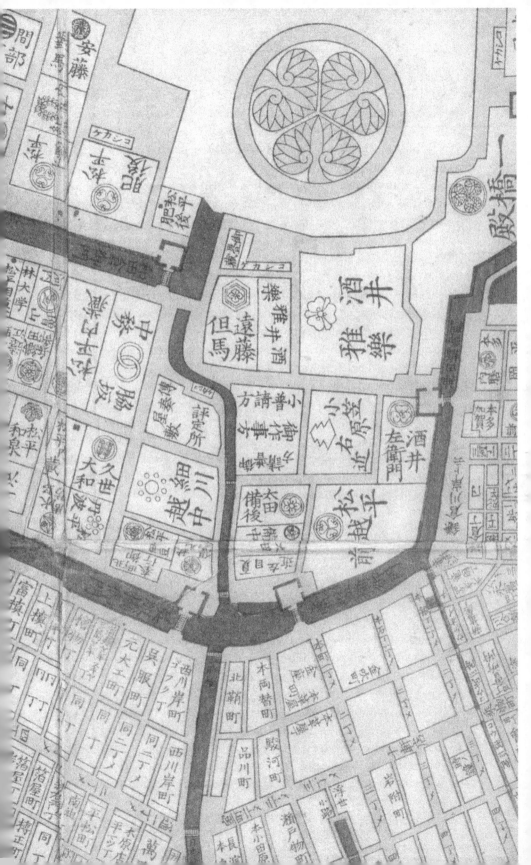

gious establishments were hardly cartographic inventions. Without any gross distortion, the model appeared to distill empirical data into commonsensical categories and almost inevitable order.

Once made, moreover, the prototype was a template. It could inspire any number of new maps of Edo that updated or amended the model, as well as any number of new maps of other cities, which translated the classification and style of the Edo map into a model of citiness itself. Similarly, the cartographic information could be repackaged and amplified in quite different texts—in street directories, say, or in guidebooks, itineraries, personnel registries, and the like. So, too, with all foundational taxonomies. One gazetteer or personnel roster could engender the next. One genre could mutate into another. And, indeed, much of the information library depended on just such synergy. Information expanded because investigators learned to gather and manage it structurally in accord with examples.

The curious effect, however, was that the cartographic models generated knowledge even as they standardized—and thus constricted—the categories of knowledge. Investigation could be routinized by the categories it had to fit (or the blanks it had to fill in). Timely data could be absorbed into apparently timeless frames, and consequently stripped of any disturbing novelty. The problem is succinctly conveyed in the phrase "newly revised," which became a commonplace in the titles of the information library. The words insisted that something in a text was new enough to merit special attention, though not quite new enough to merit a fresh beginning. Something fundamental survived—something susceptible to revision rather than reimagination. A basic constancy trumped a superficial volatility. Yesterday resembled today. Tomorrow was predictable.

If conventions simultaneously generated and standardized knowledge, they also simultaneously described and prescribed experience. Maps, and all taxonomic schemes, require order and focus, dominant and subordinate motifs, the elision of unruly material. They require, in effect, organizing ideas that discipline evidence into normative structures of meaning. The ideas behind official Edo maps, like the ideas behind national maps, are straightforward enough: this is the shogun's city, ordered by a status system that exalts military houses over those of common townspeople, where religious institutions take primacy over commercial institutions. And when commercial mapmakers reproduced the model, they reiterated—and normalized—this message about social hierarchy.

Sheer momentum surely helped keep the model going, as did a verisimilitude that masked or muted its ideological content. The genius of Tokugawa (and all) maps derives from their conflation of verifiable realities with value-laden interpretations—a conflation that made status boundaries appear as natural as rivers. The interpretations buried in the maps were also more diffuse than my bald synopses suggest. Readers could play with various meanings or try to look beyond meaning altogether to make maps fit their expectations. And, indeed, expectation remains the most powerful preservative of models. Mapmakers and map users learn to expect the kind of maps they are accustomed to seeing. In the end, then, the strength of models is their facility to frustrate, as either unthinkable or perverse, the revision of their underlying conceptions. An alternative representation of Edo would have required not so much new evidence as a new vision. Had commercial mapmakers accorded privilege to commercial wards rather than martial mansions, they would have projected a rival plot: this is a financial and mercantile capital (say), administered through the neighborhood associations of townspeople, where entertainment is a major enterprise. For that leap, they needed no fresh data. They needed a radical philosophy.

But radicalism is tough and nowhere natural. The publishers and authors of the information texts were men of their day. Observation for them, as for most observers, was not inherently linked to skepticism. The conventions of social analysis they inherited from the regime bore the hallmark of authority, and thus encouraged deference—particularly as foundational stories lacking coherent foils. Insofar as they grasped the equivalence between convention and ideology, moreover, the writers were likely to be believers. Those of samurai origin came from the organization and tended to be well schooled in a Confucianism that convincingly rationalized the polity. Geared to the market and guided by the tropes at hand, other writers (and their publishers) had little incentive to reconceive the terms of reference that made their texts intelligible.

The conventionality of the information library made it "public" in yet another fashion peculiar to political discourse in East Asia. The Sino-Japanese term *kō*, normally translated as "public," designated both the persons who embodied legitimate authority and the domain of right conduct and right thought. Its antithesis, the *shi*, or "private," indicated the (selfish) self and the domain of ego-driven conduct and deviant thought. Congruence with official norms located most of the information texts in the public sphere of right knowledge. Not only accessible to a public of consumers and descriptive of a public under investigation, the texts also captured a public as it was meant to be. In effect, they were complicit in the ideological work of a regime that remained, if selectively, comfortable with the publishing industry. Tokugawa officials released some of their most important maps to printing firms, cooperated in the publication of shogunal personnel rosters, and generally tolerated a high level of disclosure concerning what might seem sensitive information—about everything from transport and police barriers to official travel schedules, production figures, and court and monastic allowances. They apparently understood that in the routinization of such material—and in its projection of a polity both united and universal—knowledge could be put in the service of indoctrination.

Among the chief disclosures of the information library, then, are the rules of the game. In their points of convergence and common denominators, the texts expose the proper knowledge that organized the world of writers and readers in early modern Japan. Precisely because of their conventionality, the texts illumine what popular audiences were meant to take for granted, what they could and should know—what, in sum, they were being taught about collective identities.

One startling revelation is the breadth of proper knowledge and the density of the collective identities constructed through it. By the time the family encyclopedias began to appear in the late seventeenth century, the frames built by official cartography had been filled and expanded so copiously that the dimensions of a presumptively basic education—or what I call "cultural literacy"—stretched wide. The digests assembled information in all the cartographic categories (from castle town to famous place), digressing into any number of (loosely) related topics: the structure of the imperial court, the chronology of imperial and military rulers, the calendar of major rituals throughout the nation, the rudiments of poetic composition, the lexicons of natural history and material culture, the distribution of famous art objects, the organization of amateur arts groups, the itineraries of basic tours, and much else.

The digests reflected the growing quantities of public information gathered by growing numbers of investigators. Set in motion by the official surveys, and formed by official tropes, these worldly reckonings nonetheless overtook the models. In the process, they disturbed the conventionality of the information library. The shogunal personnel rosters, for example, juxtaposed against the hereditary privilege of daimyo the professional competence of the samurai and commoner officials who competitively filled administrative posts. The urban directories awarded primacy to the market and to the freedoms, attendant on expertise and wealth, that assailed both social hierarchy and social community. Tour guides claimed both open access to a huge cultural landscape and an egalitarian custody of its meanings for any competent viewer. And family encyclopedias defined a cultural literacy that supplanted status claims as the grounds of social membership.

Like the many manuals of instruction, they also conveyed the message that individuals could fashion themselves: skills were learnable, proficiency was a matter not of calling itself but of prodigious application. Anyone with the time and money could buy education—not just basic schooling but training in philosophy, medicine, poetry, calligraphy, music—and become a gentleperson.

In short, we find in the information texts a steady, often subversive, strain against fixed notions of social structure. Without dislodging the lexicon and master plots of conventional knowledge, investigators looked widely enough at disparate experiences to diffuse expectations about the norm. Hence, as we read their texts, we find not only the conventions but surprising departures. Writers offered readers both plural and mutable identities. They also rattled certainties. In their attention to the mundane, they raised unspoken questions about what mattered: was low life as important as high life and a hierarchy of value so clear? In their attention to observation, they raised questions about authority: could purely textual scholarship be trusted? And did claims about the verifiability of information equalize the relationship between the writers who collected it and the readers who were implicitly invited to test it? In their attention to the variability of social practice, they raised questions about change: were the norms elastic enough to contain rupture?

The gravest question raised by the information texts concerned limits: where, if anywhere, was inquiry to stop? Was investigation to defer to established learning or the wisdom of rulers or the mores of communities? Surely travel routes and planting schedules and the like belonged to the proper domain of investigation. But what about the justice of the law or the well-being of commoners or the distribution of grain? Although convention and conventional expectation could forestall novelty, the momentum of discovery might easily lead from the investigation of marriage rituals to the investigation of infanticide, or from the investigation of bureaucratic structure to the investigation of bureaucratic competence.

The limits of the information library were real enough in practice. Most obviously, information tended to stop at domestic borders. Chinese books, in Chinese and in translation, did selectively make it into print in Japan; and Japanese authors did incorporate secondary knowledge of China into encyclopedias, scientific texts, and other material. Maps of China, as well as maps of the world, were also published, although, again, on the basis of secondary and increasingly anachronistic sources. Western books reached shogunal officials through the port of Nagasaki and sometimes circulated among broader communities of scholars. In general, however, the stringently enforced prohibitions against foreign travel—and the careful oversight of foreign books imported at Nagasaki—kept low the volume of immediate and practical information about outside worlds. None of it was based on the observations of Japanese authors.

But, given the explosion of the information library, it is the limits on domestic inquiry that are most interesting and hardest to explain. The texts stopped short at two internal borders. They did not convert social knowledge into social science by analyzing the effects of the data and the systems they described. And they did not convert information into news by reporting on events and opinions. While the new library enlarged knowledge exponentially and disturbed norms inexorably, it never shifted register from observation to commentary. It remained in the realm of the *kō*—a realm of proper thought and action seemingly removed from the partisanship of private (*shi*) feeling.

We shall continue to grapple with the reasons, which tend to be more fugitive than transparent. Censorship surely mattered: the regime worked to suppress—first through suasion, gradually by law—the treatment of sensitive subjects, which included military households, foreign affairs, Christianity and other heterodox beliefs, and disturbing current events. Self-censorship seems to have been more powerful than official intervention, however, in a publishing industry that tested the bounds of tolerance very gingerly.[46] The critical constraint on the information library seems to have been prevailing agreements—or compromises implicitly forged with the regime—about the division of labor. In the world of letters, social commentary moved into the academies and intellectual circles where learned men generated critiques that circulated in manuscript and increasingly in printed books. Although typically written in Chinese and published after a delay, those books signaled both the richness of the debate about the polity and a consensus that debate had a place in the print forum.[47] Beyond the academy, commentary also moved into popular fiction and drama, where a guise of make-believe sanctioned long, disturbing looks at social topsy-turvy. The fecundity of academic and artistic criticism of the status quo discourages any notion that the information library hewed to convention simply owing to inertia and deference. Dangerous subjects were on the early modern mind, but they were channeled into safer streams of analysis.

Still, the information library was hardly a safe place. We are surprised by its limits only because it went so far. Breaking monopolies on knowledge, the texts reached beyond status-bound audiences of insiders to an open realm of consumers. Information became common property. Spilling profusely across mundane experience, the texts portrayed a society bigger than the polity. Here the danger was greatest, for writers insinuated that relations of power fit into the broader, dynamic structures of a society with greater precedence and a longer life than any particular government. By making that society visible to itself, in empirical treatments that were both holistic and animated by detail, the library of public information shaped an early modern mind habituated to self-consciousness. Social knowledge created contexts for social criticism.

THREE

Maps Are Strange

A COLLEAGUE CALLED ME one day to ask where he could find a medieval map of Kyoto—or, really, a good reproduction of any original drafted between, say, the twelfth and sixteenth centuries. He needed it fast. So one quick reference would do until he could examine the full record later.

Well, the record is blank. There are no surviving maps of Kyoto made in the medieval period (and no later reproductions either, only artful imaginings). Indeed, I don't think maps of Kyoto were made at all in the medieval period.

My colleague's certainty that I could direct him to a map (he asked, after all, not whether but where he could find one) represents a triumph of conviction over experience. A master of the medieval archive, this friend might have suspected that something he had never seen might well not exist. Still, he distrusted his knowledge of the sources to believe that maps he had not found himself were surely findable—just overlooked in his own reading. Nor is he alone. Ever since I began my work on cartographic history, fellow faculty and students have asked for references to old Japanese maps of military campaigns or provincial administrations or pilgrimage circuits or sea routes. And, like my caller, they have been astonished to find nothing of the sort.

In good measure, I suspect, my friends assume that any variety of cartographic material must be out there somewhere because they know Japanese mapmakers were active in the classical and medieval periods. Extant maps from these eras are actually numerous enough (well over two hundred, according to modern censuses) to suggest that Japan had one of the more robust cartographic projects in the premodern world.[1] As my friends also know, mapmaking became a stunningly prolific enterprise in Japan after 1600—an enterprise presumably dependent on established practices.[2] Hence notions about a continuous and diverse cartographic tradition, in which maps of provincial administrations or pilgrimage routes would appear unexceptional, seem only sensible.

My colleague's assumption about Kyoto seems particularly sensible. If maps were being made at all in medieval Japan, surely Kyoto must have been a prime target. A giant city by contemporary measures (with a population of over 100,000), Kyoto remained the imperial capital in the medieval period and, after 1338, served as the capital of the Ashikaga shogun as well. It was the center of a vast religious establishment, the hub of regional (and sporadically international) trade, and the destination of most domestic travelers (from pilgrims to litigants, officials to students, and migrant laborers to beggars). Writers certainly found Kyoto a muse, for the city was home to the literary elite that tracked its daily rhythms in diaries and celebrated its landscape in poems. Painters, too, routinely captured scenes of the capital—in mandalas of temples and shrines, screens and scrolls of seasonal flora, and illustrations of historical (and fictional) tales. A common subject of representation, and already in the tenth century the focus of maps that traced its lovely symmetry as a synecdoche for the imperial state, Kyoto would appear irresistible to medieval cartographers.[3]

But quite apart from knowledge about early Japanese cartography and Kyoto's power as a subject, I imagine my colleague's search emerged from unconscious, and widely shared, convictions about mapmaking itself. Believing mapmaking to be inherent in the human experience, many of us simply expect to find good cartographic evidence from the past. We assume that once a society acquires even rudimentary cartographic skills, it will go on to produce maps, more or less regularly, in response to the many needs—of travelers and explorers, soldiers and conquerors, governors and judges, builders and landholders, pedagogues and ideologues—that maps serve so elegantly.

The problem here is a leap rather than an error in judgment; for our basic assumptions about cartographic practice are sound. Cognitive scientists have shown that mapping—the ability to perceive complex spatial relations and abstract them into mental diagrams—is, for all its manifold sophistication, a function lodged in the human cortex and detectable in young children before the mastery of language. So, too, historians have shown that mapmaking—the actual representation of space in cartographic signs—is common to most societies, including preliterate societies. Some of the evidence is spectacular in its antiquity (cadastral maps appear on Babylonian clay tablets from roughly 2,300 B.C.E., for example), some in its scientific precosity (the Greeks had produced a celestial globe by the fourth century B.C.E. and a graticule for longitude and latitude by the second century C.E., for example). But across the centuries and the continents, almost all cultures have left a record of cartographic enterprise. Attention to the science of cartography (to mathematical and astronomical calculations, surveying technologies, and precision in scale and projection) has been notably erratic. Yet scientific competence is only one facet of the cartographic craft, neither precluding by its absence nor guaranteeing by its presence the pursuit of mapmaking. What is clearest from the record is a social investment in cartography so broad and various that maps figure conspicuously among the graphic artifacts prevalent across cultural boundaries.[4]

Not so startling, then, are impressions that maps must have been, if not ubiquitous, at least commonplace in the past—common enough to extend to a great metropolis like Kyoto and to persuade us that while maps of this medieval capital may no longer survive, they were undoubtedly made, only to be lost in the wastes of time. Here, however, is the leap in judgment that obscures one of the strangest, most tantalizing, aspects of cartographic history—its unevenness, its many lacunae. Although people before the modern era clearly could make maps, and did make a great number of them, mapmaking in individual societies appears to have been selective and irregular, far from comprehensive and routine, until rather recent times. Historical surveys demonstrate that premodern mapmaking was both widespread and, in the aggregate, close to exhaustive in subject matter. Local histories tell another story.

In the case of Japan, most extant maps from the medieval period chart small units of private landholding (usually the estates of medieval proprietors), with limited attention to surrounding areas. Insofar as modern scholars can uncover their purposes, the maps concentrate on issues of internal administrative importance (reclamation, irrigation, the distribution of resources) and local conflict (principally disputed boundaries). They were certainly not drafted as aids to travel, trade, regional governance, military maneuvers, or the like. Nor do such cartographic aids exist elsewhere in the medieval archives of Japan. We find no maps of large territories—of districts, provinces, or circuits. We find no maps of coastlines or waterways, no maps of battle or conquest. And we find no maps of towns—not one port or market or temple city or administrative headquarters. Kyoto is hardly unique in its absence from the record. The remaining evidence suggests no habitual recourse to maps for spatial understanding.[5]

Extant maps are only a sample, doubtless a miniscule sample, of the maps actually drafted (or traced against sand and sky) in medieval Japan.

Still, the void in the archives warns us that a diverse cartographic practice was unlikely. Would almost everything except landholding maps have disappeared without a trace? However quixotic the fate of old things, is it probable that maps of some scope and collective significance—maps of *not destroyed* Kyoto or the home provinces, say—would have perished entirely, while maps of village reclamation and irrigation have survived rather well? Absences in other sources raise warnings too. Travelers do not allude to maps in their diaries, and governors do not invoke them in their documents. Even medieval narratives rely on words, never on cartographic sketches, for their painstaking coverage of the geography of war and peace.

The case of Japan is not unusual. In England, where searches for cartographic material have been particularly thorough, scholars have identified only about 35 domestic maps produced before 1500. Local maps that predate 1500 seem similarly few elsewhere in Europe: about 15 have been recovered from the Low Countries; roughly 10 from France; and fewer than 20 from central Europe. The Italian evidence is comparatively rich (including a number of city plans and district surveys), but no internal maps of early vintage have been found in Spain, Portugal, Wales, Scotland, and Ireland.[6] Surely many maps have been lost and many others—sketched for passing purposes—were never meant to last. The small figures nonetheless hint at a limited rather than a routine cartographic practice.

So, too, do the subjects of extant maps. The British material includes simple national maps and pilgrimage itineraries, but it concentrates on discrete land issues (water pipes, property registration, and ownership disputes). There is no evidence of urban or regional cartography, of transport or defense surveys. By contrast, the Italian material suggests an administrative interest in plotting cities and districts, as well as a certain antiquarianism and civic pride, insofar as some of the city views (especially of Rome) were drawn heroically, with plentiful historical details, for display. Yet absent here are the property maps and itineraries we find in Britain. In sum, the various samples disclose distinctive patterns and emphases in mapmaking. Cartography appears to have been locally selective in function, highly particular in execution, and necessarily limited in consumption.

If we take the lacunae seriously, and thus imagine that mapmaking was somehow an uncommon practice in many societies, we open the question of why. In the case of Japan, we move from my colleague's question—where can I find a medieval map of Kyoto?—to its obverse: why are there no medieval maps of Kyoto? Put another way, if you can map one thing (in the instance of a proprietary estate, quite a complex thing), why not map many more things as well?

From the vantage of early modern evidence, we can frame the question more broadly: when mapmaking does become pervasive in a society, what accounts for the shift? Why does a rather limited practice of mapmaking mutate into a more versatile practice? The drama of the change deserves emphasis, for it was not incremental but abrupt. One census of 225 extant maps assigns 31 to the Nara period (710–784), 13 to the Heian period (794–1185), 55 to the Kamakura period (1185–1333), 15 to the period of the Northern and Southern Courts (1336–1392), and 111 to the later Muromachi and Warring States periods (1392–c. 1600).[7] The absolute numbers can mean very little, since we have no way of calculating what must be considerable loss. The production curve, however, is strangely flat (with a dip in the late classical period), and it actually declines if we assign higher rates of attrition to the maps of earlier centuries. In any event, there is no quantitative evidence of sustained expansion and no anticipation at all of the coming explosion. By 1700, thousands of Japanese maps—on virtually every domestic subject and in virtually every format—had issued from government offices, commercial publishers, and the ateliers of painters. In Europe, the transition from limited to vigorous mapmaking occurred earlier than in Japan, closer to 1500. But there, too, change was more dramatic than incremental. Across the medieval–early modern divide, difference and discontinuity in mapmaking prevailed over gradually adaptive expansion. Something happened.

The circumstances of the early modern world obviously differed enough from those of the medieval world to suggest explanations. We have noted numerous factors in the case of Japan that impinge on mapmaking: the emergence of a strong state and a commercial publishing industry; significant increases in urbanization, literacy, and travel. Foreign encounters clearly mattered as well. European traders and missionaries, present in Japan from the mid sixteenth century, brought with them both foreign maps and new cartographic learning. They also provoked, through their representations of alien worlds, a heightened consciousness of "our country." A "Japan" assumed its strong cartographic profile as attention to the globe and lands that were "not Japan" reoriented the geographical imagination.

But unless we confuse circumstances with causes, the factors contributing to cartographic change in early modern Japan do not explain the change itself. They may account for the increased volume, variety, and circulation of maps. They do not constitute a formula for the transformation—on the order, say, of state + printing + urbanization + literacy + travel + foreign encounter = strong mapmaking. In medieval Japan, after all, we find an ancient monarchy and durable shogunal institutions, a monastic printing tradition, a giant capital with a literate elite, a steady traffic of warriors and monks, and an intense consciousness of the foreign world of China. Are we to conclude that these features were insufficiently developed to generate a regular and diverse mapmaking practice? If so, how much development is enough? Insofar as roughly quantitative measures influence outcomes, we would expect mapmaking to expand proportionately with the variables. But in Japan, as elsewhere, a seemingly flat rate of production changed suddenly and increased geometrically.

We might be tempted, then, to edge away from putatively measurable changes in literacy or travel volumes to emphasize the habits and attitudes that affect the reception of media. People in medieval Japan were clearly accustomed to exploring space through the mediation of guides and scouts and informants along the way. They had learned to rely for geographical information on hearsay and the accounts of previous travelers, sometimes on instincts honed by experience. And when they translated space into texts, they leaned toward the unfolding narrative of the diary or travelogue, the lyrical focus of the poem, the specificity of the painting. The abstract economy of the map was not necessarily an attractive alternative. Thus, for example, the reluctance of medieval European sailors to trust navigational charts over the authority of personal memory suggests some resistance to cartographic innovation. Long after the invention of Portolan charts around 1300, navigators continued to rely on pilots' rudders—verbal logs of each discrete journey—for guidance in their travels. In this wariness about a new medium, the cartographic historian P. D. A. Harvey finds "a way of thinking quite different from our own"—a particular spatial imagination that marginalized maps in favor of words, pictures, the viewing eye, and the privilege of witnesses.[8]

This sort of observation, probably true enough and appealing to our sense of the mystery of the past, is nonetheless risky. Many forms of verbal and graphic media, variably abstract and literal, coexisted in a medieval world with a complex spatial imaginary. Hence while we might argue that habit discouraged a general conversion to maps (as it continues to do among many moderns), we could hardly demonstrate that some inherent aversion to sign systems foiled the cartographic mind. That mind was obviously, if selectively, at play. And even if we were ready to accept the notion that a distinctive medieval psychology impeded mapmaking, we would be left with a question about historical circumstances: why and how did it change?

However we figure the cleft between medieval and modern psychology, Harvey's association between mapmaking and "a way of thinking" remains a critical move. The association reminds us that mapmaking is a mental, rather than a strictly technical, practice—one that requires a logic specific to the medium. Drafters cannot make maps until they can impose a cartographic "way of thinking" on space. This elementary observation prods our attention away from context to text—away from the historical circumstances surrounding cartographic practice to the map itself and its internal attributes. We need to know what a map is, really; for only by understanding the formal properties of the medium can we understand what it takes to use it.

Such formal inquiry will suggest that any mapmaker, in any situation, faces one basic challenge: to reduce space to generic attributes. This challenge is inherently ideological rather than mechanical. Cartographic technique can serve mapmakers only after they have constructed spatial classifications—or what I call a spatial politics. And these classifications are not necessarily transferable from one space (such as a proprietary estate) to another (such as a city or a province or a country). Hence mapmaking will not become generalized in a society until the ideological work of classifying many different kinds of space has been undertaken successfully. Here is the core of my argument. The difference between medieval and early modern map production does not turn on differences in cartographic skill or social context alone. It turns on the ability of ideologues to think generically about the space of the nation. I have already indicated the success of the Tokugawa shogunate in this task. But to understand the nature of the task, we must look more closely at what a map is and what a map does. And then we must ask why the regime was actually able to impose a cartographic logic on Japan, since mapmaking is neither instinctive nor universal in early modern states. An abstract consideration of mapmaking will consequently lead back to a consideration of the historical circumstances that enabled Japanese conquerors to think categorically about their conquered territory.

Maps fall somewhere along the great spectrum of graphic material that represents space and spatial relations. Distinctions in this material—between maps, landscape drawings, architectural plans, and mandalas, for example—are matters of definition and hard to make convincingly. Welcoming the fuzziness, some cartographic historians use the map rubric elastically to include most graphic treatments of space. Others use the term "map" more or less narrowly, though often without clear delineation, since specificity can obscure the variety of the cartographic craft. In recent years, historians have been particularly wary of exacting definitions (requiring attention to scale and projection, say) that exclude or denigrate as "primitive" much premodern mapmaking.[9] But if we are to understand the nature of the mapmaker's challenge, we must have some sense of the peculiarities of the medium. While acknowledging the perils of the exercise, I offer a general characterization of the type of source of concern to me:

> A map is a form of graphic representation that takes as its frame of reference the physical environment, which it normally treats from an aerial perspective, with some attention to verifiable spatial distribution. Furthermore, a map relies on a combination of codes—particularly an iconic code—to construct that environment.

Although the first sentence covers a great deal of material, the second narrows the field. By "code," I mean an internally systematic body of signs. In the case of premodern and early modern Japanese cartography, the most important codes are the iconic code, the linguistic code, and the presentational code.[10]

The iconic code is the body of signs that inventory the environment—that identify all the features of a space that a mapmaker chooses to represent. (These signs sometimes appear in a map "key.") Common iconic signs include lines (variously used to signify roads, rivers, and so forth); figures (such as circles to signify cities); and hachure or color blocks (such as deep tints to signify government buildings). Figures on premodern and early modern maps are often pictorial but usually standardized enough to work as icons.

While the signs within the iconic code are potentially infinite, all share three characteristics. First, they are reasonably stable within the context of any given map. Hence, in figure 11, a medium gray building shape refers always and only to a library, and a white shape always and only to a building reserved for administrative offices. Instability often does occur in practice, especially with lines, although virtuoso treatments by mapmakers tend to clarify the signification: lines can be light and dark, thick and thin, and so forth.

Second, and critically, iconic signs are generic. The icons signify categories of spatial interpretation, reducing the many and discrete compo-

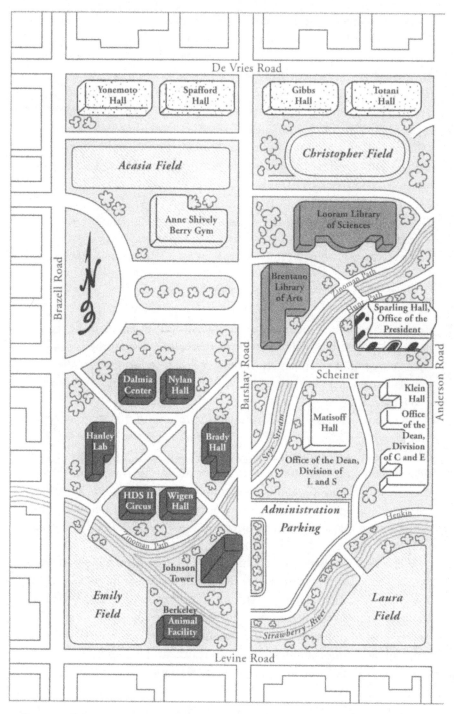

FIG. 11. The imaginary Angelica College, Angelica, California. Map by Deborah Reade.

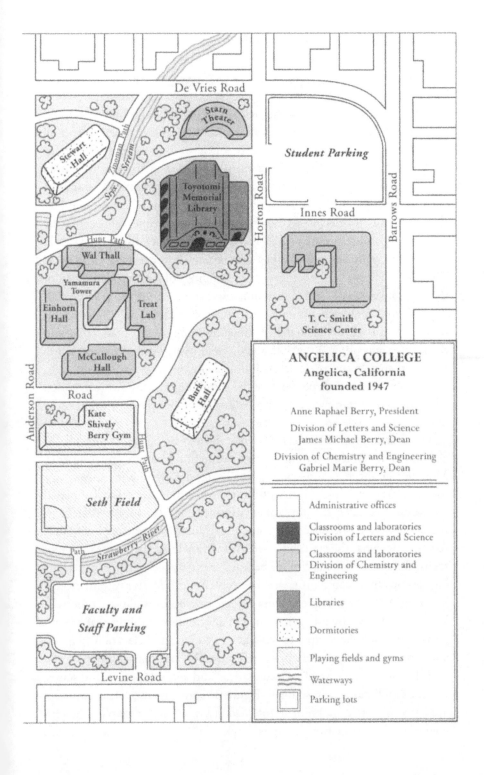

De Vries Road

Starn Theater

Student Parking

Stewart Hall

Toyotomi Memorial Library

Horton Road

Innes Road

Barrows Road

Hunt Path

Wal Thall

Yamamura Tower

Einhorn Hall

Treat Lab

T. C. Smith Science Center

McCullough Hall

Road

Burk Hall

Anderson Road

Kate Shively Berry Gym

Seth Field

Path

Strawberry River

Faculty and Staff Parking

Levine Road

ANGELICA COLLEGE
Angelica, California
founded 1947

Anne Raphael Berry, President

Division of Letters and Science
James Michael Berry, Dean

Division of Chemistry and Engineering
Gabriel Marie Berry, Dean

Administrative offices

Classrooms and laboratories
Division of Letters and Science

Classrooms and laboratories
Division of Chemistry and
Engineering

Libraries

Dormitories

Playing fields and gyms

Waterways

Parking lots

nents of an environment to certain limited, fixed, and putatively standard variables. Figure 11 uses icons to construct the imaginary "Angelica College" as a place with administrative offices, classrooms and laboratories, libraries, gymnasiums and playing fields, dormitories, and parking lots. This selection of categories excludes other categories (underground power systems, rare trees, trysting spots, food carts, high crime areas), just as all maps exclude most spatial features to concentrate on targets of interest. Equally important, categorical treatment reduces the particularity of even the places that do appear on the map. Figure 11 disaggregates "Classrooms and laboratories" into subcategories for the "Division of Letters and Science" and the "Division of Chemistry and Engineering" (and could, by multiplying and combining icons, make more elaborate distinctions). Still, each added icon signifies another general and abstract class of analysis. Thus the map can "say" that "the small buildings of L&S are southwest of the large buildings of C&E." It cannot say that "these old and airless buildings are unbearable in summer." It cannot say that "students crowd at noon onto the grass outside the ivy-laden buildings of the quad." In effect, the iconic signs obscure the ephemeral, move apart from affect and sensation, and strip away particular, colliding representations of mutable subjects. They essentialize phenomena by confining variables to categories. They impose pattern by replacing the disorder of experience with the order of cartographic system.

Third, iconic signs are versatile. As indicated by figure 11, they can be elaborated to convey fine and finer distinctions within environments. More important, they can be (and usually are) deployed to represent hard-to-see or even invisible features of those environments. I defined a map as a medium that takes the physical environment not as its subject but as its frame of reference because most maps move apart from the physical world to construct what the eye cannot see. At the very least, the iconic signs represent things that are hard to see because of their scale (as fig. 11 portrays a big campus that would otherwise be visible in full, let us say, only from a helicopter) or obtruding elements (as fig. 11 exposes walkways otherwise hidden, let us say, by foliage). Icons can also represent things that are unseeable but physically experienced (such as climate and elevation). Finally, and most interestingly, the icons can represent things that are invisible and socially constructed—such as boundaries, landownership, class and status, religious affiliations, and so forth. Figure 11 represents the constructions of academic hierarchy (administrators, faculty, students), discipline (letters, engineering), jurisdiction (campus, city), and, implicitly, market relations (between students who pay and staff who are paid to be at Angelica), although these are all categories of the mind rather than the senses.

In short, the iconic signs construct culture as well as land. They move not only from larger to smaller categories of analysis but from the visible to the invisible and from the framework of physical geography to the markings of politics, economics, and social organization. Hence, while maps are unsuited to highly discrete spatial messages, they are brilliantly suited to messages about spatial classification that other media convey poorly, if at all.

The linguistic code, which is common though not universal in maps, is a code of words that label the environments constructed through the iconic inventorying code. The labels of the linguistic code are also (more or less) stable, generic, and versatile. They are stable insofar as styles of identification are formal and consistent with established nomenclature. They are generic insofar as they signify reductive categories rather than particular attributes. And they are versatile insofar as categories might be multiplied to elaborate details. There tends to be more inconsistency in labels than in icons, as well as more particularity—since proper nouns invariably reflect the mediations of society. Indeed, every label is a mental invention. If the use of the water icon in figure II signifies the simple presence of waterways at Angelica, the label "Styx Stream" conveys value (this stream is not a sewer) and evokes time (this naming has a history).

Finally, the presentational code includes a host of interrelated choices about the appearance of the map—about its center and periphery, orientation, scale, size, dominant elements, volume of detail, colors, pictorial flourishes, scripts, and the like. All such choices inflect the significance of the iconic and linguistic signs; for they guide the eye, establish hierarchies of importance, and inspire attitudes toward space. But because the map encourages readers to concentrate on the busy multitude of icons and labels, the interpretive control of the presentation tends to fade from consciousness. We are not apt to notice too critically that a focus on the president's office marginalizes the animal research labs, that informal script and illustrations warm the tone of Angelica, and that subtle boundary treatments make the city a barely intimated neighbor, rather than an overpowering host to the campus. The presentational choices appear either inherent to the organization of Angelica or essential to cartographic legibility. Ideological decisions seem merely graphic.

Indeed, it is a marvel of cartographic communication that map consumers remain largely unaware of the interpretations carried by all the codes. In good measure, interpretation is masked by a blurring of the differences between physical and social phenomena and a consequent naturalization of what is arbitrary in human geography. Consider, in figure 11, the Office of the President. The signs immediately locate the reader in a (graphic version of a) physical world: a building surrounded by paths stands east of a waterway. Almost imperceptibly, culture intrudes with the labels that name the water and the paths and the building itself. Yet we are unlikely to notice (or at least to mind) this shift in register, since we take naming sufficiently for granted to find it more descriptive than manipulative, and even indispensable. Another shift in register occurs with the association, in the colophon, between the building and its key occupant, Anne Raphael Berry. Again, however, we remain in the physical world of a corporeal person with the familiar description of a name. If the link between building and person poses questions, the map answers them with seeming transparency. The iconic white color for "Administrative office" classifies the building; the label "Office of the President" identifies its particular function; and the title of "President" converts Ms. Berry into the chief officer of Angelica. In these signs we find a vast leap in cartographic register, for they move entirely outside physical representation to statements about organization and power: "Angelica College is a corporate institution that centers on the Office of the President." The shifts in register are nonetheless so gradual, the layering of icons and labels so helpfully instructive, and the conjunctions between physical and social geography so seamless that differences between nature and artifice all but dissolve. The marks of culture acquire their own near-physicality and inevitability. The presence of a president becomes as natural as the presence of water.

Many factors conspire in maps to naturalize artificial phenomena. Grounded in the representation of physical realities, the factual claims of maps are enhanced by an omniscient perspective and an attention to broadly accurate spatial relations indicative of empirical method. (In modern maps, the trappings of science—such as mathematical calculations of scale and elevation—further encourage credulity.) Paradoxically, perhaps, the reliance of maps on iconic and linguistic signs contributes most to their authority. By rejecting painterly likeness, the sign seems to reject emotion, point of view, and contingency. Figure 11 abandons pictorial statements ("cherry and redwood shade the president's window against the setting sun") to convey something more austere ("the building faces the water"). In their very departure from pictorial verisimilitude, generic signs imply objectivity. Stability surpasses variability; categories replace random details; formulaic representation captures essentials.

The burden of this discussion is that a map is a distinctive instrument of spatial representation different from a drawing or a photograph (or a poem or a diary). It is a tool of spatial classification that uses selective generic signs to reduce complex landscapes to order and pattern. It is also a tool of cultural construction that uses versatile signs to mark the invisible as well as the visible, the social as well as the physical character of space. And in these markings, the map naturalizes artificial constructions by conflating human and physical geography. Cartography operates, in sum, according to a logic unlike other media. To make a map—to choose to make a map rather than a landscape drawing—you must embrace that logic.

At the same time, however, a map is entirely like a drawing (or a photograph or a poem) in its interpretive, value-laden character. Schemes of spatial classification distill visions that are products of the imagination. These schemes, and their underlying visions, are not just attributes of the map. Nor are they obstacles or "problems" that interfere with some putative goal of objectivity. Classifiable ideas about space are the very precondition of a map's creation. Without a value-laden interpretation—without a spatial politics—cartographic codification is impossible.[11]

Yet it is one thing to work out a scheme of spatial classification and quite another to put it across. Here we encounter the problem of cartographic communication. A map communicates only when readers can relate its graphic signs to the space they represent. Part of the challenge is technical: readers must be able, with some experience, to decode the cartographic language of icons and labels as well as the presentational choices concerning orientation, scale, and the like. Hence the mapmaker must formulate a technique that a particular audience can learn to decipher— a task so implicated in local traditions of representation that no model (and thus no easy or universal method of decoding) prevails in premodern and early modern cartography. The graver challenge is ideological: readers must be able to recognize the ideas signified by the cartographic language of icons and labels. Hence mapmakers must either think like their audiences or teach their audiences to think like them. To map Angelica, for example, I used not only a technique familiar to many contemporaries but a set of ideas familiar to American academics—ideas expressed in the terms "laboratory," "dormitory," "president," and the like. In effect, I constructed a space through categories that my particular audience understands as conventional.

One of the greatest difficulties facing mapmakers is this linking of classification to convention. Inherent in mental mapping, classification is not so difficult in itself; for we all impose abstract principles of order, however inchoate or eccentric, on space. But mapmakers who want to communicate with an audience must adopt generally intelligible principles. The task is easiest (though not easy) at the level of physical geography, since mapmakers are likely to share with their audiences an agreement about essential categories for physical features. In the case of medieval Japan, these categories included "paddy," "dry field," "irrigation pool," and "mountain pass," but not (because topography is always culturally inflected) "aqueduct," "fallow," or "hunting preserve." Beyond the level of physical features, intelligible classification grows far harder. It is, nonetheless, all but indispensable; for even the most elementary map "From Here to There" requires markings that convert some general landscape into this particular landscape. So the mapmaker must interpolate additional ideas—about settlements along the way, or major landmarks, or power relations (boundaries, ownership rights, institutional jurisdictions), or some other generalizable notion.

Trouble arises when notions are too many and incommensurable, when complex local knowledge will not yield to common denominators. Observers may variously conceive and name settlements, determine landmarks, and define power relations. In such a situation, the mapmaker might go ahead and impose a code of spatial interpretation derived from personal experience. But the resulting map will be comprehensible only to those inducted into its premises and content to accept them. Hence the mapmaker might just as well abandon the map in favor of media, such as the verbal narrative, more accommodating to singularities.

In sum, if mapmaking is to be something other than a personal matter, the classification at its heart must work for an audience. It must reflect a knowledge of the world—a set of ideas about spatial meanings—sufficiently conventional to prompt recognition. Socially pervasive conventions are neither numerous nor easy to establish in most premodern societies; for they depend on an uncommon convergence of experience, perception, language, institutional structure, and cultural formation. (Think of the educational struggle involved before a child can read a map given over to the construction of continents, nations, and capitals.) The conventions that do exist, moreover, are not necessarily transferable from one situation to another. Premodern mapmakers who can intelligibly plot a village or a forest may be unable to plot a city or a province. The problem is unlikely to be a lack of a technique or even an individually cogent approach to classification. Almost certainly, those mapmakers lack a set of conventions that stretch far enough—that permit them both to imagine the very notion of city or province and to plot it coherently for an audience.

The inescapable conclusion of this discussion is that historical cartography is only in part the study of technical achievement. So, too, it is only in part the study of those contextual developments—from printing to literacy, from urbanization to increased travel—that speed the demand for, and dissemination of, maps. Because mapmaking is code-making, and because communicable codes rely on social conventions, historical cartography is very deeply the study of spatial ideology.

———

With supreme economy, the classical map of Japan attributed to the monk and engineer Gyōki captures the core ideas of the early imperial state: Japan is a coherent whole centered on the authority of a universal monarch and administered through provincial units (fig. 7).[12] The lines, labels, and presentation of the map construct this integrated political landscape by defining the profile of the archipelago against a blank white background (of water), organizing internal territory into named and bounded provinces, and fixing attention on the imperial capital, from which both provinces and roads extend outward. The masterful classification scheme—dependent only on notions of outer contour, center, province, and highway—encodes a conventionalized national space.

It is possible that a second effort to link cartography to national rule occurred in the medieval period when Minamoto no Yoritomo, founder of the Kamakura shogunate, attempted to collect local maps together with provincial land registers (ōtabumi) in the late twelfth century.[13] But if any such maps were actually drafted, none survives. Nor is there evidence of any interest among medieval rulers in revising the Gyōki model to express and enhance their own polities. Insofar as these governors formulated comprehensive spatial ideologies, they did not, or could not, reduce them to the fixed and generic signs required by mapmaking.

Instead, the cartographic record of late classical and medieval Japan focuses on small-area maps made for small audiences in discrete, typically troubled situations. So entangled in particular (and now elusive) circumstances that historians hotly debate their purposes and meanings, the maps conform to no templates indicative of routine cartographic practice—for transferring land rights or collecting taxes or plotting itineraries, for instance. They appear responsive solely, and idiosyncratically, to locally pressing needs.[14]

In these responses, individual mapmakers deployed the codes of the cartographic craft with considerable agility. Figure 12, for example, plots in

FIG. 12. Map of Hineno Village (Hineno-mura, c. 1316) in Izumi Province. A deepened gray in this reproduction indicates the area (in the lower part of the map) washed in green in the original. Manuscript, 86.4 × 58.6 cm. Archives and Mausolea Division, Imperial Household Agency, Tokyo.

simple terms a complex story about a place that is identified in an inscription on the back of the original manuscript as Hineno Village (Hineno-mura).[15] Covering a large surface with ample coloring and pictorial icons, the cartographer represents Hineno as a well-defined unit, bordered on the east (which is at the top) and the north by mountains, on the west by the Great Road to Kumano, and on the south by a river and a path. Its integrity is emphasized by the combination of perspectives that guide viewers both over and into the site. We scan the cultivated fields omnisciently from the air; look out at buildings and labels from a high, fixed vantage point in the west; and pivot around from the center to view the mountains. Thus focused intently on a subject that occupies almost all the cartographic space, the mapmaker merely gestures toward surrounding areas, which are labeled along three of the (very thin) margins.

The apparent target of cartographic interest is land use. The mapmaker represents a village seemingly dominated by cultivated fields (implicitly paddy) with bold black-and-white hachure. In contrast, the color green (which appears in the reproduction as a gray wash in the lower half of the map) indicates unreclaimed, still wild space (labeled *arano*), though it, too, is occasionally interrupted by hachure. These categories are complicated by additional, if considerably less conspicuous, signs. Several large areas of hachure are ambiguously labeled *kosaku*, which intimates "old cultivation" yet almost certainly means "formerly cultivated." These are probably lands, putatively converted to arable at one time, that have fallen out of production. Similarly, the unusual black squiggles near the middle of the map mark more unreclaimed territory (again, *arano*). But unlike the area blocked in green, this largely white space is labeled as the property of Hineno's main temple (and implicitly reserved for its use alone?).

On close inspection of the labels, the total of "formerly cultivated" and "wild" land actually seems to cover the better part of Hineno. Yet the point is obscured by the ennobling presentation, the sprawling treatment of the hachure, the substitution of squiggles for green color on temple property, and—most artfully—a flexible scale that exaggerates the eastern half of Hineno, which is accorded a position of privilege at the top of the map. Thus historians conclude, if contentiously and with considerable reliance on ancillary texts, that the map was drawn under the auspices of a local manager who sought to maximize the representation of the village's development and hence minimize the area in green vulnerable to intervention. Hineno's unreclaimed land had been donated by the proprietor to a family temple, beyond the village, which planned to exploit the resources for its own purposes. In short, the texts indicate, the map documents a power struggle between insiders and outsiders.

Yet we need not follow the twists of the texts to notice that what is made to appear a well-defined whole is also a porous part of a mutable landscape. While Hineno has expanded to the north and east of an area labeled "original public paddies" (presumably opened in the classical period), it is still—in 1316, when the map was drafted—an unstable conglomeration of arable, lost, underdeveloped, and undeveloped fields dependent on precarious waterworks (colored in blue in the original) and the labor of scattered settlers. Furthermore, it is a divided phenomenon, variously made up of "temple property," "shrine property," the settlements of the "lodge keepers" and the "hill people," the "newly opened property of [several individually named] farmers," and other fields attached to unnamed holders. The signs of the map discipline this complexity into generic features. Still, they are put in the service of a vision insistently animated by distinctions—by the conventions of spatial understanding that are inseparable from local interests.

The subject of figure 13 is not an individual village but a complete estate—Inoue Estate (Inoue-honshō)—that embraces a number of seemingly distinct, though unbounded, communities (two settlements of Kita Village, two settlements of Shima Village, and three settlements at places called Furukaki, Arama, and Morimaeda-Morihigashida).[16] Here, again, land use is important to a cartographer who meticulously notes cultivation conditions and the impact of river flooding. Yet the map is as clearly attentive to boundaries. Apparently uncontroversial are the northern and southern boundaries of mountain (north is at the top), as well as a western boundary established by proprietary fiat—a preternaturally straight line lacking topographical delineation that abruptly breaks something called the "New Estate" away from Inoue. It is the eastern boundary with a place called the "Property of Kokawa Temple" that the mapmaker bears down on with multiple labels and a line that changes in the original from brown (where dissension may have concentrated) to gray (where agreement may have prevailed). Skirting irrigation ponds, man-made streams, and river runoff—all carefully marked—the line is an attempt to divide the precious resource of water between claimants.

Inherent in local constructions of densely understood space, the specificity of figures 12 and 13 is intensified by the implicit quarrels that inspired them. Still remarkable, however, is their insularity from all but immediate contexts—an insularity typical of medieval cartography. Nowhere on either map is there an indication of the province or the district in which the

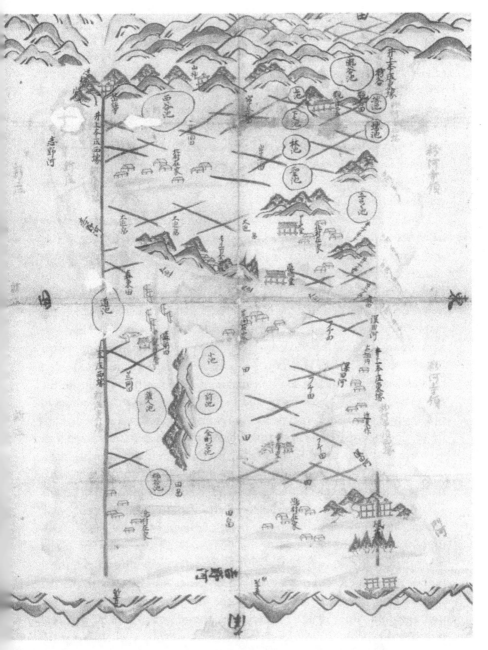

FIG. 13. Map of Inoue Estate (Inoue-honshō, late fourteenth century) in Kii Province. Manuscript, 53.1 × 65.4 cm. Zuishinin.

subject is located. Nor do general landmarks help orient viewers. There are no labels on mountain peaks or mountain ranges, no notes along the margins pointing toward towns or periodic markets in the vicinity. The names of rivers are either absent (fig. 12) or specific to the locale (in fig. 13, the Shino River becomes the Fukada River and then the Kado River before joining the Yoshino River, which was also known as the Ki River). So, too, with most roadways. While the "Great Road to Kumano" is a useful signpost at the bottom of figure 12, the outside observer cannot know—in the absence of a distance marker or even an identification of the post station in the lower left corner—just where along the way to or from Kumano the village of Hineno falls.

Hard to fix in broad geographical frameworks, the sites are also hard to fix in broad social frameworks. The maps contain no indications of scale and hence of the absolute size of the subjects.[17] They locate residential clusters with bare intimations of population density and volume; they locate lands under cultivation with only rare notations concerning area and none concerning total dimensions or productivity. As a consequence, the maps cannot support comparative observations (such as "this is a large—or a productive or a thickly settled—area"); nor can they be fitted into larger cartographic schemata. The frames of reference are strictly internal.

Wide geographical and social orientations were not the concern of the mapmakers who plotted Hineno and Inoue. But even had they wanted to situate these local sites in general frameworks, figures 12 and 13 demonstrate modes of spatial analysis that would have impeded any such effort. To make large area maps, cartographers need principles of spatial identification—principles to differentiate and integrate parts within wholes—that transcend local usage. And these were hard to come by in medieval Japan.

Clearly enough, the base units of cartographic notation were small settlements. They went by various names. Hineno was specifically a village (*mura*), a suffix also used to designate one of its neighboring places (Tsuruhara-mura) as well as two areas in figure 12 (Kita-mura and Shima-mura). But in these and other maps, small settlements often bore alternative suffixes (*gō, ho, sato*), indicative of the historical conditions of formation and sometimes of their order of magnitude in a hierarchy of local places. Most such units included scattered hamlets simply labeled (if at all) "residences" (*zaike*). With or without suffixes, however, the status of these settlements was highly variable and frequently ambiguous. Some were coherent administrative units with internal governing institutions and corporate tax obligations; many lacked formal organization among residents who maintained individually complex relations with superiors and one another. No village model prevailed in medieval society. Nor were small set-tlements common subjects of medieval cartography. The map of Hineno Village is one of only two village maps that survive from the Middle Ages.[18] Overwhelmingly, settlements were imagined as constituent parts of larger entities. Yet these larger entities were just as hard to label and fix con-ventionally.

The map of Inoue, like most medieval Japanese maps, portrays an estate (shō)—a private holding, variable in size and number of settlements, under the authority of an absentee proprietor (usually a Buddhist temple or aris-tocratic house). The suffix also marks one of Inoue's neighbors (Shin-shō) as well as one of Hineno's neighbors (Chōryū-shō). But not all estates bear the suffix (it is omitted in the case of Kumatori Estate at the northeast cor-ner of fig. 12). Nor does its presence invariably signify a proprietary hold-ing, since the term tended to survive in place-names even after particular estates were lost to legal or extralegal assault. Like villages, then, estates were porous, mutable entities. Inoue, for example, lost the boundary war implied in figure 13 and was almost wholly absorbed by Kokawa temple soon after the map was drafted (probably late in the fourteenth century). Hineno, on the other hand, belonged to an expanding holding. Together with three neighboring villages (two of them marked at the boundaries of fig. 12), Hineno Village was part of Hineno Estate, held by the aristocratic Kujō house in Kyoto. However troubled the internal politics of Hineno Village, Hineno Estate was spreading into the large area of Ueno-gō to the south of figure 12. And such elasticity was not confined to adjoining prop-erty. Many estates included "jumping land" (tobichi) or settlements nes-tled at some distance in rival jurisdictions.[19] In other cases, adjacent estates with different names belonged to the same proprietor and effectively merged in administrative oversight. (The Kujō house held both Hineno Estate and Chōryū Estate.) Indeed, proprietors' identities trumped place-names in a number of medieval maps, where labels emphasized institu-tional power over local geography.[20]

The complexities of fluid and fungible estates are only the beginning of the impediments to large-area cartography in medieval Japan. Estates made up the smaller, and a constantly diminishing, part of Japan's total landholdings. They were jigsaw pieces in a puzzle of land tenures barely represented in the cartographic record. Some estate maps do label some of those tenures. They refer to "temple holdings" (jiryō), often but not always the equivalent of estates held by monastic institutions; to "land investi-tures" (chigyō), the properties (sometimes approximating fiefs) normally held by military men; and to "steward shares" (jitō-bun), the lands wrested away from proprietors by the military deputies charged with policing their estates.[21] But these terms barely suggest the welter of tenures described in medieval documents—the tenures, for example, over "public lands" (*koku-garyō*), "steward receiverships" (*jitō-uke*), "constable receiverships" (*shugo-uke*), and domains of the "half tax" (*hanzei*).

The details are numbing. The point, however, is not that tenurial relations were irrational or inscrutable to the people who constructed and lived with them. It is, more simply, that tenurial relations were situational—many in character, specific to local negotiation, often overlapping in exercise. Particular arrangements tended to differ from one small area to adjoining areas and to resist formulaic naming and bounding. If estate cartography dominates the extant record, the fact speaks mainly to the institutional longevity of certain proprietors, the immense stakes of an old elite in sustaining the manorial system, and the relative clarity of manorial geography. Even so, surviving maps plot only the tiniest fraction of the thousands of estates that existed in the medieval period (and a tiny fraction, too, of the holdings of any individual proprietor).

This record suggests that mapmaking was hard work and required unusual provocation. Under pressure, cartographers could obviously combine icons, labels, and presentational choices to codify space with considerable legibility and persuasive power. They knew how to make maps. But they confronted a landscape so fissured by local practice and local knowledge that the common denominators indispensable to cartography were difficult to stretch beyond a few square kilometers. And even then, the terms of reference addressed only the intimate audiences already prepared to follow their meanings.

Complicated systems of landholding are normal, of course, and need not preclude ambitious mapmaking—not, at least, if some ambitious ideologue is ready to work out a general code of spatial understanding. Here the Kyoto conundrum becomes salient, since we might imagine that mapping the capital would have appealed to any number of powerful men eager to impress a vision of order on the medieval city.

In practice, Kyoto, too, was a fissured landscape—broadly divided between the variously contentious and cooperative structures of the imperial court and the military shogunates, and finely divided by multiple structures of clientage and proprietorship. While the medieval shogunates had gradually assumed (most) police power over the city, jurisdiction over taxation, commerce, and residence was scattered among hundreds of property holders and patrons in the aristocratic, military, and religious communities. Several estates lapped at Kyoto's outskirts, and numerous temple and shrine precincts—many of them large, autonomous settlements—dotted both the city itself and its perimeter. But notions such as "perimeter," and even "city," can misrepresent a space without clear boundaries or pervasive urban features. Farmland remained common in medieval Kyoto, as did huge, country-like villas, only slowly cut down by alleys and commoner neighborhoods dedicated to trade. The splendid grid of the classical capital had long since succumbed to natural disasters, migration onto the superior land east and north of the original site, the peripatetic habits of wealthy builders, and the proprietary politics of opportunistic elites. The space of Kyoto, no less than the space of the jigsaw countryside, resisted any clean and simple classification.[22]

Mapmaking might well have been attempted by a visionary—an emperor, a shogun, a great temple abbot or proprietor—able to imagine the capital holistically and tame its awesome intricacy into genera. Yet clarity is not necessarily a virtue. The cartographic visions potentially available, and advantageous, to any individual Kyoto notable would inevitably have expressed a spatial politics anathema to others. Too many fraught decisions—about where to center and bound the subject, which institutions to label (and how), what jurisdictional claims to acknowledge—made the always ideological task of mapmaking particularly challenging in the capital. Either because they could not see past its intricacy or would not jeopardize a fragile coexistence by acts of cartographic belligerence, rival powers in Kyoto chose to do without maps. Not until the early sixteenth century, when civil war had already torn apart the city and vitiated the authority of most of its elites, would painters capture Kyoto on paper. Even then, they used artful dodges—a bird's-eye perspective that transcended boundaries, heavy cloud cover that erased many sites and framed others as isolated vignettes—to convert the capital not into cartographic genera but a kaleidoscope of genre scenes.[23]

In sum, cartographic code-making in Japan moved away from large subjects by the middle of the classical period. The complexity—the anticonventional specificity—of political landscapes figured profoundly in mapmaking choices. But significant, too, I believe, was an appreciation of ideological ambiguity. Neither in Kyoto nor across the country did governors enforce universal spatial classifications. Particularity prevailed.

—

Around 1600, particularity began to yield to the general classification of space that enabled a vigorous cartographic practice. Because the change depended on the comprehensive code-mindedness of new rulers, the question is where their spatial politics came from. The overarching source of change was civil war, which broke familiar tenurial relations and thus erased the tortured geography of medieval politics. But the immediate source, felt in the bone of every combatant, was radical disorientation. Before we turn to their maps, and the astonishing effort made there at reorientation, we must consider for a moment the crises that led conquerors to cartography.

Gradually but surely, the civil wars that opened in 1467 undid medieval structures of landholding. The estate system, with its hierarchies of income rights, had effectively collapsed (leaving many aristocrats and religious institutions close to penury) long before Toyotomi Hideyoshi terminated manorial privileges during the 1580s.[24] So, too, the tenures of titleholders in the Ashikaga shogunate—their receiverships, taxation privileges, office lands, and claims on public properties—had lost all but a nominal cogency for anyone lacking the brute power to defend them. The jigsaw pieces of the medieval polity came unglued under pressure from local warriors of disparate backgrounds, all of whom sought direct control over territories removed by force of arms from superior jurisdictions. For over a century, though, the wartime landscape remained as riven as the medieval landscape. Strongmen carved out domains that changed hands and borders in the course of unending campaigns.[25]

Among the more successful lords, the men we call daimyo, a model of local rule nonetheless began to emerge. Around the middle of the sixteenth century, exceptional warlords managed to secure sizable territories and institutionalize domainal governance. They compiled law codes, collected cadastral registries, and began to systematize taxation and conscription. They relaxed controls on commerce, developed infrastructure, and initiated large-scale riparian projects. They developed chains of military and administrative command. Driven by a need for resources, since they were only as strong as the armies and commissaries within their boundaries, these daimyo began to replace the fissured landscape of the medieval world with small states.

Thus after 1560, the diffuse contests fought by local warlords for local ascendancy assumed an increasingly regional, and finally a national, dimension. Although joined by scores of allied lords, competition focused on roughly fifteen great daimyo challengers—many of them architects of the more advanced systems of domainal governance, but some brilliant opportunists—who imagined hegemonic rule. New to this late stage of battle were both the extraordinary scale of mobilization and the ceaseless movement that resulted. From 1560 until 1615—from the time Oda Nobunaga began his quest for national power until the victory of Tokugawa Ieyasu over the supporters of Toyotomi Hideyoshi at Osaka castle—a huge military establishment was in motion. Deployment for far-flung battles was only part of the story, since each victory and defeat submitted large territories to reorganization and masses of warriors to transfer. Nor did the climactic battle of Osaka still the commotion. The redistribution of land and men common after 1560 continued past 1650 as the early Tokugawa rulers continued to reposition daimyo to enhance security, discipline reluctant allies, and promote household retainers to territorial lordship.

The sheer physical disruption of the late sixteenth and early seventeenth centuries warrants emphasizing; for our narratives of war and peace tend to slight the experience of mass movement and the resulting changes in spatial psychology. That experience was paradoxical. Wars that had been driven by local interests in locally consolidated power ceded, in the end, to national contests that made warlords into transients and domains into interchangeable commodities.

Consider some bare biographies.[26] Born to a peasant family in the province of Owari in 1536, Toyotomi Hideyoshi joined a warlord army in Tōtōmi in 1551 and subsequently returned to Owari in 1558 to serve Oda Nobunaga. Following dispersed campaigns, he received his first castle in 1573 at Nagahama in Ōmi province. By 1577, Hideyoshi had moved to Himeji castle in Harima province, which he used as a base for offensives throughout the southeastern circuit. During 1583, he established his headquarters at Osaka castle in Settsu province to spearhead his drive for national conquest in the wake of Oda Nobunaga's death. He spent much of his time after 1587 at Jurakutei in Kyoto, and, after 1593, at Fushimi castle in Yamashiro, where he died in 1598. In sum, Hideyoshi occupied five castles in four provinces over a period of twenty-five years (between the ages of 37 and 62).

Tokugawa Ieyasu was born in 1542 to an old but beleaguered house in Mikawa province and spent over ten years of his youth as a hostage in Owari and Suruga provinces. He took over Okazaki castle in Mikawa in 1560 and, as campaigns eastward expanded his dominion, moved to Hamamatsu castle in Tōtōmi in 1570 and then to Sunpu castle in Suruga in 1586. In 1590, on orders from Hideyoshi, Tokugawa Ieyasu surrendered the enormous domain that he had constructed piece by piece, battle by battle, and received in exchange a vast but unfamiliar territory, stretching into nine eastern provinces, that had been taken from the defeated Hōjō house. Ieyasu's new headquarters was the brackish, poorly developed port of Edo.

In sum, Ieyasu occupied four castles in four provinces over a period of thirty years (between the ages of 18 and 48). Following Hideyoshi's death, he used Osaka castle on several occasions; built and sometimes used Nijō castle in Kyoto and Nagoya castle in Owari; and established a retirement headquarters in Sunpu, where he died in 1616.

The majority of daimyo survivors experienced similar upheavals as a result of land gains through conquest and administrative transfers following joint campaigns or disciplinary attainders. Maeda Toshiie moved from Owari to Echizen to Noto to Kaga. Uesugi Kagekatsu moved from Echigo to Aizu to Dewa. Ikeda Mitsumasa moved from Harima to Inaba to Bizen. Kuroda Nagamasa moved from Buzen to Chikuzen. Over the course of two short generations, the Asano moved from Owari to Wakasa to Kai to Kii to Aki. And so forth. Each transfer set in motion a chain of consequences, as domains were carved up again and redistributed among other players.

We can trace the changes from a different perspective by focusing on castle towns rather than daimyo houses. During the transition from war to peace, the great castle of Fukui in Echizen fell under the successive control of the Shibata, Niwa, Hori, Kobayakawa, Aoki, and Yūki. Himeji in Harima switched hands from the Kuroda to the Toyotomi to the Ikeda to the Honda. Control over Aizu Wakamatsu moved from the Date to the Gamō to the Uesugi, back to the Gamō, and then to the Katō. And so forth.

Aggregate figures tell the same story from a loftier vantage. Following the battle of Sekigahara in 1600, 88 Toyotomi loyalists lost their domains. Subsequent redistributions of land resulted in both rich increases for Tokugawa allies and the creation of 68 new lords (former Tokugawa housemen promoted to daimyo status). Between 1600 and 1650, there would be over 200 total or partial attainders, over 300 increases in domain, and about 280 domainal transfers.[27] And each change involved the full complement of a daimyo's army and administration. Tokugawa Ieyasu, for example, moved to Edo in 1590 with something like 40,000 retainers. And quite apart from the military elite, transfer put multiplying numbers of people on the road: not just retainers and their families and subordinates, but ever-enlarging circles of service personnel and hangers-on.

Some daimyo houses survived the long process of pacification without surrendering ancestral holdings—the Mōri, Shimazu, and Chōsokabe, for example. But they were few, and the size of their holdings had typically been reduced from wartime peaks. The ideal of lordly territorial control also survived the process of pacification; for the union that emerged was more fed-

eral than centralized in form. Still, the meaning of lordly territorial control
had changed. Not only were the members of the daimyo fraternity and the
boundaries of their domains regularly recast, the link between a specific lord
and a specific domain had become tenuous—conditional on both victory
and the administrative requirements of hegemons with vast interests to
oversee. As the victors divided and redivided the spoils between allies and
vassals, the daimyo were transformed from territorial lords into lords who
could govern territory. Status and skill emerged as their critical attributes—
not the particular locations of domains, which were neither fixed nor defining. No longer just a discrete and familiar place, each daimyo's spatial universe expanded across a national landscape of conquest and alliance. He
might reasonably expect a transfer to any part of it.

The deracination of warriors who became strangers to the lands they
ruled was accompanied by institutional changes that made the very meaning of land abstract. Consider, for example, mobilization for battle. On
two occasions in the 1590s, Toyotomi Hideyoshi recruited armies approaching 300,000 troops to invade Korea. He did this by levying a systematic military tax on scores of daimyo. Here was a revolution in several
parts. Here, to begin with, was the first deployment in Japan of a national
army for purposes of foreign aggression. Arrayed together were daimyo
contingents led by daimyo rivals, who were meant to share a common purpose and a common stature as generals. Local interests and local identities
were eroded, not least by the fact that many daimyo probably came to
know each other for the first time on the staging grounds of the Korean
campaigns. More radical still was the impersonal standard of recruitment.
Hideyoshi levied manpower quotas on the basis of the mighty efforts at
cadastral registration, discussed in chapter 2, that had begun in the 1580s.

Thus, for instance, the daimyo Mōri Terumoto showed up for the first
Korean campaign with 30,000 soldiers not because that was the normal
size of his force or the number he felt like bringing. Nor did the figure
convey anything individually significant about Terumoto—about his complex relations with Hideyoshi or his history in the province of Aki. Mōri
Terumoto rallied 30,000 soldiers simply because his domain had a total assessed yield, determined by cadastral registration, of 734,000 *koku*. His
military tax for the Korean invasion was four men for every 100 *koku*
($7,340 \times 4 = 29,360$).[28] In effect, the size of his army associated Terumoto
with calculable wealth rather than any particular territory, with mobile resources that were subject to national levy rather than locally strategic interests. If domainal transfers undercut spatial attachments by making the lord
of "this place" into the lord of "a place," the formulaic computation of pro-

ductivity and military taxes converted place itself into an impersonal site of income.

One mystery of the unification years is the complicity of the daimyo in initiatives seemingly injurious to themselves. Although cooperation in campaigns was driven by the logic of force and reward, cooperation in programs of cadastral registration surpasses any obvious calculation of advantage. Certainly, Hideyoshi's policy put hegemonic muscle behind surveying efforts that many daimyo had been pursuing for years, both as an expression of local suzerainty and a medium of rational extraction. Still, compliance with Hideyoshi's standards signaled fealty to the overlord and consent to an expanding agenda of containment.

In practice, cadastral registration proceeded erratically. Procedures were variable, measures inexact, and oversight inconsistent. Thorough execution of the project would take several generations.[29] But for all its predictable problems, from its inception, the enterprise subordinated the daimyo to a centralizing regime that generated guidelines for registration and required surveyors to submit registers to Toyotomi representatives. Hideyoshi then used the information to issue the formal vesting documents that confirmed a daimyo's status, specified the value of his domain, and established the hierarchy of command utilized for the Korean campaigns.

Yet more transformative purposes inspired cadastral registration as well, for it enabled two projects of social engineering: the disarmament of non-samurai and the relocation of samurai from villages to castle towns. Because the cadastres listed cultivators, and thus served as approximate registers of the agrarian population, they separated the workers on the land, who would be disarmed as permanent village residents, from the fighters, who would retain their swords but move to cities. And because the cadastres provided gross totals of agrarian productivity, they established a foundation for the salary system necessary to support a samurai class divested of land rights. Hence in complying with the cadastral project, daimyo effectively committed themselves to demobilizing cultivators (a critical resource for battle) and denying customary privileges to their warrior core (a group consequently facing alienation, possibly demoralization). The daimyo committed themselves, in short, to collective disciplines that reduced their own war-making potential.

Why did they consent? We begin to understand, I suspect, if we see them not as limitlessly rapacious warlords but as increasingly alarmed protagonists in contests that threatened to destroy them all. The threats came from all sides—most clearly from fellow daimyo (whether declared enemies or predatory allies); often from family members (ready to succeed through parricide and fratricide); endemically from vassals (practiced in the arts of defection and rebellion); and increasingly from commoners (engaged in uprisings as well as breakaway movements for autonomy). From the 1560s on, moreover, the always pervasive contests among such adversaries acquired a new and obliterating character, inasmuch as the consolidated campaigns of the unifiers—backed by substantial firepower—brought swift and total destruction to many of the most eminent houses of the era. The daimyo, who generated a climate of terror, lived with terrors of their own.

The settlement forged haltingly first around Toyotomi Hideyoshi and later around Tokugawa Ieyasu was an escape from the terror by men who chose a federalist compromise over the likelihood of annihilation. However invidious to any particular daimyo, the containment policies of the hegemon served as corporate sureties of nonaggression within the full company of lords. They also restrained internal threats. Relying on their collective will and the power of the overlord, the daimyo were ready to impose institutional discipline on the subordinates they feared. They sent inspectors into settlements uniformly conceived as administrative villages and held to account for methodical reporting of resources and methodical taxation. They stripped samurai of land and cultivators of weapons. They also, with variable thoroughness, enforced the regime's edicts against changes in status and residence. The daimyo effectively entered a mutual protection alliance, with consequences graver for their subjects than for themselves.

Hence, during the late stages of warfare, the spatial experience of warriors was altered by more than the physical deracination of transfer and the numerical abstraction of land into yields. The gradual institutionalization and convergence of governance amplified the lord's role as an administrator bound as surely to his fellow daimyo as to the samurai he converted into salaried officials and the producers he converted into registered subjects. Space was the arena of rule, assigned by circumstance.

Two different processes—one of disorientation, one of reorientation—were thus joined in the sixteenth century. On the one hand, warfare wiped out not only the geography of the medieval polity but many of the petty lordships formed in its wake. Sweeping campaigns and mass transfers made governors into strangers in their own lands. On the other hand, administrative change advanced a model of integration. Cadastral surveys translated land into a master language of villages and productivity totals; subsequent documents of investiture situated local governance in domains (*ryōchi*), formally granted by the overlord to subordinate lords. Further sorting occurred with the emergence of the castle town as the hub of domainal power. Compelled by the Toyotomi regime to reduce their multiple fortifications, and by the Tokugawa regime to destroy all but a single headquarters each, the daimyo became powerfully associated with their capitals. Indeed, the names of castle towns came to designate the domains themselves. Here, in the integral practices of a nascent state, were conceptions of space that disposed strangers to the categorical and universalizing logic of the map.

But if a new spatial psychology is a precondition of mapmaking, it is not a sufficient explanation, particularly in a situation of grave volatility. When the conquest regimes first undertook their cartographic surveys, cadastres remained incomplete, transfers proceeded apace, samurai had barely begun the passage from village to town, and fixed castle headquarters were few. Nothing was clear and stable, least of all the hegemonic order itself. The Korean wars of Hideyoshi's late tenure, the succession wars of the Tokugawa transition, the persistence until 1640 of rebellion, the threat of foreign aggression—all such dangers precluded confidence that any coalition could hold.

To initiate a cartographic project in this context of trouble, the conquest regimes required exceptional vision: a national story to frame their new spatial tropes in an ideologically compelling fashion. They also needed provocation: a sense of mission to sustain work unattempted since the classical period. First, we turn to the framework, then to the purpose.

Early modern mapmaking began in 1591 when Toyotomi Hideyoshi ordered all daimyo to submit summary cadastral records (*gozen-chō*) and maps that illustrated them.[30] At one level, the demand for the records was surely designed to speed and routinize registration by prodding at least superficial estimates of production from all locales. Its form, however, was surprising. Hideyoshi did not order up the individual cadastres made for individual villages (the *kenchi-chō*), which, in any case, were to be forwarded to him as a matter of course. He wanted, instead, synoptic statements about larger areas—specifically, districts (*gun* or *kōri*). Similarly, the daimyo were to take the district as the basic surveying unit for the maps they were meant to produce. Maps of districts, in turn, were to be collated into maps of provinces. Departing from the antecedent work of village registration, the initiative represented a spatial politics of a novel and encompassing order. Key to the enterprise was its focus on the district.

In taking the leap from small- to large-area analysis of land, Hideyoshi might logically have targeted the daimyo domain. Such a decision would have presented technical problems for cartographers, since most domains remained fluid in boundary and assignment. Even the most stable, moreover, were not neat parcels but sometimes scattered and always intermixed properties that included lands reserved for a daimyo's collaterals and great deputies, and sometimes for religious and courtly institutions. The domains also varied so enormously in size (with valuations ranging from 10,000 to over a million *koku*) as to make comparison through graphic illustration provocative. Still, those domains were the governing units of the age, the subject of investiture documents, and the indispensable currency of federal alliance.

Districts, by contrast, were holdovers from a lost world. They belonged to the hierarchy of place defined in the early classical period when the country was divided into provinces (numbering 66 by the ninth century), subdivided into districts (numbering over 600), and further subdivided into administrative villages that subsumed households. With the exception of the province, all these units had begun to mutate in size and administrative character by the late classical period. And although many survived as place-names, they had lost most salience to governance and landholding by the late medieval period. Even the province became little more than a label during the era of warring states. Why, then, map a new polity within the structures of an ancient state?

The immediate appeal of the district was certainly practical, a point suggested by figure 14, a tiny detail from a map made around 1596 of Kubiki district in Echigo province (within the domain of the Uesugi house). The original is one of only two maps that survive from the foundational cartographic project.[31] In general, the returns from Hideyoshi's 1591 order for cadastral summaries and maps appear predictably partial. Documents of 1593 indicate that daimyo in 29 provinces had submitted the cadastral reports (although largely in the form of individual village cadastres rather than district summaries), while maps had come in from 13 provinces. Not unreasonable for work still at an early stage, the response probably mounted in subsequent years but remains hard to measure, since old cartographic material was often discarded once it had been superseded. We nonetheless see in figure 14 the essential premises of early modern mapmaking.

Huge in size and small in scale, the full Kubiki map covers the eastern portion of one of Echigo's seven districts—a total of 358 villages laid out on a surface measuring 340 × 586 centimeters. Implicit here is one of the at-

Fig. 14. *Kubikigo ezu* (Map of Kubiki), in *Echigo no kuni kōri ezu* (The District Maps of Echigo Province, c. 1596), detail with seven villages, including the settlement around Unmon temple. (See sheet 38 in the facsimile produced by Tōkyō Daigaku.) Manuscript, 340 × 586 cm. Courtesy of the Yonezawa City Uesugi Museum.

tractions of district units: they were big, but not too big, and more consistent in size than the daimyo domains. The fairly limited scope of the district allowed some attention to land use, especially to paddy (signified here by rice shoots) and dry field (signified in the original by a thin green wash), in a fashion suggestive of cadastral registers. Indeed, the Kubiki map looks sufficiently like an illustration of the cadastres to intimate an almost natural progression from the field list to the field diagram. At the same time, however, districts were large enough to accord substantial overviews of both major physical features (the mountains, rivers, bridges, and roads that Hideyoshi ordered mapmakers to represent) and *many* social settlements (including towns and religious complexes). Because the Kubiki map covers not one but 358 villages, it cannot be a field diagram. The need to crowd all sites into a single composition enforces an economy of detail that exposes the gross rather than the fine features of sites reduced to sameness. The impression of uniformity is achieved partly through iconic signs, which level the landscape into common properties, but particularly through village labels, which uniformly specify village names and assessed yields (and, typically, both the number of residences and population totals). The emphasis shifts away from a complex specificity to the integral properties of place. Repetition produces monotony. The standardization pursued through the cadastral project achieves graphic representation as village after village categorically fills the district space.

The focus on the district also obscures internal boundaries, since attention centers on village units and yields rather than the sheer dimensions of holdings.[32] Kubiki is treated holistically as a territory that absorbs its village parts in a continuous landscape—one linked by roads and paths (signified by slashed lines), not cut up by property lines. This is no medieval jigsaw of atomized pieces that appear prior to the final composition. At the same time, however, the meaning of the territory remains ambiguous. Just how does this landscape fit into the geography of daimyo and domain? What *is* Kubiki?

It is a neutral ground. And here is the critical appeal of district units: they detached the land base from the jurisdictional superstructure. The very arbitrariness of the district, which was old but incidental to rule, made it a largely formal unit of cartographic surveying. If time and forgetting had made district boundaries hard to establish, all the better. They could be pushed around for administrative convenience. Because districts were smaller than even the smallest domains, plotting their borders was more procedural than the fully politicized challenge of demarcating domainal holdings. Use of the district unit consequently converted space into a large plane, or visual field, to be blocked out in the fundamental categories of landmarks, settlements, and yields. Once the plane had been defined, the operations of power could be superimposed through additional cartographic signs, which clarified the relations between base and superstructure. Jurisdiction was an overlay.

There is an implicit relationship between base and superstructure in the Kubiki map: the village generates resources that some lord has quantified and now controls. There is an explicit relationship as well; for each village label includes the name of the man or institution currently vested with those resources. But by according primacy to the resources and mapping them within reified district units, the base was imagined apart from any fixed and inevitable tie to any particular lord. Jurisdiction could vary without reconfiguring foundations. Thus the Uesugi could be transferred from Echigo to Aizu in the first month of 1598 without altering the cartographic constants. Labels alone had to be updated. The deracinating experiences of war had already snapped most connections between individual daimyo and individual territories. The genius of district-level mapping lay in the graphic expression of this reality. Unlike medieval cartography, which began with jurisdictional units and local troubles, the early modern project deferred representations of power until durable frames were in place.

The representation of power was nonetheless the consuming objective of the new regimes. And it required units more elaborate than districts. Hideyoshi was apparently building a master scaffold for national cartography: his 1591 orders called for maps of the provinces to subsume maps of the districts. But if they were made, they do not survive. We must look, then, at Tokugawa material to understand the full framework of early modern cartography and its practical utility to the hegemonic order.

In 1604, just a few years after Hideyoshi's death and the first of the great succession battles that gave him a tentative hold on the realm, Tokugawa Ieyasu ordered daimyo to submit another set of cadastral and cartographic documents. Generally following Hideyoshi's example, he called both for summary statements of the productivity figures and field dimensions of individual districts (described this time as gōchō) and for maps of individual provinces (not, in this case, districts). In charge of the cartographic project were two overseers, who appointed deputies to supervise mapmaking in each province. Although the material surviving from their surveys is both incomplete and locally variable in execution, the convergence in extant maps indicates a reasonably clear conception of the enterprise.[33] Most important was the focus on the province—again, a unit from the classical period that deflected boundary anxiety away from daimyo domains. Provincial boundaries occasioned livelier contention than district boundaries, but the not unwelcome task of resolving them enhanced the role of the regime as a national arbiter.[34]

Figure 15 is a detail from a map of Echizen province, probably completed around 1606.[35] While the map is a large one (272 × 229 cm), it is smaller in size and much larger in scale than the Kubiki district survey. The result is a more compact and legible representation, in which detail steadily yields to concision.

The principal sacrifice of detail occurs in the representation of physical geography. Early Tokugawa cartographers were clearly concerned with coastal surveying and sufficient land measurement to produce maps roughly to scale. They were also concerned with internal waterways (portrayed in the original with blue lines and sometimes marked by bridges and ferry crossings) and roads (portrayed with red lines and sometimes marked by distance measures). Otherwise, their provincial maps indicate

FIG. 15. *Echizen no kuni ezu* (Map of Echizen Province, c. 1606), detail centering on Kitanoshō castle in the northwest of the province. Manuscript, 272.3 × 228.5 cm. Courtesy of the Matsudaira Bunko Collection, Fukui Prefectural Library.

only bald distinctions between lowland and mountain (portrayed in green and sometimes marked by passes), without close attention to land use. Topographical features would continue to dominate local cartography and did intrude with greater frequency on the provincial maps produced by later Tokugawa surveys. Still, physical data remained both limited in most large-area cartography and subordinate in emphasis to representations of social and political geography. Indeed, the social and political relations of land—not the land itself—constituted the essential subject of official cartography until the early nineteenth century.[36]

If the topographical detail of the Kubiki map disappears from figure 15, the legacy of district-level surveys is nonetheless pronounced. The province of Echizen is divided into its constituent districts, each marked iconically by both boundary lines (purple in the original) and a rectangle containing labels. The labels provide the name of the district, the total of its assessed yield, and the total number of villages it subsumes. Within each district, moreover, oval icons represent each of those villages. Color-coded by district, the ovals contain more labels: the name of the particular village and its registered productivity. A legend in the northern corner of the map lists the 12 districts of Echizen, provides a key to the color code, and summarizes the land data: the total yield of Echizen is just over 680,327 *koku*, which includes slightly more than 30,762 *chō* of paddy and 13,557 *chō* of dry field, which is divided among a total of 563 villages.

To a significant extent, then, the provincial map is a collation of district maps (and a graphic illustration of the cadastres). Information is highly distilled, however, as villages become points in space—uniform ovals, apparently equal in gravity, fixed in quite approximate locations. Differences and divisions among them fade into bare statements of name and yield. The point of this radical reduction comes clear as the provincial map, greater in scope than the district map, links the village to an overarching structure of power. The Echizen map focuses on the castle of Kitanoshō, which dominates the cartographic field with its size and pictorial treatment. The fulcrum of the map's bird's-eye view, Kitanoshō is also the alpha point for measuring space. At the border crossings where roadways pass from Echizen into neighboring provinces, the map notes the distances from this castle headquarters. Here is the site of control. The notations in the Kubiki map concerning local investitures are stripped away to reveal the paramount daimyo.

Some provincial maps explicitly tie the base to the superstructure by color-coding the village icons to indicate the domains, rather than the districts, in which they are located. Others add to the village icons small symbols keyed to specific daimyo lords. Still others label castles with the total productivity figures of the daimyo's holding.[37] The Echizen map dispenses with such signs, probably because the whole province fell, exceptionally, within a single jurisdiction (that of Tokugawa Ieyasu's second son, Yūki Hideyasu). Yet in all cases, the prominent treatment of the castle towns identifies the nodes and the dynamic of power: flowing inward from the village to the castle is the wealth signified by yields; flowing outward from the castle to the village is the authority of the lord assigned those resources.

In a very few of the early provincial maps, light-colored lines trace the physical boundaries of some daimyo domains. Overwhelmingly, though, official cartography embraced a radiant conception of rule. As villages were measured by their resources rather than their borders, so, too, were daimyo domains. Centered on castles, but not delineated as fixed territorial units, those domains flowed within the armature of districts and provinces to take in the assets accorded them.

The imposition of daimyo power on a stable foundation allows provincial maps to tell an elegantly coherent story. Within an enduring topography of mountains, valleys, rivers, and roads, the land supports a vast, seemingly timeless society of villages—each known, located, and named; each productive in standardized terms that convey membership in the polity and relationship to the centers of power and prestige. These centers are important castle cities—each known, located, and named; each headed by a daimyo whose authority is expressed by agrarian harvests and radiant throughout the society producing them. The maps either expunge everything mutable (village and domainal boundaries, the details of land use) or situate variables within stable frameworks. Thus an individual productivity total can change without disturbing the standard for land valuation. A village can appear or disappear without disturbing the array of ovals. A daimyo can be replaced, a castle headquarters relocated, and a domain reconfigured without disturbing either the notions of daimyo domain and castle town or the frames that support them. The formal units of classical geography discipline the unstable geography of lordship. Seeming fixity transcends volatility because the classifications of the map—province, district, village, assessed yield, castle town, daimyo—define so purely the spatial constants that they can absorb change as transitory or superficial.

But, of course, those classifications are the black magic of cartography. They derive from the spatial politics of hegemons who were learning to detach power from territorial boundaries, to abstract authority into castle nodes, and to flatten agrarian society into revenue-generating villages. The nuances of this spatial politics would be expressed in national maps, where the full framework of hegemonic cartography emerges.

Figure 16 is a large-area detail from a map of Japan assembled, probably from the late 1630s, on the basis of a continuing series of provincial surveys ordered by the Tokugawa regime in 1633 (for a small-area detail, see fig. 9). The new surveys, and subsequent surveys of the provinces as well,[38] hewed close to the original project. But because they were conducted with greater oversight and clearer guidelines (concerning scale, color codes, and required entries), the resulting maps could be more easily collated than their antecedents into a national whole.

That whole is something rather different, though, than the sum of provincial parts. While large in size (370 × 434 cm) and generous in scale (ranging from 1:26,000 to 1:32,000), this representation of the nation required the ever-greater distillation of local information. The provincial units survive. Indeed, with their vivid color blocking (in the original) and their conspicuous labels, the provinces define the internal geography of the country. Gone, however, are both districts and villages. The 12 rectangles and 563 ovals of Echizen (as well as the 630 rectangles and tens of thousands of ovals elsewhere) are effaced. In their stead, the provincial plane is punctuated by the solitary, stand-out images of castle towns. Each is marked iconically by a bright white box and labeled with a place-name. All were also tagged originally with paper slips identifying the daimyo holder, his title, and the total registered productivity of his domain (though many slips have been lost over time). In effect, the base dissolves entirely into the superstructure. Castle, lord, and resources fuse here to construct a dominion, still radiant and unbounded, that converts the agrarian landscape into aggregate integers. hm hm hm

This severe simplification has the effect of separating castle towns from exclusively local economies and local political relations to reorient them in a national constellation of authority. The standardized icons and labels of the castellans suggest a body of peers linked not simply to individual domains but to one another—and to the regime that has imposed the standards in a seemingly total system of rule. The names of the daimyo help recover the particularity of power, while simultaneously implying larger structures of union by evoking often long genealogies. More to the point, they transform an otherwise abstract polity into a convincing realty: personally named lords—each dangerous and proven in war—have taken their place in an orderly constellation of confederates.

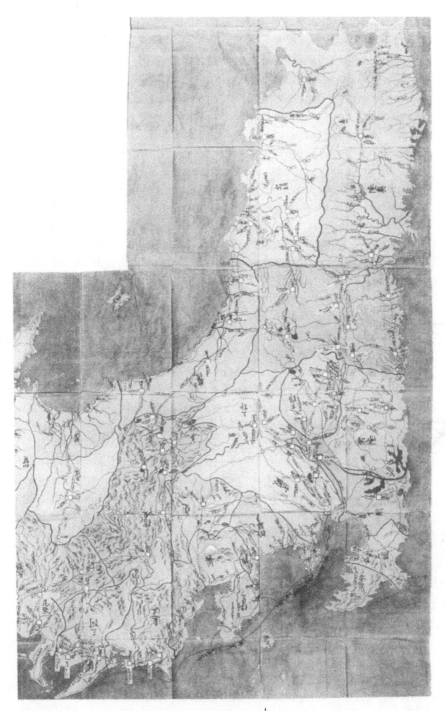

FIG. 16. *Nihonzu* (Map of Japan), compiled by the Tokugawa shogunate c. 1640, detail featuring the central and eastern provinces. Manuscript, 370 × 433.7 cm. National Diet Library, Tokyo.

The cartographic attention to castles and castellans was hardly inevitable. The emphasis in local maps on fixed geographical units and the village base might have been preserved by illustrating land use in general terms, marking the districts, and attaching productivity figures either to those districts or to the provinces (in the style of the Echizen summary). The need for representational economy might have been served by signifying only the greater castle towns, particularly those held by Tokugawa collaterals, and consigning the remainder to an index. But by featuring instead all those white boxes and their detailed tags, the national map identifies individual castellans as the ultimate and indispensable centers of local meaning. It also identifies the collective body of castellans as the instrument of a universal polity. Once the foundational maps had decoupled domains from fixed boundaries, national cartographers could select as critical the association between resources and jurisdictional control and then strip away the scaffold of districts and villages. Castle hubs and individual holders might still change (hence the use of paper tags), but the superstructure now encompassing them, represented by the sum of the white boxes, provides constancy.

Despite this attention to the political system, the pull of the center remains curiously unpronounced. While the Tokugawa castle towns are slightly exaggerated and the surnames of collaterals are ubiquitous, none of the choices in cartographic presentation glorifies the new regime. Edo is no focal point. Heraldic insignia are absent. The value of the vast Tokugawa domain is unmentioned.

Dramatic treatments of the Tokugawa presence might have been superfluous, of course, since hegemonic power is everywhere implicit in the overarching classifications and prodigious information of the map. The sheer scope and consistency of the knowledge assembled here speak to the control exercised originally in cadastral registration and expanded through decades of cartographic surveying and resurveying. Leaps in systematic data collection are particularly apparent in the logistical details of the national map. Instead of land use, the map represents major and minor roads (with regular distance markers), mountain passes, post stations, rivers and tributaries, ports, ferry crossings, bridges, and fords. Conveyed here is the seeming accessibility of all places in a country where frontiers have been vanquished by a transport infrastructure and masterful knowledge of it. Mobility, integration, and penetration—these are the messages of a map that levels harsh terrain and local difference into uniform, unifying systems.

By foregrounding the systems rather than the shogunate, the polity appears as a corporate affair, lacking any single target. Hence the decision may reflect security concerns, since figure 16 was drafted in the 1630s, when rebellion threatened to undo a still fugitive union.[39] Leaving impressions of Tokugawa power to inference rather than explication, the map discourages challenges to that power through concealment of its reach. Hegemonic authority blends into the parade of white boxes.

Significantly, though, hegemonic authority blends into more than the white boxes. Keeping the shogunal profile low, and expressing the dominion of the daimyo through nodal castles rather than bounded domains, the mapmakers accord visual privilege to the provinces. Had the federal settlement been the sole concern of official cartography, we might have expected provinces to fade away as easily as districts and villages once they had served their purpose in the foundational surveys. They are retained, however, and retained flamboyantly. Nor is the provincial order the only ancient feature of the national map. Figure 16 is striking in its general fidelity to the Gyōki-style conception of classical Japan. The outlines of the three major islands and several smaller ones are marked starkly, and in isolation from neighboring countries, against a background of ocean. So, too, the country is centered on the home province of Yamashiro, despite the geographical and political logic of shifting the focus east. And it is connected by the highways of the seven classical circuits (lined in red in the original), which cross the full classical spectrum of sixty-six provinces. The polity of a new regime blends into the cartographic landscape of the imperial state in a portrait of complex balance.

It blends, too, into a landscape of culture. In addition to castles and the logistically important sites of ports and post towns, the national map marks a number of "famous places" (*meisho*)—sites accorded name and fame for their beauty, their sacred and historical resonance. Some of these places, particularly notable temples and shrines, appear on early provincial maps. Many more of them—including scenic landmarks, the ruins of lost cities, mausolea and grave sites, old battlegrounds—would fill the successive maps of official and (especially) commercial cartographers. Figure 16 includes the seemingly indispensable signs of a historical culturescape—the Ise shrine, for example, Mount Fuji, Mount Kōya, and Mount Yoshino.

Figure 16 consequently tells a rich story of multiple, overlapping parts. Within the space of an ancient nation bounded only by sea, where the capital and provinces of an imperial past continue to organize memory and meaning, a company of castellans—united by common allegiance—governs a registered and highly productive countryside that is integrated by a universal polity, a dense infrastructure, and a shared culture.

The juxtaposition of messages here, within the frames of the imperial state, indicates that use of the provincial (and district) units was not simply a practical convenience for early modern mapmakers. Those units apparently fitted an ideological conception of the national space. We return, then, to the motives underlying the cartographic project and the holistic vision animating it. We return to Toyotomi Hideyoshi and the use of an ancient model to map a regime of conquest.

Remarkably and persistently, this parvenu had associated his settlement with the throne rather than military institutions. Hideyoshi himself ruled under the courtly titles of imperial regent and great minister of state, following his adoption into the aristocratic Fujiwara house; and he oversaw the promotion of virtually all his daimyo confederates to honorary court offices as well. He also pursued a policy of courtly restoration—returning the emperor and major aristocratic families to solvency, rebuilding the imperial palace, reviving court ceremonies. And with particular tenacity, Hideyoshi attended to the reconstruction of Kyoto, where he presided over his government from a marvelous mansion erected on the grounds of the ninth-century palace complex. He cleared a large zone for new aristocratic and military residences and repaired religious compounds. He paved new streets and built fine bridges. After consulting savants about the historical character of the city, Hideyoshi surrounded Kyoto with a stone and earthen rampart that conformed to the original plan for the capital.[40]

Work on the wall, and the finishing touches of Kyoto's restoration, took place in 1591, just months after Hideyoshi's domestic campaigns concluded and the first experiment with peace began. In the same year, Hideyoshi arranged the elevation of his heir as imperial regent, preparing for a gradual transition in rule. In that year, too, he ordered the daimyo to prepare cadastres and maps based on the district and provincial units of the classical state. His intention, clear from contemporary documents, was to present the maps to the emperor. The precedent was a series of eighth- and ninth-century decrees that had similarly required local officials to draft provincial maps for delivery to the throne.[41] Once more, Hideyoshi looked to the past to buttress his hegemonic power.

But what led him to mapping in the first place? If an ancient precedent was attractive once the decision to map had been made, the reasons for the decision itself are not so obvious. The lift in imagination toward an endeavor abandoned by national administrations for close to a millennium requires more than sensitivity to precedent. Here the international context seems critical, for Hideyoshi lived in a map-minded age that tied geographical power and knowledge to graphic expression. European traders and missionaries had introduced navigational charts, maps, and globes to Japan since the middle of the sixteenth century and subsequently undertook their own surveys of the Japanese coast. Chinese maps were circulating in Japan as well, used by European, Chinese, and Japanese traders alike.[42] Hideyoshi was undoubtedly familiar with some of this material: in 1591, for example, he received a personal copy of the 1570 world atlas of Benjamin Ortelius. This was the year he initiated his own cartographic project. This was the time, too, when he embarked on a belligerent foreign policy in a world that was no cartographic abstraction to him.

"Throughout Our Country of more than sixty-six provinces," Hideyoshi wrote the Ryukyu court in 1590, "I have pacified all people and governed with mercy and affection. . . . Henceforth, even if a land be thousands of miles distant, I shall deeply achieve amity and so build with foreign lands the spirit of the four seas as one family." Soon thereafter, Hideyoshi announced his intention to conquer China in a letter to the viceroy of the Indies; demanded submission from the Spanish governor of Manila; and ordered Taiwan to deliver tribute. In 1592, he began licensing Japanese merchants to trade with Vietnam, Cambodia, Thailand, Taiwan, the Philippines, and Macao. In 1593, he invaded Korea.[43]

For a man obsessed with the international order, the new cartography of the age must have seemed a fit instrument to express control over the place he routinely called "our country." Yet the enterprise he initiated put as much emphasis on an indoctrinating process as on an edifying outcome. Instead of professional efforts aimed at a swiftly executed national map, Hideyoshi conceived of mapmaking as a localized and incremental program founded on daimyo, legions of field deputies, and painstaking collations of evidence. So, too, the first three Tokugawa shogun repeated the orders for district-level cadastres and provincial-level maps, making locals key parties to an unfolding cartographic undertaking. The effect, at one level, was certainly an expression of control (especially since the Tokugawa orders announced the succession of a new heir and reaffirmed the subjection of their daimyo).[44] More deeply, though, the labor itself—corporate, ongoing, repeated—was an instrument of conversion. Precisely because union was fractious and unfamiliar, cartography served the conquerors by instilling a fugitive idea of cohesion, not by reflecting any palpable reality. Here was the sense of mission sustaining an unlikely project.

Indoctrination began with the cadastral tropes of village and yield, the investiture tropes of domain and castle headquarters, which were lifted now from verbal texts to become the visual codes of collective recognition. The framework for a comprehensive spatial politics, however, was old. By yoking national cartography to the imperial geography of district and province, Hideyoshi turned again to the classical emblems—monarch, capital, titles—that had helped legitimate his own fragile authority. Yet in this instance the stakes were greater than personal or household survival. The mapmaking of Hideyoshi and his successors not only normalized a nascent polity but invented, and instructed countless participants in the very imagining of "our country."

In discussing the cartographic projects of European powers in Southeast Asia during the nineteenth century, Benedict Anderson observes that the "colonial regimes began attaching themselves to antiquity as much as conquest." They drew "'historical maps,' designed to demonstrate, in the new cartographic discourse, the antiquity of specific, highly bounded territorial units." And they then laid claim to that ancient territorial dominion as inheritors or guardians—rather than as conquerors—of the tradition.[45] A similar appropriation occurred in the hegemonic mapping of early modern Japan. The Toyotomi and the Tokugawa did not so much copy as revive the Gyōki-style image in order to ratify their own rule. But by linking land to ancient names, and by reaffirming the centrality of an old imperial capital to a cultural order of provinces, the hegemons also insisted on the (fictive) integrity of the nation and the (imagined) continuity of its history. Concealing the newness and the violence of hegemonic rule, figure 16 situates the polity within a timeless framework and thus represents the rulers themselves as custodians of an enduring commonwealth.

The Tokugawa shogunate released the national map drafted in the late 1630s to commercial publishers, who issued it, unrevised, as a woodblock atlas.[46] Revision did ensue briskly, as printing houses hired popular artists (not cartographers) to make the map attractive. Over succeeding generations, rival firms also brought out numerous variants—all presented with distinctive artistic details and brought up to date with timely corrections. The basic conception of the nation, however, remained the same.

Figure 17 is a large-area detail from Ishikawa Ryūsen's *Nihon kaisan chōrikuzu* (Map of the Seas, Mountains, and Lands of Japan)—a map so popular that it was revised and reissued for a century and more after 1689

FIG. 17. Ishikawa Ryūsen, *Nihon kaisan chōrikuzu* (Map of the Seas, Mountains, and Lands of Japan, 1694), detail featuring the central and eastern provinces. Edo castle is at right. The highways, punctuated by post stations, receive prominent treatment. Woodblock, 81 × 71 cm. Courtesy of the East Asian Library, University of California, Berkeley.

(see fig. 3 for a small-area detail).[47] Unconcerned with scale and topographical fidelity, Ryūsen cuts to the quick of the social and political story of the model. The story has four familiar layers. First, Ryūsen lays out the classical order of provinces—each clearly colored, bounded, labeled, and (reminiscent of local cartography) defined in a rectangular box by its gross productivity and the number of districts it contains. Western Japan and the imperial capital of Kyoto remain dominant in the full composition, if better balanced by the eastern provinces and the shogunal capital of Edo (which appear in this detail). Against this backdrop, Ryūsen then represents the military order of castle towns—each marked iconically by a square or a circle and labeled with its name, the name and title of its holder, and the gross productivity of his domain. Edo receives somewhat exaggerated treatment, although neither the value of the Tokugawa holdings nor any other sign of exceptional shogunal privilege is shown. Next, Ryūsen proceeds to illustrate the infrastructure that links the provinces and castle towns. The highway circuits are paramount, each punctuated by post stations, although we also find lesser roads, ferry routes, and ports. Finally, Ryūsen fills the landscape with mounting numbers of famous places, many pictorially illustrated. If he departs at all significantly from the official model, it is in this emphasis on sites of name and fame.

Overwhelmingly, though, the map repeats the message of the model by constructing a union between past and present, power and culture, center and locale, institution and person, nature and artifice, Kyoto and Edo. The ancient province situates the new domain; the historical landmark enriches a landscape of castle towns; the profile of local rule conforms to a national pattern; the particular man administers resources calculated by formula; the highway penetrates a rugged terrain; the imperial city tethers an eastern shogunate to the west. This entangling of messages creates a seductively thick realm of meaning for viewers. Some might dutifully read the map as a statement of cohesion in which the parts all reinforce one another. Others might variably concentrate on cities, transportation, military power, imperial history, or points of local pride. But the very mixing of messages within simple cartographic frames gives the map a seeming truthfulness that allowed it a two-hundred-year run in the geographical imagination.

Not at all coincidentally, the Ryūsen map, like the official model, also defines the properties of the nation. "Japan" is the place constituted by the provinces and highways of the imperial state; the daimyo, castle towns, and registered productivity totals of the Tokugawa polity; and the "famous places" of a long, putatively common experience. Culture, power, and history fuse here to create the national space. Implicit, too, is a presumption that "Japan" is a place where rice agriculture—the standard for evaluating productivity—establishes the economic and social base. These properties certainly comprise a territory, although not one conceived of in purely territorial terms. Land itself, unmarked by culture and power and history, became the subject of early modern cartography only when the inspired maverick Inō Tadataka undertook strictly topographical surveys in the nineteenth century. In earlier maps, Japan appears as a landscape of human fabrication. *a w*

And, to return to the beginning, a landscape of cities. This country with only one metropolis in the mid sixteenth century, this country of farmers, who still dominated the population in the mid twentieth century, appears in early modern maps as an urban world. Castle towns embodied the political transformation wrought by conquest and, very swiftly, became the focus of cartographic activity. The enterprise was speeded by direct shogunal surveying of Kyoto, Edo, and Osaka, and by daimyo surveying, under order, of their individual headquarters. But official and commercial efforts intersected as publishing firms worked from city plans, and with city magistrates, to generate their own early maps of the three great urban centers for streaming populations of migrants.[48]

Mitigating the challenge was the binary politics that organized castle towns such as Edo and Osaka. Both were new cities under the unqualified jurisdiction of the shogun, whose immense castles overpowered the scene. Both were zoned to define the privilege of military retainers and the subordination of the commoners who fed and clothed and housed them. Both were laid out with networks of moats and canals, elaborate port and warehouse facilities, and sections reserved for temples. Both were built, in sum, to encode relations of power and hence invited the codification of maps. If the persisting fidelity of cartographers to the hegemonic blueprint remains arresting, early mapmakers relied unsurprisingly on the tropes that underlay urban rule—"castle," "martial residence," "commoner ward," "temple ward." Nowhere more vividly than in castle towns did the disciplines of state find the physical expression conducive to cartographic representation.

But what of Kyoto? Why was this imperial city, unmapped since the classical period, so readily mapped after 1600? To a remarkable extent, the story of the imperial capital replays in miniature the story of national mapmaking. There, too, civil war erased the medieval geography of proprietorships as the firestorms of coup, invasion, and uprising propelled residents into two fortified enclaves surrounded by rubble and the sporadically cultivated fields of squatters. Claimants to military authority were variously in flight and under siege, penurious aristocrats unable to defend themselves against either tax withholding or the collapse of the estate structure, and religious institutions at war with overlords and one another. Replacing this embattled capital, moreover, was a city that belonged no less than the rest of the country to a new spatial order. Its architect was Toyotomi Hideyoshi, who set about rebuilding after establishing his own representative as sole governor of the city and dissolving the residue of the old order by

FIG. 18. *Shinpan Heian-jō narabi ni Rakugai no zu* (Newly Published Map of the Citadel of Heian and Its Surroundings, 1672). The imperial palace and the area reserved for nobles occupy the upper right; Nijō castle and the headquarters of martial administration are center left. Streets appear in white, the wards in black. The wall built by Toyotomi Hideyoshi separates the city proper from its out-reaches (Rakugai), which are given pictorial treatment. Woodblock, 70.5 × 50.5 cm. Hōsa Bunko, Nagoya.

eliminating the manorial claims of aristocratic and religious proprietors. Emperor and nobility, now vested with landed stipends by the Toyotomi regime, occupied a sort of royal ghetto laid out around the reconstructed palace in the northeast of the city. A magnificent castle complex became the center of the military quarter in the west. Temples were relocated and rebuilt in three designated areas. And within the compass of the new city wall that defined metropolitan boundaries, Hideyoshi added and repaired streets to restore the classical grid. Most of them connected the ever-increasing wards of the commoners who were drawn to the city by tax freedoms and military customers.[49] *but y no map?*

Kyoto emerged, in consequence, as a legible city, in which seeming restoration (of palace, noble residences, grid, and wall) laid bare a hegemonic order (of castle, temple zones, and commoner wards). Gone were the multifarious jurisdictions and social complexity that had long foiled cartography. The same spatial politics that animated national mapmaking was now coded into the capital. Ancient frames situated a new polity with generic properties. Ideological work made mapping (prolifically) possible. No one calls me for leads to early modern maps of Kyoto. They are everywhere.

FOUR

Blood Right and Merit

WE KEEP IN THE LOCKED and climate-controlled treasure room of Berkeley's East Asian Library a body of texts that don't really belong there. These are personnel rosters of the Tokugawa administration—texts printed so prolifically in the early modern period (in tens of thousands of copies annually) that surviving examples still flood used bookshops in Japan. The pleasure in handling the texts is the pleasure of leafing through commonplace material. Beaten up, dog-eared, dirty, and covered with marginalia, these books—known generically as "Mirrors of the Military [Houses]"—saw heavy use and plenty of travel time in the sleeves and sashes of their owners, who kept them handy for reference.[1]

Like maps, the rosters of military officials were ubiquitous in the Tokugawa market. Indeed, they much resembled maps, at least early on, in the type of information they offered. The first printed rosters, which appeared around 1643, were succinct, single-volume catalogues of all current daimyo, each described in categories familiar from official cartography. Individual entries covered the daimyo's family name, his personal name, his court title, the total registered productivity of his domain, the name of his castle headquarters, and the name of the province where his domain was located. Included, too, were sketches of each daimyo's principal family crest.[2]

Although they invariably covered the same basic material as the models they were updating, the compilers of later rosters added the address of each daimyo's primary residence in the capital of Edo and the names of his major deputies there. And from the 1660s they began producing multivolume editions that parsed each lord in what would eventually number forty-four categories. No longer simple variants on maps, the rosters became encyclopedic treatments of lordly anatomy. Most of the additions amplified the personal and family profiles of each daimyo. They specified his court rank and honorary office, as well as his title, sometimes his age, the names of his

FIG. 19. *Edo kagami* (A Mirror of Edo, n.d.). In this sample page from an early (and well-used) Military Mirror, each daimyo is identified by crest; surname, title, and personal name; the name of his castle town and the province in which it is located; the registered productivity of his domain; and the names of his chief deputies in Edo. Courtesy of the East Asian Library, University of California, Berkeley.

father and heir, the paternity of his consort and sometimes his mother, the names and revenues of increasing numbers of major retainers, his genealogy (with notes on prominent ancestors), his ancestral and clan names, the locale of the ancestral home, and the name of the family mortuary temple. A second significant group of additions concerned the daimyo's life in Edo, where he was obliged to attend annually on the shogun. Entries included the addresses not just of each lord's primary residence there but of secondary and tertiary residences as well. They went on to note the schedule of his attendance on the shogun, the distance he traveled from his domain to reach Edo and sometimes the route, the list of gifts he presented to the shogun, and the name of the room in Edo castle where he was received. Further additions covered insignia. Successive Mirrors introduced sketches of both principal and alternative crests, lances and processional regalia, horse fittings and sails.

As the entries concerning the daimyo exploded in volume, the rosters also expanded in conception. From 1659 on, compilers began to cover the officeholders in the Tokugawa bureaucracy. These were the men, some of daimyo rank but most from the lesser levels of Tokugawa retainers, who staffed the shogunal institution in Edo, other areas under direct shogunal administration, and properties reserved across the country to produce shogunal revenue. Each entry in the bureaucratic lists began with the title of a particular office, the amount of any supplementary allowance accompanying appointment, the number of subordinate functionaries (*yoriki, dōshin*) in regular service, and sometimes the dates of scheduled meetings. Each entry continued with the names of incumbents and chief deputies, indicating their addresses and stipends. Entries frequently included crests and often the names of an incumbent's father and predecessors in office. The bureaucratic rosters concluded, finally, with lengthening lists of commoners in direct service to the shogunate. The full inventories were prodigious: a Military Mirror of 1683 includes the names of over 1,700 officials in 215 job categories.[3] The number of subordinate functionaries, enumerated under each office entry but personally unnamed, was larger by a considerable factor.

Mighty in size and scope, the rosters disclose the systematic imagination at work in the cadastral and cartographic surveys. But here the very rulers who had objectified and standardized the realm of the ruled—computing land values by formula, distilling the social landscape into generic classifications, sorting the population into status groups governed collectively by decree—became objects themselves of categorical knowledge and public scrutiny. Certainly, the maps of the regime had put martial power freely on display, although in an economical code and a complex presentation where hegemony blended into the geography of history. The Mirrors, with the lens of a microscope rather than a telescope, revealed the grain of power.

In these close treatments of military personnel, the rosters taught their users how to think about authority. Much as the maps inducted consumers into a particular spatial ideology, so the rosters schooled the public in a particular political rationality. And much as the maps offered disparate analyses of space within a seemingly coherent framework, so the rosters conveyed competing visions of authority within a seemingly integral structure. The rosters were, on the surface, simple catalogues of incumbent officials. But pervading these matter-of-fact lists was a conception of rule—its sources, attributes, and organization—as complex as any explored in high philosophical discourse, and, precisely because it found expression in a deceptively utilitarian form, all the more provocative. That conception was bifurcated. In the lists of daimyo, readers found an authority diffusely grounded in history, heredity, honor, and ritual. In the lists of shogunal officeholders, readers found an authority grounded superficially in status privilege but more deeply in administrative function and professional responsibility. As textbooks in a governing system and the qualifications of governors, the rosters provided a conflicted education. Government was made, alike, of blood right and merit.

Intricate in conception, the polity was nonetheless knowable. The most compelling message of the Military Mirrors, as of the maps, was that the systems constructed by resourceful designers were proper objects of common knowledge. The rosters put charts of power on the market. Anyone with the cash could buy a copy; anyone who took the trouble could find a discard.

—

The Military Mirrors originated as commercial ventures responsive to urgent practical needs, unlike commercial maps, which derived from official models. The timing of their appearance tells the story of their genesis. In 1622, the third shogun, Tokugawa Iemitsu, obliged all daimyo to send their wives and heirs to live permanently in Edo. In 1635, he converted a once informal practice into law by requiring that most daimyo themselves be present in Edo for specified terms of annual service. In 1642, he extended the order to all daimyo.[4] The first personnel rosters, known as Directories of the Great Crests, were printed around 1643.

The mass movement of the daimyo and their entourages to Edo threw into forced proximity, and routine ceremonial encounter, an elite both ill-acquainted with itself and in flux. "The martial holdings of the realm are hard to fix," wrote an official from Tosa, "for year by year, individuals suffer from disinheritances, attainders, succession failures, and both increases and transfers in domain."[5] In an effort to get things straight, self-appointed registrars like the Tosa official appear to have assembled the prototypical rosters. If they resembled their printed successors, these were probably current lists of daimyo, complete with sketches of the family crests that served as critical clues to identity. Consulting the rosters as one might consult a field guide to the birds, viewers could distinguish martial officials through their markings.

The shift by the early 1640s to commercially published rosters was undoubtedly driven by a mounting demand among military men for timely information about peers they had to recognize and do business with. (Hence the emphasis on crests, addresses, and resident deputies.) That demand was enormous in a capital where the military population approached 500,000. And the information itself was apparently unobjectionable. The basic six-part description of each daimyo was already making its way into commercial cartography, while the labeling of daimyo mansions in the city was already common in maps of Edo. Small wonder, then, that seemingly simple matters of fact with such obvious utility to the large elite of the capital should be arranged in convenient handbooks distributed on the market.

The market proved so exceptionally strong that the original Directories of the Great Crests evolved, in response to competition and a taste for novelty, into mini-encyclopedias. By the last decades of the seventeenth century, over ten firms were luring consumers with varying formats, new details, and adamant claims to accuracy. They launched their material under splendid titles—The Military Mirror of the Realm, The Military Mirror of the Great Peace, The Complete Military Mirror—and they introduced it with assurances of up-to-date improvements on the editions of rivals. Noting that information could change daily, some even promised to enter handwritten emendations for readers unable to wait for scheduled revisions.[6] Competition narrowed in the eighteenth century, when regulation of the publishing industry accorded control of the Mirror market to the Izumoji and Suwaraya. Nonetheless, these firms continued to renew and extend coverage in editions with vast annual runs.

Military men must have remained their primary audience, but hardly an exclusive one. From the early stages of the venture, the merchants of Edo were likely buyers of rosters that, with wonderful convenience, located the residences and identified the staffs of important customers. As the enterprise grew, the voyeurs of Edo and its outreaches surely joined the consumer pool as well. Filling their editions with sketches of everything from crests to horse trappings, publishers appealed to spectators who, aided by such cues, could knowledgeably watch daimyo on parade. To judge from the rosters now in the Berkeley library, the sport was popular; for their owners checked off species as if building lifetime lists of sightings. Publishers also tailored their formats—cramming vital data into small volumes handy for travel, extracting notes on the wealthiest daimyo for cheap, souvenir editions—to suit different tastes. Peddlers and sellers of secondhand books expanded circulation. For readers simply curious about their betters, the out-of-date material dumped by cognoscenti might still serve well enough for casual reference and entertainment. Discards too numerous even for the resale market must have been handed down to servants or used as stuffing in sliding walls.

As a result of these developments in content and audience, the rosters became something rather different, of course, from utilitarian catalogues for insiders. Swollen with information that was more ideological than practical, they emerged as almanacs of official life for insiders and outsiders alike. And even the earliest versions—which recapitulated each daimyo's weighty claims to honor—surpassed pragmatic considerations to convey and normalize a political vision. Market forces alone did not shape the rosters. Hence questions surrounding the enterprise press. Who provided the information available in the Mirrors? And why? We don't know. But it's not hard to guess.

Compilation of the rosters posed two challenges, really. One involved principles of coverage: how were military officials to be ordered and categorized? The second involved information gathering: how was good data to be acquired? Commercial publishers were ill equipped to address either challenge independently.

By the time the first rosters appeared, official cartography had established basic categories for describing the daimyo. Even so, publishers of the Mirrors lacked a template for organizing these lords into a verbal text—for deciding an order of precedence among them. They also lacked a template for filling out their secondary attributes—for deciding which details, beyond the basic categories, to include and exclude. What, after all, constituted a daimyo? Were publishers to be guided by their own discretion and curiosity? And when they moved into the bureaucratic lists, the publishers entered uncharted territory. No model at all guided them in imagining and then formulating an administrative structure of officeholders.

Significant here is the fact that the Tokugawa polity was a dynamic, and long an improvisational, arrangement among men. Neither a constitution nor a code of administrative law defined political relations, the prerogatives and constraints of authority, and the terms of officeholding. Nowhere do we find a gloss on the title of shogun or anything resembling a job description for daimyo. Founded on conquest and alliance, the polity very gradually took form through oaths of loyalty, shogunal decree, customary practice, and the case law of Tokugawa magistrates. Thus what appeared telegraphically in the maps and comprehensively in the rosters as a "system" of governance reflected an experiment rather than a blueprint.[7] Because the system was being put together even as the rosters were being assembled, compilers had to consult some*one*—not some legal formulary—to sketch the ligaments of power.

And once the principles of coverage had been decided, the compilers still faced the challenge of assembling data. Again, they had to rely on some*one* for most information; for while observation might provide a portion of their material (concerning insignia, addresses, travel itineraries, and the like),[8] the greater part, especially in up-to-the-minute form, required communication with willing informants (concerning ranks, titles, consorts, and the like). If these informants came from individual daimyo and bureaucratic households, their numbers would necessarily have been large to start with, and exponentially larger as time went by.

The conclusion seems inescapable that the Tokugawa administration itself was the major supplier of Mirror material. Certainly, the shogunate was at least passively complicit in the enterprise, since its police could have shut down presumptuous publishers and silenced their collaborators. But active engagement appears indispensable to the thorough treatment of officeholders (right down to legions of hawkers, drummers, gardeners, and dentists) and the consistent treatment of daimyo (all parsed with startling congruity, whether by court rank or travel schedule or ancestry). If observation and interviews did contribute to the entries, such activity ill accounts for the coordination of data (in the tricky handling of daimyo surnames and joint investitures, for example) or its punctual revision.[9] The very magnitude of the Mirror project evokes a master collaborator.

It is in the structure of the rosters, however, that shogunal control seems most pronounced. Their striking feature is an essential sameness. Although the Mirrors emerged without a model to describe a polity without an administrative code, and developed among competitors avid for novelty, the variations between them remained chiefly cosmetic. Thus even as publishers worked tirelessly to improve legibility and utility (changing layouts, breaking material into separate fascicles, adding tables of contents and indexes), real differences in coverage tended to be temporary: the fresh detail of one publisher usually appeared in the subsequent editions of rivals. Some notion of standard fare—of a correct and complete Mirror—prevailed. Some notion of a normative system—with conventional features and stable definitions—had emerged.

Certain variations did occur from the beginning and persisted over time. Thus, for example, the firms of Izumoji and Suwaraya (which monopolized roster production following the organization of printers' guilds in 1722) continued to circulate slightly different material. The Izumoji entries on daimyo, which grew to forty-four categories, included sketches of household seals and the insignia used on horses. The Suwaraya entries, which grew to thirty-six categories, included the dates when daimyo acceded to office and the sites of their warehouses in Kyoto, Osaka, and Fushimi.[10]

But these are differences of a kind. That they existed at all indicates a concern with the appearance of distinction and commercial rivalry. It also indicates official mediation. Insofar as anyone could collect sketches of horse trappings or addresses of warehouses, differences among Mirrors were preserved artificially, almost certainly by a shogunal warrant that tended to favor the Izumoji (whose head served as official bookseller to the shogun). A shogunal hand appears firmest, however, in the conservatism and conformity of the story the Mirrors told. Avoiding anything genuinely revealing (concerning, say, the variable size and attrition of daimyo armies or the debt levels and trade volumes of individual domains), the texts repeated in their finally decorative additions—so redundant as to make difference insubstantial—a single narrative.

The story of the daimyo emerged in two phases, which correlate closely with the regime's emerging conception of lordly, and its own, identity. The symmetry suggests that the shogunate used the Mirrors in calculated acts of publicity to inculcate in a primary audience of military men and a secondary audience of common readers a normal understanding of authority. If market demand created the context for Mirror production, a complicit regime created the text.

A description of the Kanamori that appears in an early roster titled *Gomon tsukushi* (A Collection of the Great Crests, 1656) is typical of the entries during what we might consider the first phase of daimyo definition. Below the prominent crest is a name, "Kanamori Izumo no kami dono," which is amplified by the small characters "Shigeyori" to the left. The notation "60,000 *koku*" appears in the upper right; the notations "Hida Province" and "Residential Castle: Takayama" appear in the upper left. Here is the compound formula of the daimyo's being. He is simultaneously the head of a martial house (Kanamori), a particular man (Shigeyori), and an honorary aristocrat (Izumo no kami) entitled to a deferential form of address (*dono,* or lord). He is also a governor within the classical, Kyoto-centered order of provinces (Hida); a territorial lord in control of agrarian wealth (60,000 *koku*); and a castellan within the shogunal order of command (Takayama). Furthermore, he is subject to public display in the form of heraldic insignia (the crest).[11]

Like the cartographic portrayal of space, this portrayal of identity is diffuse in meaning. The daimyo is fitted into ancient frames of honor even as he belongs to an ascendant federation of generals. He is situated in a local place even as he is folded into a centralized system. But what remains arresting in this depiction of complex attachment is the prominence of the individual man. Not only do crest and name control attention, the very organization of the daimyo fraternity emphasizes personal contingency over impersonal structure.

Compilers of the early rosters had to decide, as cartographers did not, how to line the daimyo up. They might have settled on a geographical order that identified individual castle towns, and then the daimyo who held them, province by province. Such a scheme would have made the domain itself the hinge of the polity, prior in importance to the person in residence.[12] Alternatively, compilers might have settled on an institutional order—determined, say, by title or genealogical precedence—and then inserted the daimyo into that hierarchy. Such a scheme would have made the organs of state or house superior to the person. Compilers might even have arranged the daimyo mechanically, in phonetic or birth order, in which case the rosters would have implied parity among peers in a seemingly unstratified collectivity.

Instead, the rosters lined the daimyo up in order of the registered productivity totals of their domains—in order of sheer material and territorial power. These figures, startling in their variety and, at the time of the first publications, their instability, acknowledged the force of history. The polity was an invention of the many particular players, big ones elevated over small, who had cut up the landscape through conquest. In sum, the volatile relations of men were prior to the structures of place or institution. The Mirrors were so urgently needed in the 1640s precisely because the political players themselves—and hence the organization of place and institution—remained in motion.

In arranging lords by the standard of wealth, the compilers of the rosters conformed to official practice, doubtless through some combination of shogunal suasion and deference to precedent. Elite conceptions of prestige were clear enough; for we find in both the documents levying troops and the protocols governing ceremonies a rank system dictated by physical resources. As mobilization orders listed daimyo according to the size of their armies (and thus the size of their domains), so receptions and processions arrayed participants in accord with registered income.[13] The investitures that simultaneously expressed the martial value and the military threat of a daimyo also determined the ritual deference awarded him. Here, in effect, was a wartime hierarchy of command—one dictated by the variable of force, not by any impersonal constant.

This hierarchy survived in the rosters throughout their run of over two hundred years. Nonetheless, it was steadily undercut by information that converted the daimyo from dangerous generals into baronial symbols—from actors into icons. The expanding rosters reflect the effort, long under way but accelerated by the third shogun, to impose peacetime disciplines on wartime rivals by codifying the very meaning of "daimyo," a term more evocative than exact ever since the Middle Ages. In a memorandum (*oboe*) of 1634, the regime captured a basic definition by describing "great lords" as men vested with lands assigned a minimum productive capacity of 10,000 *koku* and subordinate to the administrative supervision of the Tokugawa senior councillors (*rōjū*).[14] The actual terms of rule emerged jaggedly, and over time, in oaths and statutes that obliged the daimyo to maintain armies for the shogun's use, forebear from treason, seek consent for military construction and marriage, conform to the rules of propriety, and "follow in all things the laws of Edo" (in matters ranging from foreign relations to sumptuary behavior).[15] Yet not until the years after 1640 did two fundamental principles of mature peacetime rule become clear. These principles, one concerning succession and one concerning ritual attendance in Edo, would organize the continuing relations of shogun and daimyo. They would also organize the expanding Military Mirrors. First, the principles, then a return to the Mirrors.

In 1641, under the leadership of the Confucian tutor Hayashi Razan, Tokugawa scholars compiled a group of annotated genealogies for the Japanese imperial line, the Chinese imperial lines, the Kamakura shogun, the Muromachi shogun, and the houses of both Oda Nobunaga and Toyotomi Hideyoshi.[16] In the same year, the Tokugawa regime ordered Ōta Sukemune to oversee a comprehensive genealogical project covering all current military families in Japan. Barely twenty months later, in the ninth month of 1643, Sukemune presented the completed work, *Kan'ei shoka keizuden* (The Genealogies of the Houses of the Kan'ei Period), to the third shogun.[17] It comprised two sets of 186 volumes (one in Chinese, one in Japanese) and accounted for 1,419 houses. The basic data came directly from martial houses themselves, which had been required to collate family documents, prepare genealogical tables, and submit both the documentation and the tables to the authorities. Teams of scholars subsequently corrected and verified the texts. After settling on the prime ancestor of each house, they also divided the entire martial community into three major lineage groups (Seiwa Genji, Heishi, Fujiwara) and one miscellaneous category. Finally, they fitted all families into the many branches of trunk lines that derived in every case (if only through finesse) from an emperor or aristocrat of the classical period.

As ambitious in its way as the cadastral and cartographic surveys, this undertaking, too, used encyclopedic knowledge in the service of control. Having vetted the family histories of the military elite, the regime produced master genealogical tables that awarded primacy of place to the Tokugawa house, traced back through twenty-six generations to the Seiwa emperor (r. 858–876). To emphasize the preeminence of the Seiwa lineage, all other Genji (descended from the emperors Montoku, Murakami, Saga, and Uda) were consigned to the miscellaneous category.

Still, the ranking of pedigrees remained only one purpose, I think the lesser one, of editors scrupulous about historical details. Placing the Genealogies in a scholarly tradition dating to the classical period, they submitted all the documents to the scrutiny of exegetes and exposed their many lacunae and inconsistencies in the final text. With equal fidelity, they acknowledged the pervasive crises—wars, assassinations, coups, betrayals, martial intrigues—that tempered the fiction of continuity with the reality of disjunction. Despite the errors inevitable in labor done fast, this punctiliousness lent the Genealogies authority throughout the early modern period. More immediately, it altered the portrayal of the Tokugawa shogun, who became not just predestined inheritors of lineage rights but masters of their troubled times. They were victors.

By yoking a story about ancestry to a story about history, the Genealogies achieved a deep purpose, which is disclosed in the preface. "How truly revealed [in these genealogies] is the fulfillment in our time of the Great Peace," Ōta Sukemune writes. "When we know the official service of the various houses, we cannot forget the depth of our obligations. When we know their meritorious deeds, we must think of our duties to the ancestors. In doing so, we shall venerate immortal virtue and the way of loyalty and filial piety for a million generations to come."[18] Through these numbing platitudes, the preface passes a paradoxical verdict: history made us, but history is finished. It was the deeds of ancestors that achieved the Great Peace. Yet because peace is now complete, only remembering is left. "In our time," the descendants of mighty actors must simply venerate their immortal virtue. In effect, the editors assign the ancestors a greatness founded in historical agency and their successors a votive function rationalized by genealogical obligation.

As the text goes on to illustrate, history climaxed quite specifically during the generation of Tokugawa Ieyasu. The biographical notes, often prodigious even for distant ancestors, expand in volume to describe the individual household heads contemporary with the regime's founder. They conclude with variations on an indispensable statement: "Then Munetoshi [or Mitsutsuna or Nagamasa or Yukinaga or whoever] entered the service of [or paid homage to, attended upon, was received by] the Daigongen [Ieyasu]." Thereafter, most notes become all but perfunctory records of ceremonial matters. The point is clear. Through many paths cut by myriad progenitors, the grandfathers of the current martial elite arrived in common at the omega point of the Tokugawa peace. Now their descendants are not only in the family business, their business is the family—remembering it, honoring its defining alliance with Ieyasu, and continuing its tradition of loyalty for a million generations. The message is stasis.

Tokugawa Iemitsu presented the Chinese text of the Genealogies to the ghost of his own grandfather, Tokugawa Ieyasu, at the shrine in Nikkō where he was deified under the title "Great Avatar who Illuminates the East" (Tōshō Daigongen). Several years earlier, in 1636, Iemitsu had completed an extravagant reconstruction of the shrine buildings for the twentieth anniversary of Ieyasu's death. And two years after presenting the Genealogies, he would preside over ceremonies to elevate the Nikkō mausoleum to the first rank of national shrines—on a par with the shrine to the imperial ancestors at Ise.[19]

At the time of these activities, Iemitsu was preoccupied with the ordeal of succession. Ill, tormented by dreams, and already twenty years in shogunal office, Iemitsu had a very young heir (born in 1639) and a volatile confederacy (threatened in 1637–38 by the Shimabara rebellion).[20] He sought shelter in ancestor worship. On the one hand, he continued to propagate Ieyasu's cult in a series of commemorative rituals focused on the founder's divinity. On the other, he commissioned the Genealogies to celebrate *all* the martial ancestors who had joined the founder to make the peace. The quintessential role of Iemitsu and his daimyo alike, these actions proclaimed, was that of heir. Their job? To produce and safely install the next generation of heirs.

It was in the 1640s, then, that Iemitsu relaxed succession policies to place a premium on the peaceful continuity of the military houses (and thus on the staying power of the shogunate itself). Although the Tokugawa had once confiscated the domains of daimyo who failed to identify heirs in a timely fashion, such attainders slowed to a trickle as lords were permitted to select successors until the moment of death (even, with the proper seal on a document, posthumously).[21] Here was a reversal of the often belligerent strategy of containment that had put the daimyo's very survival at risk. During the third generation of Tokugawa rule, the need for stability replaced the need for force. And the family replaced the man as the pivot of the polity.

Reinforcing the ritual character of the daimyo's role was the policy of periodic attendance in Edo. It had many purposes (not least a heightened control over daimyo compelled to squander wealth, disperse manpower, and invest half a lifetime and more in the shogun's city) and many consequences (not least the conversion of Edo into a giant metropolis at the center of a national economy). In essence, through, the policy was a glue. It held together through routine physical witness a settlement otherwise expressed in the long-distance documents of command. And it belonged, despite the impersonal character of much public administration, to an old tradition of body and gift politics. The delivery of hostages, the exchange of brides and concubines, the swearing of oaths, the calibration of clothing and material display to social privilege—all such elite practices insisted on the direct performance of political relations.[22]

Once in Edo, the duty of the daimyo was to see the shogun—to be physically present at the receptions and ceremonies of the ritual calendar—and to give and receive gifts both splendid (horses, swords, fine silks, precious metals) and rare (perfect tree mushrooms, confections, bean pastes, mountain herbs, seaweeds, teas, radishes). In these performances of homage, the claims of family established precedence. The shogun received his men in rooms reserved, in order of intimacy, for relatives, daimyo with hereditary attachments to the Tokugawa, and daimyo whose ancestors had allied with Ieyasu late and from independent land bases. For the purposes of castle ritual, the hierarchy of landed wealth yielded to a hierarchy of blood and historical association with the Great Avatar. The claims of family were reiterated, moreover, in ceremonial obligations extending beyond the castle: daimyo accompanied the shogun to services at Nikkō as well as the Tokugawa mortuary temples of Kan'eiji and Zōjōji.[23] Combined in these commemorative displays were the two principles that ordered Tokugawa Iemitsu's policy toward the daimyo: they were bound by ancestral obligations focused jointly on their own forebears and the founder of the regime; and they were obliged to bear continuing witness to this union through periodic attendance on the incumbent shogun.

These principles organized the presentation of the daimyo during the second phase of the Mirrors' development. The earliest rosters had put across a polity that was universal (covering all the lords of the realm) and coherent (combining in each lord the same attributes of honor). Still, they retained the punch of news by delivering ever-changing information about lords who might not last the year. The later rosters told a story about continuity, even predictability, in a fixed elite defined by family and ritual service.

Consider the entry on the Mōri house in a Mirror from the turn of the eighteenth century.[24] The entry opens with an abbreviated chart of the "Mōri Lineage," beginning with the prime ancestor Ōe no Hiromoto (1148–1225), who descended from an aristocratic house and served the shogun Minamoto no Yoritomo as head of his chancellery. He is identified

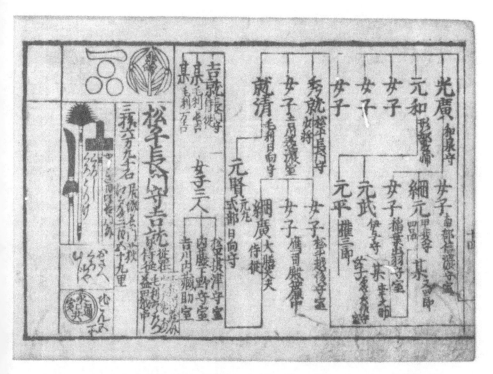

FIG. 20. *Gorin bukan* (A Military Mirror of the Great Forest, 1701), published in more abbreviated form than the 1705 work by the same title discussed in the text, which concludes its account of the Mōri lineage with Matsudaira Nagato no kami Yoshinari (father of Matsudaira Yoshihiro). On this sample page of the (longer) Mōri entry, we also find two of Yoshinari's predecessors (Tsunahiro and Hidenari) and a number of collaterals. Courtesy of the East Asian Library, University of California, Berkeley.

by his court rank and titles as well as his position in the Kamakura shogunate. Noting that Hiromoto's first son was "Mōri Mutsu no kami" (hence indicating the change in surname), the chart then skips several centuries to arrive precipitously at Mōri Takamoto (1523–1563), progenitor of the principal Mōri line of the Tokugawa period.

Following Takamoto, the chart identifies the four subsequent heads who preceded the incumbent daimyo, noting court ranks, titles, and offices in each case. Exceptionally elaborate details are provided for Mōri Terumoto, who submitted to Tokugawa Ieyasu following the battle of Sekigahara in 1600. In addition to this main lineage, the chart also follows several branch lines and singles out fifteen Mōri daughters who made auspicious marriages to daimyo, other military officials, and courtiers.

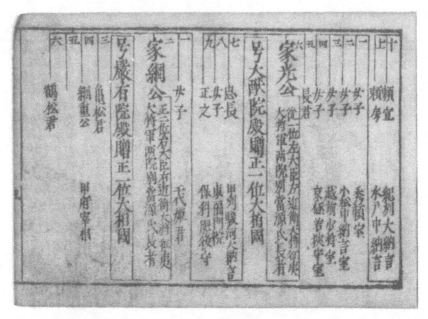

FIG. 21. *Gorin bukan* (A Military Mirror of the Great Forest, 1701), partial chart of "The Tokugawa Lineage" beginning with the Seiwa Emperor and concluding

The entry proceeds from the lineage to the incumbent daimyo, identified by surname and personal name, Matsudaira Yoshihiro, as well as court title, office, and rank. His consort is the "Honored Daughter of the Princely Former Imperial Regent, Junior First Rank, Takatsukasa Kanehiro." The entry provides sketches of three of the incumbent's crests and locates four of his mansions in Edo (one of them just within the Hibiya gate of Edo castle). It also names eight of his major deputies and three of his "castle representatives." The entry continues with the registered productivity of Yoshihiro's domain (over 369,000 *koku*); the name and location of his headquarters (Hagi castle in Nagato province); and the distance of his castle from Edo (259 *ri*). It indicates that the Mōri domain, enduring for "generation upon generation," has centered on this particular castle since Keicho 5 (1600). In the event that readers have skimmed the opening lineage chart too hastily, the entry closes by recapitulating the full names and titles of Yoshihiro's predecessors at Hagi.

The data in this long entry has the perverse effect of occluding the person of the daimyo. The story of family succession is paramount. Twice—in the original chart and the concluding list of castellans—the incumbent is linked to a chain that will continue with the transition to his heir. His

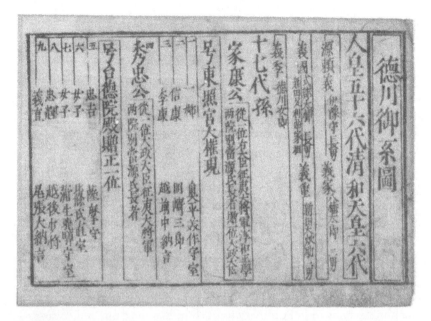

with Ietsuna (d. 1680). The genealogy continues on the following page. Courtesy of the East Asian Library, University of California, Berkeley.

house is also linked to others: to the classical aristocracy through Ōe no Hiromoto, Yoshihiro's union with the Takatsukasa, and the noble marriages of female relations; to the martial elite through Hiromoto and a startling number of nuptial alliances (five of Yoshihiro's aunts became the consorts of daimyo). The critical connection is to the Tokugawa. The incumbent's history as lord of Hagi dates from Ieyasu's victory at Sekigahara, when his great-great-grandfather submitted to the overlord. And his surname appears neither as Ōe nor Mōri but as Matsudaira, a Tokugawa family name bestowed on allies as a mark of honor. One more indication of the shogunal hold on Mōri history appears in the treatment of its branch lines. Following the entry on Yoshihiro, the roster lines up four lesser Mōri daimyo, whose domains, the notes make clear, were carved out of a once consolidated family holding after 1600. If the roster acknowledges the great wealth of Yoshihiro and the collective eminence of his house, it also exposes a forced diffusion of resources resulting from the Tokugawa conquest.

The relationship between the Mōri and the Tokugawa is also a matter of parallel treatment. As later rosters emphasize daimyo genealogy, so they elaborate entries concerning the incumbent shogun (often absent in the prototypes) to trace his line to the beginning of time. Thus they declare that "fifty-six generations of human emperors" led to the Seiwa emperor (858–876), whose descendents five generations later included Minamoto no Yoriyoshi (995–1082). Yoriyoshi begat Yoshiie who begat Yoshikuni who begat Yoshishige who begat Yoshisue. And Yoshisue's descendents fifteen generations later included the Posthumous Dainagon Minamoto no Hiro-tada (1526–1549). His first son was the omega point: the "Great Avatar who Illumines the East, Lord Ieyasu, Junior First Rank, Minister of the Right, Great Shogun who Subdued the Barbarians, Head of the Junna and Shōgaku Academies, Chief of the Genji Clan, and Great Minister of State with the Posthumous Senior First Rank." The charts then continue the shogunal succession to the incumbent, noting the ranks and titles of all brothers, the marriage alliances of all sisters.[25]

Implied in such charts was a certain parity between the shogun and the daimyo. Yes, the shogun was first in prestige. Yes, he transcended any cate-gorical summary (of his castles, his revenues, his deputies) that might con-fine him to the world of ordinary lords. But, like the daimyo, he was pre-eminently the heir to a house that encumbered him with endless obligation. He was also the father of an heir, whom the Mirrors represent, in the terms of a conventional daimyo, with rank, title, consort, deputies, a specific investiture (350,000 koku), and a castle headquarters (Fuchū, later known as Kōfu, in the province of Kai). And he was entangled, too, with collateral lines—particularly the three great Matsudaira houses head-quartered at Nagaya, Wakayama, and Mito. These collaterals appear in the Mirrors directly after the shogunal entries to confirm the precedence of the extended Tokugawa establishment. Yet, together with the lineage chart, the presentation of the branches constructs a family story different only in eminence from the family stories of the daimyo.

It is in Edo that the stories converge. The gravitational pull of the center is felt most powerfully as the rosters combine greater family detail with lengthening references to the system of alternate attendance. Formed by individual histories, the daimyo collectively form a union in the capital. Thus the description of Mōri (or Matsudaira) Yoshihiro makes him as much a man of Edo as a man of Hagi. He retains no fewer than four man-sions in the capital, one of them in the outer circle of the shogun's castle. Eight major deputies attend him there, while Hagi is entrusted to surro-gates. Indeed, together with Yoshihiro, Hagi enters the magnetic field of Edo: the castle town is defined not only by its province but its distance from the center. And although Yoshihiro's entry lacks a synopsis of the route that connects the shogun's castle with his own, most notes on the daimyo do include itineraries (the highways and ports and lodgings they use, the provinces and cities they pass, the distances they cover on each leg of the journey).[26] Daimyo geography is binary—organized by two destinations and the very public travel between them that announces dual attachments. The official schedules of daimyo attendance in Edo began to appear in Mirrors published after 1712. So, too, did lists of the gifts they exchanged with the shogun and (after 1745) the locations in Edo castle where they were received by the shogun.

These last details, which conjure mental pictures of the daimyo in action, are somehow startling in catalogues otherwise given over to what a daimyo *is* rather than what he *does*. But these things, the Mirrors suggest, are really the same. The ceremonial attendance of the Edo daimyo on the shogun—at the right time, in the right room, with the right gifts—is both expression and confirmation of his privileged status. He enacts who he is. Being a daimyo, with its lapidary layers of significance, is his job.

The point is suggested again by the increasing attention in the rosters to daimyo regalia: to secondary crests, lances, spears, standards, the decorative umbrellas carried in processions, and the insignia used on uniforms, ships, sails, and horses. This array of visual signs, hardly necessary for simple identification, implies parading and watching. It implies that the daimyo manifests his honor in rich regalia and then performs that honor in flamboyant marches, which serve as the public counterpart to the private enactment of status in Edo castle. Proceeding to and from the capital, the shogunal residence, the Tokugawa mortuary temples, and one another's mansions, the daimyo are men not only of Edo but of the streets.

In their treatment of regalia, the Mirrors effectively present themselves as celebrity guides. Instead of addressing insiders with increasing amounts of practical information (concerning the size of daimyo retinues in Edo, say, or the names of their principal purveyors), they address an audience of spectators with lengthening inventories of both symbols and honors. The symbols invite informed watching, while the honors provide the incentive to watch. Here, the Mirrors say, is a big creature: a wealthy castellan, a descendant of an ancient house, a continuing link in an eminent family chain, a bearer of an aristocratic title, a lord in the shogunal circle of prestige. He is important in his very being. Look at him.

This identification of the daimyo with his symbols converted him into an icon—a figure of parade and public consumption. Certainly, his person continued to matter in the Mirrors, although in the context of the family dramas of birth and marriage and succession. Certainly, too, variation among the daimyo mattered in the Mirrors. In a fashion doubtless delectable to cognoscenti, the rosters marked fine and gross differences in wealth, pedigree, rank, title, and access to the shogun. But here, again, variation occurred across a fixed spectrum in a closed community of privilege. Finessing any concern with active leadership and governing responsibilities, the Mirrors ultimately reified the daimyo by tying their real (or sufficient) relevance to honor. The transformation undertaken by Tokugawa Iemitsu, who cast his daimyo as heirs and ritual performers, found expression in commercial texts.

—

At the same time that compilers of the Mirrors were elaborating the familial and ceremonial roles of the daimyo, they began tracking the personnel of the shogunal administration. The two lists in the Mirrors—one of daimyo, one of officeholders—were sufficiently different in kind to describe, and focus attention on, two distinctive orders of power. In the daimyo order, a power of hereditary privilege but inchoate practical application attached to individual iconic figures with lifetime tenures. In the bureaucratic order, a specifically administrative power, demarcated by a job title, attached to the office and devolved through appointment upon officeholders, many with limited terms.

Like the evolving definition of daimyo, the creation of orderly catalogues of officeholders owed a great deal to Tokugawa Iemitsu. A peacetime overlord without experience in battle, Iemitsu had inherited a wartime organization adapted fitfully and exigently to a national civil rule. Hence he struggled, in stabilizing a regime no longer absorbed with conquest, to regularize both the institutions and the procedures of governance. He identified the principal organs of shogunal administration and specified their responsibilities. He reorganized the shogunate's military guard and police units. He streamlined the management of Tokugawa finances and landed property. He established a hierarchy of official posts and the minimum income levels required for appointment. In sum, Iemitsu rationalized a once motley and improvised system.[27] By 1659, when the Mirrors first introduced the lists of officeholders, that system looked not just big but marvelously coherent—each job numbered and named in a descending order that covered a remarkable range of activity.

The very size and coherence of the administrative structure (in appearance if not in fact) help explain the willingness of the regime to publicize the lists through commercial publication. Much in the manner of the daimyo catalogues, the catalogues of officeholders conveyed an enormous amount of practical information to military men themselves, even as they projected an image of the state, at once edifying and orderly, to general consumers. Yet the edification value of the bureaucratic lists had deeper reach than the daimyo lists; for they engaged the self-interest and self-knowledge of a substantial population that became both visible to the public and invested in the public as a result of the circulation of the rosters. This population included all persons from many stations who were potentially active in official life. And it loomed at least as large as the daimyo in the regime's calculus of survival. Hence, in disseminating the office rosters, the shogunate was recruiting loyalty on a grand scale. The effect was contradictory: when they exposed the stake of jobholders in the polity, the Mirrors also exposed a political rationality founded in professional service rather than ancestral fealty. By juxtaposing the daimyo and bureaucratic rosters, the Mirrors suggested conflicting answers to basic questions. What is the role of government? Who is eligible to serve?

The lists of officeholders typically appeared in the Mirrors, following the lists of daimyo, in separate fascicles that were headed, if at all, with bare titles such as the "Honorable Offices." They varied by publisher and edition, partly to reflect small but steady changes in the numbers of job titles and jobholders, as well as the rank order among them. They varied, too, in the detail of their entries; for publishers continued to load the office lists, like the daimyo lists, with additional notes (concerning, for example, dates of appointment and dates of meetings, the responsibilities of officials, the names of their predecessors, and their secondary regalia). Two durable principles of organization nonetheless prevailed. Thus, for example, *Honchō bukei tōkan* (The Right Mirror of Japan's Martial Lines, 1691) begins by covering all offices and officials headquartered in Edo (#1–139), proceeds to provincial posts (#140–212), and concludes with a list of commoners in service to the shogun (#213–219).[28] Within these groupings, moreover, the Right Mirror lists offices in descending order of putative prestige—an order that conforms roughly, though not exactly, to the income levels of their holders.

This arrangement of offices by geography and import discourages any easy sorting of the regime's main functions—into, say, the categories of defense and policing, finance, adjudication, urban administration, and the like. Councillors, guardsmen, city magistrates, pages, supervisors of public works, flag bearers, inspectors, drummers—all are interspersed in rosters that describe wide spheres of official jurisdiction without differentiating them very clearly. Yet the careful reading and rereading of regular users would have disclosed patterns of activity indicative of reasonably clear missions.

First, and obviously, readers would have recognized the more or less familiar workings of a martial house—a great house, to be sure, but one conventionally preoccupied with castles to keep, a landed domain to oversee, and a military force to maintain. Conspicuous throughout the Right Mirror, then, are the staffers of the shogun's household administration—from his more eminent deputies (councillors, chamberlains, masters of ceremony, comptrollers) to a host of lesser attendants (secretaries, couriers, escorts, pages, standard bearers, hawkers, grooms).[29] The primary locus of this administration is Edo castle, which is served by a long litany of caterers, provisioners, lacquerers, carpenters, gardeners, physicians, entertainers, and other guardians of the shogun's physical welfare. But the shogunal establishment also encompasses, as the catalogue of provincial offices indicates, a network of castles and castle administrations in Kyoto, Osaka, Sunpu, and Echigo. And supporting this formidable presence are vast landed resources in the twenty-four provinces where the Right Mirror identifies Tokugawa intendants. Supervising the intendants are the various financial magistrates and regional coordinators (all based in Edo) who were responsible for the Tokugawa treasury.

The martial complement of the shogunal house looms particularly large in the Right Mirror. Loftiest in rank is the great guard of twelve units, each led by a captain and four divisional commanders, which served primarily in Edo, with rotating assignments in Kyoto and Osaka. Close behind are a bodyguard of ten smaller units that protected the person of the shogun and an inner guard of ten units that attended castle ceremonies and accompanied inspection teams in the provinces. The roster also identifies a new guard of six units responsible for policing Edo castle. Below these principal bodies, a large number of additional military units punctuates the lists of both Edo and provincial officers. Some are attached to particular stations in Edo castle (individual gates, compounds, and suites) and the Edo environs (Kawaguchi, Nakagawa). Some perform escort duty (mounted or on foot). Many specialize in particular weapons (the lance, the bow, the pike, the musket). And many operate as permanent divisions at sensitive provincial posts under shogunal control (such as Kyoto, Osaka, Sunpu, Echigo, Nikkō, and Hachiōji). The roster includes, too, a substantial cohort of assemblymen (*yoriai*)—landed retainers of the Tokugawa who lacked current office but stood ready, at least in theory, for military service.

But as clearly as the Right Mirror describes the workings of a landed martial house, it describes something larger as well. For one thing, it describes a metropolitan authority; for, like all castellans, the shogun governed the cities that housed his headquarters. Thus readers of the roster would have noticed, apart from castle keepers, the high-placed urban magistrates, and extensive support staffs, who were stationed throughout Tokugawa castle towns. Especially in Edo, the roster accounts for a dense urban administration, including officers in charge of engineering, construction, public works, water supply, fire control, crime control, and prisons. For another thing, the Right Mirror describes a hegemonic authority; for, alone among lords, the shogun exercised powers of surveillance over both his confederates and the imperial court. That power is intimated by the preeminence of the senior councillors (whose jurisdiction extended, as later Mirrors would specify, to the daimyo and the aristocracy). It is apparent in the offices of the great inspectors (who toured daimyo domains to enforce compliance with shogunal policies); the Kyoto deputy (who oversaw the throne); the three units of palace guardsmen (who policed the imperial household); and the masters of ceremony (who presided over the reception of daimyo and courtiers at Edo castle).

Still, the scope of Tokugawa rule was hardly exhausted by these enlarging categories of administration. Bearing in on readers of the rosters was a plethora of job titles impossible to attach to either conventional lordship or urban and hegemonic functions. Although the Right Mirror sprawls into many arenas of governance, it highlights four particularly important areas of public interest: religion, transport, coinage, and adjudication.

High on the list of Edo-based officials are the magistrates of temples and shrines, who exercised ultimate administrative and judicial authority over the lands, residents, and clerical hierarchies of the country's Buddhist and Shinto establishments. Lower on the list, but similarly significant of the regime's jurisdiction over religious activity, are the examiners of Christians, who superintended the annual interrogations, conducted nationwide, designed to preclude the practice of the Christian faith. Officeholders in the provinces include magistrates in Japan's most sensitive religious centers: Nikkō to be sure, but also Ise (the site of the imperial shrine to the Sun Goddess) and Nara (the original capital of metropolitan Buddhism in Japan).

Threaded through both the Edo and provincial lists are the officials in charge of transport networks and commercial nodes. The Edo list accounts for numerous magistrates of highways, roads, ocean and river traffic, and ships. It also includes barrier magistrates responsible for the highway stations where monitors checked travelers and their documents.[30] Prominent among provincial officials are the magistrates of Nagasaki (controlled directly by the shogunate as the sole port for Chinese and European trade), Shimoda (the inspection point for all maritime traffic around Edo Bay), Fushimi (hub of the river system linking the Kyoto area to the Inland Sea), and Sakai (a secondary port for the Osaka area).

The roster indicates the regime's control over the country's principal deposits of precious ores by identifying in the provincial list the magistrates of Sado (site of Japan's major gold mines) and the magistrates of Iwami and Tajima (sites of major silver mines). It indicates shogunal authority over the mint, as well as rates of exchange for metals, by identifying the magistrates of copper coins in the Edo list and the gold and silver guildsmen in the list of commoner officials. The former supervised the production and distribution of legal copper issues; the latter manufactured legal tender in gold and silver.

The judicial apparatus of the shogunate, although never fully distinguished from administrative jurisdictions and hence dispersed among many particular magistrates, came to center on the office the roster identifies as the tribunal (*hyōjōsho*). There the regime's principle civil officials (including the magistrates of Edo, finance, and temples and shrines) decided major cases unresolved at lower levels. These cases involved parties of all stations, from courtiers and daimyo to commoners. They also involved charges of all kinds, from treason and rebellion to sexual scandal.[31]

Only the savviest readers of the Right Mirror would have known the particular duties of most officials. And even they would have been unlikely to sort out the particular spheres of official activity in a fashion agreeable to the modern eye. Indeed, the roster's intermixture in a rank order of apparently disparate offices warns against any modernist conception of this early modern regime. There is no clear demarcation here between the operations of a martial house and a civil administration; no strict separation of powers or differentiation of functions; no obvious delineation of boundaries between hegemony and society or between shogunal and daimyo authority. The regime is nameless in the Mirrors, and remains hard to label today, because it expanded dynamically and operated simultaneously on many levels. Jobholders staffed the organs of what was, at once, a house, a lordship, a military command, a metropolitan administration, and a statist institution.

Yet in representing this very breadth and complexity, the Right Mirror exposes the capacious national role assumed by a protean government. A lordly dominion had expanded to take in a public province of common resources and integral functions. The regime's reach may have been most apparent to readers in the list of provincial offices; for there its specifically territorial claims—ranging from Sado to Nagasaki, from Ise to Nara, from Dewa to Hizen—reveal a pervasive geographical presence. Still, the list of core officials in Edo conveys more surely the radiant power of a center that ignored borders to claim oversight of the nation's monarchical and religious institutions, transport and trade systems, and monetary and judicial operations.

Although the grave practical limits on this power are not a subject of the Mirrors, its conceptual limits are. They came chiefly from the daimyo; for in juxtaposing the lists of domainal lords with the lists of shogunal officeholders the Mirrors represent a federal system divided, if none too specifically, among local and central jurisdictions. But limits are also set by the specificity of the office lists. However raggedly the Right Mirror intersperses disparate posts, it is clear about the priorities of the regime (established by the rank order) and the defining importance of definite work. The personalism of an enveloping lordship mutates, here, into the structuralism of a government that assigns bounded functions to job-centered functionaries.

Work becomes, really, the subject of the text—work that is broken down into 219 categories, named in descriptive titles and addressed to specialized activities. Readers did not find in the rosters a vague body of overarching ministers with obscure portfolios. They found, instead, an elaborately classified organization with specifiable, and therefore selective and accountable, purposes. The regime staked out particular territorial interests (excluding, for example, such significant ports as Kagoshima and Hiroshima) and particular governing operations (excluding, for example, food distribution, education, and paper currency), and on that basis appointed a workforce focused on the job.

Certainly, the Right Mirror sketches a number of offices in broad strokes. What, actually, *was* the scope of the Edo city magistrates or the financial magistrates? What, most curiously, was the function of the senior and junior councillors who head the job list? By the early eighteenth century, the Mirrors began to supply answers for readers outside the inner circles of rule. They came to include, in separate sections, the equivalent of supervisory charts, which indicated for each major office the subordinate offices reporting to it.[32] Lined up below the senior councillors, for example, were the fifteen or so units they controlled directly. Scrutiny would indicate that these chief executive officers of the shogunate were charged with final oversight of the imperial court, the daimyo, the principal guardsmen, Tokugawa properties, the city of Edo, major construction projects, land distribution, and temples and shrines. This jurisdiction was large and only roughly delineated. The supervisory charts nonetheless portray the governing system as a system—one that translated priorities into jobs and organized jobs by lines of accountability. This arrangement was so elaborate, moreover, as to bear the mark of invention: neither natural nor inevitable, the structure was made up.

And then it was staffed. The primacy of job over man is the most arresting feature of the office rosters, for it abraded the status order of the Tokugawa world.

The Tokugawa shogun was lord to two distinctive groups—his daimyo confederates and his housemen. The daimyo were treated comprehensively in the rosters as both scions of great families and heads of specific domains. The housemen were another story.

Like the daimyo, the Tokugawa entered peacetime with a substantial army that was never demobilized. The survival of the samurai had originally been a condition of cease-fire, since the long-tentative alliances between hegemon and daimyo depended on both a balance of force among them and the local control of local troops. Created by wars, the daimyo stood ready to wage more. They also remained wary of fighters who had delivered their victories and might wreak havoc if discharged summarily. Yet even as the peace acquired momentum and redundant soldiers a punishing cost, the entitlements of warriors grew more firmly entrenched. They had become inextricable from the social and moral order of the regime.

Through a combination of legal statute and Confucian rationalization, the Tokugawa settlement developed as a hereditary status system. The system had urgent practical purposes: to secure the power of the martial elite as a birthright; and to fix the labor services of peasants and other subjects as a birth obligation. It assumed ethical valences, however, as thinkers of diverse background (from the shogun's tutors to the schoolmen of popular academies) masked coercion as virtue. In a rich discourse focused on the moral necessity of hereditary distinction, they associated status discipline with devotion to the ancestors, fidelity to honorable callings, and the organic interdependency of the social body. Central to this discourse, as both a problem and an exemplum, was the martial community. The problem derived from the shrinking role of fighting men: the very persons the status order was designed to protect lacked opportunities appropriate to their ancestry. Hence the literature diminished the military profile of samurai to emphasize their role as gentlemen called to leadership. As exempla, they discharged their obligations by displaying the exemplary character that privilege permitted and required them to cultivate. Character could be variously formed (through education, emulation of superiors, physical regimens) and variously employed (in governance, learning, voluntary public service). But it was, in itself, the justifying property of men who upheld the social order by embodying humanity, loyalty, ardor toward duty, devotion to principle, and reverence for forebears.[33] Thus, however burdensome a population too large to employ and too expensive to maintain, the samurai became too entangled in the regime's ethos to sacrifice. They stood collectively for the hereditary power that no daimyo was prepared to surrender. And once imagined as gentlemen, they stood collectively for the civilizing values that made power rightful. To demobilize them would have been to tear at the sense of the system.

So together with the daimyo, the Tokugawa house carried on its books a huge retainer complement stratified by rank and remuneration. At its apex were roughly 1,500 men vested with lands that ranged in assessed yield from 500 to just under 10,000 *koku*. Another 4,500 men, some with land but most on stipends, received annual incomes valued at 100 to 500 *koku*. Roughly 16,500 men received stipends below (typically *well* below) 100 *koku*. In addition to this complement of approximately 22,500 retainers, a much larger group of rear vassals and marginal attendants brought the total number of Tokugawa samurai to something around 60,000—all putatively ready for military service.[34]

Like the daimyo, the retainers belonged to the martial elite and, if in of ten meager portions, enjoyed the distinction of vested incomes and social privileges (mainly in treatment before the law). Unlike the daimyo, their distinction did not extend reliably to employment or even to participation in the regime's ceremonial life. While a few dozen landed retainers were received by the shogun at Edo castle, the overwhelming majority lacked ritual functions that confirmed their honor. They lacked publicity as well. No roster of the shogun's retainers was ever published. Nor is there evidence that any such roster circulated among insiders in manuscript copies. Toward the end of the Tokugawa period, publishers did issue catalogues of the loftiest housemen, about 250 of them, who held lands with assessed yields over 3,000 *koku*.[35] The rest remained invisible.

It is easy to imagine something akin to a peerage list that would have identified a substantial number of retainers (all those above the 100 *koku* level, say) with suitably ennobling notes about their fathers, heirs, and

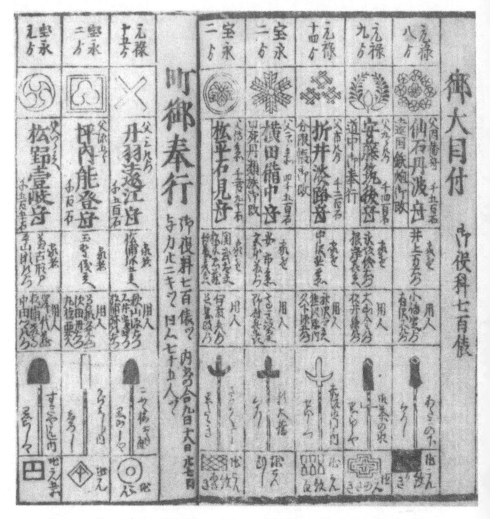

FIG. 22. *Kansei bukan* (A Military Mirror of the Kansei Period, 1789). In this sample from a comparatively late Mirror, the entries for both the great inspectors (*ōmetsuke*) and Edo city magistrates (*machi onbugyō*) specify the amount of the office allowance as well as each official's crest and regalia, date of appointment, father's name, income, and major deputies (*karō* and *yōnin*). The entries for inspectors also include their previous appointments. The general entry for magistrates includes the number of functionaries (*yoriki* and *dōshin*) assigned each official and their monthly meeting dates. Courtesy of the East Asian Library, University of California, Berkeley.

crests—something, in effect, that would have acknowledged the prestige of martial status itself. It is also easy to imagine an office roster, akin to a daimyo roster, that would have lined up retainers in status order and then entered, as a secondary matter, all current job titles—a roster that would, in effect, have made the retainer complement both prior and superior to the job structure. Instead, and surely in accordance with intelligence provided by the regime, the publishers put jobs first. And because jobs were far fewer than retainers, housemen entered both public life and the public record quite selectively through official appointment.

Who, then, received appointment?

Some of the most powerful posts in the shogunal administration—including those of senior and junior councillor, Kyoto deputy, and keeper of Osaka castle—were reserved for daimyo, identifiable to readers of the rosters by investitures over 10,000 *koku*. While daimyo appointees tended to come from a select group of families close to the Tokugawa, their very presence in office contributed to the impression of national integration. The Mirrors portray a regime that, having laid claim to vital functions of state, assigned its confederates to corporate governance and thus entwined the interests of center and locale. Precisely because those interests were often opposed, the structural inclusion of daimyo acknowledged the management of conflict as inherent in a workable union.[36]

Still, the overwhelming number of posts went to Tokugawa retainers, identifiable to readers of the rosters by investitures below 10,000 *koku*. The insistent entry of those figures exposed a tight relationship between the status order and the office structure. Because investitures appeared as a defining attribute of jobholders and axiomatically distinguished samurai from commoners, the Mirrors represented official appointment as a near monopoly of the military establishment. (Thus, investiture = military status = access to appointment.) The Mirrors also exposed a relationship between rank and job assignment. Because the prestige of an office corresponded to the size of an investiture, and because the latter depended on a man's station in the company of retainers, the Mirrors seemingly represented as symmetrical the hierarchy of birth and the hierarchy of office. (Thus, hereditary rank = specific investiture = eligibility for particular posts.) In effect, the lists of shogunal officials, like the lists of daimyo incumbents, appear to describe a closed system—one pushed by the iron laws of hereditary succession toward atrophy.

Certainly, the office rosters acknowledged the claims of family by identifying the fathers of many jobholders, as if confirming that both a suitable income level and a notable patrilineage fitted these men for appointment.[37] In general, however, the rosters bore out the status claims of samurai to office while unsettling strictly hereditary principles of employment. The absence of extensive personal data in the entries—concerning heirs and consorts, for example, or genealogy and clan names—offered a quick clue to differences between daimyo, who were defined by their households, and administrative personnel, who were defined by their functions. Differences became clear in the evidence of selective appointment.

Fastidious readers of the early rosters would have noticed, year by year, changes in the surnames of jobholders. By the early eighteenth century, even casual readers could not have missed the principle of change. Most Mirrors expanded to include the dates when major appointees took office. Densely annotated Mirrors also indicated both the prior positions held by incumbents and the names and terms of their predecessors in current posts. So, for example, a roster of 1713 identifies four incumbent great inspectors (ōmetsuke) of the provinces: Sengoku Tamba no kami, appointed in 1695 after previous service as provincial inspector of muskets; Yokota Bitchū no kami, appointed in 1705 after previous service as examiner of Christians; Matsudaira Iwami no kami, appointed in 1704 after previous service as magistrate of highways; and Nakagawa Awaji no kami, appointed in 1712 after previous service as inspector of daimyo retainer registries. Following the entries on incumbents, the roster lists thirty-three of their predecessors as great inspectors, with terms dating back almost a century.[38] None of the predecessors bears the same surname as an incumbent.

Such detail tended to accompany only a few dozen of the greater offices (particularly those with responsibilities for other units). But it carried the message that those offices did not pass, either automatically or even much in practice, from father to son; that they entailed not sinecures but limited terms; and that they required harrowing in lesser posts. The volume of different surnames among incumbents and predecessors also implied an eligibility pool large enough to make selection significant (and unemployment among peers a problem). And because selection did not occur on a fixed schedule according to a predictable rotation, and hence in a mechanical fashion designed to accommodate most candidates, it appears to have been driven by qualitative criteria. In short, some competitive principle was at work.

The criteria for appointment were not a subject of the rosters. Indeed, they remain impossible to capture formulaically in a system that, lacking an examination or training regimen, was variably responsive to a man's talent, patrons, background, and sheer enterprise. Plainly enough, though, the rosters represent the context of recruitment to office, rather than ascription, as normal. More startlingly, they acknowledge the imperatives of rank as inadequate. By the 1680s, the rosters noted that individual offices carried particular "office allowances" to supplement the hereditary stipends or land grants of their holders.[39] Such perquisites, which went with most posts by the mid eighteenth century, enhanced the distinction of jobholding and helped cover official expenses, while conceding that the remuneration of most housemen was inadequate. They also lifted retainers from lower income levels and ranks to higher income levels and ranks and thus fitted them for offices above their birth station. The recruitment pool for any particular position became elastic—especially since office allowances tended to exceed the minimum incomes required for most posts.

Indeed, the relationship between rank and jobholding had been elastic from the beginning. Readers of early and later rosters alike saw remarkable disparities in the income levels of men holding the same office. The investitures of great inspectors, for example, ranged from 500 to 2,000 *koku;* of Edo magistrates from 500 to 3,000 *koku;* of pages from 200 to 5,000 *koku;* of attendants from 100 to 5,000 *koku;* of guard captains from 200 to 19,000 *koku.*[40] The minimum requirements were set low, making possible the appointment of compelling candidates of comparatively modest rank, while high ceilings expanded the positions that wellborn retainers could accept without loss of face. The introduction of office allowances, which all but erased the minimum requirements, opened up an already flexible system. Conservative rather than radical, the reform permitted men to be effectively bumped up in station during their official terms, and hence did not supplant the status and rank order. Even so, the increasing income disparities apparent in the later rosters unsettled any notion that birth station (and the consequent size of the investiture) was the defining property of either jobworthiness or actual jobholding.

Plenty of jobs in the shogunate did pass routinely, if not inevitably or exclusively, through families. Most of them were hidden from readers of the rosters, for they involved the support services of attendants (*yoriki, dōshin*), rear guardsmen (*banshū*), and other lesser workers who went unnamed in the office catalogues. Because the rosters focused on officials with investitures of over 100 *koku,* appointments at lower levels, where hereditary succession was common, escaped public notice. But hereditary succession to higher offices was hardly unknown, a point that would have been obvious to readers of the rosters who compared entries over time. Those offices tended to fit two categories. Many entailed specialized work requiring the professional formation that typically began within families— the work of secretaries, archivists, scholars, physicians, musicians, gardeners, and carpenters, for example. Thus appointment to such offices appeared less a consequence of ancestral entitlement than exceptional training in ancestral callings. Operating here was the principle that animated the status order of farmers, craftspeople, and other commoners: fidelity to calling through mastery of an assigned skill resulted in the good society. Still, appointment was no monopoly. New surnames regularly appeared in, and old surnames disappeared from, the lists of the regime's most specialized personnel.[41]

Heredity more insistently determined appointment to a second group of offices that required not exceptional training but exceptional dignity. Operating here was quite a different principle of selection, which exposed the tension at the heart of the status order: recognition of (some) entitlements remained indispensable to the regime's stability. High on the rosters of jobholders, for example, were the great attendants (*otsumeshū*)—twenty to forty or more daimyo, assigned a special waiting room in Edo castle, who were invited to be present at routine ceremonies. Following them was a body of "equivalent" attendants, a roughly equal number of daimyo who bore mention but no responsibility. The attendants came from daimyo houses historically closest to the Tokugawa but rarely invested with major domains. And their appointments, involving only perfunctory service, acknowledged their prestige—in the stead of great territorial power—within the federation.

So, too, the regime elevated as masters of court ceremony up to twenty heads of the "high houses" (*kōke*). Up to twenty more were identified in the rosters as "equivalent" masters of court ceremony without active duties. The high houses were families defeated in wartime but revived with small stipends as Tokugawa retainers because of their lustrous reputations during the medieval and warring states periods. Their names—Imagawa, Hatakeyama, Takeda, Hino, Rokkaku, Yamana, Uesugi, Oda—conjured up fabled histories that the regime artfully subsumed under its own. Those heads of the high houses who became masters of court ceremony did do real work; for they served as the chief protocol officers for all imperial embassies to Edo. But the regime gave them official prominence and named a score of backups to exploit their pedigrees, assuage memory, and knit the present to the far past.

Another hereditary group conspicuous in the rosters was the large body of landed retainers identified as assemblymen (*yoriai*). In general, the title extended to all high-ranking housemen—those with investitures ranging from 1,000 to 9,800 *koku*—who otherwise lacked official appointments.

Their numbers varied but tended to be high: the Right Mirror names about 190 assemblymen and later rosters up to 400. Yet only a fraction, usually designated as "assemblymen in attendance," had duties. Together with the daimyo, they participated in the system of alternating residence in Edo and hence appeared ceremonially before the shogun. The great majority had no formal responsibilities whatsoever.[42]

The appointment to essentially titular offices of the great attendants, the high houses, and the assemblymen indicates the regime's need to honor men of unusual historical and hereditary distinction by inventing positions for them. Indeed, padding and redundancy are apparent throughout the rosters, particularly among the pages and the huge guard units assigned to all but identical posts. A shogunate with too many peacetime soldiers bloated the system with too many gratuitous jobs.

Yet this bloating is the interesting point. Appointment mattered. Sheer membership in the lord's retainer band—with the chivalric distinction of name, pedigree, investiture, and status privilege—was insufficient in a lordship that had become a government. A job in that government had emerged as a critical source of honor. And (just as critically) the honor depended on the principle of selectivity. The regime did not expand offices indefinitely to accommodate all candidates. It did not obscure the focus of most offices on specialized work and competitive recruitment with the honorary sinecures. It did not ameliorate status anxiety with some sort of inclusive retainer list, thick with heraldry, that rivaled the office rosters. By choosing bloating over these alternatives, the regime grounded the prestige of unavoidable favors (whether to assemblymen or guardsmen) in a generally selective system of appointment. Titular assignments did concede the claims of blood. But the compromise between blood right and competition, arresting because it existed at all, is the more arresting because it bent in a certain direction. When the regime needed to dignify a claimant for attention, it found him a job.

Reflecting a consensus that ancestry was not enough to solace the samurai, a minor intellectual industry emerged to buck them up. In a massive military encyclopedia of 58 volumes (over 2,000 pages in modern print), the philosopher Yamaga Sokō assembled the knowledge presumptively at the core of the samurai's privileged status.[43] The *Buke jiki* (Records of the Military Houses) covered history (18 volumes, including hundreds of extended biographies of military leaders and their major followers since the twelfth century); battle strategy (10 volumes, including analysis and maps of all key engagements); documentation (6 volumes, including the archives of major houses of the warring states period); law (2 volumes, including all legal formularies since the seventh century); geography (3 volumes, including administrative divisions, highways, and maps); and culture (15 volumes, including the ceremonial calendars, language, etiquette, official posts, diet, clothing, housing, military equipment, and arts of the Japanese warrior). By imagining military men as a society and giving them a culture, Yamaga Sokō taught samurai who they were, even as he provided a curriculum they were meant to master. Being a samurai entailed *knowing* law and ceremonial requirements and the like, and hence *deserving* access to office. Pedigree alone was not qualification enough. Yet even in the absence of office, knowledge rationalized privilege. Samurai need not fret.

Nonetheless, the popular literature reinforced the job fixation of the personnel rosters by emphasizing the work rather than the hereditary honor or superior knowledge of military men. Neither basic dictionaries nor encyclopedias contained entries on "samurai" or "household retainers." Instead, they categorized the military community in terms of general appointments, such as "elder councillor," "magistrate," "intendant," and "mounted attendant." They also defined appointment holders as workers. Thus the intendant, for example, "conveys laws to the people and administers affairs in the lord's territorial holdings. His duty is paramount. Acting with compassion, he puts selflessness above all. If he impoverishes the people through greedy indulgence, he dishonors his lord, exhausts the people, and destroys the country."[44] Embedded in presumptions about moral character, this definition is equally embedded in presumptions about spheres of duty, accountability, and hard toil. The attendant is no fancy notable but a laborer for his lord, his country, and (invoked three times) the "people."

Whether through Yamaga Sokō's exhortation to learning or the dictionaries' exhortation to service, the samurai were projected into a public arena of duty bigger than vassalage. Yet it was in the Military Mirrors that this recalculation of identity occurred most visibly and persistently as, year after year for two centuries, the shogun's men appeared in the role of jobholders. The community of Tokugawa retainers chiefly knew itself, and was known to general readers, in professional rather than status categories. And by colluding in this enterprise, and hence attaching to office both outward distinction and inner esteem, the regime recast itself. It became the source of public appointment, not just personal fealty; the custodian of the public arena, not just a lordly dominion. By allowing the personnel rosters to convey its public face, moreover, the regime focused its appeal for loyalty on those invested in appointment—first, on those who held office or hoped to hold office, and more broadly on those who looked to the shogun and his officials for accountable public administration.

Among those who did and might hold office were commoners. The Right Mirror includes over 280 townspeople, with names and addresses, in seven categories of shogunal appointment. Although they appear at the end of the list, no visual clue separates them from samurai appointees. Nor is their work so different in distinction, or even in kind, from the work of numerous samurai jobholders. Many occupy weighty positions as keepers of the shogunal warehouses, chiefs of carpenters, ward elders, principal drapers, and holders of the gold, silver, and vermilion monopolies. Many provide specialized services to the regime as painters (fifteen members of the Kanō house) and sword connoisseurs, for example. The greater number purvey specialized goods (such as swords, lacquer, clocks, incense, sake, sweets, and oil) and provide ritual entertainment (as dancers, noh actors, and musicians). Categories and numbers would mount steadily in later editions of the Mirrors to take in more commoners serving the regime outside Edo—from the eminent officials of the imported thread monopoly to the innkeepers of licensed highway lodgings—and more and more privileged purveyors (of everything from books to Seto pottery).[45]

Here, again, one might sense bloating by a shogunate happy to distribute favors to important clients. If so, the telling point is the regime's need to ingratiate itself with townsmen and its willingness to use public appointment for the purpose. But clearer than the padding is the expertise of each commoner recorded in the Mirrors. Whether they worked at the indispensable jobs featured in the early rosters (such as warehouse managers and masters of the mint) or at the seemingly lesser jobs added in the later rosters (such as innkeepers and lapis carvers), townsmen with official titles commanded obvious skills. Some of their contributions were crucial to the polity, many indistinguishable from those of samurai, all more tangible than those of assemblymen. Rather than a form of ingratiation, then, the incorporation of the commoners appears to bear out the professional, work-centered emphasis of the office rosters. It also expanded exponentially the recruitment pool of those hopeful of office in what looked like a big and bigger public government. Most provocative, this incorporation unsettled another certainty. By following the lists of iconic daimyo with lists of specialized and competitive jobholders, the Mirrors counterposed the claims of ancestry and merit. By concluding the lists of samurai jobholders with lists of commoner jobholders, they exposed the fault lines in status boundaries.

The Military Mirrors made no editorial statements about jobs and duties in the manner of the dictionaries or philosophical discourse. Nor did they tell anyone how Tokugawa rule actually worked. Idealized outlines of a formalized system, the rosters abstracted a normative order from dynamic practice. And, to be sure, they look orderly—with their procession of daimyo and samurai and commoners, all symmetrically delineated by status, privilege, function, and income. So all the more striking is the popular education they served up, in many billions of pages, about a public administration, national in its dimensions, that depended on professional expertise and promoted commoners to office.

FIVE

The Freedom of the City

THE JAPAN OF EARLY modern maps is a place not of hills and farms but cities. As political geography replaces most physical features, and agrarian production figures swallow the village landscape, the country seems a mass of urban points—the castle towns of daimyo, the ports and post stations that connect the polity, and the famous sites that intimate a common culture. Very quickly, these cities became the consuming subject of commercial cartography. The urban world dominates the work of early modern Japanese mapmakers, something that would have been unimaginable for their medieval predecessors.

The generic and categorical vision of the city that made urban cartography possible came from new conquerors. And it depended on a contrast: the city was not a village; city people were not villagers. Villages were places of agricultural production, where fields were measured and harvests evaluated in formal cadastral documents. Villagers were the locally registered producers who paid taxes on those harvests. Thus the urban scene belonged, by elimination, to other status groups pursuing other activities—preeminently, in the martial capitals that organized local power, to samurai living in official quarters on official stipends and discharging obligations to their lords. Supporting this elite throughout the urban network were the merchants, craftspeople, and disparate workers who were excused from agriculture and qualified to enter the city market by reason of their indispensable functions, from casting gold to engineering canals, from dressing hair to selling sex. Cities emerged in the official mind, then, as distinctive residential and work zones for populations with distinctive, nonagrarian legal identities.

They emerged, too, as sites of unitary and comprehensive jurisdiction. The medieval city, a complex bundle of proprietorships where multiple powers had shared the privileges of rule, was gone. The dominant centers of early modern Japan were castle headquarters under the integral control of daimyo or shogunal magistrates. The remainder (ports, commercial hubs, religious centers) were administrative townships assigned either to shogunal deputies or, when jurisdiction remained local, to municipal officials of the daimyo.

In practice, cities remained porous, particularly for temporary laborers in good times. Still, a variety of controls organized the membership of urban communities. Commoners were accountable to the constellations of neighborhood authorities who supervised housing transactions, communicated and enforced statutes, and assigned collective responsibilities (for fire patrols and monetary offerings to superiors, for example). They were also accountable to the many official and unofficial bodies that regulated employment—guilds, trade associations, labor foremen, and overseers of certain status corporations. But once integrated into the structures of neighborhood and work, residents became city people (*machikata*) under the rule of urban law and urban magistrates.[1]

Clear notions about residence, function, and jurisdiction resulted in the lucid maps that put cities in mind and on paper. Invariably depicted as a web of streets, each labeled neighborhood by neighborhood in a continuous whole, the physical space of the city situated a society plainly understood as a status order. A basically binary code of signs separated the martial elite from commoners. The lodgings of the former—marked by the individual names and regalia of residents—stood apart from those of the latter, marked only by distinctive colors (typically white or black). Labels and color blocking also identified religious institutions and, in the case of Kyoto, the courtly aristocracy. But the city remained, in essence, the space of dominant ruling communities supported by subject commoners, who lived and worked within the color-coded neighborhoods signifying nonagrarian enterprise. In the maps of castle towns that accounted for most cartographic production, power radiated from the lord and his retainers. In maps of ports and other centers, the offices of military magistrates focused attention.[2]

The synoptic conception of citiness, which the regime framed and maps distilled, became the departure point for a long, restless inquiry into the urban experience as artists and writers made cities the central subject of early modern representation. In paintings and prints, fiction and poetry, drama and burlesque, they explored with near obsession, and piercing contemporary detail, the question left by the urban juggernaut: what happens when strangers are massed together and everything is for sale? Accounts of urban life also crowded the library of public information, although there authors began with the prior question that had animated mapmakers:

what, really, *is* a city and how is it ordered? For the insiders who needed to navigate the labyrinth day by day, and for the outsiders who came for profit, prayer, and entertainment, these authors took the measure of the material city in a swelling number of texts: street directories, trade directories, religious directories, calendars and almanacs, lists of famous products, sales catalogues, rosters of actors and prostitutes, and guidebooks of all kinds.[3] Such texts followed the lead, and relied on the master outline, of the maps; for they, too, approached the city as an inventory challenge. And they, too, used the streets to control the count. But in the directories, those streets did not situate a status system, which virtually disappears from view. They situated a society bigger than the polity.

To some extent, we might read the directories as ripostes to the maps—as reverse views of the city with an alternative perspective on the status system. Diminishing the presence of elite communities, the directories fill in and out the spaces left blank by cartographers to stress the role of common residents. They examine their quarters ward by ward; catalogue goods for sale item by item; and flesh out tradespeople name by name. More than a change in emphasis, this close treatment of commoners also muddles the categories of maps. Generic conceptions of status and work collapse under the weight of specificity: craftspeople are not just craftspeople but weavers and dyers and embroiderers; makers of flutes and lutes and drums; lathers of cypress and paulownia and zelkova. And the status hierarchy itself is disturbed by both the honor accorded commoners (in deferential terms of address, for instance) and the glancing notice given military men—who appear undeserving of much notice in inventories lovingly reserved for persons of skill.

Polemical readings of the directories nonetheless miss the sprawl that defeats any singular interpretation of the city scene. These texts differ from the maps not so much in their reverse view of the city as in their ground view. The vantage point of the map is high, its code system reductive, its presentation centered. The peculiar genius of the medium lies in its clarity and economy: limited graphic signs, deployed on limited surfaces, abstract a coherent structure—one observed from the air—from the myriad properties of space. But the writers of the urban directories were walkers. And their texts move at the speed, and with the darting eye, of the walker. Their cities are low. They are also diffuse and decentered, experienced from multiple vantage points. Mainly, they are thick. With the luxury of seemingly limitless pages, writers wrote and rewrote the city, coming back to spill out more thoughts in supplements. The city, and an understanding of it, was always unfinished.

Some of the most ambitious efforts to capture urban life appeared toward the end of the seventeenth century, when writers began to fold the multifarious material that had earlier been distributed among more specialized texts into single, sweeping surveys. Merged in these compendia were street and commercial directories, personnel rosters, guides for sightseers and pilgrims, calendars of events, lists of religious institutions, lists of natural landmarks, lists of historical artifacts, necrologies, and much else. And to deliver such heroic data, the compendia embraced the categorical logic of cartography. If they differed in viewpoint from urban maps, the urban surveys—like most texts in the information library—relied on taxonomic order. But their categories were not boxes, which sort one thing from another; they were threads, which weave one thing to another in patterns that change with the light. The first survey of the imperial capital was called the *Kyō habutae* (Kyoto Brocade). The counterpart for the shogunal capital was the *Edo kanoko* (Dappled Fabric of Edo). Neither Mirrors nor maps, these compendia used textile metaphors to evoke the connections that make cities hard to tear apart and the colors that alter with shifting perspectives.

So instead of sorting the city into status groups, the texts pick out the interwoven strands of the urban texture—concentrating on religious institutions in one section and popular piety in another; attending to the time of the festival calendar in one section and the space of pleasure seeking in another; lining up neighborhoods in one section and their tradespeople in another. With each new chapter of the surveys, the compilers appear to start a new walk with a new itinerary, threading through familiar terrain that takes on fresh highlights. And in tracing the multiple strands of the cityscape, the compilers also summon up the multiple attachments of city people. As a resident of the imperial capital, I might find myself many times in the Kyoto Brocade—as a householder in a particular ward, a practitioner of a particular trade, an adherent of a particular temple, a patron of a particular festival, a client of particular merchants, a fan of a particular actor, a follower of a particular tea master, and a sightseer at old battlegrounds or famous graves. Like the strands of the city, I would have many identities and relations, variously determined and voluntary, vertical and horizontal, institutional and commercial, long and short in duration, close and distant in intensity.

Yet these relations do not constitute some seemingly organic social union; for the urban surveys tend resolutely toward raggedness rather than a fine weave. They explore a plural society best captured by overlapping inventories, not a totalistic one unlocked by a master code. Indeed, their recurring motifs—the market and the stranger—disperse notions of any reliable social coherence.

The Kyoto Brocade, first published in Kyoto in 1685, was compiled by the local printer and *haikai* poet Kojima Tokuuemon under the sobriquet Koshōshi.[4] Four years later, Koshōshi brought out a supplement, the Rewoven Brocade of Kyoto, which contained material he had been unable to cram into the original.[5] Both Brocades were big, six fascicles each, but they were popular enough to be updated and revised for generations. They also inspired knockoffs. The Dappled Fabric of Edo, a close cousin of the first Brocade, appeared in 1687. Variants on the later Brocades, burdened with ever heavier titles, succeeded in short order—notably the Great Expanded Dappled Fabric of Edo: Omnibus of Famous Places, compiled by Fujita Rihei and published in 1690.[6] Compilers turned out similar surveys of Osaka in the late seventeenth century and other cities throughout the eighteenth.[7] All the while, the publication of more specialized urban manuals—from shopping directories to tour guides—proceeded briskly.

Although the surveys vary in content, their coverage tends toward convergence, as if some combination of mimicry, inertia, and commonsense had produced agreement about essential urban properties. Thus we find in the original Brocade a rough blocking out of the topics that would continue to organize the textual cityscape—or what becomes, in Koshōshi's exposition, six overlapping cityscapes. The *physical city,* particularly in its secular guise, is the subject of volume 1, where Koshōshi lays out streets, natural landmarks, and auspicious sights. Then he travels through the *city of history,* with its memorials and remains and inscriptions, in the opening sections of volume 2. He proceeds, in the same volume, to the *city of ritual,* as if to connect the contemporary reenactment of seasonal ceremonies, popular pilgrimages, and the annual processions of the Gion festival with a living past. Shifting into an institutional register, Koshōshi then describes the *city of shrines and temples* in volumes 3 and 4, where he accounts methodically for the foundation and administration of hundreds of sanctuaries. The organization of religion leads, in turn, to the organization of prestige, power, and labor: volume 5 takes on the *city of hereditary honor,* with a catalogue first of the courtly aristocracy and then of those daimyo who maintained residences in Kyoto; and volume 6 takes on the *city of work,* with a catalogue first of governing officials and then of merchants, craftspeople, and providers of services.

But while coverage appears more consistent than not, the arrangement of the urban compendia tends to change from edition to edition, as if successive compilers (or even the same compilers of successive revisions) refused to fix the city's properties in any inevitable order of value or connection. They start with different topics—sometimes streets, sometimes natural landmarks or history or governing personnel—and they go on to mix and redistribute material in new combinations. Reflecting an interest in freshness, these choices also declare that the order is artificial: cities don't have beginnings and endings and linear linkages. To drive the point home, the surveys include long, long tables of contents, which invite readers to abandon the compilers' sequence altogether and head directly for favorites.

Given such license, I adopt an artificial order of my own to limn several of the great subjects of the texts: the past, the street, the specialist, the gathering.

The Past

The urban surveys open in a scolding tone. "In the Capital of Flowers," the compiler observes in the preface to the Kyoto Brocade, "imperial rule has flourished without interruption throughout the ages." Here, "left and right, boundlessly in all directions, range venerable sites, famous remains, shrines, temples, and the residences of gentle and common people." Here, "east and west, range the teaming shops and concerns of famous masters, famous artisans, merchants and men in official service." And yet, Koshōshi concludes with asperity, "how few are those who really know these places." So, too, the compiler of the Dappled Fabric of Edo laments that "while many go to pray at our shrines and temples, they are ignorant of old things, foundations, and history." Nor do his contemporaries know much of our "famous places and venerable sites," "the enterprises of the masters and artists," and "the shops of famous artisans and merchants." Although daunted by the "truly inexhaustible" subject before him, the compiler consequently takes up an account of what he calls the Plains of Musashi to "fend against forgetting and the loss of legacies." He echoes the Kyoto chronicler who, in an effort to amplify the knowledge of his audience, "inquired year after year into the old and sought out the new," finally weaving "the warp and weft of these colored strands into a brocade of the capital."[8]

The compilers have clearly come to praise their cities. Their prefaces sound the theme, repeated throughout the texts, that cities are marvelous landscapes full of famous sites and famous shops. Not here will readers find a dark world they must be warned against. But one source of urban attraction—the constant regeneration of the scene by travelers and migrants and residents of many stations—is a source of loss as well. City people have no memories. Volatility and an enchantment with "the new" have resulted in plain ignorance: hardly anybody *really knows* old things. For the compilers, it is knowledge that makes the landscape marvelous, since meaning is to be found in thick temporal layers. It is knowledge, too, that connects the living and the dead in mental and physical space alike. So these men who have come to praise their cities have also come to resurrect their ghosts.

They do so, despite the waspish prefaces, in a profligate spirit of pleasure. Historical recall saturates their texts, not as some pedantic labor but as an almost instinctive, and exhilarating, mode of orientation. In otherwise matter-of-fact inventories of urban features, the compilers of the surveys cannot hold back the etymology of a street name, the origins of a festival, the foundation story of a temple, the classical poem that made an unexceptional waterfall a landmark. The past forever breaks through the surface of today as they pause to remember a priest who loved a particular cherry tree, an imperial regent who built a particular bridge, a Zen master who mediated on a particular rock.[9] Nowhere is novelty a thrill. Even in accounts of the contemporary theater, the compilers trace antecedents back to distant patrons and performers.[10] Like the narrator of Margaret Atwood's novel *Cat's Eye,* they imagine time as "a series of liquid transparencies, one laid on top of another. . . . Sometimes this comes to the surface, sometimes that. . . . Nothing goes away."[11]

But nothing is really transparent either. What seems effortless recall is closer to sleight of hand, for the cities the compilers describe as old were mostly new. Edo, long a brackish backwater, had been laid out by its Tokugawa builders after 1590. Kyoto, obliterated by the firestorms of war, had been remade after 1580. Together with most urban centers of the seventeenth century, both capitals were physical creations (no less than political creations) of the early modern state. The emphasis in the urban surveys on continuing pasts proceeded, then, more from desire than from factual fidelity. The compilers wanted those pasts enough to contrive them. And while they were guided in this task by formidable models, their motive appears peculiarly populist: to project a shared urban space through a shared history.

In part, the surveys evoke images of a long past by equating genealogy with continuity, standard practice in institutional narratives. Thus, the first main entry of the Kyoto Brocade is a selective list of emperors, which indicates in each case a monarch's numerical position in the imperial line and the site of his capital. The begats conclude with the fiftieth emperor, Kanmu, who chose Kyoto as the imperial center in Enryaku 13 (794), or, as the compiler puts it, "eight hundred ninety-one years before this, the second year of Jōkyō (1685). Truly, [the foundation for reigns of] ten thousand years, and ten thousand years, and tens of thousands of ten thousand years."[12] Much in the same fashion, the first main entry of the Dappled Fabric of Edo is a list of Japan's military rulers. It starts with Minamoto no Yoritomo (number one, r. 1192–1199), runs through the subsequent Kamakura and Muromachi shogun, includes five Oda and Toyotomi leaders, proceeds seamlessly to the Tokugawa shogun, and concludes with the incumbent, Tokugawa Tsunayoshi (number thirty-six, r. 1680–1709). Then the envoi: "The Honorable Regime [will prosper] for tens of thousands of years."[13]

This martial inventory overlooks both ruptures in rule and the irrelevance of Edo to pre-Tokugawa regimes. But the imperial model itself is a nice piece of equivocation, because those eight hundred ninety-one years covered persistent succession rifts, periodic war, efforts both to relocate the capital and usurp the throne, and substantial redistributions of power. No matter. By defining governing institutions as human lineages (which can always be fitted together somehow), the chroniclers transcend the breaks. They also impute longevity to the capitals of rulers—literally, in the case of Kyoto, or figuratively, in the case of Edo—since the presence of the incumbent and the reenactment of succession rituals lift space into a timeless continuum of "tens of thousands of years."

Religious institutions are made old through similar associations with antecedents. Among the temples and shrines of the two capitals, many had been recently established (especially in Edo) and many others relocated from former sites. Almost all were dominated by new buildings. Still, the compilers of the urban surveys adopt the conventions of the religious foundation story to link sanctuaries with whatever traditions they can recover. They concentrate on identifying founders and patrons, preferably ancient notables invoked, if not in record, at least in legend. As default positions, they recycle old miracle stories, assign branch temples the pedigrees of their headquarters, and situate obscure places on venerable pilgrimage circuits. Not infrequently, they conjure up the past through icons—statues or paintings said to have been owned or made by Prince Shōtoku or the abbot Kūkai or some other luminary.

Driven by origin myths, the institutional genealogies in the surveys tend toward boilerplate predictability. Every place had seen an old emperor or an old shogun; no sanctuary lacked an ancestral holy man or a treasure.

Because relics were moveable and their sites incidental to stories of continuity, these accounts also tend to diminish the significance of physical space. The emperor Kanmu and the abbot Kūkai belong to rhetorical litanies, not any particular piece of soil. But the compilers recover the ground of the past through two additional approaches to space that specifically connect it to time. Particularly important to Koshōshi, the compiler of the Brocades, was the model of historical geography.

This emerging discipline, influenced by Chinese gazetteers of the Ming dynasty and pursued principally by Confucian scholars (many of them samurai), combined documentary research with empirical investigation to expose the contemporary traces of past activity. One of its most distinguished practitioners was Kurokawa Dōyū, a physician and classicist who left employment as a doctor in the Hiroshima domain to pursue geographical studies of Kyoto and the home province. By 1682, he had completed in draft the *Yōshū fushi* (Record of Yamashiro), a twenty-five-volume encyclopedia of the capital region that was published, in Chinese, during 1686. Aspects of Koshōshi's work—specific entries on historical materials, as well as a general attention to the scholarly record—suggest that he may have relied on Dōyū's research in preparing both the Kyoto Brocade (Brocade 1) and the Rewoven Brocade of Kyoto (Brocade 2).[14]

Indeed, a number of Koshōshi's entries reek of the academy. Brocade 2, for example, describes the metamorphosis of the classical capital into the city of his day and offers learned counsel on suspect or mistaken attributions for surviving artifacts.[15] Mainly, though, Koshōshi scavenges the scholarship to pull up wonderful lists of mortuary monuments, site remains, and old things (each item accompanied by exact directions to its location).

He summons the ghosts early in Brocade 1 through a list, with 133 entries, of the local tombs, memorials, and commemorative portraits of Kyoto's notable dead. The list expands in Brocade 2 to 311 entries, now broken down into eleven categories: emperors, empresses, princes, nobles, military leaders, warriors, priests, poets, important women, specialists in the arts, and "miscellaneous." Largely free of dates or historical narration, the entries are anecdotal in texture and fluid in organization, which is only roughly chronological and quite flexibly categorical. (Look for Murasaki Shikibu, the aristocratic lady-in-waiting who wrote the *Tale of Genji,* among the poets.) They are also familiar in tone, treating the dead from many ages and many stations as collective ancestors. (Blended comfortably together into the pantheon are Kakinomoto Hitomaro, Kōbō Daishi, Izumi Shikibu, Kumagai Naozane, Taira no Kiyomori, Nichiren Shōnin,

Rennyo Shōnin, Toyotomi Hideyoshi [and his mother, sister, consort, and concubines], Sen no Rikyū, Kanō Motonobu, and Hon'ami Kōetsu.)[16]

Brocade 1 follows the necrology with a list of seventy-four "old places," the sites primarily of famous residences, most visible only in imagination, where dead luminaries—including many commoners of artistic distinction—had lived. That single list becomes, in the next Brocade, fifteen lists, with hundreds of entries. They identify the sites and remains of former capitals, palaces, detached and temporary palaces, castles, battlegrounds, military mansions, villas, huts, hermitages, and miscellaneous dwellings. Koshōshi reserves a category for places associated with divine apparitions, and another for historically fabled displays of nature (the late-blooming cherries of Ninnaji, the fireflies of the Uji River, the fall maples of Takao).[17]

Old things come after old places. In Brocade 1, Koshōshi begins modestly with thirty-nine "old plaques"—large inscriptions, appearing on wooden boards above temple gates, that had been carved from calligraphic models in the hands of (mostly imperial) patrons. In Brocade 2, Koshōshi adds thirty-eight items to the original list of plaques and goes on to survey eight more categories of surviving stuff: Buddhist icons with unusual histories (sixteen entries, including three far-flung statues of Kannon carved from the same piece of zelcova wood harvested at the Kamigamo shrine); Buddhist icons once owed by notables (thirteen entries, including a Kannon from the collection of Emperor Shōmu); other religious treasures (eighty-one entries, including a full canon of Buddhist texts from Korea, deemed a "masterpiece," in the possession of Kenninji); old manuscripts (twenty-four items, including a map of a Taira landholding and the "poem cards" completed at one of Toyotomi Hideyoshi's poetry parties at Ryōanji); old bells (six entries, including a Chinese "masterpiece" at Rokuonji); old towers (twelve entries, including the Gold and Silver Pavilions); buildings erected through special donation (ten entries, including the main gate at Daitokuji, funded by the poet Sōchō and the tea master Sen no Rikyū); and portraits (fifty-two items, including paintings of the empress Bifukumon'in and the monk Mujaku).[18]

There is in the sheer load of the lists (here plaques and there bells, here ruined hermitages and there battlegrounds) something of a magpie quality. Certainly, Koshōshi was a hectic collector who raided whatever material he could find to produce a big and bigger account of the city. Even when he finally cuts off his inventories, readers sense an interruption, not an ending: our compiler has, for the moment, quit his catalogues to go to press (warning that additional material is too unwieldy to permit anything like exhaustive coverage). But the effect—deliberate, I think—is kaleidoscopic rather than tedious or overwhelming. The institutional lineages shatter across a memory-saturated landscape with neither a controlling chronology nor a single key. Hence multiplying categories and entries break metahistory into disparate pasts freely available to the curious. Readers can selectively explore the huts of tea men, the graves of renegade warriors, the remains of lost palaces, and the masterpieces of imported art. They can variously cast themselves as connoisseurs of objects, adepts of martial or imperial lore, tomb counters, or proto-archeologists. And they can embrace Koshōshi's presumption that the past belongs to them.

Finally, however, the sense of social connection between past and present owes less to the scholarship on historical geography than the tradition of the "famous place." Literally a "place with a name" (*na no aru tokoro*), the trope arose early in the classical period to describe sites summoned to recognition by a poet's notice. Most were natural landmarks remarked on for a beauty uncommon in its elegance or austerity, grandeur or poignance: the Moor of Saga, the Stream of Hirozawa, the Hill of Ogura. Yet naming extended gradually to the human scene—gardens and arbors, sanctuaries and mansions, battlegrounds and ruins. Here, too, the distinction of a name derived often enough from physical beauty, but when poets evoked the deeds of ancestors in space, it came from historical memory as well.

Even so, named places escaped any static past to figure, invariably, in lively social practice. Drawn to artistic life by poets, they animated continuing poetic dialogues that required practitioners to inflect established toponyms with fresh meanings. The first lists of famous places appeared in tenth-century handbooks called "poem pillows" (*uta makura*), which supplied aristocrats with the images as indispensable to composition as pillows to bodies. Famous places also inspired painters, who interpreted and reinterpreted them on screens, scrolls, albums, and fans. If, over time, poets and painters reified famous places in a self-referential art, physical encounter remained vital to yet other social pursuits. City-bound aristocrats built their ceremonial calendars around viewings (of spring blossoms, summer moons, autumn color, winter snow), outings (for morning skies, evening air, river boating, cormorant fishing), and both the near and far travel associated with pilgrimage, festivals, and religious rites. For these activities, they chose sites already made famous by their predecessors or newly assigned a "name" by their own approbation.[19]

Because the experience of place changed with time, so did the currency of named places. Some sites disappeared from the poem pillows, others were folded in. And as names flowed increasingly from popular sociability, new lists—now generically labeled "famous places"—began to appear in the medieval period. They subsumed the poem pillows while taking in any number of sites with local cachet.[20] Still, the names were generated and kept in play by diverse performances that resonated with past associations without demanding historicist attitudes. Never entangled in dates, time lines, or dense factual contexts, fame found expression in the dynamic transfer of images across generations of artists, travelers, pilgrims, and pleasure seekers.

The literary representation of famous places, which spread from poetry to the diaries and travel accounts of medieval writers, expanded into commercial tour guides during the early modern period. In a world of motion, markets, and popular publication, sightseeing became sport—celebrated in such early highlights of the guide genre as *Kyō warabe* (A Child of Kyoto, 1658), a survey of eighty-eight sites by the poet and physician Nakagawa Kiun, and *Edo meishoki* (An Account of Edo's Famous Places, 1662), a survey of eighty sites by the Buddhist priest and commercial writer Asai Ryōi.[21] Both texts conceived of the city as a landscape loaded as no other with famous places. To see things worth seeing, they declared, go to town. And since more was better, the authors of urban tour guides continued to inflate entries (in Edo's case from 12 in 1621 to 1,043 in the nineteenth century) and thus to bestow name and fame with some abandon on all manner of old and new landmarks: not just sanctuaries and palaces and graves but theaters, brothels, daimyo mansions, commercial establishments, and busy intersections (such as the Bridge of Edo).[22] Not much escaped. Early modern writers kept within the tradition by tying sites somehow to time— to the classical dancers who presaged contemporary entertainers or the medieval tea peddlers who gave way to contemporary merchants. So, too, they tied sites to repetitive social performance—digging up old poems for newly famous places and distant precedents for present-day ceremonies.[23] But social performance also extended in their texts to the novel recreation of tourism. Equipped with guides and leisure and curiosity, the early modern pleasure seeker could keep fame in play by simply looking around.[24]

The influence of the tour guide on the city survey is immediately apparent in the virtual equation between urban space and famous place— a point driven home in titles like the Great Expanded Dappled Fabric of Edo: Omnibus of Famous Places. The larger legacy of naming is most apparent in the surveys' lists of topographical features. The first volume of the Kyoto Brocade inventories 274 such features, both natural and manmade, in twenty-two categories such as "ponds," "waterfalls," "rocks,"

FIG. 23. "The Otowa Falls at Kiyomizu Temple," from Nakagawa Kiun, *Kyō warabe* (A Child of Kyoto, 1658). Courtesy of the East Asian Library, University of California, Berkeley.

"trees," "hills," "valleys," "rivers," "plains," "islands," and "bridges." The Dappled Fabric of Edo opens with sixteen similar lists. Individual entries name a site (the Pond of Osawa, the Waterfall of Otowa, the Stone of Benkei, the Mount of Atago) and then explain the "naming" (*na o tsuku*). Glossing the "Turtle Well" in Edo, for example, the compiler of the Dappled Fabric tells readers that the name is a "very old" one inspired by the "occasional surfacing there of large turtles." He adds: "Its pure water was used in the tea ceremony until the time of the great Meireki fire, when muskets and military gear were stashed in the well for protection. Since the water became metallic from equipment that fell to the bottom and could not be retrieved, it's now good for hardly anything." The combination of big turtles and stashed weapons makes this well, he concludes, "truly awesome" (or "awful"). It is located in "Kanda Suda ward, at the mansion of Lord Nagai of Kai Province."[25]

The names glossed in the urban surveys come variously from poems (sometimes quoted, sometimes associated with an author or anthology), legends, and folk etymologies. Yet they invariably link a place to the fame of social recognition and thus recapitulate the classical practice of claiming the landscape through proper nouns. The topographical categories recapitulate the tradition as well; for their antecedents include the poem pillows, which also sorted toponyms into the categories of "hills" and "valleys" and the like. By emphasizing such physical features, moreover, the compilers of the urban surveys not only recover past practice but celebrate what is most durable in the urban scene. The lineages of rebuilt sanctuaries or the memories kindled by ruins and graves offer abstract images of continuity. In rivers and rocks and forests and valleys, the images become tangible.

Yet these places are not just notable sites worthy in themselves of notice. Nor are they shrines where viewers are meant to venerate the dead or the natural world. If the ghosts of famous places care about being remembered, the compilers of the urban surveys seem little worried about them. They tie sites to names and stories—the "old things" they want readers to *really know*—because knowing serves the knower. Tales of turtles, tea water, metallic taste, and the Meireki fire induct city people into membership in the living organism of the city. The landscape has a history that knowledge permits them to join. City people also share the landscape itself. Although located within the mansion of Lord Nagai of Kai, the Turtle Well is older than Nagai, a fixture in the public mind and implicitly accessible to some public traffic. Precisely locating each site in their catalogues, the compilers imply a corporate trusteeship over famous places.

The cities they offer readers, then, are not thin or alien spaces discovered yesterday and possessed by the privileged. As they create a continuous past despite discontinuity, so the compilers create a past held in common despite social cleavage. The pantheon of ancestors and their material patrimony belong not just to the lineal descendants of the dead or the current owners of their objects but to anyone who cares to appropriate them. Named and knowable places can orient any city person in a tradition and a continuing collectivity. Yet the need of the compilers to construct that tradition and that collectivity returns us to the beginning. Knowing, *really* knowing, matters not so much because people are ignorant as because society is fragmented. Newcomers and strangers, in numbers too large for the intimately exchanged knowledge of any organic community, are offered the alternative knowledge of public instruction. Denied any natural inheritance of their landscape, they must claim it now through learning.

The streets

To explore the places of putatively collective memory, readers had to learn to navigate the city—a skill the compilers of the urban surveys, taking nothing for granted, were ready to teach. The pedant in Koshōshi led him to begin Brocade 2 in the style of the provincial gazetteer. There he sets Kyoto within its environs by describing eighty or so neighboring settlements (with notes on land areas, population totals, building totals, and assessed yields). There, too, he names all the districts and villages in Yamashiro province, delineates boundaries, and identifies highways, mountain passes, rivers, other natural features, and entries to the capital.[26] In Brocade 1, a laconic Koshōshi passes over Kyoto's outlying areas and heads straight for the navigational challenge at hand. Right after the imperial genealogy, he attacks the city streets.

First, he names each of the thirty-two avenues running north to south, then the forty-eight avenues running east to west. Subsequent entries list fourteen major roads just outside the city proper, as well as forty-four lesser streets, more like alleys than avenues, within the city grid. A final section on the urban layout glosses the popular but informal names, most with historical associations, that insiders use to designate various areas of Kyoto. Each of these parts has a counterpart in the Dappled Fabric of Edo, although there the entries appear in the fifth volume.

This treatment of basic urban anatomy derived from the early street directories—particularly the *Kyō suzume* (Kyoto Sparrow, 1665) and the *Edo suzume* (Edo Sparrow, 1677)—that grappled with cities by taking readers down every single block of every single roadway. The first entry in the Kyoto directory, for example, offers a synoptic view of the easternmost artery within the capital grid.

> Kyōgoku Avenue is now known as the Avenue of Temples (Teramachi). North of Teramachi is a small settlement at the Kurama barrier and, on the west bank of the Kamo River, another group of village houses. Just south of those houses is the ward of Saihō temple at the northern extremity of Teramachi Avenue. Proceeding south along Teramachi, until it joins Fifth Avenue and Matsubara Street, you find many temples along the eastern side of the thoroughfare. The shops and home of commoners appear only on the western side.[27]

Following this synopsis, the Sparrow works through each of Kyōgoku's sequential wards or neighborhoods—thirty-seven of them, from the ward of Saihō temple in the north to the street's southern terminus, just by the Fifth Avenue Bridge, at the ward of the Lancers. Ward by ward, the Sparrow counts frontages, describes points of interest, and provides historical and etymological notes. Once the walk down Kyōgoku is done, the Kyoto Sparrow undertakes similar walks down every other street in the capital. Here, a typical entry about a ward on Nishinotōin, and another well story:

> Just inside the ward of the Willow Water stands the former residence of the tea master Ota Jōshin. The famous water from the well there surpassed all water elsewhere and near it grew a willow. But when the water lost its preeminence for use in the tea ceremony, Jōshin moved to Ittsuji in Kitano. The willow eventually died and was replaced by a mulberry. The well is still called Willow Water, however, and people from the area continue to draw water from it.[28]

The urban compendia condense the street notes of the Sparrows by redistributing much of their discursive material to other sections (concerning temples and shrines, for example, or festivals and historical remains). They nonetheless include the street and ward lists, together with a fair amount of etymological information, as an indispensable definition of the city scene. Maps, apparently, will not suffice.

Certainly maps present problems, not only for the many readers helpless before graphic material but for all readers puzzled by their inevitable lacunae and distortions. Hence we might regard the street directories as narrative cartography designed to ease travelers through navigational trouble—particularly in Edo, a semi-radial thicket of erratically named roads where maps best served those readers who knew already where they were. We might regard them, too, as guides to urban argot. Their lists of ward names, which organized city geography more insistently than street names, convey vital information more legibly than maps, where labels are often too cramped to stop the eye.

Yet this stopping itself, enforced by the slow litany of names, is probably the point. For modern readers jaded by urban life, street and ward inventories can grow tedious fast.

> The Avenue of the Asakusa Bridge runs from the bridge at the south to Oi-wake fork in the north. The avenue includes the Miscanthus ward, the Heavenly Kings ward, the Hira ward, the Morita ward, the Hatago ward, the ward before Monju temple, the ward of the Black Ship, Suwa ward, Komakata ward, the ward of Lined-up Trees, the Bamboo ward.[29]

For early modern readers, such deliberateness seems to have abetted an approach to the city more alert than our own to its peculiarity and localism. Whatever the navigational utility of the lists, they function basically as primers on the street. Thus, on the one hand, they teach newcomers how to figure out the very notion of a street by traversing its length. Step by step, over and over again, the lists limn urban arteries as continuous thoroughfares, packed with enterprises, where the public can move freely. On the other hand, they expose each individual street, to insiders and outsiders alike, as a distinctive place. Kyōgoku Avenue is no generic phenomenon, so familiar or predictable that readers are to take it for granted, but a particular artery that feeds from the Kurama hills to the great bridge over the Kamo River at Fifth Avenue, binding along the way a long line of temples on the east front with the lodgings of commoners on the west. No other street is like it. And much of its character comes from wards that also differ one from another.

Above all, the emphasis in the urban literature on wards acknowledges the membership of commoners in the polis. Formed, in general, by the properties facing any single thoroughfare between intersections, the ward emerged in early modern cities as a unit of self-government constituted by householders and administered by corporately selected officials.[30] This political identity looms largest in materials concerning Osaka. Maps of the city from the late seventeenth century signify with icons or color both local ward associations and the larger ward federations to which they belonged. And street directories published after 1679 list the names of the commoner "elders" and "deputies" who, chosen among local ward officials, oversaw those federations (Kita-gumi, Minami-gumi, and Tenma-gumi).[31] Wards are not coded in maps of Kyoto and Edo (perhaps because of their number and complexity). Nor are ward officials identified in directories of Kyoto and Edo before the eighteenth century (perhaps because of their frequent rotation). But the hundreds of ward names capture in shorthand the primacy of neighborhood to social organization. Some derived from streets (the "upper ward of Ogawa Avenue"), most from landmarks or trades, historical personages or circumstances (the "ward of the Young Pine," the "ward of the Drapers," the "ward of Izumi Shikibu," the "ward of the Old Castle"). The naming itself, and the fusion of the names with urban definition, converts the street into a site of commoner politics.

The street is also—and emphatically—a site of commerce. Although shops receive attention in the Sparrows, business is not a major motif of entries that range capaciously over landmarks and lore. Business moves to the center in the Kyoto Brocade and the Dappled Fabric of Edo, where the description of each thoroughfare concludes with a "Great Summary of the Trades of This Street and Its Wards." Among Kyōgoku's residents are

> carvers of bone and horn, dealers in dolls, dealers in votive paintings and collages (*oshie*), dealers in mortuary tablets, dealers in combs, booksellers, dealers in stone memorials, sellers of sundries, dealers in Buddhist rosaries, dealers in white face powder, dealers in pole boxes and cases, sculptors of Buddhist statues, dealers in writing brushes, makers of papier-mâché objects, forgers of short swords, workers of Chinese leathers [tiger skins], dealers in tanned leathers, dealers in towels and wrapping cloths, dealers in koto musical instruments and their strings, dealers in samisen and their strings, dealers in bows and arrows, dealers in archery gloves, dealers in fans, dealers in lances, dealers in lumber, and dealers in inkstones.[32]

So, too, the compiler of the Dappled Fabric of Edo concludes his first street entry, concerning the Northern Avenue of the Bridge of Japan, with an identically titled "Great Summary." Among residents there are

> lacquerers, dealers in ink and writing brushes, dealers in silk thread, booksellers, dealers in raincoats, dealers in mirrors, dealers in fans, dealers in Buddhist goods, dealers in swords, mounters and binders [of paintings and books], dealers in Buddhist robes, printers, dealers in koto, dealers in samisen, carvers of bone and horn, cake makers, dealers in mortuary tablets, dealers in paper, dealers in candles, dealers in heavy brushes, dealers in baskets, dealers in lacquer goods, and dealers in Chinese-style straw hats.[33]

Fig. 24. "Lacquer and Houseware Seller," from *Jinrin kinmōzui* (An Illustrated Encyclopedia of Humanity, 1690). National Diet Library, Tokyo.

Uniting the notions of street and trade, these summaries also tell a story about the profusion and specialization of urban commerce—apparently a good thing. The city is thick not only with places of name and fame but with goods of name and fame as well. And they deserve equal notice.

Like the naming of places, the naming of objects had a long tradition. The leading primer in the Middle Ages (the *Teikin ōrai*) instructed the children of the elite in a basic social lexicon that included a fair sample of the country's "famous products" and "famous manufactures." Listed there are twenty-two items from the Kyoto area (figured silk from the Ōtoneri guild, dyed stuffs from Rokujō Avenue, needles from Anegakōji, turnips from Higashiyama, pottery from Saga) and another forty-one from over thirty different provinces (rice wine from Bingo, carp from Ōmi, stirrups from Musashi, crepe paper from Sanuki, salmon from Hokkaido).[34] Such items acquired name and fame because of an excellence expressive of local genius. Optimal conjunctions of nature and artifice yielded certain superior goods—often commonplace ones made rare by their quality—that conveyed the virtue of human work. The producers themselves remained

fame

anonymous and their materials (of soybeans for a famous paste or persimmons for a famous dried sweet) as humble as not. It was a putatively communal skill in husbandry and craft that created a realm of distinction in which fine turnips lined up with fine brocades, fine carp with fine stirrups, fine barley with gold-flecked lacquer.

Stimulated by connoisseurship and market sense, a once limited practice of naming became a minor industry after 1600. As famous places kept multiplying, so did famous products and manufactures. In the Kyoto area alone, they numbered about 700 by the mid seventeenth century.[35] This proliferation was particularly influenced by what would later be called "the study of production" *(bussangaku)*, a multifaceted inquiry into natural and human resources that assumed both diverse purposes (from scientific learning to economic development) and diverse forms (from botanical taxonomies to agricultural handbooks).[36] Some of the foundational works— Kaibara Ekiken's *Yamato honzō* (Flora and Fauna of Japan), Miyazaki Yasusada's *Nōgyō zensho* (Complete Book of Farming), and Hitomi Hitsudai's *Honchō shokkan* (Culinary Mirror of the Realm)—quickly found their way into commercial print. But many of the most ambitious "studies of production" were too vast in size and local in detail for publication. Most came from daimyo seeking a practical grasp of their own domains. They began to require of surveyors not only basic cadastral information but extensive reports, village by village, on topographical features, human and animal populations, marketable resources, processed goods, and manufactured products. An exemplary standard was set by the gazetteers of Aizu Wakamatsu, initiated by the daimyo Hoshina Masayuki. In addition to catalogues of resources (such as hawks, wild ducks, salmon, trout, and carp) and products (such as lacquer ware, wax, paper, rice cakes, and various woven goods), the Aizu materials provided extended notes on social life—from local festival calendars to marriage and burial customs.[37] Such intensive local surveys in turn inspired efforts to distill core information for general consumption. Scholars and writers began assembling data on folk rituals into national almanacs.[38] They also began compiling national inventories, organized by province, of major resources, products, and manufactures.[39]

Here, in the convergence of production studies with market growth and popular publishing, was the great stimulus to the naming of goods. With commendable alacrity, commercial writers converted lists of local products into the lists of "famous things" that filled guidebooks, gazetteers, and even the margins of maps. Long lists got longer, moreover, as the interests of publishers coincided with the interests of traders, tourists, and local boosters. Hence a mini-genre of guides to named goods—with titles like the *Shokoku meibutsu kanoko* (Dappled Fabric of Our Famous Things)—took off in the eighteenth century. Primers followed right behind. While geographical textbooks had long included basic lists of products, primers such as *Banmin chōhō meibutsu ōrai* (Everybody's Treasury of Famous Things) focused sole attention on the country's resources, arts, and crafts.[40] They taught popular piety toward the land, even as they introduced children to economic values and, perhaps, the lure of consumption.

But there was also music in the names of famous things and surely sheer pleasure in sounding the litany: safflower-dyed silk, gold-lacquered saddles, trumpet shells from the beach of Imai, ginko nuts from Kōfukuji. In *Kefukigusa* (Feather-Blown Grasses, preface date 1638), the *haikai* poet Matsue Shigeyori luxuriates in the words of the material world as he builds what was for its time a phenomenal list, numbering over 1,800 items, of the "old and new famous things of all the provinces." Insisting that the vocabulary of art break with overrefinement to embrace common experience, Shigeyori demonstrates in copious examples how typically simple things can be used in an adamantly contemporary poetry. His manifesto urges followers to discard flaccid old images in favor, say, of a seasonal reference (if in the sixth month) to the "flowers of the eggplant" or a spatial reference (if to the northeast) to the "clams of Musashi." The interest of his examples tends to shrivel, though, in comparison with the strange, lovely lists themselves. Here, the famous things of Matsumae: hawks, hawk feathers, saltwater crane, dried salmon, herring, herring roe, smoked whale, kelp, sea otter, seals, bearskin, deerskin, sea lions, fur seals, dried udo, dried tofu, powdered gold, and magnets.[41]

Similarly playing on the music of marvelous things, the "Great Summaries of the Trades" in the Brocade and the Dappled Fabric make the street a combined center of enterprise and fascination. They invoke the trope of famous goods to connect work with virtue; and they insinuate comparisons with the famous place to project shops as sites of sightseeing. But the lessons of the street, which began with navigation only to spread across politics and commerce, are not yet finished. Giving name and fame to products was an old tradition. Giving name and fame to producers—and sellers—was alien to a tradition of anonymous skill. In their final volumes, the compilers of the surveys alter the landscape by identifying tradespeople in contexts of honor. Home to shops, the streets are home as well to estimable shopkeepers.

After concentrating for the better part of four volumes on place and time, Koshōshi puts people up front in volumes 5 and 6 of the Kyoto Brocade. Volume 5 is an institutional honor roll. It opens with the nobility, treated much in the manner of the "Courtly Mirrors" that had emerged around the mid seventeenth century in imitation of the military originals. Imperial princes come first, followed by roughly 200 male aristocrats in rank order (from the junior first rank through the senior sixth rank). Written to formula, the entries include surname, personal name, clan name, principal crest, age, address, and income. Next are 18 imperial abbesses and roughly 250 officeholders in the courtly bureaucracy (identified, much in the manner of shogunal officeholders, by job title).[42]

Volume 5 proceeds from aristocrats to daimyo, naming about 150 lords who kept mansions in Kyoto. Again, the entries are conventional (name, title, castle headquarters, registered productivity of the domain), although they add salient local details: the address of each daimyo's Kyoto residence and the name of his permanent deputy there. The entries also include the name and address of each daimyo's "official draper," the privileged merchant immediately responsible for providing the ceremonial wardrobe but often broadly engaged in the commercial (and sometimes the personal and political) affairs of his patron.[43]

Kyoto's men of hereditary privilege now covered, Brocade 1 turns to Kyoto's working men in volume 6. Still hewing close to the Military Mirrors, it begins with a list of the fourteen major officeholders in the shogunal bureaucracy who served in the capital and its environs—from the Kyoto deputy and the Kyoto magistrate to the guard commanders at the palaces and the intendants of Tokugawa house lands. The official list concludes with commoners appointed (with stipends) to shogunal posts, such as the head carpenter and the keepers of the warehouses at Nijō, Ōtsu, and Takatsuki.[44]

Thus far, the human inventories of Brocade 1 conform to models. The next move challenges the models. Seemingly small, even all but inevitable, the move bridges and blurs distinctions between elite and common, official and nonofficial workers.

Under a new heading, but without any dramatic visual break, Brocade 1 turns in volume 6 from shogunal officeholders to the "Various Masters and Artists" of Kyoto. There are roughly 250 of them, all identified by full name and address, who are grouped into forty-seven categories. They spe-

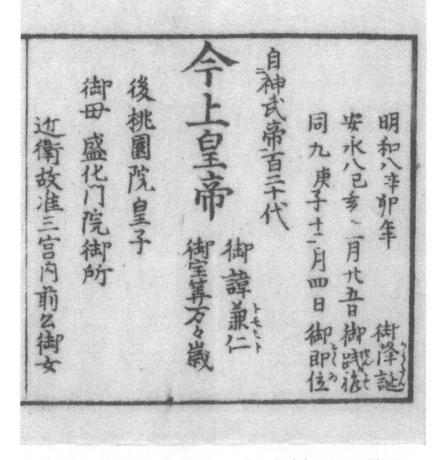

FIG. 25. Entry on "The Incumbent Emperor" in *Kyō habutae taizen* (The Kyoto Brocade Omnibus, 1768), noting the dates of his birth, succession, and formal accession; his place in the imperial line (the 120th generation since Jinmu); and his personal name (Tomohito). The entry also identifies his father, mother, and consort. Courtesy of the East Asian Library, University of California, Berkeley.

cialize in metiers such as medicine (seven categories, from pediatrics to acupuncture); Confucian and Shinto studies; poetry (including classical verse, popular verse [*jige uta*], linked verse, and *haikai*); handwriting; calculation; board games; flower arrangement; tea ceremony; kickball; painting (both secular and Buddhist); connoisseurship (of swords, calligraphy, rubbings, paintings, and miscellaneous objects); cooking; eyebrow pluck-

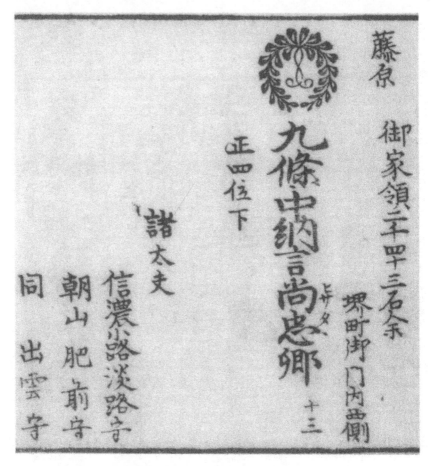

FIG. 26. Entry on "The Middle Counselor Kujō Hisatada no kyō" in *Kyō habutae taizen* (The Kyoto Brocade Omnibus, 1768), identifying his clan (Fujiwara), income (over 2,043 *koku*), address, age (13), rank, and major attendants. Courtesy of the East Asian Library, University of California, Berkeley.

ing and earwax removal; gardening; noh and *kyōgen* dancing; and music (five instruments, from flute to drums).[45]

Following the masters and artists, Brocade 1 goes on to the "Various Traders and Famous Craftsmen"—roughly 700 persons, again identified by name and address, who are grouped into 166 categories. Leading the list are specialists of greater prestige: the gold, silver, and vermilion guildsmen, selected drapers, tea dealers, handlers of Chinese silk imports, and makers of weights and measures. But then the catalogue surges in a more random order across the many dealers and makers of (generally fine) products. Merchants tend to appear before craftspeople and better before lesser items. Things of a kind (military gear or tea equipment, for example) also tend to appear in sequence. Still, any systematic sorting in this list is less obvious than the plenitude of activity it describes. The juxtaposition of disciplined specialization with prodigal creativity, which characterizes the Brocade's earlier lists of ward enterprises, occurs here on a grand scale.[46]

Thus among the items offered by Kyoto's traders and producers, readers find goods fashioned of gold, silver, copper, bronze, lacquer, lapis lazuli, mother-of-pearl, coral, cypress, and sandalwood. They find fans, screens, scrolls, poem cards, incense, exquisite papers, brushes, inks, inkstones, and pigments. They find mirrors, bells, altar goods, ritual objects, Buddhist statues, musical instruments, wood carvings, stone work, and dolls. They find books and specialized booksellers (who deal, for example, in poetry, theatrical texts, Confucian texts, and Buddhist texts, sorted by sect). They find a confounding array of things for the tea room (not only precious tea caddies but the brocade bags meant to hold them; not only implements carved of common woods but implements carved of cryptomeria; not only window blinds but the rustic sedge shades meant for simple-seeming huts). They find tortoiseshell combs, wigs, white powder and other cosmetics, local and imported medicinals, rare trees and plants, blades and swords and saddles. They find exquisite cakes, birds, and crustaceans. And they find plain and figured silks, gauze, gossamer, brocades, padded robes and dance costumes, Chinese fabrics, embroidery, and appliqué.

In assembling these lavish lists, the compiler of the Brocade continues to rely sufficiently on the format of the Military Mirrors to make them seem predictable extensions of his previous lists. Koshōshi adopts the structure of the Mirrors, first lining up members of the hereditary elite, then shogunal officeholders, and finally commoner specialists. He also treats these specialists in the style of the Mirrors, incorporating their categories and abiding in general by their order of presentation (putting the gold and silver guildsmen at the head of the list of merchants and craftspeople, for example). Indeed, Koshōshi includes in his entries virtually all of the Kyoto commoners who appear as privileged clients of the regime in the shogunal rosters.

The pattern holds true in surveys of Edo as well. Conforming to the Brocade's template, the Dappled Fabric covers specialists in the shogunal capital by listing roughly 300 "Masters and Artists" in 43 categories and roughly 700 "Traders and Famous Craftsmen" in 193 categories. Here, too, the names of the regime's official clients in Edo feature prominently, as if the compiler were lifting material directly from the Military Mirrors.[47]

FIG. 27. "Miedō Fan Shop," from Akizato Ritō, *Miyako meisho zue* (An Illustrated Guide to the Capital, 1787), illustrated by Shunchōsai Takehara Nobushige. This firm carried on a traditional association between a nearby Jishū

御影堂扇折

temple and fan-making by its priests and nuns. Courtesy of the East Asian
Library, University of California, Berkeley.

But those names are not the only names, of course; for the Brocade and the Fabric depart from the Mirror model in the volume and variety of their local coverage. While the shogunal rosters confine entries to official and quasi-official personnel in the service of the regime, the urban surveys sweep the spectrum of specialists engaged in public trade. They mutate, in effect, from cousins of the Mirrors into cousins of the commercial directories that had begun appearing in the great cities during the 1670s. Forthright guides to urban enterprise for audiences of consumers, texts such as *Kyō suzume ato-oi* (More Traces of the Kyoto Sparrow, 1678) advertised hundreds of businesses in handy single-volume booklets organized (and cross-listed) in phonetic order.[48] As versions of the commercial directories, the Brocade and the Fabric take on the function of promotional material aimed at shoppers for the city's myriad goods and services.

Not entirely, though. Or, at least, not exclusively. The major consequence of the merger between Mirror and trade guide is the recalculation of social distinction. In listing the privileged clients of the regime among the various masters, artists, merchants, and craftspeople, the compilers of the surveys accord them no special mark. The job categories they monopolize (as calendar makers or silk importers, for example) receive pride of place without otherwise being set apart. The job categories they share with humbler practitioners (as everything from painters to tatami makers) mix names indiscriminately. Indeed, the compiler of the Dappled Fabric of Edo includes in his lists men of high samurai rank. Thus the head of the Sakanoue house, who appears in the Military Mirrors as the shogun's chief personal physician, with a stipend of 500 *koku,* appears in the Fabric as just another of the forty-three general practitioners who lead the inventory of the "various masters and artists." The head of the Hayashi house, who appears in the Military Mirrors as the shogun's chief tutor and principal of the Confucian academy, with a stipend of 1,700 *koku,* appears in the Fabric as just another Confucian scholar.[49]

In effect, the urban surveys put profession over rank in their inventories of masters, artists, merchants, and craftspeople. The deliberateness of the move seems apparent if we compare their lists to the most detailed records still available concerning specialists practicing in the city. For fiscal and administrative purposes, the magistrates of Kyoto kept rosters of major tradesmen and providers of services that overlap sufficiently in category and content with the Brocade's lists to suggest that Kōshōshi mined them—or variants circulating among professional people—for much of his information. But the records of the magistrates differ in a fundamental respect from the lists of the Brocade. The roster of physicians, for example,

FIG. 28. Entry from *Kyōto kaimono hitori annai* (A Self-Guided Tour to Kyoto Shopping, 1831), a comparatively late (and enormous) advertising directory, here featuring makers of and dealers in "Buddhist goods and metalwork" (including "China goods"). In addition to providing the name of the proprietor, his crest, and the shop's address, the entry in the middle of the page identifies the firm as a privileged purveyor to the shogun (*goyō*). Courtesy of the East Asian Library, University of California, Berkeley.

begins with "general practitioners receiving official stipends," noting not only their names and addresses but the size of their stipends and the constituencies they serve (the residents of the imperial palace, say). It continues with "general practitioners of the wards," noting simply names and addresses. The subsequent lists make the same distinction. "Confucian scholars receiving official stipends" precede "Confucian scholars without stipends"; "linked verse masters with official stipends" precede "linked verse masters of the wards"; and so on through many categories of masters, artists, merchants, and craftspeople.[50]

These distinctions dissolve in the Brocade, where privileged commoners (and even samurai) in service to the regime merge as seeming peers into large groups of nonofficial doctors, poets, sword makers, brush makers, and the like. The point is not that social distinction itself dissolves. It comes from an alternative source. The doctor who appears in the Military Mirrors derives honor from his patron and membership in a company of rank. The doctor who appears in the Brocade derives honor from his skill and membership in a company of professionals. Thus he bears the suffix "master" (*shi*), which recurs throughout the Brocade and the Fabric to designate both the general category of learned men and many individual artists and craftspeople. Analogous to "teacher" or "maestro," it implies an independence gained through expertise. Not incidentally, all commoners appear in the inventories with full surnames and personal names (or sometimes with artistic sobriquets), never with demeaning forms of address. Many of those surnames, moreover, are sufficiently lustrous—Kanō, Ikenobō, Hon'ami, Kanze, Gotō, Yodoya, Suminokura—to heighten the dignity of fellow specialists throughout the lists. Together, they occupy a public realm of work, seemingly self-legitimating, that confers prestige apart from elite status or elite patronage.

The contrast between Mirrors that exalt rank and urban surveys that exalt profession is imperfect, of course. The Mirrors, too, organize bureaucrats by job title and imply competition for office through skill, thus opening the way for the professional taxonomy of the surveys. And the surveys, too, capitalize on the eminence of rank. City specialists belong to a big system of exalted roles including courtly aristocrats, daimyo, and shogunal officials. They belong to an immediate system of urban enterprise featuring such great licensed monopolies as the mint and the imported silk trade. In effect, the compilers of the inventories have it both ways. On the one hand, they emphasize function over privilege: a doctor is a doctor before he is the shogun's internist. Score one for a performance-based approach to social distinction. On the other hand, they ennoble function through association with an ultimately hierarchical status order: the doctor shares in the dignity of the princes listed above him, while bestowing dignity on the humbler specialists listed below him. The compilers seem to correlate the division of social work with the boundaries of social station, essentially according to the regime's formula. Score one for an ascriptive approach to social distinction.

The compilers are obviously grappling, in their ambivalence over the claims of merit and ascription, with questions about prestige. Do urban workers have it? If so, is it equal to the prestige of others? But the more interesting question concerns autonomy: how powerful are the market and its workers?

The compilers make a strong statement about market power through the sheer number of enterprises they list, beginning with the summaries of economic activity street by street and continuing with the inventories of individual specialists profession by profession. Nor are those lists the end of the trade catalogues. Brocade 1 concludes with several shorter listings of the express messenger services run out of Kyoto, local hostels and inns for pilgrims, and public bathhouses.[51] The Dappled Fabric improves on the Brocade by adding a list, in twenty-one categories, of over seventy firms of "transporters and wholesalers."[52] We find a response in Brocade 2, where the compiler enters over 500 more traders in fifty-one categories neglected in Brocade 1. Most are transporters and wholesalers who handle particular goods (raw lacquer, fish, oil, sake, lumber, pharmaceuticals, dyestuffs, tree cotton) or a mix of imports from individual provinces.[53] Numbers and categories continue to mount in subsequent directories, particularly as compilers take greater account of mundane goods and services. In this regard, too, the Fabric is more precocious than the Brocades. Apart from both the summaries of ward enterprises and the inventories of specialists, the Fabric offers a list in ninety-six categories of trades too ubiquitous for coverage elsewhere. The compiler includes (for newcomers?) a short sample of firms within each category, noting that the entries are necessarily partial. Readers can find here selected rice sellers, charcoal sellers, dealers in old clothing, dealers in old furnishings, gardeners, roofers, shoemakers, tobacco sellers ("really too numerous for mention"), and so forth.[54]

These many catalogues of urban workers inflect the preceding lists of notables much as the rosters of officeholders in the Military Mirrors inflect the preceding lists of daimyo. So rich in job titles and real world meaning, the bureaucratic rosters tend to relegate the putatively powerful daimyo to a purely iconic sphere. Similarly, the accounts of specialists in the urban surveys seem to consign aristocrats and martial lords alike to a remote domain of blood honor. But they also, and critically, imply an independence of workers from their social betters that shogunal officeholders did not enjoy from theirs. However indispensably able, each official listed in the Mirrors appears there as a servant of the regime: he relies on an appointment (and a salary) awarded by a specific political administration built on a scaffold of daimyo. Hence, no shogunate = no employment for its staff. City workers, too, belong to a polity acknowledged in the lists of daimyo and officials. Still, the polity and the market are not congruent. Addressed regardless of social station to a public of consumers, the urban surveys put goods and services in the arena of open exchange. Like the commercial directories, and an exploding volume of advertising handbills and seasonal shopping catalogues, they declare that working people work for one another in an economy bigger than the regime. A market serving more than elites and functioning well beyond the bounds of official patronage is a market with a life of its own. No shogunate ≠ no market.

The forthright emphasis on trade in the urban surveys took on a political edge, for the texts appeared when relations between state and market had turned overtly contentious. Several generations into Tokugawa rule, it had become apparent that wealth was changing hands. Too large in number to employ fully or pay adequately, samurai on inflation-ridden stipends were in straitened circumstances. At the same time, producers and tradespeople were benefiting from an agrarian revolution stimulated by urban demand, widespread reclamation, and far-reaching improvements in farming methods. Insofar as rural taxation failed to keep pace with increased yields and commercial taxation remained limited to selective business fees, the more successful players in the market retained marginal profits that spread the demand for goods and services into the commoner population. Popular consumption joined elite consumption as a stimulant to growth and a source of gain.[55]

Certainly, wealth remained ill divided among samurai and commoners alike. Still, prosperous entrepreneurs controlled enough resources to create visible disturbances in the status order. Acquiring the appurtenances of honor, from rich clothing to fine food, they cracked the prescribed symmetry between social station and social behavior. The regime fought back with more and more sumptuary laws that insisted on a legible universe where material things remained transparent markers of place and privilege. The laws regulated food—who could eat what, when, at what cost. (Tree mushrooms were not to be sold before the first month; cranes and swans were not to be sold at all; farmers were to abstain from sake, tea, and tobacco.) They regulated housing and furnishings—the size of buildings, the height of gates, the length of roof beams, and the use of metal ornaments, lacquered moldings, carved lattices, painted walls, and fine flooring. They addressed ceremonial extravagance, horse and ox fittings, carriages and conveyances, personal ornaments and hairdressings. And with unremitting exactness, they addressed cloth and clothing. Commoners were forbidden velvet loincloths, embroidered crests, woolen jackets, gold and silver appliqué, thin silk crepe, and dappled tie-dye. Prostitutes were admonished not to wear robes with gold-thread woofs, servants not to wear brocade, sumo wrestlers not to wear silk loincloths.[56]

Striking in their admission of what affluent commoners could afford, the statutes were also entirely discordant with the message of the commercial press. They condemned in law the things promoted in print. But the coolness of publishers before the blast, which left the urban directories unchanged, points to an evolving accommodation between state and market that made sumptuary legislation a mainly symbolic exercise.

In advance of the laws, the state already had in place fundamental controls on commerce—primarily the severe restriction of both foreign trade and domestic land transactions. City people could not buy rural property and had limited access to urban real estate, reserved in the main for daimyo and samurai. The regime also confined a number of enterprises to its own monopolists, collected licensing fees from trade organizations, and impressed forced loans on the wealthiest merchant houses. On occasion, it manipulated the currency supply and tried to fix commodity prices.[57] Beyond such staple policies, however, the regime did not respond with aggressive change—in the form, for example, of universal commercial taxation, the structural reform of agrarian taxes, or (for that matter) the dismissal of redundant samurai—to the sustained transfer of wealth from military men to commoners and its own fiscal deterioration. Enforcement of the controls it did embrace was sporadic in a mercantile community given great latitude for self-regulation, not least in the areas of contract and labor recruitment.

Caution was not a bad response. Calculated or not, a toleration of private gain at the expense of a sound fisc insulated the regime from destabilizing struggles with producers and traders. Still, the concession set Japan on a distinctive course of economic development that habituated actors in the market to constrained opportunities. Allowed a fairly free hand for domestic entrepreneurship, producers and suppliers did not wage war on underlying controls and thus signal a break toward transforming innovation. Most important, they made no concerted demand for open foreign trade, a position intermittently conspicuous only in intellectual circles. Without major import and export ventures, merchants lacked incentives to accumulate investment capital through syndicates and stock exchanges, and to negotiate with the state for loans, legal guarantees for contracts, and military protection for oceangoing ships. The compliance of merchants with domestic restraints discouraged innovation as well. The absence of an open market in real property blocked another route to finance and investment capitalism, while frustrating the vertical integration of industry. One more factor conducive to conventional business practice, of course, was prolonged peace on both the national and international fronts. The state faced no urgent need for substantial tax increases, huge loans, and economic re-organization; its financial agents faced no transforming need to assemble the capital for and underwrite the technology of war. In short, the state and the market reached an accommodation, in a peacetime context, that suppressed seminal contests and left the real power and potential autonomy of trade untested. The regime undertaxed and underregulated commerce of a routine nature; entrepreneurs did without substantial access to foreign contacts and real estate.

As a consequence, economic development proceeded along the conservative trajectory indicated in the urban surveys. Traditional craft manufacture, which entered a proto-industrial stage late in the Tokugawa period, continued to organize production. After agriculture, wholesale and transport became the biggest sectors of the economy, although they were dispersed among many regional networks and concentrated in rice. The professional sector expanded, particularly in education and medicine, but included no established legal or notarial community. While extremely sophisticated at the level of interregional trade, financial institutions took no deposits and extended in a makeshift fashion to a host of brokers, money exchanges, trade associations, and lay and religious lending societies.[58]

Systemic constraint stalled growth during the eighteenth century. But if the economy reached and even surpassed its limits, popular consumption made the difference. While the regime reconciled itself to chronic indebtedness and insults to the status system, a culture of consumerism took hold in the commoner population. Exquisitely refined at higher reaches, it was grounded in the trade in basic commodities (such as processed foods, fertilizers, tools, cloth, bedding, and paper) and the array of goods indispensable to gift giving (such as cakes, tea, fine fish, and sake). The urban surveys artfully associated production and exchange with virtue. Traders dealt in the "famous things," from good persimmons to good silk, that conveyed the bounty of the land and genius of producers. Specialists themselves were "masters" and "famous artists" and "famous craftspeople" who shared their laudable skills, in Confucian scholarship no less than tatami making, with audiences educated to discrimination. Their shops were "famous places" that lined up on a par with the "venerable sites, famous remains, shrines, and temples" that all city people should "really know." And the entire world of commercial enterprise fitted into an honorable social order of princes, daimyo, and officials. This convention-rich valorization of trade helped deflect the heat of the sumptuary laws. Yet in the unabashed advertising of the inventories, where things became desirable and tradespeople professional, the implicit subject remained consumers. The legitimacy and the power of the market, the inventories indicated, depended on buyers rather than rulers.

The baldest commercial literature of the seventeenth century made this point through parody. Even as they mimicked the codes of honor employed for daimyo in the Military Mirrors, the rosters of actors and prostitutes also appended evaluations (and eventually outright rankings) of these entertainers. Hence they carried the logic of promotion to a subversive conclusion: the attributes of honor were only part of the calculus of success, which depended finally on skill and the judgment of the audience. And because those attributes were so vulnerable to appropriation, they might just be altogether artificial in an economy where buyers made decisions.[59]

The urban surveys did not so overtly expose the battle between a polity founded on ascription and a market premised on competition, between a polity founded on obedience and a market premised on choice. The contrast was nonetheless latent in texts, written for sale themselves, that tracked the professional specialists whose services were also for sale.

[marginalia: So they're breaking status but also enforcing it w/ the history/past stuff no?]

[marginalia: The gathering?]

[marginalia: Ooms? how they each treat obedience vs choice?]

A number of tourist handbooks from the seventeenth century include in their titles the phrase *hitori annai*, which might mean "a solitary traveler's guide" but better describes a "self-guided tour." The phrase appears, too, on the reverse side of many maps, where publishers inserted lists, tailored to various timetables, of must-see sights.[60] Readers could find, for example, itineraries for one-day tours or three-day tours or the like. Since excursions tended to be sociable affairs, even for pilgrimage, "solitary" alludes less to the traveler's company than the traveler's freedom. Accompanied by a text, the stranger needs no insider experience or roadside advice to get along. Invited by a text into disparate sites, the stranger can also select at will places to visit as a spectator. The traveler is solitary not because alone but because anonymous, not because lonely but because disconnected.

Inherent in cities because of their size, the experience of anonymity comes to the fore of early modern texts as print itself makes communication impersonal. The market that connects author and reader, and the sellers and buyers who dominate urban activity, also makes the stranger the prototypical city person—free to pass through shops; free, too, to appropriate history and historical sites, to walk any street and every ward. *Homo urbanus* is a consumer with access to the scene. Social encounter goes along with consumption and, indeed, emerges as a leitmotif in guides (and prints and paintings) that focus on urban commotion—busy streets, thronged bridges and intersections, mobbed theaters and pleasure spots. But this is the encounter of the crowd, the audience, the moment, the passing conversation, the business transaction.

In several sections with peculiarly mixed and modern messages, the urban surveys nonetheless offer readers something approaching community—one constructed of ritual life. This is not the internal community of neighborhoods and religious congregations; for, without breaking into the daily experience of their members, the surveys present the wards primarily in a commercial guise, the temples and shrines in an institutional guise. Entries on the latter, for example, proceed from historical to adamantly administrative matters (personnel, income, sectarian lineages, subordinate units), leaving unremarked the functions of ministry (devotional schedules, say, or the charitable practices of lay organs). Instead of exploring the filiations of small social groups, the compilers offer their readers a community of porous boundaries and transient membership.

It takes shape in volume 2 of the Kyoto Brocade where, after lists of old tombs and old places and old things, the compiler provides the annual ritual calendar of the capital and a description of the Gion festival. The volume continues with outlines of five local pilgrimage circuits (which take devotees to thirty-three places dedicated to Kannon, forty-eight to Amida, six to Jizō, twenty-one to Shinto deities, and twenty-nine to Benzaiten) and inventories of famous icons, statues, and relics in ten categories. The volume closes with the monthly schedule of prayer and abstinence for persons making special novenas to Kannon and Yakushi, as well as a chart of distances from Kyoto to twenty-four (generally nearby) locations, almost all of them pilgrimage sites. For ballast, the compiler throws in a list of fifty-three measurements (nostrils two feet wide, ears ten feet long, and so forth) pertaining to the monumental Buddha and Buddha hall built by Tototomi Hideyoshi in Kyoto in 1595.[61] Similar categories are covered in the Dappled Fabric of Edo, in volume 2 of which the compiler includes the annual ritual calendars of both the shogun's castle and the commoner wards; a description of the Sannō festival; lists in ten categories of locally famous icons; and the novena schedules for Kannon and Yakushi.[62]

In contrast to the institutional accounts of temples and shrines, the entries concerning novenas, pilgrimage circuits, and icons of beloved deities highlight religious *practice*—practice of a particular kind. They represent the city as a site of intense popular piety expressed not only (or even primarily) in institutional adherence but in itinerant worship detached from both sect and formal organization. The circuits entail sequential devotions, at the individual traveler's pace, in sanctuaries consecrated to a particular divinity. A pilgrim in Kyoto, for example, might call on Kannon first at Rokkakudō, then at Shimo-Goryō, and on, finally, to the thirty-third stop at Seiwain. Devotees might also improvise their own itineraries by moving among the twenty-one sites famed for statues of Jizō, say, or (if in Edo) to the twenty-four sites famed for statues of Inari. In doing so, they would join elective communities of belief formed, in action, on the road. Broadcasting the circuits and the sites, the surveys make cities concentrated arenas of religious connection where dedicated and more casual worshippers can unite voluntarily in passage.

The community offered in the annual ritual calendars is of a somewhat different order; for it emerges from simultaneous practice while leaving purpose obscure. Formalized by the classical aristocracy and adapted by the medieval military, such calendars originated in the planting and harvest rites of rural society. In each of these cases, they were designed to forge, through ceremonial routine, groups invested in maintaining themselves. Thus they focused on the recurring special events—from seasonal celebrations to religious feasts—that affirmed both internal cohesion and exclusive membership.[63] So, for example, the "Annual Ritual Calendar of Edo Castle," which the Dappled Fabric records in abbreviated form, highlights the receptions sponsored by the shogun for the daimyo and, reciprocally, the processions undertaken by the daimyo to the shogunal mausolea at Nikkō, Zōjōji, and Kan'eiji. General interest in these processions (abetted by shogunal interest in selective publicity) may explain the appearance of the castle calendar in the Fabric. Yet it was also used to situate the succeeding entry, the "Annual Ritual Calendar of the Wards," where the compiler borrows the prestige of an elite model while confounding its clarity of purpose.

Urban writers began formulating calendars for city people in the wake of provincial gazetteers that listed the annual rites of villagers.[64] This precedent, and broad acquaintance with court and martial practice, surely stirred the presumption that *any* collectivity must share *some* schedule. But what kind? And why? Unlike villagers and courtiers and daimyo, city people had neither an established ritual life in common nor any basis for one, insofar as corporate identity was not indispensable to corporate survival. Too vast in number to constitute an intelligible group, they remained a centrifugal population both quantitatively and qualitatively different from a few hundred farmers or nobles or domainal lords. So in groping toward some ritual definition of this urban mass, writers came to reconceive the motives for ceremonial calendars and redefine the attachments of groups.

The "Annual Ritual Calendar" in the Kyoto Brocade lists almost two hundred events. Most take place in the capital and its environs, some in nearby towns (Sakamoto, Ōtsu, Uji), and a few in more distant locales (Nara, Sakai, Osaka, and even Edo). All are religious, though they cover the range of officially recognized Buddhist and Shinto faith (omitting, then, marginalized and underground practice). Most entries concern a specific event at a specific place: the reading of the Daihannya sutra at Eikandō on 1/16, for example; the penitential rites at Tōfukuji on 2/1; the chanting of mantras to Amida at the Senbon Enmadō on 3/14; the horse races at the Kamo shrine on 5/5; the festival at Wakanomiya Hachiman shrine on 8/15. In a substantial number of entries, however, the compiler indicates a practice undertaken concurrently at many sanctuaries. Devotees visit shrines to Benzaiten on 1/7 and Inari on 2/1. They mark the death anniversaries of Hōnen Shōnin from 1/19 to 1/25; Sugawara no Michizane on 2/25; Kōbō Daishi on 3/21; Kūya on 11/13; and Shinran Shōnin on 11/22. They mark the death and transcendence of Shakyamuni on 2/15 and celebrate Ebisu, the god of good fortune, on 10/20.

Although it includes significant departures from the Brocade model (more later), the ward calendar in the Dappled Fabric of Edo also concentrates, in its eighty-five entries, on religious events. Again, most entries (all local) guide readers to specific sanctuaries for specific rituals on high feast days: the opening of the Great Gate at Zōjōji on 1/16; the Sanja Gongen festival at Asakusa on 3/18; the festival of Nakagawa Myōjin in Akasaka on 6/15; the Yotsuya Tennō festival on 6/18. But, again, many entries are more generic in nature. Thus the calendar notes that townspeople make their New Year's visits to Yakushi between the eighth and twelfth days of the first month, to Hachiman on the fifteenth, to Enma on the sixteenth, to Kannon on the eighteenth, to Tenjin on the twenty-fifth, and to Fudō on the twenty-eighth. "Various temples, including Zōjōji, exhibit images of Buddha's death" on 2/15. On 10/13 devotees make offerings before images of Nichiren Shōnin at "Lotus temples throughout Edo"; and between 11/22 and 11/28, they commemorate the death of Shinran Shōnin "at the Honganji temples and other Shinshū chapels."

Immediately striking in both calendars is their scope. As schedules of religious events, they are highly selective; for the Brocade compiler had to choose among thousands of ceremonies at local temples and shrines and the Fabric compiler among a smaller though still formidable number. But as schedules of collective urban activity, intended for general consumption, they are big—too big to outline a ritual life in common. Nobody, let alone a cohesive group, could cover the territory, spare the time, and cultivate the

FIG. 29. "The Yasurai Festival at Murasakino Ima Miya on the Tenth Day of the Third Month," from Akizato Ritō, *Miyako meisho zue* (An Illustrated Guide to the Capital, 1787), illustrated by Shunchōsai Takehara Nobushige. Courtesy of the East Asian Library, University of California, Berkeley.

interests necessary to do more than sample the activities in the lists. In this very bigness, then, the calendars declare a difference from the models. Rather than bounding a corporate body defined by shared and exclusive practices, they stretch eclectically to include both disparate events and their disparate participants in the unbounded field of urban membership and ceremonial life. The communities of the city emerge dynamically through choice as people gather to do the same thing at the same time. This simultaneity sets ritual events apart from pilgrimage. So, too, does motive.

Marvels of judiciousness, the calendars manage to mention most popular forms of devotion (such as New Year's greetings of the gods); the bigger personality cults (formed around teachers such as Kūkai and Shinran); the range of authorized Buddhist sects (from Tendai to Zen); a representative selection of practices (from sutra reading to mantra chanting to dancing); a good sample of large and small, famous and obscure sanctuaries; and most of the fabled events at historically renowned sites (from the horse racing at Shimogamo to the Sanja festival at Asakusa). This obliging coverage suggests that while faith itself may be sufficiently pervasive among city people to ground the urban calendar, the forms of faith are sufficiently diverse to require broad acknowledgement.

Still, the calendars treat religious commitment as only one motive for ritual attendance. Studded with appeals to the uninitiated, the entries provide notes on the background of events, their conduct and duration, and the various sites where moveable feasts occur. Participants need not be in the know already to join the proceedings. As if luring in spectators, the compilers remark, too, on the performances and displays entailed in celebrations. The Fabric informs readers that they can see flower arrangements at Nishi Honganji and Hōonji on 7/7; dancing at the Ōji festival on 7/13; sumo at the Asakusa Zaō Gongen festival on 7/15; and noh at Kanda Myōjin on 9/18. They can climb a miniature version of Mount Fuji at Komagome on 6/1 and hear the *hinzasara,* an unusual plucking instrument, at Asakusa Kannon on 6/15. Throughout most such activities, they can visit shops and stands selling tea, rice cakes, sushi, and special sweets.[65]

Rituals become, in effect, pageants open to anybody—not only the ardent but occasional worshippers, seekers of entertainment, holiday revelers, tourists, and sightseers. Above all, the texts suggest, they are occasions for being at the center of the action. The compilers remark repeatedly on the "great crowds" who gather at ceremonies, on the "convergence of high and low, old and young, male and female alike." The biggest events in the shogun's capital draw in throngs the Dappled Fabric describes as "All Edo."

So, for example, "all the tradespeople of Edo" join in the Ebisu festival on 10/20. The Shiba Shinmei festival on 9/16 attracts "all people high and low." And "all the children of Edo" participate in the Tanabata festival on 7/7.

These references help sort the calendar a bit by drawing attention to ritual denominators more common than not. Some events do appear to summon the collectivity, though still as permeable and voluntary gatherings requiring no qualifications, barring no strangers. The chief such events are the Gion festival of the Yasaka shrine in Kyoto (6/5–6/14) and the Sannō Gongen Festival of Hie shrine in Edo (6/14–6/15), each given pride of place in the local calendar through a comprehensive inventory of its floats. The Brocade names, numbers, and describes the thirty-three floats of Gion; the Fabric, the forty-six floats of Sannō Gongen. By specifying in all cases the names of the wards providing the floats, the texts fuse the festival with the particular neighborhoods surrounding the sponsoring shrine that have made it their own. Yet they also translate the festivals into civic productions through publicity. The celebrations expand elastically from core supporters to the outer circles of townspeople and spectators who follow the crowd in a spirit of religious devotion or neighborliness or pleasure or longing.

Indeed, the pleasure principle is pronounced in the Dappled Fabric, for there the compiler moves outside religious ritual to draw in secular recreations. From the mid sixth to the late eighth month, townspeople take boats from the Ryōgoku Bridge to enjoy the cool of the evening. On 7/26 and 9/13, they combine boating with moon viewing. And on 8/15, "all Edo" goes to the water to watch both the moon and the fireworks.

Seasonal recreation is combined, moreover, with seasonal shopping. Between 12/17 and 12/19, the market at Asakusa Kannon sells the New Year's decorations that everyone in Edo seeks out. Between 12/26 and 12/30, the shops of Naka-bashi sell the children's arrows that the gods will bless at New Year's. All Edo shops again for the children's festivals of 3/3 and 5/5. During the five to ten days preceding each celebration, consumers can buy dolls in court dress or armor throughout the Doll ward (and at other specified locations). Nor is moneymaking the monopoly of merchants: the Brocade lists "exhibitions" (*kaichō*) of normally hidden icons that temples and shrines put on periodically for paying audiences

The all but inevitable overlay of commercial and ritual activity is less interesting, however, than the insinuation throughout the calendars of a market mentality. Big and eclectic, the calendars offer both access to and seemingly equal standing in the ceremonial life of cities to any anonymous

FIG. 30. "Blossom Viewing at Omuro," from Akizato Ritō, *Miyako meisho zue* (An Illustrated Guide to the Capital, 1787), illustrated by Shunchōsai Takehara

花の香ふ
夜のぬく
歳みのり
本の下屋
尾の
まんく

貴久

新古今

御室花見

Nobushige. Courtesy of the East Asian Library, University of California, Berkeley.

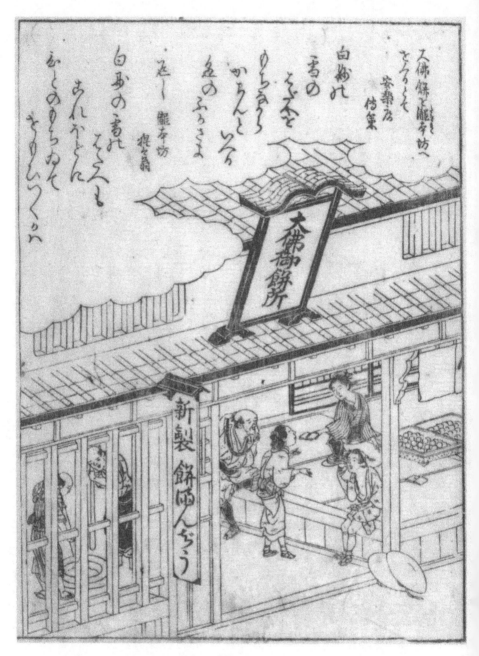

FIG. 31. "The Great Buddha Sweet Shop," from Akizato Ritō, *Miyako meisho zue* (An Illustrated Guide to the Capital, 1787) illustrated by Shunchōsai Takehara Nobushige. This shop capitalized on proximity to one of Kyoto's main tourist

洛東大佛餅の濫觴は朝
方廣寺大佛殿建立の砌
より氏はうやまつて變化
其實義まつて有ることは
糸粉方さて陸放翁の煮餅
東地の湯餅ふとふふ
名品ど唐孤汎他の類様版は
正水乳まつて代々にらつ後
一て遠近ふ其名を

attractions, the Great Buddha erected by Toyotomi Hideyoshi. Courtesy of the
East Asian Library, University of California, Berkeley.

spectator with any individual motive. Ritual is not put on sale, nor is the participant merged with the consumer. It is, rather, a context of apparent freedom that unites the presentation in the urban surveys of market and ritual encounters.

Because ritual engages crowds in a voluntarily shared and simultaneously sought experience, it holds out the promise, which the market does not, of community—of "all Edo" becoming a union. This is the promise the compilers also hold out in their representation of history-drenched cityscapes where "famous places" and popular knowledge of them can ground strangers in a common past. The promise nonetheless concedes the inherent disconnection that accompanies freedom. Choices, not obligations, bring city people together for transitory gatherings.

Whether choice appeared exhilarating or disturbing to readers, it remained the theme of texts that substituted the motley fabric for the cartographic model of urbanity. The city of maps was a place of status hierarchies, occupational and residential zones, visual order, and comprehensive control. The city of the Brocade and the Dappled Fabric was a place of loosely woven strands and random patterns detectable in different lights to different eyes. Certainly, the compilers relied on a strong warp of streets and wards, religious and governing institutions. But the weft—of commercial enterprise, historical legacy, and ritual activity—traced images of ambition and taste. The market rivaled the regime as a source of autonomous power. The past offered all residents a rightful patrimony. The ritual calendar redefined community as voluntary attachment. The social identities so clear in cartography are many and mutable in the urban surveys, which took as their subject the opportunities of consumers and strangers.

SIX

Cultural Custody,
Cultural Literacy

SEVERAL SUMMERS AGO I traveled around Kyoto following a tour guide written in 1706 by the Confucian polymath Kaibara Ekiken. I brought with me a late seventeenth-century map of the capital region and, to help with reference questions, an all-purpose family encyclopedia published in 1692. Unlike the material I have surveyed thus far, the guide was compelling as a short work (two spare fascicles) that takes readers by the hand to achieve a single, clear goal. No sprawling directory or roster or atlas, it focuses with pedagogical intensity on getting the consumer through a job. It suggests, then, how a practical text was meant to work and what expectations author and reader might have brought to their encounter.

Ekiken introduces his guide, *Keijō shōran* (The Excellent Views of Kyoto), in an irritable (and chauvinistic) tone, familiar from the Kyoto Brocade:

> Our Japan [*waga hi no moto*] surpasses other human realms in the mildness
> of its climate, the richness of its soil, the refinement of its people, and the
> wealth of its resources. But many of our people [*wagakuni no hito*] are not
> mindful of these facts. . . . They do not know that men of China called our
> land the "land of the gentlemen" and the "land of the immortals." And as
> for our imperial capital, even those who live here do not know that it is
> peaceful and tranquil surpassing all other provinces. We are like "insects
> surfeited with luxurious grasses heedless of good fortune."[1]

Part of the good fortune is a good library. Citing by title the texts already available to lead travelers through the city proper, Ekiken focuses on Kyoto's outreaches—the suburban area of Rakugai, which embraces such fabled locales as Uji, Fushimi, Ōhara, Atago, Takao, and Arashiyama. And to blanket the territory, he sets out seventeen walking tours, each meant to take a day and, probably, to follow one upon another in the prescribed se-

FIG. 32. "A Tour Guide to the Famous Places of the Capital," from Akizato Ritō, *Miyako meisho zue* (An Illustrated Guide to the Capital, 1787), illustrated by Shunchōsai Takehara Nobushige. Here both a human guide and a guide book instruct the traveler. Courtesy of the East Asian Library, University of California, Berkeley.

quence.[2] Most itineraries cover fifteen to twenty individual places, require twenty to thirty-five kilometers of hiking through often steep hills, and demand (to judge from my experience) twelve to fourteen hours. The obedient traveler will follow Ekiken through roughly 320 sites spread across roughly 450 kilometers of trails. For tourists who can take more, Ekiken appends as a sort of postscript a long list of additional sightseeing opportunities in the vicinity. Seventeen days of work, he implies, represent no more than a good beginning.

Ekiken turns out to be a more affable guide than the tone of his introduction suggests. Never, though, does he surrender authority over the landscape and its viewers. In a preparatory outline of the itineraries, he remarks of the third day's tour, for example, that "Today you will travel from Kyoto to Fushimi, returning via the Takeda Road. Be aware that the round-trip entails about six and a half *ri* [over twenty-five kilometers] and includes along the way a great many places you should see. So start early in the morning."[3] Ekiken knows his routes and his roads and his distances and his travel times. He knows what to see. He knows where to catch a boat, find a shortcut, stop for a meal or a night's lodging. He knows just how to arrange logical walks that bring travelers back to their departure points by the end of the day. And he knows when to get up in the morning. With seeming omniscience and empirical control, he leads his followers not to discovery—for what mystery or surprise could remain in a landscape fully mastered?—but induction into the community of knowers. Exploration appears to be finished. It remains only to arrange the data.

And Ekiken arranges the data, instructively, for "ordinary people," the *bonnin* who can count on their guide for all the information they need. He writes in a simple, declaratory Japanese full of phonetic reading aids. He writes, too, in a manner of helpful initiation, presuming an audience of newcomers. Thus he pauses, after summarizing the seventeen itineraries, to orient readers in their base camp, Kyoto proper (Rakuchū). Having disavowed in the introduction any interest in writing a downtown tour guide, Ekiken nonetheless includes in his Kyoto remarks a list of some fifty sites worth visiting. But his main concern is navigation. He runs through the major streets of the grid, defines the city's boundaries and internal divisions, and, most important, tells novices how to ask and follow directions in the local argot. Dutiful readers who learn Kyoto's codes "will find it easy to get around without any confusion."[4]

Once on the road, Ekiken takes travelers to and through successive sites in economical, unlabored entries focused on highlights. Here, a sample.

Tōfukuji is a great temple ranked among the Five Mountains. It has extremely extensive grounds. The temple was founded by Shōichi Kokushi Enni, who is commemorated every year on 10/16. The temple holdings include an image of the death of Buddha by Chōdenzu as well as many other old paintings and old writings that people can see. In recent years, many people have been coming to view the autumn maples at Tsūten Bridge. [5]

Ginkakuji is built on the site of a residence of the shogun Ashikaga Yoshimasa, Higashiyama-dono. It has a beautiful garden with a miniature lake. There is a two-story tower, the Silver Pavilion, built by Yoshimasa. The Tōgudō, also built by Yoshimasa, has a tea room that was the first such formal space for conducting the tea ceremony. You should see it with a temple attendant. On the hillside above the buildings, fires are burned every year on 7/16 to form the character "great" [as part of the *obon* rituals that welcome the spirits of the dead for a summer reunion with the living].[6]

Ninnaji, called Omuro, is a temple with an abbot who is an imperial prince. You should see the main building with a guide [*michibiki*]. Within the grounds there are many double cherry trees that are regarded as the best in Kyoto and its environs—equal to those of Yoshino. They bloom every spring for over ten days, when many people come to view them, crowding in day after day. Bringing food and sake, and curtaining off enclosures, many visitors also lay out banquets for themselves under the flowers. High viewing platforms are available as well. People who love cherry blossoms should come three times for viewings—at the beginning, middle, and end of the season.[7]

Ishiyama has a Kannon hall flanked by any number of large, strange rocks, standing as if in a stone forest. Hence the name, Stone Mountain [Ishiyama]. In the eastern part of the hall is the Genji room where Murasaki Shikibu is said to have written the *Tale of Genji*. There is an inkstone in the hall used in writing the *Genji*, which, unusually, has two wells side by side. The collection also includes a portrait of Murasaki, two poems written by her, calligraphy by Konoe Nobumoto, and one volume of the Daihannya Sutra attributed to Murasaki's hand. You should ask a temple priest to show you these things. Downhill from the Kannon hall, you will find extensive quarters for monks and, by the river, lodgings for travelers. During the fourth and fifth months, fireflies attract and amaze visitors from far and wide.[8]

Jakkōin, located in the Grassy Fields of Nishinotani, is a convent where the former empress of Takakura'in, known as Kenreimon'in, lived as a nun after taking her vows. There is a wooden statue of her here, and her grave is be-

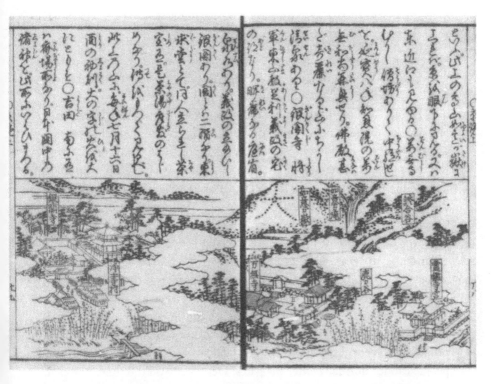

FIG. 33. The Silver Pavilion and surrounding landmarks, from Kaibara Ekiken, *Keijō shōran* (Excellent Views of Kyoto, 1718). Courtesy of the East Asian Library, University of California, Berkeley.

hind the convent amid several imperial mausolea. It was in the mountains just beyond that the royal nun went to gather bracken, as described in *Tales of the Heike*. In summer these mountains are thick with green trees of great beauty. Those ready to give themselves over to simplicity, who love green shade and find luxuriant flowers unappealing, should come here.[9]

As this sample suggests, most entries in the Excellent Views concern religious institutions, although Ekiken also singles out villages, natural landmarks, vista points, mountain passes, grave sites, castles, and the like. But whatever the subject, he wants it *seen*. Loaded with the imperative "must see" (*mirubeshi*), this is no tour of walls and rooftops viewed from a distance. Ekiken prods his readers into sanctuaries to look at buildings, altars, icons, paintings, documents, inscriptions, gardens, ponds, waterfalls, mortuary monuments, bridges. He seems particularly high on statues (of Murasaki, Kenreimon'in, thirteen of the Ashikaga shogun, the sixteen

Arhats, Tamuramarō, Hideyoshi, Kōdaiin ...). And he is unfailingly high, however sensitive to those who hate flowery flamboyance and love somber green, on seasonal color—cherry, double cherry, plum, peach, camellia, wisteria, mountain rose, daphne, maple. An ardent natural scientist (and author of *Yamato honzō* [Flora and Fauna of Japan]), Ekiken lingers, too, over fireflies, mandarin ducks, cranes, and various other birds and insects. Yet he remains circumspect with his readers, including enough details to set the scene without substituting words for vision or dictating reactions. He does remark that certain things are "beautiful" (the main halls at Inari and Bukkokuji, for example) or "very old" (the Kōryūji Buddha, the Kamigamo shrine) or "very big" (Hideyoshi's Buddha, the Chion'in cemetery) or "very long" (the veranda of Sanjūsangendō, the platform of Kiyomizu) or rather "odd" (the Ishiyama rocks, Hideyoshi's ear mound, the sites of gruesome executions). Still, these are tantalizing rather than coercive observations. The active seeing of the traveler is the point of a text in which eyes, certainly not feet, preoccupy the author.

Seeing presumes access, of course, and on this important matter Ekiken is punctilious. Early in the text, when he checks off notable sites in Kyoto proper, he directs readers to the imperial palace with a warning: "Ordinary people cannot normally enter the gates. Depending on the time, however, there are certain days when you can gain permission to look around." So, too, "it is hard to look around the retired emperor's palace and the retired empress's palace."[10] A few sites on his suburban itineraries pose problems as well. Myōhōin "cannot be entered without permission," Shōren'in is "hard to see if you don't know somebody," and the upper temple at Daigo is "closed to women."[11] Although such counsel discloses an author mindful of potential trouble, it often seems surmountable. Except for women wanting to visit upper Daigo, Ekiken at least holds out hope that even the most rarified sanctums are penetrable with the right connection or on the right day. Trouble also seems rare. Since this learned insider invites readers into other sites without cautions, they presumably enjoy the right to enter virtually all of the hundreds of places alluded to in his text—including temples with princely abbots, isolated convents, and imperial graves.

They also appear to enjoy rightful access to treasures. Yes, travelers may need to recruit (and pay) an "attendant" or a "guide" to see collections of "old paintings" and "old writings" and "old documents" and "inkstones" and such. But Ekiken tells them what's what, directs them to intermediaries, and orders them to proceed. Viewing rights to rare things are not a matter of "permission," simply of savvy.

Nor are viewing rights dependent on social qualifications. Status figures in the text only insofar as "ordinary people" are encouraged, just like anybody else, to see everything to be seen. Religious filiation figures not at all. Often enough, Ekiken identifies temples by sect and notes major icons and rituals, though as points of commonplace information. Imagining an audience of sightseers rather than pilgrims, he uses a secular, matter-of-fact tone to lead travelers comfortably from Zen to Lotus to Tendai temples. Whether or not they stop to pray (which is apparently of no concern to the author), they are meant to take stock of natural and man-made things as intrinsically interesting objects of observation. Much of that interest derives from historical connection—connection, for example, to the ghosts of Murasaki Shikibu, Kenreimon'in, Ashikaga Yoshimasa, and many others (among them Jingō, Tamuramurō, Kanmu, Toba, Saga, Daigo, Izumi Shikibu, Giō, Kiyomori, Shigemori, Go-Shirakawa, Saigyō, Shinran, Hōnen, Go-Daigo, Musō Kokushi, Hosokawa Katsumoto, Hideyoshi, Suminokura Ryōi, Sen no Rikyū, and Hayashi Dōshun). Yet here, too, history is not the property of affiliates, of those partisans or followers or descendants or housemen or status equals who have some privileged claim on a past uniquely theirs. Names are a collective property as, indeed, are the literary works that Ekiken unremarkably invokes to situate them: *Tales of Ise*, the *Tale of Genji*, *Tales of the Heike*, *Tales of Uji*, the *Collection of Poems Ancient and Modern*.

As if to confirm rights of common access, Ekiken forever emphasizes the normalcy of travel. His is a landscape of lodgings and teahouses, of distance markers on the roads, of guides ready to display Murasaki's inkstone. Above all, his is a landscape of crowds, sometimes identified as "ordinary people" but more often as "pleasure seekers" (*yūjin*). They gather to view maples and cherries and fireflies, join festivals (at the Kamo shrines, Inari, and Atago, for example), mark comings-of-age (at Hōrinji, for example), see the sights, remember the dead, enjoy the commotion. They also gather to eat and drink—not just at picnics but at the temple restaurants Ekiken singles out for their excellent vegetarian cuisine, developed for monks but widely offered to the public as well. At An'yōji in Maruyama, "the cuisine is prepared in accord with personal requests and includes the temple's 'famous specialties'—soy paste soup, pickled plum, persimmon cakes, and bean curd. Pleasure seekers come here in great numbers."[12] In effect, the travelers who follow Ekiken along the road are also following their many counterparts, who have made excursions a normal practice for normal people. One travels because one can. Because people do.

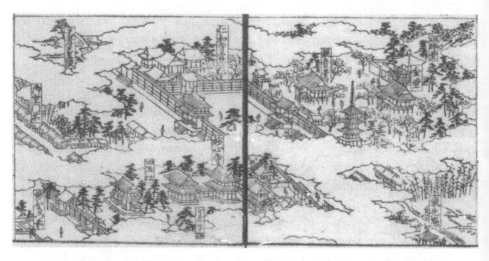

Fig. 34. Ninnaji and surrounding landmarks, from Kaibara Ekiken, *Keijō shōran* (Excellent Views of Kyoto, 1718). Courtesy of the East Asian Library, University of California, Berkeley.

They do so widely, moreover. And if they follow Ekiken, they do so thoroughly. His guide is hardly a selective survey of Top Spots for people in a hurry. Nor is it a thematic survey of linked spots for people with agendas. Ekiken does not arrange a hike to cover, say, the places associated with Heike and Genji partisans in the twelfth century. He has no "classical tour" of old court remains; no "battleground tour" of wartime monuments; no "famous man" tour built around a Hōnen or a Hideyoshi; no "mausoleum" or "relic" or "poetry" or even "cherry blossom" tour. Although Ekiken covers all such interests along the way, he does not, will not, sort space into anything other than geographical categories.

He accordingly achieves two effects. More obviously, the landscape and its parts become a depository of many converging meanings as nature, ritual, ghosts, and multiple histories intersect. At Ginkakuji, visitors find the hand of Ashikaga Yoshimasa, the origin of formal tea rooms, a marvelous garden, and the character carved by fire in the hills that is the center of Kyoto's festival of the dead. They move next to Yoshida, a site filled with imperial inscriptions, where the "myriad gods of heaven and earth" congregate in "3,132 god seats representing all the shrines of Japan's 68 provinces." And they then proceed to Hyakumanben ("one of four principle temples of the Jōdo sect"), Shōgoin (once the residence of a prince, now a headquarters of mountain ascetics [*yamabushi*]), and so forth.[13] For Ekiken, space is the bank of time and activity. Although he sometimes uses chrono-logical dates to mark that time, he prefers vague markers ("long ago," "in the middle period," "recently," "now") that suggest a fusion of experience in place. Thus travel cannot be arbitrarily guided by celebrity or themes, for it is an encounter with the total accretion of the land's meanings.

That land is not only thick, it is large and continuous. Because Ekiken breaks up itineraries into numerous individual stops, each with a label in the text, readers may at first think of the tours as beads strung on the rope of the road. The actual walking feels more like carpet sweeping. Ekiken blends one site into the next, extends boundaries into surrounding hills and plains, incorporates roadside scenery and settlements into the tour, and leads his followers to panoramic outlooks that fold all points together. And as walk follows walk for seventeen endless days, travelers discover the second effect of Ekiken's approach: they gain hold of the full landscape. Freedom of access expands from particular temples and their treasure rooms to the space of the journey. In the process, the notion of the "fa-mous place" all but falls away.

Ekiken does use the term, although sparingly and in a purist sense to in-dicate sites mentioned in "old poems." Given the profligate invocation of fame in both the titles and the contents of other tour guides, this parsi-mony seems to reject the celebration of discrete places holding some unique appeal in favor of attention to a landscape universally steeped in significance. With over three hundred stopping points and counting, sub-urban Kyoto can only be diminished by any selective concentration on the "famous place." Nor is suburban Kyoto special, except for the numbers of people who travel thereabouts. Writing repeatedly and reverently about lo-cal geographies, particularly about his home province of Chikuzen in northern Kyushu, Ekiken insists on total immersion in the space of the country.[14]

This is the space he calls "our Japan" in his introduction. And its resi-dents are "our people." If Ekiken focuses in the Excellent Views on one part of the land, he regularly summons the whole with references to "Japan's sixty-eight provinces" and the connections between local sites and wider contexts. Thus, for example, Imagumano enshrines the avatar of Ku-mano, Mimurodoji is one of the stops on the western circuit of the thirty-three Kannon, and Mukō no Myōjin is on the pilgrimage route from cen-tral Japan to Atago.[15] Yoshida welcomes all the gods of heaven and earth in small pavilions representing over 3,000 shrines throughout the country. Ekiken also likens local sites to what he takes for granted as national stan-dards of reference—Fuji, Ise, Yoshino, Kōya, Tōdaiji, Tōfukuji, Kasuga. Integrating the Kyoto area into a "Japanese" framework that readers are meant to share, the author assumes popular custody of "the land of the gentlemen."

Certainly, much in Ekiken's guide recalls the two Brocades. There, too, a vast historyscape of old graves and old things and old places is laid before the reader. There, too, anonymous crowds of newcomers and strangers are accorded a seeming freedom of entry into ritual sites. There, too, limitless places of note, which become almost synonymous with the cityscape itself, hold disparate lures for worshippers, sightseers, pleasure seekers, shoppers, and crowd followers. But with their many inventories reassembled from many sources, Koshōshi's Brocades take the measure of the city while leaving obscure the access of ordinary people to it. His lists—of historical features, landmarks, temples and shrines—may simply be lists. Do they constitute an urban encyclopedia or an urban guide?

What is murky in the Brocades becomes clear in the Excellent Views. And the contract between Ekiken and his readers is explicit enough to throw into relief the radical assumptions underlying much of the library of public information. For his part, Ekiken offers authoritative guidance to a big landscape that the public can enter at will. He confirms the fact of access as a precondition of the entire enterprise of travel. He also detaches access from particularistic motives, allowing "pleasure seekers" an open range of activity. And he detaches access from social qualifications as well, presuming for "ordinary people" the privileges accorded elites. One qualification is nonetheless indispensable. From his readers, Ekiken demands not just seeing but informed seeing. Cultural custody is exchanged for cultural literacy. The freedom of the traveler is yoked to the discipline of knowledge.

The modern reader is likely to feel vertiginous leaps between elementary and sophisticated levels of discourse throughout the Excellent Views. Ekiken tells his audience when to wake up, how to follow directions, what to eat, where to catch a ferry. He glosses even the simplest characters phonetically, withholds even the most modest challenges grammatically. Never, though, does he explain a name or a term. The ordinary people who take up his solicitous text are expected to know many things.

They are meant, for example, to know dozens of names of emperors, empresses, princes, monks, priests, nuns, military rulers, generals, writers, artists, dancers, tea masters, and scholars. They are meant to know the names of provinces, cities, major rivers, and mountain passes. They are meant to know important historical events and the era names of imperial reigns. They are meant to know aristocratic and clerical titles, the names of sects and deities, the ranking system of Zen monasteries, and the vocabulary of religious architecture and iconography. They are meant to know the titles of significant literary works. Even if Kyoto's sites are unfamiliar, they are meant to know the many famous places across the country to which these sites are regularly compared, from Kōya to Kasuga. And, of course, they are meant to know basic trees, flowers, birds, and insects.

Most of the texts I have discussed require implicitly high levels of cultural fluency. Still, we might well imagine a consumer of the Brocades or the Fabric or the Military Mirrors skipping among sections to select out material immediately useful and easy to decode. In the Excellent Views, the demands are so pervasive as to make the text near useless without good grounding in the nomenclature. Certainly, travelers could speed by unfamiliar references or turn to local people for help. It was doubtless the rare user of the guide who absorbed its information effortlessly. The text nonetheless sketches assumptions about common knowledge that construct quite a particular kind of reader. The impersonal "you" whom Ekiken addresses as an audience ("'you' should get up early," "'you' should see the main hall") is not just any competent reader who buys or borrows books. This "you" is one of "our people" who knows enough of "our country" to undertake the responsibility of the road. This "you" is the new collectivity of knowledge that binds together an otherwise centrifugal society of consumers and strangers.

Ekiken's text acknowledges the freedoms so conspicuous in the urban literature. His readers are mobile and solitary. They travel voluntarily as spectators and enter crowds anonymously as a public. They buy food and lodgings and advice in a well-developed market geared to consumption. They experience, at least on the road, a social leveling at odds with any status system. They belong not to a *Gemeinschaft* of integral communities but to a *Gesellschaft* of money and voyeurs, opportunity and taste. But to tame freedoms with obligation, Ekiken's text also imagines the bond of peoplehood. It is founded not on a specific social or a political system, not on a religious creed, not on an overt contrast to or anxiety over some alien, other people. It is founded on the ordinary "you" who commands common information about "our country" and then claims that country through experience. The new collectivity is founded on a mindful piety toward the land.

Throughout his career, Ekiken remained, above all, a teacher. Both a schoolmaster and a writer of educational texts for children, he was absorbed by ethical formation and its linkages to practical learning. And while the Excellent Views may seem an almost frivolous digression from his philosophical and scientific work, it cuts to his core interest in cultivating the human heart through the observation of nature, the study of the past, and sympathetic encounter with all persons.[16] But precisely because he was a sleepless pedagogue, the assumptions about cultural literacy in his guide may seem ambitiously inflated. What is most interesting, though, is their convergence with the curriculum of mundane reference works.

—

The reference text I carried on my own travels with Ekiken was *Banmin chōhōki* (Everybody's Treasury), published anonymously in two fat fascicles in 1692.[17] It belongs to an enormous genre of instructional books, most of them just beyond the level of school primers, that addressed adolescent and adult audiences seeking general as well as more specialized learning. Although elastic, the genre centers on texts known as *setsuyōshū, kinmōzui,* and *chōhōki*. The *setsuyōshū* are dictionaries, ranging from elementary to erudite, that typically group words according to the categories of Chinese encyclopedias (such as cosmology, geography, anatomy, clothing, tools, animals, birds, fish, insects, and the like). Because many came to feature long and longer supplements—on political geography, society, history, and etiquette—they resemble desk encyclopedias.[18] So, too, the *kinmōzui,* or "illustrated lexicons for the ignorant," combine several functions by providing detailed glosses, both verbal and pictorial, of specific vocabularies. What I call the Illustrated Encyclopedia of Humanity *(Jinrin kinmōzui),* for example, defines almost 500 types of work and workers in nine general categories. Similar lexicons disaggregate and define the nomenclature of individual arts, professions, and avocations (such as the pursuit of pleasure in the brothel quarter). They consequently expand from word lists into pedagogical surveys of their subjects.[19] The *chōhōki,* finally, are "treasuries" that assemble information on diverse themes in topical form. Many cover a particular skill—such as letter writing, calligraphy, poetic composition, the conduct of the tea ceremony, healing practices, child raising, cooking, geomancy, or spell casting—in simple, systematic, and heavily illustrated style. Many others cover a variety of skills pertinent to a particular group—such as young men, young women, newlyweds, and housewives. Still others, like Everybody's Treasury, serve as more or less universal digests of more or less indispensable common wisdom.[20]

Despite the sometimes considerable differences between the texts, the dictionaries and illustrated lexicons and treasuries address a great many similar topics. At least as a foundation, moreover, they tend to repackage a standard body of knowledge. Its contours are sketched by the contents of Everybody's Treasury:

1. *Summary of the Emperors of Nihon.* One hundred fourteen genera-tions, from Jinmu to the incumbent, each identified by number, name, father, and birth order; each placed in time by counting the to-tal number of years separating his or her accession from the accession of Jinmu *and* the total number of years separating his or her accession from the near-present (Genroku 4, 1691, the year before the publica-tion of the text).

2. *The Palace.* A list of leading members of the current imperial house-hold.

3. *The Investitures of the Nobility.* A list of eight members of the regental houses (*sekke*) and one hundred fourteen members of the next-highest-ranking aristocratic houses (*seiga*), each identified by name and the value of his official vestiture (covering a range for the *sekke* of 2,043 to 1,500 *koku* and for the *seiga* of 1,355 to 30 *koku*).

4. *The Abbots of the Imperial, Regental, and High Noble Houses.* A list of princely and noble abbots (and one abbess), who are identified by sect, temple, title, name, and investiture.

5. *The Five Mountains.* Lists of the (putatively) five major Zen monas-teries in India, China, Kyoto, and Kamakura, as well as a list of the five major Zen convents in Japan (with the addition of a sixth, super-numerary monastery—Nanzenji—in the case of Kyoto).

6. *Court Offices.* An outline with phonetic readings and glosses of roughly 200 aristocratic offices and titles.

7. *The Annual Ritual Calendar.* A list by month and day of over 400 annual events, principally religious ceremonies held in Kyoto.

8. *Meeting Dates for Various Artistic Gatherings.* A list of the monthly dates, places, and sponsors for gatherings of groups pursuing the arts of linked verse, *haikai,* noh chanting, flower arrangement, kickball, the board games of *go* and *shōgi,* and archery.

9. *Account of the Holders of Famous Objects Used in the Tea Ceremony.* A list in twenty-two categories of several hundred renowned items—tea caddies, tea bowls, whisks, censers, scrolls, and the like—which are identified by their own names, the names of the men who own or owned them, and sometimes their historical provenance.

10. *Linking Conventions in Verse.* A discussion of the rules governing opening and succeeding stanzas in the contemporary practice of linked verse.

11. *A Convenient Guide to the Extended Almanac.* A twelve-year almanac, covering the years equivalent to 1692–1703, which includes such information as the place of the year in the sexagenary cycle, the incidence of long, short, and intercalary months, the dates of winter solstices and the intervening solar time markers (*sekki* and *chūki*) between them.

12. *A Brief Record of the Imperial Era Names of the True Dynasty (Honchō).* A list of 222 successive era names in use in Japan from the time of their adoption during the reign of the thirty-seventh emperor ("1,005 years after the accession of Emperor Jinmu") until the near-present (Genroku 4), with notes on incumbent monarchs, the date in the sexagenary cycle when each era name was selected, the numbers of years intervening between its selection and the near-present, and the dual era names used during the period of the Southern and Northern Courts.

13. *Record of Military Leaders.* A numbered list of thirty-six successive martial rulers, from Minamoto no Yoritomo to Tokugawa Tsunayoshi, in each case with notes on his father and birth order, the number of years he held power, his death date and age, his posthumous titles, and other details.

14. *The Provinces, with Notes on Daimyo, Castles, and Productivity.* A list of sixty-three of the provinces (unaccountably omitting Awaji, Iga, Izu, Noto, and Satsuma), indicating in each case the names of local daimyo castellans (a total of 202), the names of their castle towns, and the registered productivity of their domains.

15. *The Provinces of Nihon, with Notes on Productivity.* A list of all sixty-eight provinces (including the often omitted islands of Iki and Tsushima), which records individual productivity figures and then concludes with summaries: for example, total national productivity, over 22 million *koku;* total provinces, 68; total districts, 604; total villages, 908,868; total paddy, 90,047,801 *chō;* total shrines, 27,700.

16. *Orthography in Classical Verse.* Detailed guidance concerning the use of the phonetic syllabary (*kanazukai*) in Japanese poetry (*waka*), including correct character choices when declining adjectives and conjugating verbs.

17. *A Dictionary for the Ages.* Lists of several thousand words, in Chinese characters with phonetic readings, grouped into nine categories: miscellaneous, trees and grasses, fish and birds, insects, animals, humans, anatomy, injuries and illnesses, and food.

18. *The Names of the East-West Streets of Kyoto.* A list of forty-eight street names, organized from north to south.

19. *The Names of the North-South Streets of Kyoto.* A list of thirty-one street names, organized from east to west, followed by brief notes on the history of the capital and classical topography.

20. *Distances to Various Places.* A list of distances from Kyoto to twenty-four nearby locations.

21. *The Seven Highways of Kyoto.* A list of the major roads leading in and out of the imperial capital, with notes on important sites along the way.

22. *The Highway to Edo with Current Portage Rates.* A list of the fifty-three stations of the Tōkaidō, originating in Kyoto, with notes on the distances between stops and the rates for porters, animals, and ship transport.

23. *Chinese Measures* (Tōshaku). A guide to everyday divination, derived from classical Chinese measures.

24. *The Production Stages for Long and Short Swords.* A brief outline of the smelting and forging process (arranged under the categories of "wood, fire, water, earth, and metal").

25. *Poems on the Eight Views of China.* Poems in both Chinese and Japanese, with illustrations, concerning one of the major tropes of East Asian painting: the eight views of the Rivers Hsiao and Hsiang.

26. *Poems on the Eight Views of Ōmi.* Poems in both Chinese and Japanese, with illustrations, concerning one of the major tropes of Japanese painting: the eight views of Lake Biwa in Ōmi province.

Stitched together from disparate sources according to the taste and opportunity of the compiler, the entries of Everybody's Treasury have a comfortable motley quality. Catalogues of tea booty interrupt catalogues of rulers; a selection of topographical poems concludes lists of topographical data. The compiler neither bullies his readers with an arch narrative that insists on the importance of the information nor focuses single-mindedly on any particular curriculum. He likes a certain sprawl, which makes the Treasury appear just that—a depository of facts, rich but random, for curious seekers of knowledge. Still, the text is orderly enough to convey a pedantic purpose.

Aside from the twelve-year almanac, the compiler dodges what we might consider practical intelligence. We find here no tables of weights and measures, no information on currency exchange rates or rice prices or rainfall or bureaucratic routines (concerning applications for travel papers, for example) or the like. The data that does appear useful, moreover, is too sketchy to matter much. Anyone who really wanted to navigate Kyoto's streets or the Tōkaidō highway, say, could find much better guidance elsewhere. Indeed, anyone absorbed by any of the Treasury's topics—from aristocratic organization to poetic composition—could explore the library of public information for far fuller treatments. Hence the text declares itself as an overview, neither immediately utilitarian nor especially thorough, of the general knowledge available to "everybody" (literally, "the myriad people"). And while the entries may jolt in sequence and wander in focus, their consistency in emphasis also suggests a presumption about the general knowledge expected of "everybody." The Treasury attends to institutional structures on the one hand and to conventional civility on the other. Its readers are meant to care about both the social form and the social practice that organize the place variously named Nihon and Honchō.

The institutional entries tend to cluster around four intersecting subjects: the court (items 1, 2, 3, 4, 6); the historical and current military establishment (13, 14); the geographical scene (15, 18, 19, 20, 21, 22); and the calendar (7, 11, 12). These are big subjects and, given the directions of the information culture, reasonably obvious ones for a basic reference work. To a remarkable extent, the coverage also reflects Kaibara Ekiken's presumptions about the domain of common knowledge. If the Treasury occasionally disappointed me when I wanted help with the references in the Excellent Views, it usually held up. Here Ekiken's readers could find clerical and aristocratic titles, era names and a lucid dating system, the rank order of Zen monasteries, the geographical basics, the names of all past and present rulers, and (in the dictionary) a good sample of challenging terms. Aside from its considerable reference value, though, the Treasury inevitably tells its own stories about "Japan." And some of them are surprising.

One story, borrowed from national cartography, concerns the integrity of the whole. This sense is most vivid in item 15, where the compiler breaks Nihon into circuits and provinces only to recover, beyond all local divisions, a series of national totals. The country embraces 908,868 villages, which produce annual harvests valued at over 22 million *koku*. Its people work about 90,000,000 *chō* of paddy and worship at 27,700 shrines.[21] Yet the integrity conveyed by these large (and dubious) figures is a leitmotif throughout the entries. Daimyo and their castle towns become subsets of comprehensive provincial tallies. The imperial era names mark the time not of a house but of a universal dominion (Honchō). The ritual calendar belongs to everyman rather than a specific body of nobles or martial lords. As if to sharpen the profile of a national collectivity, the compiler also introduces the occasional contrast to foreign worlds. Thus the ranking Zen monasteries of Kyoto and Kamakura, which cap a domestic hierarchy of Rinzai temples, are juxtaposed against their putative counterparts in China and (in an artful leap) in India as well. Poems in both Chinese and Japanese concerning eight fabled views of China's landscape are followed by poems in both Chinese and Japanese concerning eight fabled views of Japan's landscape. If these entries imply certain international filiations in culture, they insist on national variation. They also convert the local sites of lake and monastery into corporate symbols of an "us."

In their rarity, the foreign allusions of the Treasury draw attention to the text's preoccupation with this "us," a body evoked not only through images of the whole but in appeals to time. Focused on court and shogunate, the institutional interests of the compiler zoom in on succession. One hundred fourteen generations of human emperors and thirty-six generations of military leaders link the present to the past. Unsatisfied with the generational count alone, however, the compiler keeps calculating years—both backward and forward—in an exceptional effort to track linear time. The first emperor, Jinmu, we are told, ascended the throne 2,352 years before the present. The current emperor ascended the throne 2,347 years after Jinmu and 5 years before the present. Similarly, moving toward the middle of the list, the fiftieth emperor (Kanmu) ascended the throne 1,442 years after Jinmu and 910 years before the present. The sixtieth emperor Daigo ascended the throne 1,558 years after Jinmu and 794 years before the present.[22]

The compiler does include in a separate list all the imperial era names used, since the equivalent of 645 C.E., to date time in Nihon. But there again he appends calculations that were never part of the official calendar and rarely a matter of informal practice. Thus, for example, he tells readers that the Taihō period began in the fifth year of Emperor Monmu's reign and 991 years before the present (the equivalent of 701 C.E.). The Kenmu period began with the accession of Emperor Go-Daigo, 358 years before the present (the equivalent of 1336 C.E.). These ubiquitous glosses acknowledge the near impossibility of keeping in mind over 200 era names, let alone their duration and sequence. More to the point, they insist on the linear conception of time missing from an official dating system that lacked alpha or omega markers.

The effect is to bring genealogy into history. The decision entailed problems, of course, since it exposed the fault lines in the early imperial tree: quite a few of the first sixteen monarchs have implausibly long reigns and lifetimes. After holding the throne for over a century, for example, the sixth emperor appears to have passed power to a natural son who held the throne for seventy-six years. But if any luster is lost in these disclosures, it is recouped by the demonstrable longevity in rule of the forebears' collective progeny: misty origins give way to a historical succession traceable not only in names and generations but in countable years following one on the next. The interest of the compiler in historicity is confirmed, moreover, by biographical notes. Emperors are identified by their fathers and birth order; military leaders by fathers, birth order, the duration of their tenures, ages at death, and numerous other details. Again, something may be lost— first of all any presumption that power passed predictably and without trouble from incumbent to heir. Particularly apparent in the handling of military rulers is a cold-blooded candor that situates men remorselessly in crisis. And it carries a complex message about the long past invoked by the Treasury.

Readers find, for instance, that the fourth leader of the shogunate founded by Minamoto no Yoritomo was an eight-year-old aristocrat from the Kujō house who was transported from Kyoto to Kamakura and inducted into office (after some months' hiatus) following the assassination of the third shogun and the end of Yoritomo's line. The "Record of Military Leaders" also records the diversion of shogunal succession from Kujō scions to imperial princes; the delegation of shogunal prerogatives to deputies in the Hōjō house; and the replacement of both princes and deputies by new men from the Ashikaga lineage. They, too, faced assassination, nonlineal succession ordeals, and final collapse. The last Ashikaga, the Treasury tells us, was inducted into office and then deposed by Oda Nobunaga who, following fifteen generations and 239 years of Ashikaga hegemony, succeeded to martial dominion. Nobunaga lasted for ten years before mortal attack. His heir lasted for three years before usurpation by Toyotomi Hideyoshi. And Hideyoshi lasted for fifteen years, including the nominal tenure of a nephew he condemned to death. The five-year-old son who succeeded him lasted for eighteen years until an unexplained suicide at the age of twenty-three. Next, and thirty-second in the line of military rulers, appears Tokugawa Ieyasu. Depending on how you look at it, the

Treasury points out, Ieyasu ruled for either two years (his tenure as shogun) or fourteen (his tenure as both active and retired shogun). In any case, those years overlapped with the putative ascendancy of Hideyoshi's heir—whose end, even the dimmest reader must conclude, was not voluntary. The Tokugawa succession appears uneventful in the Treasury, unless the reader accurately detects trouble in the count of Ieyasu's term and the need in several cases to elevate younger sons to shogunal office.[23]

The Treasury's account of imperial succession is not quite so candid. But even there the identification of a monarch's father and birth order intimates persistent volatility in accession politics. Thus, for example, the catalogue of emperors reveals that two competitive lines provided emperors, in alternation, for fifty and more years. It conceals the eventual war between them, and the maintenance of two rival courts for six decades, by listing only the emperors of the "northern" line who resided in Kyoto. The reader nonetheless discovers the crisis in the list of era names (item 12), which acknowledges the prolonged use of different calendars (each recorded) by dual monarchs (each named) in two imperial centers (Yoshino as well as Kyoto).[24]

In his brief and formulaic accounts of emperors and military leaders, the compiler of the Treasury cannot convey at all fully (even were he inclined to do so) the tortured course of power. Yet there is enough truth-telling in his time lines and biographical details to alter the character of the simple genealogical lists normally found in primers, gazetteers, urban directories, and the like. The basic plot survives: very long chains of rulers have exercised authority for at least a millennium (in the case of the throne) or four centuries (in the case of the military). By historicizing that plot, however, the compiler makes succession an ongoing achievement of will, fraught with violence and negotiation, which enters into a national life; for the actors are many and the outcomes dynamic. Succession emerges, in effect, as a continuing story of the "us" who constitute not just a target of genealogical edification but a party to consequential struggles. And the names in the chains emerge as historical players worth knowing, not just jumbled syllables in a family mantra.

Unlike the *Kan'ei shoka keizuden* (Genealogies of the Houses of the Kan'ei Period), the foundational text produced by the Tokugawa shogunate, Everybody's Treasury includes no preface that tells readers what to think. Thus while the official account describes the commotion of history in the past only to claim a transcendence of history in the present, the compiler of the Treasury lets audiences go ahead and imagine more commotion. He appears more interested in the resilience that makes Nihon cohere than the metanarrative that ossifies it. He is also interested in the disparate sources of resilience. Whatever the investment of Tokugawa (and imperial) genealogists in their own stories, the Treasury compiler has a supple investment in a Nihon with multiple centers of value.

His institutional material itself is complex. Clearly, for him, the throne occupies the paramount place in the national calculus of meaning. The list of emperors leads the Treasury's inventories, followed by accounts of current palace occupants, the incumbent heads of noble houses, and princely abbots and abbesses. The compiler also throws in a daunting list of aristocratic titles, no doubt because he had easy access to the data.[25] The nurturing of a popular consciousness of courtly anatomy is nonetheless arresting. Inducting common readers into once esoteric knowledge and hence projecting to them something like a real and living nobility, the compiler seems to invoke an at least latent loyalty to the throne. Still, the court remains only one part of a national entity that includes both the central shogunal administration and local daimyo governing from over two hundred castle towns (item 14). These structures of rule operate, moreover, within a cultural geography of circuits, provinces, and districts, which are detached from and antecedent to contemporary political administration.

In a departure from the model of the Military Mirrors, Everybody's Treasury subsumes the daimyo under the provinces. Space comes first. Perhaps to emphasize the autonomous integrity of the spatial order, the Treasury names the provinces twice: first to situate the domainal system, second to frame the account of rural productivity (item 15). The production figures—together with total counts of villages and paddy acreage—layer a geography of agrarian wealth onto a geography of ancient names to fuse Nihon with its human and physical resources. This Nihon is, moreover, a land of dense religious and ceremonial life, one intimated by the entry on Zen monastic institutions and the reference to 27,700 local shrines, but evoked most clearly by the annual ritual calendar. A prodigious sampler of rituals rather than a guide to any uniform national practice, the calendar represents (like its counterparts in the Kyoto Brocade and the Dappled Fabric of Edo) a sphere of open encounter, loosed from status or employment or residence, where participants form elective communities. Critically, this sphere of freedom is created by diffuse religious activities, not by anything resembling statist or political festivals. Not here are shogunal processions or imperial birthdays or daimyo commemorations. The time of the year, no less than the space of production, organizes a Nihon separable from superstructures.

Thus in its inventories of institutional data, Everybody's Treasury associates general knowledge with disparate nodes of meaning—a dynamic history, multiple tiers of rule, a cultural and economic geography, a religious and ritual life. The whole is not one-dimensional or monochromatic. Nor it is constructed only of institutions; for the compiler's attention to the arts puts social civility close to social structure in his curricular hierarchy. Punctuating the Treasury's institutional data are sections on artistic gatherings (item 8), tea objects (9), linked verse (10), classical verse (16), lexical proficiency (17), and topographical poetry (25 and 26). Why in the world are such sections included?

Readers familiar with other Treasuries might have found the entries predictable, since much of the genre focuses on handy instruction in the polite arts. The texts teach board games, for instance, and flower arrangement, decorative gardening, and painting. But absolutely fundamental, to judge from their converging emphases, is some proficiency in calligraphy, letter writing, gift giving, poetry, and tea. The subjects of numerous specialized texts, these five practices are also at the core of the generalized Treasuries that cover multiple bases for audiences of young men, young women, and housewives. Any aspirant to basic cultivation, the texts suggest, really must know how to wield a brush, write a letter and fold and address it correctly, compose a proper poem with apt seasonal allusions, offer the right gift on the right occasion with a suitable presentation, and both serve and receive tea in an acceptable fashion.[26] The rules are rugged. Form is crucial. The promise is social competence. And the promise extends to anyone ready for the everyday disciplines of everyday arts.

Not surprisingly, tutors in the fundamental arts made up the better part of urban teaching establishments. And the paraphernalia for these arts made up a fair part of urban trade. Shops teamed with fine papers, poem cards, brushes, ink, inkstones, ornaments for gifts (stands, ribbons, paper flowers), the gifts themselves (good fish, exquisite cakes, almost every kind of sake), and the stuff of the tea ceremony (caddies, bags for the caddies, bowls, whisks, water holders, censers, vases, trays, artworks). Marketers of education collaborated with marketers of goods to convert the luxury consumption offensive to authorities into acts of decorum and discrimination.[27]

But if the artistic entries in Everybody's Treasury conform to the expectations of the genre and prevailing directions in educated taste, they also orient artistic learning in a far broader context than personal improvement. Mixing lists of tea objects with lists of rulers, the compiler lifts culture from the domain of enrichment to the domain of requisite national knowledge. Certain forms of civility, no less than generative institutions and geographies, appear inherent in the construction of Nihon.

There is a seeming combination of opportunism and calculation in the compiler's choices. He may have included "The Meeting Dates of the Various Arts" (which comes straight out of a Kyoto directory)[28] simply because the section provides a clever bridge between the previous entry (concerning the *dates* of annual rituals) and the succeeding entry (concerning the *art* of tea). Yet the entry makes an equally clever, marvelously economical statement about artistic practice: it is diverse (ranging from poetry to kickball, noh chanting to archery); pursued by amateur groups who gather once or twice a month according to published schedules; and worth knowing about. No matter that the meetings occur in Kyoto and probably involve an inner circle. Readers anywhere become familiar with the principle of artistic sociability.

And, in the list of tea objects, they become familiar with the principle of artistic competition. Standard fare in any number of urban directories and gazetteers, the list reappears throughout the library of public information as a seemingly captivating piece of entertainment.[29] Its appeal surely derives, in part, from the singling out of treasures that bear famous names and fabled histories. But the appeal is compounded by the connection of fabulous objects to the powerful men said to own them—including, distantly, the Ashikaga shogun, and, more recently, the Tokugawa collaterals of Owari, Kii, and Mito, the daimyo of dozens of domains, and, occasionally, the heads of great merchant houses. However out of date, the list appeals to a timeless curiosity by identifying both the things men covet and the men who obtain coveted things. In that conjunction, the Treasury also links taste to value, ambition to discrimination, private cultivation to public performance, and inert matter to the transformative recognition of connoisseurs who know how to give things life.

When he turns to the next subjects on his artistic list, the compiler actually takes on skill itself, using abridged versions of introductory poetry manuals to acquaint readers with the rules for composing linked verse as well as the thirty-one syllable poems (*waka*) at the heart of the classical poetic tradition. The entries cover the principles of prosody—syllabic meter, lexical and syntactic choice, the balance between upper and lower stanzas, the scope of prescribed imagery, for example—in sufficient detail to enable both informed reading of verse and technically accurate writing. They also suggest in their specificity that poetic composition is the prime expression of cultural competence, too important for mere glancing treatment even in a summary of general knowledge. A certain logocentrism is reinforced by the dictionary, appearing right after the section on classical verse, which addresses an essentially learned, Sinophilic, and antiquarian vocabulary. Described as a lexicon of the "myriad ages," the entry assigns words a role similar to generational continuity: they bind succeeding ages insofar as antecedents remain known and honored. Mastery of them provides access to old texts; continued invocation of them prevents the erosion of cultural legacies. Finally, the concluding entries in Everybody's Treasury make a synoptic statement about the arts and the nation. Having opened his text with a list of the emperors, the compiler closes it by evoking the space of Nihon—juxtaposed against the space of Kara/China—through pictures and poems. Knowledge of this space, and fit description of it, spreads beyond institutions to works of artistic invention.

Everybody's Treasury focuses less emphatically than other texts in the genre on basic tutelage. There are no lessons here on letter writing and gift giving and brush handling and the like. Yet the attention to active poetic skill, and the presumption of at least passive familiarity with other cultural practices, puts civility squarely into the equation of common learning. The forms of that civility—classical verse, linked verse, tea, and the "various arts" mentioned in the list of "meeting dates"—belonged to elite, venerable, and often esoteric traditions. Significant as their translation into a popular arena, however, is their representation as living arts that belong to contemporary and sociable practice. Instead of offering a digest of great old poems, the compiler offers a digest of rules for writing new ones. Instead of listing tea objects alone, he links things to the collectors who invest them with meaning and put them to use. Learning words, gathering in amateur clubs, blending verse into routine correspondence, serving tea—all such activities define a Nihon captured as critically in topographical poetry as in official genealogies and production totals.

——

Early in the eighteenth century, instructional texts came to include works aimed explicitly at status groups. The Confucian scholar Nishikawa Jōken, for example, wrote two bestsellers—*Chōnin bukuro* (The Townsman's Satchel) and *Hyakushō bukuro* (The Farmer's Satchel)—that adjusted practical advice and moral guidance to place in the hierarchy of power.[30] Certainly, the rhetoric and reality of stratification sound throughout much of the library of public information, from the status coding of maps to the status differentiation of personnel directories. But Kaibara Ekiken's tours for "ordinary people" and the Treasury's counsel for "everybody" move with a powerful countercurrent. Nowhere do such texts deny the status order, but neither do they anywhere acknowledge station as inextricable from social definition or instrumental to social learning. Such texts imagine an undifferentiated audience united by national knowledge, motivated by unspoken contracts. Ekiken offers his readers cultural custody of the landscape in exchange for cultural literacy. The compiler of Everybody's Treasury offers membership in the "us" of Nihon to readers invested in both historically grounded institutions and dynamically renewed standards of civility. The social controls of the status order mutate here into the cultural disciplines of education. This ambivalent form of liberation seems characteristically modern, except that the statist component of knowledge remained comparatively small. "Our country" and "our people" were made up of time, place, ritual, poetry, and inkstones. *not really*

challenging power

SEVEN

Nation

I BEGAN THIS BOOK by staking out a temporal boundary. The "library of public information" that took shape after 1600 signifies, for me, a quiet revolution in knowledge—one separating the early modern period from all previous time. In empirically grounded accounts of contemporary, often mundane experience, investigators created from fissured parts an integrally conceived Japan. Commercial publishers also circulated those accounts to open audiences of consumers, who were implicitly entitled to information, familiar with its frames of reference, and invested in self-discovery. Profound changes in the mode and volume of investigation thus entailed no less profound changes in communication.

Produced for the market, the new texts depended for intelligibility on a cultural literacy shared by anonymous readers. By the turn of the eighteenth century, the rudiments of this literacy were coming clear. Disparate material—whether the family encyclopedias that assembled basic learning for "everybody" or the travel guides that assumed such learning among "ordinary people"—outlined a body of knowledge expected of the general reader. This knowledge was emphatically situated in "our country," regularly identified with "our people."

The course of the information revolution bent with its different movers. It started, clearly enough, with the state. Across a landscape stripped by war of medieval tenures, the Toyotomi and Tokugawa regimes used cadastral and cartographic surveys to plot a new union. If gradually and imperfectly, they oversaw the first efforts in Japan to measure, evaluate, and register resources to standard. Then they mapped onto this physical foundation a consistent political geography. The results were immediately practical; for the surveys enabled penetrating changes in relations of power (the systematic investiture of daimyo, the separation of classes, and the conversion of samurai into urban salarymen). The results were broadly ideological as well; for the surveys both enacted and gave graphic form to Nihon as a whole made intelligible through inclusive conventions. Not least important, the surveys inducted large numbers of participants—investigators and investigated alike—into an exemplary logic: social phenomena were amenable to inquiry, knowable through observation, and communicable through taxonomic analysis.

Inveterate record keepers, Tokugawa officials continued to act on these legacies in surveys not only of land but of population and commercial activity.[1] Crucially, though, they tended to treat their data as internal intelligence, never deploying it widely to indoctrinate or mobilize the body of the ruled. A "public" created by the surveys as an object of impersonal scrutiny and aggregate analysis remained, in the eyes of the regime, just that. Hence, in two critical respects, the state ceded control over information to the market. Declining official publication of its own material (whether maps, production figures, transport details, or personnel charts), the state relinquished to commercial printers the circulation as well as the presentation of knowledge. Increasingly relegating its inquiries to routine matters, the state also relinquished to independent investigators the pursuit of new knowledge. The legacies of its revolutionary surveys—indeed, the leadership of the information revolution itself—passed to private enterprise.

The commercial texts that embodied the revolution did hew close to the holistic imagery and conventional lexicon of state cartography. Nihon was a place of castle towns radiating power over the countryside, barriers and post stations dotting official highways, cities zoned by class, and villages defined by registered productivity totals. Implicit in these tropes, and explicit in ubiquitous references to officialdom (shogun, daimyo, bureaucrats, licensed tradespeople), was a state-centered orientation that encouraged the regime's toleration of private publishing. Still, the polity tended to recede as investigators filled the book market with broadly social accounts of everything from agronomy to medicine, rural manufacture to urban trade, historical geography to demimondaine geography. Converting information from a tool of governance into a source of instruction and entertainment, they also converted the "public" from an object of surveillance into a subject of service—an audience with demands to meet, desires to kindle, wealth to spend. And in exploring the reaches of social activity for this audience, writers and publishers not only obscured the primacy of the polity but disturbed its values. The subtle messages of the information library turned on mobility and money: learning of all sorts was accessible; the self could be improved; professional competence mattered; the good society produced and consumed myriad excellent goods; almost anything was for sale; a fascinating world awaited the stranger. In short, a commercial literature put across an economic system of value.[2]

The library of public information was hardly monolithic: it addressed a prolific subject matter, as well as a complex readership, in many voices. It spoke to basic learners with primers and lexicons. It spoke to specialists and connoisseurs of all kinds with accounts of ethnographic and botanical research, say, or poetic and artistic practice. Yet it also filled a middle ground with the perennial texts I have surveyed here—maps, itineraries, personnel rosters, urban and commercial directories, gazetteers, travel guides, family encyclopedias, and the like. And as the referents in these perennials became a standard currency of communication, the information revolution entered a new stage. However disparate their subjects and readers, writers came to assume a core learning—what I call a cultural literacy—that ranged across the history, institutions, and mundane civility of Nihon. They began, too, to conflate cultural literacy with membership in a collectivity conscious of itself—a collectivity, for Kaibara Ekiken, that enjoyed custody over the time-drenched landscape of a shared patrimony. Because it represented a coherent territory and posited a collective people, I have equated this core learning with "national knowledge."

The phrase stirs trouble along another temporal boundary. The genesis of public information may mark a defensible divide between early modernity and previous eras. But by assigning the information revolution a national character, I appear to assail the later, more vigilantly guarded divide between early modernity and modernity proper; for many scholars treat national formation as an invention of the quintessentially modern mind. So now I grapple with the mixed meanings of nation to explore a second temporal frontier: the one separating the early modern from the modern experience.

"Nation" is a protean concept. And nations assume protean forms. Still, scholars examine this variety more readily in space than in time— recognizing multiple versions of the nation across the globe while dating most of them to the rather recent past.[3] In the case of Japan, they usually reserve the concept for the convulsive achievement of the Meiji era: the construction of a centralized constitutional state; the establishment of territorial sovereignty within an international system of states; and the indoctrination of subjects into a patriotic culture.[4] Insofar, then, as we consign Japanese nationhood to the nineteenth century, I court anachronism by imputing national knowledge to the seventeenth.

But labels are heuristic devices, after all, that help organize inquiry rather than hallowing absolutes. By making "nation" a synonym for the modern order, we forfeit its descriptive and comparative utility. At one level, the label sorts variables through definitions (as often as not contentiously) to illumine gross patterns of human association. Implicit in my summary of the Meiji achievement is a prevalent if conservative formulation of the nation that highlights the conjuncture of three elements: "nation" signifies the congruence within a bounded territorial dominion of a paramount state institution and a cultural consciousness of membership.[5] This conjuncture of territory, state, and culture is hardly limited to the Meiji era, however; we also find it in the Nihon of the information library. And the naming of that Nihon as a nation helps clarify the otherwise elusive coherence of the library's new and common subject. It also avoids vacillating substitutes like "proto-nation," which either deflect early modern change into invisibility or make it a precursor of Meiji. Since "proto-nation" implies stages of development connecting incipience to ripeness, the term has the perverse effect of conjoining the histories of the Tokugawa and Meiji periods as necessary complements.

Obviously, though, the two histories followed discrete trajectories. And it is this difference that labels can help clarify as well, for their power is ultimately comparative. Just as definitions of the nation sort variables to illumine a general likeness among cases, they invite scrutiny of those variables to illumine the particular unlikeness among cases. Every nation, distinctively configured of distinctive elements, is peculiar. So, too, early modern Nihon. In stretching the temporal dimension of nationhood, I imply no sameness between the Tokugawa version and its Meiji successor. Nor do I construct a continuous (let alone a precocious) narrative of development. I am interested, rather, in putting historical variants of the nation in tension and thus detecting the differences that loom larger than convergence. So even as I use the national label to separate early modern Japan from its medieval past, I probe the distinctive conjuncture of state/territory/culture that separated early modern Japan from its Meiji future. To withhold from modernity any original or exclusive hold on nationhood is not to deny its awesome, disturbing novelty. The challenge is specifying that novelty without distorting its antecedents.

For orientation to the early modern nation, I turn again to the fiction of Ihara Saikaku, whose parodic account of Oman's family treasure we sampled in chapter 1. My text this time is *Nihon eitaigura* (The Eternal Storehouse of Japan, 1688), a collection of thirty stories about moneymakers, most of them thinly disguised caricatures of real-life contemporaries. We follow here the story of a gallant named Shinroku.[6]

—

Disowned by his wealthy merchant father for profligacy in the brothel quarter, Shinroku hits the road to recoup his fortune and turns a quick profit by peddling the ashes of a dead dog as "burned wolf powder," purportedly a cure for "nervous indigestion." Then he builds what will become fabulous wealth by foisting hand towels on pilgrims at an Edo shrine. He ends happy. "For shrewdness he was considered in a class of his own. People took Shinroku's advice on many matters, and he became a treasured asset in his locality."[7]

Saikaku uses this tale of a swindler's wit as light armature for heavy ornament, mainly the spatial detail of the travelogue. The action starts in Kyoto, Shinroku's home; moves to Fushimi, his first refuge; and continues along several different highways leading to Edo, his destination. The itinerary includes Fuji no Mori (a "famous place" where Shinroku is soaked by snow); Ōkamedani and Kanshuji (post stations where he steals tea and a straw cape); Ono village (where he finds the dog's carcass under a persimmon tree); Otowa hill (where he burns the dog); the Osaka barrier (where he begins fobbing off the wolf powder on fellow travelers); Oiwake (where the Fushimi highway joins the Tōkaidō); and Hatchō (by which point he has realized big gains). Proceeding along the way, Shinroku passes the Seta Bridge, Kusatsu, Mount Kagami, Oiso, and the Fuwa barrier. Then he takes the Mino road to Owari, "hawking his powder around every town and village on the Tōkaidō" until "at last, on the sixty-second day after leaving Kyoto, he arrived at Shinagawa," just outside Edo. Readers are already alert to Shinroku's dual passage through space and time, because, we are told, he had spent New Year's Day enjoying "Uba cakes" in Kusatsu and welcomed spring at Oiso shrine, "its trees white with sacred festoons."

Having gotten his hero to "the great castle town of the shogun," Saikaku indulges in new digressions: Shinroku finds shelter at the gate of Tōkai temple where he overhears the life stories of three fellow miscreants turned beggar. One is a brewer from Tatsuta who had gambled local profits on prospective riches by relocating to the Gofuku ward of Edo, "alongside all the high-class sake stores." But there he was outclassed, and finished off, by dealers in sake from Kōnoike, Itami, Ikeda, and "the long-established, powerful Nara breweries" (which matured their drink in cedar casks). A second beggar, an Edo native, is an "outcast in practice, even if not registered as one with Kuruma Zenshichi's guild," having managed to exhaust a fortune in house rents through extravagance.[8]

A third beggar, a man of Sakai, is described as "past master of a thousand arts." Actually, if we count down Saikaku's list of this character's pursuits, he is past master of seventeen: calligraphy (which he studied under Hirano Chūan); the tea ceremony (studied under Kanamori Sōwa); Chinese verse as well as Chinese prose (studied under Gensei of Fukakusa); two forms of Japanese linked verse, *renga* and *haikai* (studied under Nishiyama Sōin); noh dancing (studied under Kobutake); drumming (studied under Shōda Yoemon); classical Confucian scholarship (studied under Itō Jinsai); courtly kickball (studied under Lord Asukai); chess (studied under Gensai); the koto (studied under Yatsuhashi Kengyō); the flute (studied under Sōsan); chanting for the puppet theater (studied under Uji Kadayū); dancing (studied under Yamatoya no Jinbei); the art of love (studied under the Shimabara courtesan Takahashi); and "revels with boy actors" (studied under Suzuki Heihachi). Alas, this "pleasure-seeker of exquisite refinement" learned nothing of the abacus or the scales and ended up cursing his parents, who "had omitted any instruction in the elements of earning a living."[9]

These recitals done, Saikaku rushes to the finish. Shinroku introduces himself to his fellows; listens to counsel that he should never have come to Edo ("meeting-place for all the sharpest men in Japan"); takes tips on breaking into trade (by burning shell into lime, shredding seaweed, selling hand towels); and, in return for the advice, distributes some of his wolf powder profit. The beggars respond with joy ("Your luck has come!" "You'll make a pile of money as high as Mount Fuji!") and Shinroku turns to the towel trade ("honest work"). Within ten years rumor has it that he is worth five thousand gold pieces.[10]

⸺

Saikaku's fiction is a close cousin of the texts of the information library. It, too, focuses on a contemporary and mundane world—the commonplace here and now of readers. And it, too, observes that world with what appears an empirical exactness. The action of the tales may flout routine, but Saikaku locates his drama in thick physical settings that convey a sense of realism. He names real names, from temples to castles, from urban wards to individual firms. He loads the senses with allusions to cedar-cured sake, wet straw, burning fur, amulets white as late snow or spring plum. He creates recognizable protagonists—declined by age, job, income, and family—who speak real-seeming patois, spend real-seeming money, attend in privies and baths to real-seeming bodies, and deck themselves in real-seeming loincloths and rain capes.

Indeed, such details can overpower plots we might generously describe as perfunctory and characters rarely stretched past one dimension; for the interest in Saikaku's fiction centers on visually and verbally dense vignettes that put character types on display for the entertainment of knowing audiences. In Shinroku's story, the vignettes unfold as picaresque comedy, a rake's progress. In other stories, they convey comedies (and tragedies) of manners—studies in the style (the dress, deportment, diet, conversation) of exemplary protagonists. Yet knowingness itself, exchanged between a writer with virtuoso command of imagery and readers ready to recognize it, is always a source of pleasure; for vignettes remain lifeless unless voyeurs can decode their signs. In the end, the mutually congratulatory play of knowledge between author and audience rivals storytelling as the point of Saikaku's art.

Most of this knowledge mimics the content of standard texts from the information library: commercial maps, family encyclopedias, commercial primers, and urban directories. And much of it in Shinroku's tale turns on geography. A ruined rich boy from straitlaced Kyoto heads for freewheeling Edo, morphing along the way from a "fox with his tale exposed" (at the Fox Shrine in Fushimi) to a titan of wolf powder set on "fresh ideas for trade" (at Tōkaiji, a temple founded by the equally enterprising Tokugawa at Shinagawa, or "Commodity River"). For adepts, Saikaku deploys the place-names of the journey with a verbal bravura—replete with puns, syntactical breaks, poetic reversals, lexical and metaphorical linkages—that makes heady Shinroku's passage from (literally) naked fear to a confidence capable of leading him up a Fuji of fortune. For readers of middling proficiency, he packs in the more familiar literary conventions—litanies of the road (*michiyuki*), seasonal tropes, pivot words, "poem pillows"—that nudge burlesque toward art.[11] But the spine of the tale is a basic list of toponyms presumably familiar to most readers.

The catalogue of names in Shinroku's tale is long, a total of forty-one, and multiplies many times for readers who get through the full text of the Eternal Storehouse. In a near-comprehensive survey of space, Saikaku takes us from Sakata in the snow country of Dewa to Funai in the tropical bay of Bungo; from the whaling harbor of Taiji on the Kii peninsula to the Japan Sea port of Tsuruga in Echizen. En route, he pauses at most of the storied spots of the early modern landscape: for example, the foreign trade entrepôt of Nagasaki, the principal rice exchange at Kitahama, the vista points of Ōmi, the burial grounds of Mount Kōya, and the brothel quarter of Shimabara.

Even savants are unlikely to recognize every name, since delight derives from the author's virtuosity and the audience's surprise. But Saikaku uses a scaffold of social and political geography to permit easy navigation of the text. His space is organized by the official transport system (of highways, barriers, post stations, and ports); the administrative structure (of castle towns, wards, villages, and hamlets); and the cultural conventions (of provinces, famous places, and religious sanctuaries). Presumably versed in this coherent spatial order, readers make out odd references by analogy with what they know.

So, too, they follow the complementary lists of temporal festivities and famous products that lace Saikaku's spatial catalogue. As Shinroku marks the New Year with Uba cakes in Kusatsu and spring with blossom viewing at Oiso shrine, other characters participate in such festivals as Gion, Tenma, Mizuma, Bon, and Buddha's birthday. As Shinroku's tale alludes to Nara sake, other tales allude to Sugiwara paper, Ueda pongee, Nishijin brocade, Tango yellow fish, Ise crustaceans, Sakai firearms, Yodo carp, and Ōtsu needles. Not infrequently, Saikaku inventories the noteworthy firms that deal in noteworthy products—the individual timber merchants of Edo, say, or the cotton merchants of Yamato. In a tour of Osaka rice brokerages, he runs down all the concerns in the area of Nakanoshima: the houses of Oka, Hizenya, Kiya, Fukaeya, Higoya, Shioya, Ōtsukaya, Kuwanaya, Kōnoikeya, Kamiya, Binzenya, Uwajimaya, Tsukaguchiya, and Yodoya.[12] Alternatively, Saikaku inventories the specialties of individual urban neighborhoods. Thus one of his narrators marvels, following a fire in Edo, at the swift recovery of the drapers of Honchō, the silk firms of Tenma ward, the paper merchants of Sakuma ward, the fish dealers of Funa ward, the rice dealers of Kome-gashi, the lacquer wholesalers of Amadana, the sandal makers of Furetere ward, and the silversmiths of Shirogane ward.[13]

This attention to employments recurs in Saikaku's sketches of individual characters, for jobs figure first in social anatomy. Saikaku numbers among his moneymakers dozens of different workers: tea peddlers, harpooners, textile stencillers, lathers of mulberry wood, and traders in everything from fans to lobsters. And when he turns in other collections of stories to the samurai, he delivers a full spectrum of magistrates, councillors, guardsmen, pages, and masterless "men of the waves."[14] Jobs identified, Saikaku declines his characters by what they own and how they cultivate themselves. Their better possessions include any variety of old and new luxuries (porcelains, scrolls and screens, lacquer, rare plants, and rare woods) but tend to concentrate on clothing (of sharkskin, fur, crepe, damask, velvet, satin, pongee, or figured silk, variously dyed, tinted, painted, embroidered, and flecked with precious metals and stones). Their cultivations tend to replay the long repertoire of arts pursued by Shinroku's new acquaintance, the complete aesthete from Sakai. Character after character, "often a humble clerk," rises in the world and then "acquires the elements of Chinese and Japanese verse composition, kickball, archery, the koto, the flute, the drums, incense blending, and the tea ceremony, and by associating with the best people . . . even loses his vulgarities of speech."[15]

Such gleeful lists interrupt the action as virtually parallel plots. Pitched to aficionados, they also take in a general audience schooled in the tropes—and the endless inventories—of the information library. Sometimes Saikaku dips verbatim into that library: the diversions of the Sakai aesthete mimic too closely for mistake the catalogues of artistic endeavor in urban directories (down to the identification of real-life master teachers). Yet throughout his work Saikaku rehearses the well-established categories of gazetteers and the like to limn a field of common knowledge: social and political geography, the ritual and festival calendar, famous products and manufactures, the range of human employment and specialization, the notable forms of luxury consumption and artistic cultivation.

In short, Saikaku expects his readers to know many things. Like Kaibara Ekiken's *Keijō shōran* (The Excellent Views of Kyoto), discussed in chapter 6, Saikaku's fiction presumes cultural literacy—a framework of references that orient readers in a recognizable and shared world. The content of this literacy varies somewhat from Saikaku's tales to Ekiken's guides to the family treasuries to other commercial texts. But the overlap remains arresting enough to expose the conventions that make space legible and variety intelligible. In the hands of popular writers, the reference matter of the information library mutates into a standard currency of communication. It enables the easy, telegraphic conversation of Saikaku's characters (on the order of "I did well enough selling the local sake in Tatsuta but couldn't make it against the Nara vendors in Gofuku ward"). It binds his anonymous readerships (who can laugh at overdoses of tea training or mind-numbing numbers of rice brokers). The impersonal scrutiny of the investigator becomes the collective self-scrutiny of a narrator.

Thus linked in content and purpose, the cultural literacy presumed by an Ekiken or a Saikaku also shares a defining premise: it unites an elective and elastic community of knowledge forged by ambition and opportunity. If particularistic attributes (of birth, station, sex, age, and residence) influence opportunity, they do not construct the audiences authors project as "ordinary people" or "everybody" or a corporate "you" who share the writer's elevated vantage point. Nor do they prepare audiences for outlooks that are resolutely panoramic. Ekiken's guides cover the big space and big time of many actors and activities. Saikaku's stories cover a bigger space and a nearly complete range of contemporary roles. From snow country to tropical harbors, from whalers to money lenders, the Eternal Storehouse blankets too much material to encompass by any specific, ascriptive formation. The texts appeal, instead, to the general knowledge of a general readership—one that needs to know many things broadly but none very deeply. Ekiken assumes familiarity with monastic building types but not architectural fine points; literary classics but not arcane manuscripts; flowering trees but not tropical grasses; renowned Buddhist teachers but not obscure abbots. Saikaku trips lightly over myriad facets of work without worrying about the mechanics of the futures market, the hybridization of rice, the exchange rates of precious metals, the techniques for lathing zelkova, the handling of the pike and the halberd. Ekiken and Saikaku operate at the level of the illustrated lexicons and compendia of the information library. And they posit mixed audiences, say of cloth merchants from Sakai and samurai guards from Kanazawa, ready to comprehend experience (the history of a Kyoto temple, the enterprises of a Japan Sea port) across boundaries.

Now to the question: do those mixed audiences and crossed boundaries signify a nation?

TERRITORY

Saikaku's title *Nihon eitaigura* (Eternal Storehouse of Japan) resonates with other titles we have encountered—*Kyō habutae* (Kyoto Brocade) and *Edo kanoko* (Dappled Fabric of Edo), for example. Here, again, a whole, now Japan, is an array, now a storehouse, of parts that retain their specificity. Shinroku takes no allegorical journey across a featureless, composite landscape. His path is a matter of forty-one named places, changing food and festivals, snow-heavy pines and leafless persimmon trees, companions savvy about cedar-cured sake from Nara and high-ranking courtesans from Shimabara. Indeed, throughout the Storehouse, Saikaku steeps every locale in color. Nagasaki is a crowded import market teeming with "Chinese textiles, medicinal herbs, sharkskin, and tea implements of every kind"; Ōtsu is a "shipping port for the northern provinces," where "girls from the Shibaya quarter are summoned to provide entertainment for the brokers' clients at all hours of the day and night."[16] Throughout the Storehouse, Saikaku also attaches every character to a home. We learn the origins of the beggars at Tōkai temple, the merchants who buy boxes at fancy noh performances in Kyoto.[17] Shinroku himself is no blank slate. He may reinvent himself in Edo, but we know just where he came from and how he got there.

It is not just the imagery of his title, then, that links Saikaku's landscape to the space of the information library; for both geographies are simultaneously sprawling and particular. The Edo of the Dappled Fabric spills in exhausting categories across a huge terrain, but always with an emphasis on detail: the names of neighborhoods, the addresses and trades of shopkeepers, the miracle stories of temples, lore about famous wells. The Kyoto suburbs of Ekiken's Excellent Views fill seventeen days of methodical hikes, but always to reveal novelty: the graves of individual luminaries, the haunts of exceptional fireflies, the icons of rare size or antiquity, the forests of strange rocks. In these and other texts of the information library, nothing is deprived of distinction. Little is left out without regret. And hardly anything is sorted by importance. As the regular rearrangement of the urban directories foils notions of urban hierarchy, so the topographical orientation of Ekiken's tours foils any singling out of top spots. Saikaku follows suit. His tales lurch from site to site, in a sequence more poetic than geographical. And if he tends to make Edo a magnet (here "all the provinces rub shoulders"), he offers casual praise (usually flavored with salt) of most places. So, for example, Osaka is "the foremost trading center of Japan"; Nara, the only spot "in a world of sham and deceit" with "the constancy of the autumn rains"; Ōtsu, "a picture of prosperity and bustle"; Ise, "the province of the gods"; and Sakai, "a city of millionaires in hiding."[18] The insistently particular places of a sprawling landscape are also many, scattered, and tough to rank.

So what draws this landscape together? What binds the whole that Saikaku names so clearly in his title and invokes so often in his text—with seemingly effortless references to the "customs of Nihon," "the leading merchants of Nihon," "the sharpest men in Nihon," "the commerce of Nihon"?

Saikaku is a storyteller, of course. Hence his whole is constructed, in the first instance, by fiat. He simply invents a Nihon as the common world of his stories and then puts it across to readers through the omniscient gaze of a narrator. Assuming the vantage of the voyeur, this narrator observes Shinroku and his adventure. He observes other protagonists and their adventures. He observes scene after scene. And he recounts them all for an audience that can rely on the narrator for easy entry to the story world. Readers of disparate background may lack experience of wastrel heirs or highway life. No matter. The narrator becomes a guide, showing what he sees without presuming that the onlookers have been there before. Bundled together, the scenes of his narrative become space open to those onlookers as a shareable territory. They, too, are invited to claim it imaginatively as their own. So a space made whole by the unifying eye of the guide is ultimately made whole by its putative accessibility: this is the common ground, taken over as public, that an audience can know.

The rhetorical construction of a world is hardly the monopoly of storytellers, however. The cartographers who plotted Nihon for the Toyotomi and Tokugawa regimes worked with real material—a physical space, controlled by visible force, which they surveyed empirically with tools. But like the storyteller, they converted their material into a common world through an omniscient vantage and a unifying narrative structure. Graphing on small paper a huge space detectable only by a mental eye, they organized it with boundaries, labels, icons, color-coding, and all the other magic of their craft. And with their signs, they told a story: Nihon is one. An act of fiat of a high order, mapmaking made a country by declaring it a country.

Other authors of information texts participated in the construction and reconstruction of Nihon as they, too, seized a vantage on a rhetorically organized world. Much in the manner of Saikaku, Kaibara Ekiken becomes a narrator-guide who observes scene after scene, recounts each for onlookers presumed to be new to it, and bundles them all into a single accessible landscape—this time, Kyoto's environs, treated as a subset of "our country"—that readers are meant to make their own. Its integrity derives neither from necessity nor sameness but from an encompassing narrative gaze. Writers, like "sparrows" and "mirrors," transfer their wide, clear vision to readers.

There is more. Having staked out a fictive "Nihon" for collective appropriation, Saikaku binds it together with a narrative grammar as well as a narrative perspective. A structure of linkage—like the structure of cartographic signs—orders the frequently strange places of his landscape. This spatial syntax is the body of tropes that fit the particular into a whole with putatively common features. Its categories are the categories of cultural literacy, derived both from official cartography and the multiplying taxonomies (covering work and cultivation, famous products and manufactures, landmarks and holidays) of the information library. Thus the discrete stops along Shinroku's path belong to a Nihon constructed from official highways, famous places, and ritual calendars (just as the discrete stops along Ekiken's itineraries belong to a Nihon constructed from official highways, famous places, and ritual calendars).

It is these tropes that convert Nihon into something more than a rhetorically invoked space. In themselves, they are abstractions. They are also manifold. Different writers and readers might assign them different weight, particularly associating Nihon with, say, its shrines or name-and-fame-bearing products or martial scions. But once embraced at all, the conventions do more than conjure a physical space: they require it. Nihon becomes the place where those shrines are built (and can be seen), those products are produced (and can be sampled), and those scions are buried (and can be memorialized at grave sites). Nihon is not dispersed ambiguously in a penumbra but situated emphatically in a territory—one bounded by the reach of its conventional parts.

For the state, this territory conformed to the demonstrable space of rule secured through conquest, imposed through confederates, and defined through surveys. It extended across the sixty-six provinces of the classical polity, as well as the tip of Hokkaido—where the shogun vested the Matsumae house with trading rights to Ezo, or Ainu, goods. Trouble stirred over outer borders as the Matsumae pushed northward into core Ezo lands and the Shimazu exerted influence southward over the kingdom of the Ryukyus. But boundary trouble (endemic to state development) tended to clarify rather than confuse an internal cohesion expressed by castellans, registered yields, and highways. If fuzzy about the span of Matsumae, maps discriminated easily enough between this interior and an outside. Labels along the perimeter marked near neighbors: China, Korea, the Ryukyus. Distance charts listed more remote lands: Siam, Cambodia, India, Holland, England. . . . All were non-Nihon.[19]

The state's conception of territory appeared prominently in commercial maps, gazetteers, and encyclopedias. It also resonated throughout virtually all texts in myriad references to daimyo, castles, highways, post stations, barriers, urban wards, and rice revenues. Real mastery of state geography was probably rare among readers. Rarer, surely, was an orientation toward space that made the polity primary or even secondary. Shinroku and his audience had their minds on the cakes of Kusatsu, the sake of Nara, the sharpsters of Edo. Kaibara Ekiken had his mind on Murasaki's inkstone and Ninnaji's cherries. But the point is not that the territory of Nihon was uniformly conceived of in the texts. The point is that their spatial syntax— derived from politics and expanded by social conventions—invariably denoted a specific, physical place where the syntax made sense. Non-Nihon was the place where the syntax of provinces and castles, shrines and sake, broke down.

There is more still. Made whole by a narrative vantage and a narrative grammar, Saikaku's Nihon is also made whole by mobility, by active and ceaseless interconnection. His narrator gives readers mental access to the territory. His presumptions about cultural literacy reaffirm that access: readers can learn, and are meant to know, many things about the territory. But it is not just by mind, not just by congruent practices of governance or ritual celebration, that Nihon is integrated. It is drawn together by the motion of people and things. Himself a man of the road, Shinroku finds in Edo the aesthete from Sakai (who has trained with teachers from all the great cities) as well as the entrepreneur from Tatsuta (who has been undone by rivals from Osaka and Nara). His route passes inns and tea stalls meant for travelers, all familiar with itinerant peddlers. The Eternal Storehouse rattles with traffic. High livers from Kyushu import silks and sacred waters from Kyoto. Aficionados from Sakai visit Kitano for noh performances. A marketing breakthrough in Echizen—wrapping bean paste in lotus leaves—influences trade across the provinces. Izumi ships laden with rice voyage along the northern coast before returning to Osaka.[20] In effect, Nihon becomes not just a commonly accessible mental ground but a practically intertwined space of exchange, where ideas, goods, ships, tourists, traders, and wanderers can and do move.

The information texts repeat the theme. Ekiken writes for ordinary strangers to Kyoto in need of advice about lodgings and local argot, who are numerous enough to demand reissues of his guide. An early version of the Dappled Fabric of Edo lists over seventy firms (and counting) that dealt in the transportation and wholesaling of provincial goods; an early version of the Kyoto Brocade lists express messenger services as well as the local hostels and baths that welcomed travelers. Everybody's Treasury lists not only the post stations but the portage fees of the Tōkaidō, not only the highways leading out of Kyoto but the tourist centers they connect. The prototypical representation of a Nihon in motion appears in the Military Mirrors: the binary geography of daimyo ever en route between Edo and their domains complements the axial geography of officeholders ever en route between Edo and the many outposts of shogunal oversight. Yet far from singular, this political commerce is the model and catalyst for the multiplying commerce, from labor to entertainment, that follows.

Within limits. The space of mobility can coincide with the space of "our country" because travel and travelers remain essentially domestic. Nihon is neither elastic nor porous: insiders do not freely spread Nihon-ness across boundaries; outsiders do not freely circulate non-Nihon-ness within them. Moving exclusively through the sixty-six provinces, Saikaku's protagonists encounter only provincials. They sometimes struggle with local dialects but never with unfamiliar languages. They observe fabulous fabrics but none with an alien cut, fabulous hair ornaments but none for use in an alien coiffure. Almost all fine things, moreover, come from locally notable places—lacquerware from Yoshino, silk crepe from Akashi, tea from Uji, crustaceans from Ise. Variation belongs to closed systems.

Non-Nihon is not absent from Saikaku's world. On the one hand, his narrators inventory the goods from China and Southeast Asia arriving through Nagasaki: confections, silks, medicinal herbs, sharkskin, aloes wood, sandalwood, various curios.[21] On the other, they draw many of their prodigious analogies from Chinese history and literature—referring, in passing, to King Wen's garden, the cliffs of Lake Hsi, the "flower battles held at the court of Hsuan Tsung," the dance of Lao Lai-tzu, the daughter of the Chinese hermit Pang.[22]

In the information texts, too, objects and culture link Nihon to larger worlds. The import business receives regular mention in the personnel directories that list licensed distributors of Chinese silk and vermilion, the gazetteers and guidebooks that list foreign products available in Nagasaki, and the commercial and urban directories that list particular retailers of either general "China goods" or specific items (books, tea wares, medicinals). And this contemporary exchange replays patterns of historical exchange, for Nihon is thick with continental legacies. The Rewoven Brocade of Kyoto includes among the city's precious "old things" all sorts of Chinese bells, sutras, statues, and paintings. Imported goods abound no less in Everybody's Treasury's list of famous tea wares, Ekiken's accounts of temple furnishings, and the Dappled Fabric's notes on Buddhist icons.

To an extent, certainly, the references to goods and culture reinforce each other to evoke a cosmopolitan Nihon. A taste for continental treasure is a mark of the sophistication Saikaku approves: "It is a pitiful thing to pass a lifetime going round and round the pans of shop scales, and to know nothing of the wide world which lies beyond."[23] And sophistication can blur the very distinction between foreign and native. In their lists of antique dealers and experts ready to authenticate rarities, urban directories project circles of connoisseurs who are proper inheritors—with their educated appetites and congenial habits—of things they know how to choose and use and keep alive (and pay for). Old painting and calligraphy, bronze and porcelain belong to an unbounded tradition and any discriminating consumer.

So, too, the continental sages and poets whom Saikaku treats as mental familiars. There is doubtless some swagger in allusions that show off the author and flatter his readers. There is at least as much play, for Saikaku inserts only to parody the sort of reference mandatory in erudite discourse. Students of Mencius will first savor the mention of King Wen's garden, then laugh at the analogy with a humble plot of holly.[24] Yet the parody just heightens the presumption that civilized people know their classics (a little). King Wen is no alien from non-Nihon but a common property, just as Kyoto's Chinese statues are a common patrimony. The cultural mix is complex enough that when Everybody's Treasury juxtaposes poems about Lake Biwa with poems about the Hsiao and Hsiang Rivers (each group in two languages, with almost interchangeable illustrations) readers must wonder whether contrast or convergence is the point.

All the same, the texts temper references to a mentally accessible outside with acknowledgments of its practical remoteness. The trade goods, after all, are funneled through the single port of Nagasaki and regulated by government officials and guildsmen. Foreigners are all but invisible. Saikaku manages only hearsay allusions to Chinese merchants (they are "honest"),[25] while the information texts concentrate on the dead—Chinese monks, artists, and poets who number among the professional ancestors of Japanese followers. The import trade appears to enliven the market without much disturbing the insider networks that control and connect Nihon. There is something chimerical about a cosmopolitanism without contact.

The volume of intellectual traffic in early modern Japan deserves emphasis. Anyone interested in historical China could turn to a vast printed literature of original Chinese works, translations, and Japanese scholarship both high (from academic philosophers) and low (from compilers of biographical samplers or dynastic chronologies). Anyone interested in contemporary and near-contemporary China could turn to a selective but growing body of new titles (from fiction to science) imported through Nagasaki and reissued (occasionally in translation) by Japanese publishers.[26] Around the turn of the eighteenth century, the pace quickened. Two illustrated encyclopedias, both distilled from Chinese sources but written and printed in Japanese, provided general readers with gazetteer-like surveys of Chinese geography, ethnography, production, craft, and technology. And both went on to deliver similar (if less copious and reliable) data about other countries near and far (including Korea, the Ryukyus, Taiwan, Siam, Cambodia, Malacca, and Holland).[27]

The encyclopedias signaled an expanding interest in mundane informa-tion about the foreign world. They also signaled an expanding notion of what, beyond China, the knowable world might be. Coverage of Korea, which had long figured in the mix (through Korean as well as Chinese and Japanese texts), would increase after 1700.[28] But the growth industry was information about Europe. Tokugawa Yoshimune ended restrictions on the import of (non-Christian) Dutch books in 1720 and ordered deputies to study the Dutch language in 1740. The subsequent pursuit of Western learning—from medicine to astronomy, from military science to paint-ing—centered in specialized communities of knowledge even as it ex-tended into the popular domain. A primer of Dutch studies entitled *Ran-gaku kaitei*, which included an introduction to the language, appeared in print in 1788.[29]

Opportunities to enhance book learning with personal communication or even direct observation of foreign life nonetheless remained rare. Except for misadventure on the seas, "our people" saw foreigners only by watching processions or traveling to Nagasaki, Matsumae, and Tsushima. The pro-cessions, infrequent though sometimes spectacular, occurred when em-bassies from Korea, tributaries from the Ryukyus, and representatives from the Dutch factory in Nagasaki made their way to the shogun's castle in Edo (proceeding, on occasion, to Nikkō). They were not only observed by many spectators but commemorated in the popular prints and paintings that acquainted many more Japanese with foreign styles of dress, deport-ment, and ornament.[30] Other sightings of foreigners (at least of Chinese traders, who enjoyed fairly free movement, though not of the Dutch, usu-ally off-limits on an artificial island) occurred chiefly in Nagasaki. The port became such a tourist attraction in the eighteenth century that publishers steadily enhanced their lists of imports with more elaborate maps and guidebooks. While neither Matsumae nor Tsushima attracted similar cov-erage or comparable traffic, travel diaries concerning Ezo did appear in print after 1750.[31]

Throughout this empirical record of contact, the foreign was neither commonplace nor familiar. However disparate the observers, they con-curred in emphasizing the differences—in language, clothing, diet, house-keeping, manners—of outsiders. Imported things and ideas might be made native, but unusual styles of living confirmed distinctions among people. Striking in the record, then, is the tone of fascinated interest, never of alarm or outrage, which recalls the ethnographic approach of domestic investigators to the provincial cuisines and marriage rituals and brothel cultures of Nihon. Marvels like the thermometers and oceanworthy ships of the Dutch are unthreatening. Variety in human anatomy and civilization—the dark skins of Indonesian servants, the use of pictographs by the Ezo—is not a source of hostility.[32] Here the patterns of observation and methodical reporting common to the information culture surely mattered. The exceptional context of foreign relations mattered more. Observers could look at outsiders with detachment because, for upwards of a century and a half, outside affairs lacked urgency.

In this respect, the Tokugawa and Meiji ideas of territory were profoundly different, reflecting obverse experiences of war and peace. The early modern settlement came out of a civil war that lasted well over a century, engaged hundreds of warlords, armed hundreds of thousands of combatants, and left tens of thousands of casualties. Foreign conflict certainly attended this settlement. Toyotomi Hideyoshi twice invaded Korea. Manchu conquests in China raised fears that Japan would be invaded. Belligerent relations with European traders and missionaries augured outright battle. Astonishingly, however, the early modern peace entailed retreat: withdrawal from Korea, the reduction and isolation in Nagasaki of trading partners, the contraction of diplomacy, the prohibition of conversion to Christianity or overseas travel by Japanese subjects. Associating durable security with radical pacification, the Tokugawa regime spent its early energies on isolating foreigners and demobilizing the armies that could have fought them or each other. Farmers were stripped of weapons, samurai of land, daimyo of castles. One of the biggest war machines constructed before modern times was disassembled. And, just as astonishingly, both the domestic demobilization and the foreign retreat held. Major rebellion ceased by 1640.[33] Aggressive agitation for open borders came neither from insiders nor (until the turn of the nineteenth century) from outsiders, who lacked vital interests in a strategically obscure Japan. Hence continuing contact between foreigners and Japanese observers occurred in a largely quiet context. Engagement was low, stability high, danger remote.[34]

While both foreign incursion and foreign intelligence mounted after 1790, a full crisis in international affairs arose only in the 1850s. From that decade forward, engagement was consuming, volatility great, danger constant. And in the course charted by the Meiji government, foreign relations involved not retreat but competition; domestic policy centered not on pacification but militarization. Once again, the transformation began with civil war, although in the Meiji case, one that lasted five years, engaged limited armies of ideological partisans, and avoided massive bloodletting.[35] The differences had less to do with the gravity of internal turmoil than with the urgency of an external challenge that had catalyzed civil violence even as it required consolidated response. Provoked by fear into a fractious union, the Meiji regime took on an agenda of radical internal change aimed at creating a "rich country." The complement was a "strong army" on the model of the Western powers who had compelled the opening of Japanese ports (mainly for the servicing of ships) and then enforced a system of unequal treaties. Identifying the national interest with an international parity secured by force, the Meiji regime introduced universal male conscription and made massive investments in arms. Virtually from the outset, moreover, aggression vied in importance with defense for a regime that identified modern nationhood with colonial power. By the end of the nineteenth century, Japan had taken over Hokkaido, the Kurils, and the Ryukyus; invaded Taiwan and Korea; and defeated China in war (resulting in substantial indemnities as well as control of Taiwan).

Foreign entanglement was so elemental a fact of Meiji life that the spatial construction of Nihon could no longer be overwhelmingly internal, whether in fiction or school texts or family almanacs or accounts of silk production. Now shaped in the vortex of imperialism, the territory was both elastic and porous. And external referents—not just to relations of state but to relations of science, capital, and culture—inflected a Nihon positioned inextricably in the world.[36] Such connection nurtured deep cosmopolitan strains in Meiji society. It also encouraged essentialist conceptions of a singular "us," different from a "them," which had remained latent in early modern texts.

An us/them contrast helped frame the Tokugawa settlement, of course, since the policy of limited contact declared both the integrity of borders and the separateness of what lay within and without. Separation was accompanied by anti-Christian violence and punctuated by controversy (over bullion flow, the cost and content of foreign cargoes, the smuggling of illicit goods, and the interference of unlicensed traders). In some circles, it also nourished convictions of superiority: shogunal advisors recast a deferential posture toward China to place Japan at the center of the Asian order, while Nativist scholars sought in the Japanese classics a core system of value stripped of disfiguring Chinese accretions.[37] At issue, though, is not the existence of complex foreign relationships but their centrality to a common discourse about territory. For all but small constituencies, contact settled into peripheral rather than mundane significance. Never, between 1640 and 1790, did it provoke belligerence and hence the need to mobilize force or popular sentiment. Geographical attention focused, as a result, on internal consolidation.

In a population with no living memory of peace and limited experience of interconnection, this consolidation became the unlikely drama that dominated all formative narratives of the early modern period: the maps, the Military Mirrors, the genealogies, the war chronicles and biographies. And as the story took hold, interest expanded into the many facets of a popular life that was being linked through investigation and the conventions of political and social geography. Contrast did underlie the texts of the information library. But it derived from a basically internal tension between part and whole, rather than an explicitly external tension between us and them. The particularity of the local—of Saikaku's whaling harbors, Ekiken's green-shaded convents, the Brocade's individual neighborhoods—put the collectivity addressed by authors in tension with the multiple units organizing its attachments. Nihon emerged as a space of common access, where any pilgrim could follow a sacred route and any stranger mingle at a festival. Nihon emerged as a space of overlapping and intertwined geographies, where the circuits of religion and trade and artistic affiliation connected discrete places. Yet this Nihon subsumed without erasing the Avenue of Temples, the rice exchange of Kitahama, the burial ground of Mount Kōya, the Bay of Bungo. Shaped in the vortex not of imperialism but of warlord alliance, the early modern territory was a union of parts. Thus the information library constructed "our country" from the long, knowledge-heavy litanies of names and rituals and products that bound the whole together, not from any short, essentializing formula of faith and race that set this country apart from others.

STATE

Saikaku's protagonists are firmly situated in a territory, but less firmly attached to a state. Their world does seem saturated by a state presence (one that evokes the Tokugawa polity as strongly as their territory evokes contemporary Nihon), for some pervasive authority has organized more than administrative geography. The civil calendar is fixed, copper currency regulated, a system of weights and measures in place. Official traders and brothels are licensed, sumptuary laws enforced (or not), outcasts registered, neighborhood associations made accountable for local discipline.[38] But the authority evoked by this orderly picture remains hidden. Certainly, it does not impinge on a Shinroku, who gets by without travel papers or guarantors. More interesting, he gets by without loyalties or obligations beyond those he constructs himself.

Shinroku's seeming freedom serves the purposes of fiction, of course, and will be sacrificed—partly to the "honest work" of the towel trade, partly to the public opinion he courts (by offering "advice on many matters") and wins (by becoming "a treasured asset in his locality"). The invisibility of authority is nonetheless arresting in stories so rich in contemporary detail, however improbable their plots. We notice, then, that Saikaku names numerous real-life figures but never a Tokugawa official. His characters never see "the lord of Edo" or happen by a state ceremony or visit a shogunal monument. No state holiday marks the ritual calendar, no shogunal box is reserved at grand events. No Tokugawa image appears anywhere. Nothing bears the shogunal name.[39]

A similar disjunction characterizes the texts of the information library, which represent a clear power structure but an obscure center. In the Military Mirrors, readers could find extended accounts of administrative anatomy—from a hereditary leadership of shogun and daimyo to the thousands of officeholders responsible for roads, rivers, currency, cities, prisons, policing, engineering, finance, and the like. In any variety of text, readers could find digests of such material. Publishers also projected a well-regulated society with copies of official almanacs, tables of official portage fees on official highways, rosters of official commodities' brokers. Here, again, was a seemingly state-saturated world.

But, again, the source was hidden. If the texts enabled readers to identify the carriages of luminaries in procession, they intimated neither contact nor connection between ruler and ruled. As a practical matter, the authority that emanated outward and downward from the shogun's inner quarters also thinned at each successive remove, reaching most commoners directly through the "functionaries" left unnamed in the Mirrors. Yet as a symbolic matter, too, that authority barely reached beyond Edo Castle. The shogun's ritual calendar included no encounter with the public—whether during exceptional events (installations and interments, for example) or annual celebrations (at the New Year and the Feast of All Souls, for example). Nor, in consequence, was there occasion to enact a relationship with the public—whether between benevolent lord and filial subjects or mighty general and loyal followers. In the information library, no less than in Saikaku's fiction, the shogun (together with his daimyo and high deputies) remained a titular presence.

In fact, he was little more to most people. His voice was silent, for rarely did any shogun put his seal to laws or public correspondence. And his body was hidden, for once their wars were done, shogun confined their ritual lives to ranking warriors (and occasional ambassadors, courtiers, and

priests). When Iemitsu presented the colossal compendium of martial genealogies to Ieyasu's ghost at Nikkō, he had only a military entourage, in a
forest closed to entry. Even indirect efforts to project the shogunal person
into a public arena—as the sponsor of festivities, amnesties, almsgiving—
remained unusual. In the wake of disaster, the shogun offered consolation
or relief (if at all) in impersonal proclamations.[40]

This remoteness reflects the peculiarity of the early modern state, which
differed from its Meiji successor as deeply as early modern conceptions of
territory differed from modern variants. The crucial difference turned on
the relationship between ruler and ruled. While exercising paramount
powers of governance, the shogunate established no direct tie with subjects
and exacted no paramount loyalty from them. While demanding obedience from those subjects, the shogunate inculcated no sentiment of attachment to the person or the office of the shogun. Thus an early modern Nihon defined spatially by internal connection rather than external tension
was defined politically by a common structure of rule rather than a universal center of allegiance. And insofar as it required no universal allegiance,
the regime required no universal story of itself—on the order of the myth-
history contrived for the Meiji emperor—that might inspire popular devotion. The regime did project a story, to be sure, but one addressed with
considerable ambiguity to the elite. In consequence, it imposed lightly on
the public mind, leaving open the popular construction of national narratives. Unlike the modern state, which distorted the past into a single chau-
vinist orthodoxy, the early modern state allowed for a historicism—and for
histories of Nihon—separable from itself. First, an overview of state structures; then, a discussion of state stories.

Entangled as it was in complex, nonconstitutional alliances with emperor
and daimyo, the Tokugawa shogunate might appear to have been too com-
promised in authority to meet exacting definitions of "state." I nonetheless
use the term because the regime functioned throughout a clearly conceived
territory as the ultimate enforcer of order. The emperor may have con-
ferred the title of shogun, but it was the shogunate that policed the court,
regulated its finances, vetted aristocratic promotions, and controlled the
imperial capital itself. The daimyo houses may have enjoyed latitude in domainal governance, but it was the shogunate that appointed and disciplined their heads, established the framework of local policy, and required
annual attendance in Edo. It was the shogunate, too, that oversaw foreign
relations, coastal defense, internal transport, major cities and ports, reli-

gious institutions, mining and the currency system. Whatever its strength over time or efficiency day by day (matters historians debate), the regime established a vertical and coherent structure of power that for centuries averted divisive contests over jurisdiction. Between the suppression of the Shimabara Rebellion in 1638 and the arrival of Commodore Perry in 1853, neither emperor nor daimyo challenged the legitimacy or breached the basic polity of the shogun.[41]

My emphasis on the statist character of Tokugawa power is not, however, meant to obscure the mediated conduct of Tokugawa rule. Although the shogunate assumed paramount governing prerogatives, it discharged them indirectly. The daimyo enforced shogunal policy in their own domains, while retaining discretion over local matters (including taxation and control of armies). A host of specialized bureaucrats executed the public functions of the shogunate itself. I take both forms of mediation as systemic features of the early modern state, rather than foils to its integrity.

A third feature of indirect rule, the isolation of the shogunal person, had less to do with the regime's system of administration than its sense of constituency. The isolation was certainly compatible with the federal and bureaucratic diffusion of power. It was also compatible with the coercive and nonreciprocal relationship of the ruler to the ruled. In general, the shogunate demanded order. In its immediate holdings, it also demanded revenue. Neither demand was contractual or negotiable. Both were filtered through layers of command not to individual persons but to the corporate organs of village and neighborhood.

Still, the shogun's isolation was hardly inevitable. Authoritarian rulers, even in decentralized systems, can perform symbolically as popular leaders, using a rhetorical and ceremonial presence to project charisma (in the manner, for example, of Toyotomi Hideyoshi).[42] Such gestures need not link public consent to political legitimacy. But they do make the public a party to rule. And they do so for a reason. The public becomes a target of suasion because it can provide something the ruler wants: sheer acclaim, perhaps, or religious capital, leverage against opponents, direct military support. What the Tokugawa wanted from the public was disengagement and demobilization, not mass allegiance or populist activism. To keep this public in order, it looked to the martial elite, which remained the critical source of survival for it, and hence the constituency it courted so exclusively that access to the shogun defined honor. In time, the regime's policies of popular control would acquire the ideological trappings of a "status system," thus making the shogun's isolation appear consonant with a hierarchical principle. Before principle, though, came pragmatism: the identification of fellow generals not only as confederates but as the essential witnesses to rule.

Preoccupied with the fealty of the martial elite, the regime recruited no loyalty from, crafted no curriculum for, a public kept estranged. It issued no official documents for popular circulation and forbade mention of its own affairs in commercial texts. The regime clearly became complicit with commercial publishers in conveying a story of political integration through maps and personnel rosters. It was apparently content to see in print a good deal of information amplifying shogunal dignity: the details of its genealogy, the calendar of its ceremonies, the distribution of its graves and castles. Yet ideological suasion remained a diffuse, derivative venture. Legal statutes carried the burden of public instruction, with their broadly Confucian emphasis on deference to superiors and responsibility to callings. Otherwise, popular education belonged either to households or the wide, contentious domain of commercial pedagogy. Late to recognize an official academy of Neo-Confucian thought, and never disposed toward an examination system that would school the elite in orthodoxy, the shogunate tolerated both entrepreneurship and variety in sociopolitical teaching (excepting Christianity). Ambition, rather than any ideological machine, drove the scholarly market. Generally based on the *Classic of Filial Piety*, the learning emanating beyond the academy did identify the humane society with rightful hierarchy and submission to the collectivity. But this core ethic stressed no paramount loyalty. If the self was subordinate to elder and lord, who was the lord? And what bound the self to him?[43]

Numerous constituencies would, over time, explore the notion of social contract. Commoner grievants used an expanding battery of protest—suits, petitions, demonstrations, uprisings—to hone expectations of justice and networks of accountability. Scholars used an expanding discourse on government—its principles, conduct, and policy—to require virtue from power.[44] Grievants and scholars tended to agree, moreover, that authority was grounded in obligation, attached to office not man, and ordered in ascending (as well as descending) tiers—hence making the shogun, at least in theory, the ultimate locus of remonstration. But, in practice, lordship remained local and protest contained within tiers, channeled upward only through a superior's discretion. When the samurai visionary Ōshio Heihachirō tried to break the pattern in 1837 by leading a direct uprising against the ill-rule and rice hoarding of the shogunate, he found only negligible support. Not until the 1860s would millenarian rebellion unite huge peasant followings bent on "world renewal" and the egalitarian distribution of resources. Even then, the target was the rich, not the shogunate.[45] A combination of mediated authority and diffuse ideology kept a paramount regime remote from the ruled.

Not so in the modern era. The Meiji state differed most obviously from its Tokugawa predecessor in the constitutional centralization of authority in the monarch. It differed most profoundly in the reconceived relations of ruler to ruled. Written in the emperor's voice, the opening statements of the 1889 constitution established direct ties between sovereign and subject. They associated past achievements of the nation with "the loyalty and bravery of Our subjects"; they forecast a future in which, "harmoniously cooperating together," those subjects would share "Our hope of making manifest the glory of Our country."[46] Such mutuality and reciprocity supported an implicit contract. The emperor would "promote the welfare" and "protect the security of the rights and of the property of Our people." In return, the people would "assume the duty of allegiance to the present Constitution."[47] The main text stipulated their obligations: "subjects are amenable to service in the Army or Navy"; they are also "amenable to the duty of paying taxes."[48]

In short, the Meiji constitution conceived subjects as individuals and bound them to the sovereign through universal conscription and taxation—prerogatives indispensable to a now militarized state girding for foreign war. The consequent need for individual obedience created a need for individual loyalty. Hence the modern state adopted sweeping campaigns of education to instill patriotism in its subjects. Anchored by compulsory schooling, lessons in civics took many forms, including national holidays and ceremonies, monuments and memorials. The Imperial Rescript on Education distilled their elegantly simple message. The emperor's ancestors had "founded Our Empire on a basis broad and everlasting" and "deeply implanted virtue." Thus the emperor's subjects, "ever united in loyalty and filial piety," were to "guard and maintain the prosperity of Our Imperial Throne coeval with heaven and earth."[49]

No such message—with a singular target of loyalty, a universal sense of audience, a demagogic appeal to myth—came out of the Tokugawa regime. Like all states, the shogunate needed a legitimating story to inspire obedience. And, like all stories, its version converted a governing system into an ideological instrument that shaped behavior by engaging minds. But different states demand different stories. They also invade the mental landscape with different force. Not so paradoxically, an early modern state that excluded the public as a party to rule disturbed that landscape less than its successor.

Although simple in form, the Meiji foundation myth was vast in reach, fusing past and present, authority and morality, monarch and father. The emperor-patriarch, heir to an unbroken line old as creation itself, was not just ruler but source of virtue: he gave voice to teachings "infallible for all ages and true in all places." His subjects, in accordance with a Way bequeathed by this "everlasting" continuum of ancestors, owed him not just fealty but ardent service: all subjects had to "render illustrious the best traditions of [the] forefathers."[50] History was both heavy and prescriptive.

Themes of continuity and ancestral eminence echoed, too, in the historical masterwork of the early modern state, the *Kan'ei shoka keizuden* (Genealogies of the Houses of the Kan'ei Period). Linked to imperial ascendants as well as shogunal founders, the Tokugawa derived legitimacy from an ancient and superior pedigree. At the same time, however, the text kept foremost the exigencies of war and alliance. The Genealogies traced not one but many hundreds of martial lines, all converging at the omega point of Ieyasu's victory. Grounded in this practical achievement of union, Tokugawa legitimacy derived, ultimately, from timely and superior performance.[51] Unlike the Meiji myth, then, this foundation story put in tension the claims of destiny and agency, the plots of continuity and rupture. And while exalting Ieyasu as a peacemaker, it made no one a moral center. History, if not light, was not prescriptive either.

The historicist character of the Tokugawa story reflected political circumstances rather than scholarly rigor (which, despite the jingoistic myth, characterized Meiji academies). Instead of a mass audience of subjects, shogunal apologists addressed a small audience of near-peers—the daimyo confederates, ranking housemen, and symbolically puissant courtiers who were party to the settlement. All were indispensable to a durable peace; all were exquisitely alert to issues of precedence. Hence, in the first instance, the official story had to honor the collectivity—an effect achieved by using the collective genealogies to define the elite and acknowledge its luster. Because the great martial houses issued from imperial and aristocratic ancestors, the project intertwined civil and military prestige. So what was the source of the singular distinction of the Tokugawa? The final emphasis of Genealogies on historical contingency—on the details of conquest, alliance, submission, investiture—identified a single successor to power in an inclusive field of honor.

Following this official line, historicism tended to outweigh mythos in the early modern academy as both later shogunal apologists (notably

Hayashi Gahō and Arai Hakuseki) and their critics (notably in the Mito and Nativist schools) relied as much on evidence as on dictum to make arguments about rightful authority.[52] But the state story had consequences at least as significant in the popular domain. And most were liberating. Liberation was partly a matter of sheer disengagement: a regime that isolated its head and confined its message to near-peers simply excused the public from attention to any orthodox narrative. Popular audiences required no past that made way for one ultimate lord deserving ultimate loyalty. Nor did commercial writers construct one. If shogunal history was not quite as invisible in their texts as the shogunal person, it was not a dominant concern either. Indeed, there was no dominant historical theme. Here was another liberating consequence of the state story: the dual emphasis on ancestry and achievement made room for multiple approaches to a manifold past.

Serious readers with serious interests in history could explore the high tradition, including contemporary scholarship, through private tutors and the book market. General readers could turn to the proliferating war tales, exemplary biographies, political chronologies, anecdotal collections of lore, and historical geographies. But much of the popular readership probably received much of its casual instruction in history from the texts of the information library. History was certainly not their focus. Yet the ceaseless summons to memory—in etymologies, legends, origin stories, and pedigrees—made the texts virtual primers on the past. They rained their history down, moreover, on big audiences that were not necessarily looking for it. Anyone seeking data in the texts about highway itineraries or administrative personnel or commercial neighborhoods had perforce to learn something about historical landmarks, celebrated ancestors, or urban folklore.

History appeared in three guises in the information texts—as genealogy, as inventory, as playground. Each conveyed pieties consistent with official scholarship: Nihon is old; most institutions are continuous; long antecedents bestow dignity. Each also reflected some feature of the state story: its generous conception of ancestral honor, its acknowledgment of the discrete paths leading to Ieyasu's victory, its attention to the contingencies driving power. Detached, however, from a shogun-centered narrative, the texts featured anecdotes that imposed neither inevitable consequences nor obvious responsibilities. One of their messages, compatible with early modern orthodoxy but alien to the Meiji period, was embodied in a Shinroku able to free himself of family and home and calling: the burden of the past might, after all, be light.

Like most contemporary history, the information texts came closest to an integral story of Nihon in their ubiquitous genealogies. Most common were charts of the imperial lineage, which linked the incumbent to heavenly ancestors through a human chain more than a hundred generations long. Almost as common were charts, in two forms, of the Tokugawa lineage. Some traced blood descent from the ninth-century emperor Seiwa (through stultifyingly obscure ancestors, known only to pedants). Others traced professional descent from the twelfth-century shogun Minamoto no Yoritomo (through seven different houses, most felled by calamity). But the imperial and shogunal charts were just the beginning. Adhering to the principle that anybody worth mentioning required ancestors worth remembering, the texts brimmed with genealogical information about courtiers, daimyo, officeholders, priests, artists, entertainers, and specialists of most kinds.[53]

One effect of copious coverage was diffusion: ancestral honor appeared tensile enough to extend to all notables. But if pedigrees were more or less mandatory, they had to be easy to construct as well. Thus resourceful genealogists assigned long and eminent lineages to the daimyo, for example, by tracing succession through any combination of (direct or collateral) blood descent, intermarriage, adoption, the grant of surnames, and (on occasion) usurpation. Bending the familial framework further, they also relied on professional filiation—an old tradition in religious biography that spread to many groups in the early modern period. As priests belonged to sectarian lineages traced through disciples to founders, so any number of specialists were identified with generations of past masters in their fields. Fictive kinship bound them sometimes, as often not. The professional ancestors of the Tokugawa shogun included the Fujiwara, Oda, and Toyotomi. The professional ancestors of their bureaucrats included any predecessor in office.

Another effect of copious coverage, then, was flexibility in genealogical practice: lineage charts focused on *who* succeeded whom without requiring a formula for *how* (heredity, talent, usurpation, marriage—any approach would do) or *why* (inertia, revolution, restoration—any goal might serve). Seeming continuity was not, then, synonymous with stasis, for genealogies simply put often-vexed transitions in order, in retrospect—a point apparent even in an imperial story replete with signs of trouble (early abdication, assassination, dual courts, delayed accessions). Nor was seeming longevity or eminence a prescription for actual power. If the information texts accorded prominence to the emperor and the shogun, they specified no precedence between them. Were they competitive? Who depended on whom? The variable approach to Tokugawa succession introduced more questions. Was shogunal authority a matter of blood or martial leadership? If blood, why did the Tokugawa take seven centuries to get to the top? If leadership, did heredity matter much?

With their parallel treatments of daimyo and officeholders, the Military Mirrors appeared to offer answers by constructing separable domains of honor. One embraced daimyo lords of awesome ancestry (or defensible claims to it) who coexisted as luminaries, not rivals, beyond any absolute calibrations of rank. Representing them as heirs and icons, each responsible to enact his privilege through rites of passage and attendance on the shogun, the Mirrors also intimated that awesome ancestry did not dictate everyday duties. The second domain embraced officials of professional distinction (established through bureaucratic performance) who did execute the everyday duties of governance. Here were alternative models for the relationship between emperor and shogun. Like the daimyo, they might coexist as luminaries. Like daimyo and official, they might enjoy the interdependence of symbol and surrogate, lord and minister.

Still, the genius of genealogical practice in the early modern period lay in its pliancy and consequent ambiguity. The art made room for fictive as well as blood kin, professional as well as hereditary prestige. It obscured competition yet acknowledged change. It represented hierarchical orders of power while outlining parallel fields of achievement. In the end, the construction of genealogy remained a multifarious process open to interpretation. The Meiji nation builders would seize on the imperial genealogy and then emplot it as the singular, central story of Nihon. The outline of this story was available in the information texts. It was also dispersed among alternatives.

Dispersal—or inclusion—was the theme, too, of the inventories that constructed the history of Nihon through all manner of surviving things (from buildings to inkstones), haunting sites (from ruins to battlegrounds), resonant words (from "poem pillows" to neighborhood names), and recurrent activities (from ritual to pilgrimage). Preoccupied with "places of name and fame," and influenced by historical geographers, the authors of the information texts seemed to pursue, as Nietzsche put it in another context, the "restless raking together of everything that has existed."[54] Hence the packed surveys of Ekiken (about 320 sites along 450 kilometers of trails) and the Brocades (311 memorial objects, 74 sites of abandoned mansions, 77 old plaques . . .). "Everything," as Nietzsche says, "is blandly, equally worthy of reverence."[55]

Perhaps more to the point, (almost) everything appears available as a past. The very possibility of raking suggests that little was off-limits, that writers could reclaim from time what they would. And, indeed, they assembled a motley history with apparent freedom, referring easily to remote controversies (failed imperial restorations, for example), recently defeated houses (the Hosokawa, Miyoshi, Asai, Imagawa, Hōjō), and slain leaders (Ashikaga Yoshiteru, Oda Nobunaga, Toyotomi Hidetsugu). They alluded with particular frequency to Toyotomi Hideyoshi. Ekiken's itineraries led walkers by the bridge where the household of Hidetsugu, his first heir, had been beheaded; the mound where noses and ears carried away from his Korean campaign were buried; the temple to which his consort retired; the hill where his own remains were interred.[56]

The state itself left the past open not only through historicist practice but official conduct, and thus made it accessible to popular writers. Appropriating legacies and assimilating antagonists, the Tokugawa intermarried with the imperial family, honored Hideyoshi's widow, elevated as "high houses" the surviving heads of over forty fabled but defeated families (including the Oda), and rebuilt formerly hostile monasteries. Hence even as they secured victory with purge, the shogun pursued forms of reintegration that helped relieve history of taboo (precluding the mention of brilliant predecessors, say) and dogma (specifying the illegitimacy of competitors or the obsolescence of the throne, say). Their past was not polemical but lapidary: complex events had made way for the ultimate peacekeepers.

But this was not quite the past of the information library, where the complexity survived without the narrative. Engaged by neither an overarching story nor a consistent interpretation, the writers of tour guides and gazetteers and the like offered historical fragments that took shape as collage or kaleidoscope. Just as Hideyoshi entered their texts free of overt judgment (good or bad? hero or villain?), so the Tokugawa appeared just as more intriguing actors among many. A hectic past, once released from a narrative climax, became anecdotes and images barely tethered to chronology. Readers could sort them, evaluate them, at will.

And, indeed, they might very well dismiss them as simply old and over; for one implication of texts full of defeated houses and overthrown leaders was that time levels, or at least changes, most things. The official genealogies effectively made the same point: the Tokugawa and their allies had replaced all predecessors, who were chiefly relevant now to lineage charts. If committed to the proposition that time had stopped with Ieyasu, never again to turn on a favorite, the regime treated previous history as a scythe that had cut down the Ashikaga, the Oda, the Takeda, the Hōjō, the Toyotomi. It could honor their survivors with gestures of reconciliation because they were only that, survivors. The world was new.

Some sense of the pastness of the past seems inseparable from another prevailing approach to history in the information texts—as entertainment. Throughout a commercial literature meant variously to instruct and give pleasure to popular readerships, authors connected the historical landscape to play. Even the often starchy Ekiken made his hikes into occasions for blossom viewing, picnicking, feasting at restaurants, boating, and sighting fireflies. Addressing readers almost interchangeably as "ordinary people" and "pleasure seekers," he summoned images of the "crowds" they would join on their way, all drawn by marvelous festivals and curious discoveries (huge icons, miniature lakes). Throngs big as "all Edo" or "all Kyoto" also filled accounts in the urban directories of festivals that, however compellingly historically, offered good entertainment (wrestling, music, dancing, drama, flower exhibits), good refreshment (sweets, sushi, tea, sake), and good shopping (amulets, trinkets, locally famous products). And, whether visiting monuments or joining festivities, those crowds were engaged in "sightseeing." Without precluding piety or seriousness, the term emphasizes recreation.

Sightseeing may surely have entailed a lively connection to the past—a rooting of identity in ancestral sources, a seeking of solace against a fugitive now. For the writers who urged readers to "know, really know" the "famous places and venerable sites" of their cities, history seemed a collective heritage that might relieve atomization with community. For the more reverent visitors to those famous places, mindfulness of old names may have served as both a foundation and obligation of culture. Nonetheless, tourism is less about memory than the invention of memory. Guides objectify sites as targets for spectators and make them appealing through instruction—telling those spectators what to see, luring them with fascinating detail, promising them some sort of satisfaction. Discovery is the message. And while discovery may mutate into historical self-knowledge, it presumes an original distance—the pastness of the past—that must be bridged through exertion. Sightseers acquire memory, which is bred not in the bone but by the book.

The very opening of discovery to popular audiences resembled the work of Meiji, for it converted the past into a common property, into something emerging as "our history." Otherwise, however, the early modern version differed from the myth-history of Meiji, which the state decreed to be compulsory, timeless, and moral learning. Produced by the market, the instruction offered by the information texts was voluntary: learning, and remembering, was an option. And just what was learned or remembered, out of a huge pastiche, remained a matter of taste. Insofar as instruction was linked to sightseeing and thus to show business—with all the trappings of commerce and entertainment—history also assumed a kind of lightness. Play may not expel seriousness, but it does nudge the past toward monument and spectacle, and hence toward reification and moral ambiguity.

Certainly, the past weighs lightly on Saikaku's protagonists, who almost invariably end up apart from where they started out—in different places, in different work, with different companions and lovers, with much vaster or smaller incomes. They do so, moreover, without particularly willful rebellion against fathers and histories. Like Shinroku, many fall into change through carelessness or self-indulgence (and subsequent bootings by fathers who reject *them*). Others are guided by luck or opportunity, appetite or ambition. And all, like the beggars Shinroku meets in Edo, seem to take volatility for granted: surprise is the order of things. Judgment is slippery as well. Saikaku's narrators variously approve, disapprove, and suspend verdict on the exploits they describe. Regardless of judgment, fate is fickle. There is no telling at the outset how a good boy or a bad girl will finish up.

With their elective attachments and dispensable obligations, Saikaku's characters are limit cases of what readers may simultaneously have longed for and dreaded. So, too, the popular history of the information texts—with their pliant genealogies, aimless inventories, and playground pleasures—suggests a limit statement on the malleability of an escapable past. There were, to be sure, countervailing voices in ethics texts, household codes of behavior, emperor-centered histories, Confucian commentaries, and the like. Even so, both the fiction and the popular history represent directions in early modern thought effectively opened up by the early modern state—one that separated paramount power from the recruitment of universal loyalty, wrote exigency and agency into its official story, and left the instruction of the public to the marketplace. And when the market seized on themes of mobility in a world more new than old, it followed a master precedent.

CULTURE

While giving form to a modern nation state, the basic Meiji documents also instructed subjects in Being Japanese. They were a people "united in loyalty and filial piety" to a "Throne coeval with heaven and earth." And they demonstrated allegiance through moral and obedient conduct, including readiness to "offer [themselves] courageously to the State."[57] In short, Japaneseness entailed a contrast: "we" compose a unique collectivity, exclusive of outsiders, which is loyal to the "sacred and inviolable" emperor. Japaneseness also entailed the performance of membership: "we" enact our collective being in deeds ranging from the veneration of imperial portraits by schoolchildren to the preparation for imperial wars by conscripts.

In the early modern period, neither the contrast nor the performance that helps instill collective identity in the modern world was well delineated. The territory was defined more by internal consolidation than external competition, and hence required no formula of differentiation from non-Nihon. The state was committed to mediated authority rather than direct mobilization of loyalty and service, and hence imposed no rites of membership on the public. There existed no prescription for Japaneseness, no routine for enacting it. So whatever the connections writers projected among their readers, they did not arise from the sort of regime-driven patriotism that commonly figures (if often negatively) in modern explorations of identity.

Nor did those connections presume any essential likeness among readers; for the discreteness of experience remained the principal subject of an early modern literature that refused to level the human landscape into sameness. Insistent about the particularity of place, Saikaku was no less insistent about the particularity of person—each distinct in parentage, work, wealth, style, and learning. A Shinroku who could intelligibly trade tales with a Tatsuta brewer, an Edo rentier, and a Sakai aesthete was not a Shinroku who could axiomatically appraise sake, fathom mortgage rates, or compose Chinese verse. Differences mattered. Indeed, they lay at the heart of the information library: the very taxonomies that put difference in order also acknowledged difference as fundamental. Work, as we have seen, broke down among some 200 categories of officials; some 400 categories of prostitutes and entertainers; 47 categories of "masters and artists"; 193 categories of "traders and famous craftsmen"; 51 categories of "transporters and wholesalers"; 96 categories of humbler urban tradespeople; and untold constellations of farmers cultivating 145 separate crops.

Differences continued to multiply along many axes—sectarian affiliation, place of residence, income, patronage. Some of the most significant divided and stratified communities of learning, both professional and amateur. For seekers of expert knowledge, the information library provided specialized instruction in everything from grain hybrids to sericulture, pharmaceutical management to obstetric practice, mining to surveying. For seekers of avocational improvement, the library provided specialized instruction in love, classics, poetry, painting, music, dance, tea, flower arrangement, gardening, incense blending, and a great deal more. Much such learning was organized within rival schools. Most such schools encouraged loyalty to masters and ranked practitioners by proficiency.

In this society of proliferating discriminations, any "culture" that bridged divides could hardly have been "common." Even within the most intimate groups, after all, the finest differences (the cut of a kimono sleeve, the choice of a verb, the style of a mourning ritual) can hew the gravest chasms. Within the large, impersonal readerships of Nihon, gross differences made cultural confluence a phantasm. No one took the point better than Saikaku, who never equated a common currency of communication with the erosion of distinction. Hard on characters mercilessly observed for style, he was harder still on readers mercilessly tested for learning—by poetic quotation folded casually into prose, for example, or place-names chosen to register a protagonist's temperature. His ultimate audience consisted of fellow virtuosi from the Danrin school of poetry. And things got worse. If Saikaku's fiction offered a little something for everybody, the most elegant writing of the eighteenth century became a virtually unreadable trial of wit.[58]

In themselves, of course, the differences cutting through early modern society were not unique, for they derived from a fundamentally modern paradox: consolidation requires differentiation; rationalization increases complexity. The very agents that encourage cohesion (states, markets, urban and transport networks) also provoke fracture and alienation (bureaucratization, specialization, anonymity). Thus the social intricacy of the Tokugawa period forecast developments that would only accelerate over time, not least in the arena of culture. Disorderly in any case, cultural practice becomes scrambled in commercial economies, insofar as money and opportunity, rather than station and custom, govern choices. And the scrambling leads to ever-renewed, always doomed efforts to get things straight and put snobs in their place.

It seems remarkable, then, that integrative conceptions of society emerged at all in early modern Japan, since the more urgent provocations—pressure from a centrist state, domestic crisis, foreign threat—remained unpronounced. Remarkable, too, is their genesis in a commercial literature so alert to social division and hence undeceived about the final uncommonality of culture. Nonetheless, writers did project two forms of union, through what I earlier called a narrative vantage and a narrative grammar. Staking out a common ground that audiences could enter freely in mind or body, they appropriated both the human and the physical terrain of Nihon as knowable, shared space. Describing this common ground in common tropes, they established the formal linkages that made the human and physical terrain intelligible as a whole.

Connection was not a matter, then, of any imaginary sameness in conduct or thought, experience or sensibility. Nor was it a matter of creed. Certainly, the information texts conveyed any number of ideologically rich propositions—that (only to begin) authority radiated from lords of superior pedigree, a productive people generated bountiful (rice) harvests, civility demanded poetic skill, and naming bestowed distinction. Still, the normative assumptions implicit in the gathering and ordering of information did not quite add up to a code of allegiance required from, and defining of, "our people." Insofar as a paramount value did dominate the texts, it was a reverence for the land itself—the place of names, history, harvests, graves. Their emphasis continued to fall, though, on wide-ranging observation. And it is here that we find the peculiar culture both taught and ordained by the information library.

In a Nihon defined as common ground and signified by common tropes, knowing those tropes and something of their content constituted connection. Culture became a body of learning—encompassing political and social geography, ritual and festival calendars, principal products and employments, conventional forms of self-cultivation and etiquette, histories focused on "name and fame"—that enabled navigation and communication. A mode of managing without eliding difference, culture was accessible, at least potentially, to an inclusive "everybody." To some extent, cultural literacy surely extended beyond learning to embrace behavior— the practice, for example, of the arts so important to the writers of the many Treasuries (calligraphy, poetry, letter writing, tea, and gift giving). Cultural literacy could also find expression in savvy travel, ritual participation, and discriminating consumption. But like learning itself, such conduct remained elective and particular, a form of daily sociability rather than an official enactment of belonging.

We might wonder, indeed, whether the culture explicated in the information library entailed notions of belonging at all. Did a union based on common ground and common tropes, but lacking creed or regimen, presume a collective identity transcending social difference? Some sense of an "us" does stir in encyclopedias like Everybody's Treasury, which offered a basic curriculum about "our country" to initiate into membership "our people." This collectivity remains inchoate, however, since membership has no consequences. Kaibara Ekiken offers a clearer contract: cultural literacy entitles "our people" to corporate custody of a landscape made meaningful through knowledge. Yet here the collectivity appears static, more an inheritor than a mover of Nihon. It is in Saikaku's fiction that something more dynamic begins to emerge. And it helps unlock a promise intimated throughout the information library.

With his very choice of medium, Saikaku takes one kind of collectivity for granted. A humorist, he assumes an audience able to get a joke—not just slapstick or burlesque but parody.[59] Aimed at readers familiar with the style of the information library, his comedy relies on mimicry (of inventories and classification), exaggeration (of cultivation and consumption), and incongruity (between a fabled itinerary and a rake's progress). It treats culture as a form of social self-knowledge that enables self-mockery; a form of identity that, once clarified by the bright light of parody, becomes simultaneously a source of communion and discomfort.

Saikaku goes on to suggest that a society capable of laughing at itself is competent to judge itself. Withholding easy resolutions from plots full of mixed messages, he delivers justice (if at all) with a jolt, typically in the voice of background characters. A long-deferred verdict on Shinroku comes from the "people" who profit from his counsel and count him a "treasured asset." A premature verdict on Oman comes from a righteous narrator ("slaves to love" are "doomed to fade away and die"), only to be overturned by forgiving parents: "since [the wastrel Gengobei] is the man she loves, let us unite the two in marriage and then convey this house to them."[60] Such verdicts emerge, to be sure, from the funhouse mirror of fiction, where reversals of expectation provide the thrill. But Saikaku's punch has less to do with the nature of judgment—bad girls may end up happy, bad boys may die rich—than its source. Rather than simply foiling expectation and thus unsettling standards, Saikaku goes further: he detaches judgment altogether from ethical absolutes, official justice, or implacable fortune and entrusts it, instead, to opinion. Opinion is the basic currency of conversation that surrounds a Shinroku who receives earfuls of advice from household clerks, highway acquaintances, fellow beggars, and friends alike. It is the primary control on a Shinroku who decides in the end to curry favor with his Edo neighbors. And it is the penultimate locus of judgment on a Shinroku who, proving himself agreeable to those neighbors, gets good marks. The ultimate locus of judgment is Saikaku's audience, which is left alone to figure out just what to think about characters cut loose from moral moorings and plunged into a swirl of social reaction.

By placing Shinroku before the jury of opinion, Saikaku is clearly not counting on culture—whether in his fictional society or his contemporary readership—to decree a system of value. If it could, verdicts would not be slippery, and the stories would not be interesting. Saikaku seems, instead, to find in a collectivity linked by common ground and common referents (and self-conscious enough to get a joke) the best tribunal available to mediate mores in a world of differences.

He also destabilizes those differences enough to suggest a certain parity among members of the jury. Instability comes partly from mobility, since characters move so precipitously up and down the ladders of wealth, work, and style that position seems too tenuous to encourage security. And, indeed, warnings against complacency dominate the commentary of didactic narrators who—very much in the manner of contemporary merchant codes—urge on audiences the conservative habits deemed essential to guarding and amplifying social place: caution, industry, thrift, sobriety. Remember, they say, that the warmth of summer yields to the "chill of winter"; so avoid, they conclude, the pitfalls of lending, idling, self-indulgence, conceit, and reliance on the gods.[61] The combination here of anxiety and ambition certainly affirms the importance of distinction. It also disturbs, no less than Shinroku's perverse example, any sense that distinction is immutable.

Saikaku further destabilizes difference by separating ego and id from station, an effect achieved through his seemingly contradictory development of character. On the one hand, he assigns protagonists specific identities: each has a distinctive calling, home, and formation. On the other hand, he reduces those protagonists to stereotypes. Abandoning the complexity promised by detailed profiles, Saikaku distills character into caricature to put across his merchants, for example, as quintessential misers or dilettantes or gamblers or the like. So, too, he relies on types to portray both samurai (who range from crazed avengers of honor to cynical opportunists) and the lovers in his erotic fiction (who range from hapless romantics to professional connoisseurs).

Indispensable to the speed of his plots and the clarity of his satire, such stereotyping illustrates Saikaku's chief subject—the transforming power of money and sex—with optimal economy. And because caricature depends on the exaggeration of recognizable patterns rather than the invention of dreamlike impossibilities, it does so within a framework of greater realism than fantasy. Saikaku tells stories about avarice and luck through dissolute heirs who turn to petty connivance, not moneylenders who leverage loans into daimyo appointment. He tells stories about obsession and near-ruin through merchant daughters who fall for monks, not princesses who fall for farmers. However out of kilter, his world remains familiar enough to give bite to its transgressions and revelations.

And the bite pierces everywhere in a world where stereotypes fail to correlate with status position or social role. Saikaku offers readers no single archetypal merchant or artisan or samurai or farmer, for he ignores gross status categories to look at scores of individual players in discrete contexts. Nor, among his merchants, say, does he offer an archetypal rice broker or textile trader or moneylender; for he provides both multiple and contradictory caricatures of most such professionals, each declined too specifically to appear exemplary. Crucially, moreover, types transcend status boundaries. Indolent heirs, feckless schemers, upright householders and the like appear across the spectrum. In effect, the close delineation of identity that appears at odds with caricature is the very device that precludes the linkage of caricature to group. Person transcends ascription. The status system apportions no virtue (unlikely anywhere), controls no appetites (universal and insatiable), assigns no wealth (volatile), dictates no style (variable with income and taste), presages no fates (fickle), and determines no prestige (a matter of opinion). Saikaku refuses, too, to correlate types with locale, age, or gender. He delights in epigrammatic profiles of place without populating them to formula. He imputes significance to life stages without acknowledging any waxing or waning of the passions. And though male characters may outnumber female, his women are as abundantly drawn. In an unprecedented tour de force, Saikaku creates an Amorous Woman who narrates in her own voice a sexual progress that commences at twelve and remains unfinished (over ten thousand men and some women later) in advanced old age.[62]

Thus representing distinction as neither fixed nor predictive, Saikaku projects a fictional domain in which structural divisions recede and a collective dynamic of competition and empathy can arise. His theme, finally, is social entanglement—not only through shared knowledge and ceaseless exchange but through volatility in opportunity and commonality in psyche. And his emphasis on social opinion reflects an assumption that such bonds are strong enough to make possible collective self-regulation.

The information texts, too, undermine the structural barriers of the polity to create room for a collective social consciousness. One of their messages concerns the permeability of status boundaries, which are breached alike by the samurai who appear in the marketplace (as writers, teachers, agronomists, and doctors) and the commoners who appear in the Military Mirrors (as official guildsmen, city elders, innkeepers, and artists). Significant here is not so much the boundary crossing itself—

indispensable as a safety valve to the survival of the status system and, in any case, never very common—but the intimation of an alternative order of prestige. Expertise and importance to the regime bring selected townsmen into the ranks of officeholders; expertise and frustration within the regime send disparate samurai into the market. And whatever their status, master practitioners of medicine and other learned arts are listed together in directories of urban specialists. In sum, a professional competence tested by performance seems increasingly to figure as a determinant of identity.

Indeed, jobs consistently overpower status categories in accounts of social taxonomy. With typically perfunctory reference to the fourfold status system, the information texts concentrate on the ever-finer distinctions of work that belie clarity and simplicity in social structure. So great are distances within station—between, say, the urban magistrate and the rear guardsman, the silver broker and the rag dealer, the cotton magnate and the charcoal maker—that distances across status lines diminish as satisfactory measures of position. And so ample are opportunities to ignore station that the status order is drained of any totalistic salience. Touring, shopping, theatergoing, pilgrimage, and festival participation are all activities of crowds and strangers. Cultivating an art, hiring a tutor, following a master, and excelling in an avocation all depend on ambition, discipline, leisure, and cash. Collecting wonderful objects, wearing elegant clothes, and planting a great garden all require taste and more cash. Throughout the texts of instruction and entertainment, the information library displaces considerations of status to address the mutable and mobile self.

I am not suggesting here that these new emphases on profession, public sociability, and self-fashioning altered the immense practical impact of the status system, which until the fall of the shogunate dictated such vital matters as tax obligations, criminal liability, property rights, and eligibility for high office. Nor am I suggesting that these emphases eliminated status consciousness, which never ceased to inflect popular as well as elite discourse in the period.[63] They signify, rather, both a stretching of opportunity for personal recognition and an opening of connection to an increasingly variegated society—one, like a brocade, woven not only of station but of work, play, art, commerce, religion, and display. They signify, in effect, another version of social entanglement. In addition to the bond of cultural literacy, the information texts begin to trace a collectivity bound by aspiration, shared sources of satisfaction, and common modes of intercourse.[64]

In the Meiji era, notions of collective attachment took two striking forms, one of them alien to the experience described in Tokugawa texts, the other consistent with it. The great change came with the explosion of nationalism as foreign threat conspired with statist indoctrination to exalt Nihon, in the person of the monarch, as the primary locus of loyalty and duty. Here was a seeming erasure of difference within a collectivity of common cause, common pride in a sacred heritage, and common calling to sacrifice and service.

And here, too, was a break with the collectivity of the information library. The early modern texts did convey, in my reading, a sense of nationhood: an integral conception of territory, an assumption of political union under a paramount state, and a prevailing agreement about the cultural knowledge and social intercourse that bound "our people." They also indulged in chauvinistic pieties about "our country," a land rich in history, harvests, enterprise, taste. Yet the outside and downward pressures that later galvanized piety into patriotism were largely absent from a territory defined by internal connection rather than external competition, a state committed to mediated power rather than popular mobilization, and a culture fashioned to negotiate difference rather than enforce sameness. In this nation without nationalism, allegiance was not focused on any universal lord and belonging was not yoked to any performance of identity, whether in school or in battle.

But coercion alone did not forge the Meiji collectivity, which increasingly found expression in a voluntary popular politics. If never immune to the lure of nationalism, this politics moved radically apart from statist ideology by exposing the fierce divisions in interest that underlay putative commonalities in purpose. More critically, it denied any homology between nation and state by according to society an oppositional voice. With a torrent of debate over everything from land taxes to suffrage—conducted in all manner of fora from clubs and tearooms to newspapers and parties— political actors claimed the nation for the public.[65] Their collectivity was defined not by state-driven regimens but by shared access and the mutual labor of representation and suasion.

The evolving story of the modern public sphere is a harrowing one that features themes of tenacity and courage against a drone of police harassment, internal corruption, and state co-optation. My concern here, however, is the background story, which begins in early modernity. Although both the Meiji nation and its nationalism departed from past experience, the construction of the public—as a domain of social representation separable from the polity—connects early modern to modern history.

The obvious departure point for discussion of the modern public sphere is the imperial "Charter Oath" of 1868, which allowed some room for politics by declaring that "Deliberative assemblies shall be widely established and all matters decided by public discussion."[66] Crucial, too, is the dissolution of the status order after 1873, which altered the very terms of political participation by dissolving the equation between authority and hereditary privilege. It is easy, though, to exaggerate the significance to Meiji experience of this reform, not only because an authoritarian hierarchy influenced by birth continued to prevail, but because systemic injustice of many kinds—based, for example, on sex, ethnicity, caste, and citizenship—continued to fracture the social body. It is equally easy to exaggerate the significance to Tokugawa experience of status distinctions, not only because an ascendant market recalibrated their consequences but because social connection of many kinds—based, for example on professional association, avocational interest, leisure activity, and shared learning—continued to mitigate normative difference.

Without slighting the gravity of status discrimination, I suggest simply that the forces of alienation and empathy variously splintering and binding collectivities are hard to assess formulaically. Hence just as the dissolution of the status system did not ensure a public life in the Meiji era, so the existence of the status system did not preclude one in early modernity. In two developments—the growing friction between social structure and social practice, and the growing divide between society and state—we may find the genesis of a public well before 1868.

The sharpest evidence for a public sphere of opinion in early modernity comes from the academy, where scholars of disparate station and philosophy sustained critiques of virtually all aspects of the polity: fiscal and monetary policy, taxation, international trade, defense and foreign relations, criteria for official appointment, the rationale for samurai privilege. The sharpest evidence for a public sphere of protest comes from the village, where farmers across the country used suits, petitions, and uprisings to oppose any variety of perceived misrule: high taxes, corvée levies, commercial and transport monopolies, usurious lending rates, and the personal ignorance and misconduct of local officials.[67] And the sharpest evidence of a public sphere of letters comes from vernacular playwrights and storytellers who veiled as fiction a reality that made no sense: samurai reduced to tawdry vendettas, peasants compelled to sell daughters, honest merchants in hock, charlatans in glory.

Yet my concern is the somewhat different public sensibility—not specifically focused on opinion, protest, or exposé—that appears in the information library. The publicness of the texts derived quintessentially from their character as market commodities: written for sale and produced by commercial publishers, they were accessible to anyone with the means to buy or borrow them. Public because distribution was open, print released knowledge from discrete circles of manuscript sharers and pedagogues into anonymous readerships. Publicness of another sort emerged when authors conceived of those readers not as chance buyers but as interested subjects with needs, tastes, and longings. More than access, public denoted the discerning if impersonal "you" whom writers took as an audience to be served. And this "you" was both protean and omnivorous, seemingly ready for maps and poetry manuals, urban directories and medical encyclopedias, and dictionaries and ethnographies alike. In time, it was also a particular "us," however diffuse in reading habits, which presumptively shared a basic cultural literacy—a frame of reference supporting the discourse of Nihon. Hence more, finally, than a general audience, public denoted a self-conscious collectivity.

None of these versions of publicness coincided with official perception and, indeed, each abraded it. When referring to the social body, the Tokugawa regime projected the public as an object of rule—as an "inferior people" (*genin*) that received commands and owed obedience. In a loftier and literal sense, however, the public was the *kō*, a rich old term signifying heavenly principle, righteousness, and just authority. And this *kō* fused throughout official usage with the person of the shogun, the embodiment of public virtue. Its antithesis rather than its complement, the private (*shi*) denoted the selfishness of the self—the pleasure principle, appetite, unruliness, the confusion of hierarchy—that, always latent among the base people, was checked by the ruler.

The information library disturbed these norms at one level by replacing the "inferior person" with the participating subject. A readership of "our people" found itself in the texts as the producers of "famous products and manufactures," the lifeblood of named and inventoried neighborhoods, the professionals lined up with samurai in Military Mirrors no less then commercial directories. Readers were made custodians of the cultural landscape, rightful consumers of all available knowledge. They appeared to possess Nihon and share in its many pliable histories. Just as insidiously, moreover, the information library disturbed the norms at another level by replacing the selfish private self with the legitimate social actor. Without assailing the *kō/shi* divide philosophically, the texts simply portrayed as normal the activities of shopping, pleasure seeking, touring, personal cultivation. They took for granted an appetite for things, a competition for distinction. They made entertainment part of a mission tuned to the ambition, the unruliness of the marketplace. And they repeatedly did so, free of irony, in compendia that folded lists of shogunal officeholders together with lists of theaters and brothels.

Implicit in the contrarian publicness of the information library was a subversive sense of social structure. Again, without assailing the status system philosophically, the texts simply assumed readers with choices—about improving skills, pursuing arts, establishing ties, spending money, and spending time. Their reinforcing emphases on profession and sociability and self-fashioning, if less than a manifesto against a determinism of birth, conveyed a world too complex in opportunity, too prolific in real life courses, to be contained by any four-tier model. What connected it, in the end, was not some physiocratic Confucianism that posited the interdependence of functionally separate, yet mutually indispensable, status groups. What connected it was social commerce itself. A society bound by common ground and common knowledge was represented by the texts as the space of competition, encounter, and display—in the market, the street, the salon, the theater, the circuits of tourists and pilgrims.

The Tokugawa regime cut some slack for social autonomy, partly through accommodation with a market it needed, partly through isolation from an "inferior people" it never recruited to allegiance. Yet in the information library, as elsewhere, we find a startling seizure of initiative: writers imagined a public bigger than the polity and converted it into an "us." Cultural literacy and collective identities, nation and popular histories— these were projections not of the state but of commercial publication.

Their connections to Meiji politics were hardly straightforward. Certainly, there was a great leap from the information texts to newspapers, parties, unions, and assemblies. There was doubtless a leap, too, in the constituencies engaged, though the numbers are hard to figure. If familiarity with the information library was concentrated in an urban male readership, the rudiments of cultural literary—reiterated over generations in family encyclopedias and conveyed to nonreaders through social exchange—may have extended to the early modern majority.[68] The profound change across the Meiji divide seems nonetheless to have been enabled by a prior public consciousness that had already overridden the status order with presumptions of a collective stake in Nihon. Without it, the tenacity of a society facing spectacular political crisis defies understanding.

NOTES

ACKNOWLEDGMENTS

1. For extended discussion, see Roger Sherman, "Acquisition of the Mitsui Collection by the East Asiatic Library, University of California, Berkeley" in *Committee on East Asian Libraries Bulletin*, no. 67 (February 1982): 1–15. Also see Sherman's thesis of the same title, which was submitted for the MLS degree in the Graduate School of Library and Information Science, University of California, Los Angeles, 1980.

2. See the Preface and Introduction by Donald H. Shively to Oka Masahiko, Kodama Fumiko, Tozawa Ikuko, and Ishimatsu Hisayuki, comps., *Edo Printed Books at Berkeley, Formerly of the Mitsui Library in the Collection of the University of California at Berkeley* (Tokyo: Yumani Shobō, 1990), pp. 1–7.

I. A TRAVELING CLERK GOES TO THE BOOKSTORES

1. A good sample of booksellers' catalogues appears in Shidō Bunko, ed., *(Edo jidai) Shorin shuppan shoseki mokuroku shūsei* (Tokyo: Inoue Shobō, 1962–64). For the 1692 catalogue mentioned here, see ibid., 1: 223–317, *Kōeki shojaku mokuroku* (also called *Kōeki shojaku mokuroku taizen*, both standard titles for numerous works). There are four copies of the woodblock edition of this text in the East Asian Library of the University of California, Berkeley. For publishing and cataloguing information concerning this and subsequently cited books in the EAL collection, see Oka Masahiko, Kodama Fumiko, Tozawa Ikuko, and Ishimatsu Hisayuki, comps., *Edo Printed Books at Berkeley, Formerly of the Mitsui Library in the Collection of the University of California at Berkeley* (Tokyo: Yumani Shobō, 1990).

2. For two major studies of printing history and bookselling, see Peter Kornicki, *The Book in Japan: A Cultural History from the Beginnings to the Nineteenth Century* (Boston: Brill, 1998), esp. pp. 169–205, and Henry D. Smith II, "The History of the Book in Edo and Paris," in James L. McClain, John M. Merriman, and

Ugawa Kaoru, eds., *Edo and Paris: Urban Life and the State in the Early Modern Era* (Ithaca, N.Y.: Cornell University Press, 1994), pp. 332–52. Also see David Chibbett, *The History of Japanese Printing and Book Illustration* (Tokyo: Kodansha International, 1977), and Peter Kornicki, "Obiya Ihei: A Japanese Provincial Publisher," *British Library Journal* 11 (1985): 131–42. The names and addresses of booksellers appear in such urban directories as the *(Zōho) Edo sōkanoko meisho taizen,* in Edo Sōsho Kankōkai, ed., *Edo sōsho* (Tokyo: Edo Sōsho Kankōkai, 1916–17), 3: 1–88, and 4: 1–131; see 4: 94–95.

3. The East Asian Library at the University of California, Berkeley, holds copies of this map from the 1689, 1691, and 1694 editions. (No printed catalogue of the Japanese maps in the EAL exists as yet.) The library also holds several copies of a very similar map, Ryūsen's *Dai Nihon ōezu.* For a reproduction of a 1691 edition of *Nihon kaisan chōrikuzu,* see Unno Kazutaka, Oda Takao, and Muroga Nobuo, eds., *Nihon kochizu taisei* (Tokyo: Kōdansha, 1972–75), vol. 1, pl. 31. I have used Marcia Yonemoto's translation of the title. See, for a discussion focused on Ryūsen's *Honchō zukan kōmoku,* her *Mapping Early Modern Japan: Space, Place, and Culture in the Tokugawa Period (1603–1868)* (Berkeley: University of California Press, 2003), pp. 26–35.

4. I am guessing here, although colleagues in Japan agree that the size of most early modern maps invites viewers to walk on them. Because neither the woodblock technology nor the density of entries required maps as large as those produced, bigness itself appears to have been a desideratum. And because sheet maps were not displayed (but folded and put away), I suspect their size suited a taste for physical as well as visual exploration of the surface.

5. *Nihon ōrai,* discussed in Ishikawa Matsutarō, *Ōraimono kaidai jiten* (Tokyo: Ōzorasha, 2001), 1: 648, and reproduced in Kaigo Tokuomi, ed., *Nihon kyōkasho taikei: Kindai-hen* (Tokyo: Kōdansha, 1961–67), *Ōrai-hen,* vol. 9. Also see the discussion of geographical primers in Ishikawa Matsutarō, *Ōraimono no seiritsu to tenkai* (Tokyo: Yūshōdō Shuppan, 1988), pp. 99–129 and, for an almost exhaustive collection of texts, Ishikawa Matsutarō, ed., *Ōraimono taikei* (Tokyo: Ōzorasha, 1992–94).

6. *Shokoku annai tabi suzume,* facsimile in Asakura Haruhiko, ed., *Kohan chishi sōsho* (Tokyo: Sumiya Shobō, 1969–71), vol. 9. A 1720 variant of this text, the *Shokoku tabi suzume,* is held by the East Asian Library at the University of California, Berkeley. For a survey of geographical texts published early in the Edo period, see Wada Mankichi and Asakura Haruhiko, *(Shintei zōho) Kohan chishi kaidai* (Tokyo: Kokusho Kankōkai, 1974).

7. For a facsimile, see Ochikochi Dōin and Hishikawa Moronobu, *Tōkaidō bunken ezu,* ed. Kohan Edozu Shūsei Kankōkai (Tokyo: Kohan Edozu Shūsei Kankōkai, 1970). Also see Asakura Haruhiko, ed., *Kohan chishi sōsho,* vol. 12. For discussion, see Koji Hasegawa, "Road Atlases in Early Modern Japan and Britain," in John Sargent and Richard Wiltshire, eds., *Geographical Studies and Japan* (Sandgate, Folkestone, Kent: Japan Library, 1993), pp. 15–24.

8. *Banmin chōhōki,* facsimile in Kinsei Bungaku Shoshi Kenkyūkai, ed., *Kinsei bungaku shiryō ruijū: Sankō bunken-hen* (Tokyo: Benseisha, 1975–81), 10: 129–261.

9. Kikumoto Gahō, comp., *Kokka man'yōki,* facsimile in Asakura Haruhiko, ed., *Kohan chishi sōsho,* vols. 1–4. Two woodblock editions of this text, dated 1697 and 1835, are held by the East Asian Library at the University of California, Berkeley.

10. Asai Ryōi, *Tōkaidō meishoki,* ed. Asakura Haruhiko (Tokyo: Heibonsha, 1979). For a facsimile, Kinsei Bungaku Shoshi Kenkyūkai, ed., *Kinsei bungagku shiryō ruijū: Kohan chishi-hen* (Tokyo: Benseisha, 1975–81), vol. 8. For discussion of this text and several of the Edo sources mentioned in the following paragraphs, see Jurgis Elisonas, "Notorious Places: A Brief Excursion in the Narrative Topography of Early Edo," in James McClain et al., eds., *Edo and Paris,* pp. 253–91.

11. For a detailed history of Edo mapmaking, see Iida Ryūichi and Tawara Motoaki, *Edozu no rekishi* (Tokyo: Tsukiji Shokan, 1988).

12. *Edo suzume* in Kokusho Kankōkai, ed., *Kinsei bungei sōsho* (Tokyo: Kokusho Kankōkai, 1910), 1: 1–177.

13. *Edo kanoko* in Asakura Haruhiko, ed., *Kohan chishi sōsho,* vol. 8. The following description of the city appears in a revised and expanded edition of this text from 1690, the *(Zōho) Edo sōkanoko meisho taizen.* See citation in n. 2 above. A 1751 edition of the text, the *(Saitei) Edo sōkanoko shinzō taizen,* is held by the East Asian Library at the University of California, Berkeley.

14. For these tallies and discussion of successive Edo guides, see Suzuki Norio, "Meishoki ni miru Edo shūhen jisha e no kanshin to sankei," in Chihōshi Kenkyū Kyōgikai, ed., *Toshi shūhen no chihōshi* (Tokyo: Yūzankaku Shuppan, 1990), pp. 108–26.

15. See, e.g., Asai Ryōi, *Edo meishoki,* in Edo Sōsho Kankōkai, ed., *Edo sōsho,* 2: 1–160; facsimile in Kinsei Bungaku Soshi Kenkyūkai, ed., *Kinsei bungaku shiryō ruijū: Kohan chishi-hen,* vol. 8.

16. For a large selection of texts, see Hashimoto Hiroshi, ed., *(Kaitei zōho) Daibukan* (Tokyo: Meichō Kankōkai, 1966). For discussion, see Fujizane Kumiko, "Bukan no shoshigakuteki kenkyū," *Nihon rekishi* 525 (February 1992): 47–62.

17. Courtly rosters circulated most widely in popular reference works such as the *Banmin chōhōki* (see pp. 141–45) and the Kyoto city directories. See, e.g., the *Kyō habutae,* ed. Shinshū Kyōto Sōsho Kankōkai, *(Shinshū) Kyōto sōsho* (Kyoto: Rinsen Shoten, 1969, second printing 1976), 2: 155–77. Woodblock editions of the *Kyō habutae* (1811) and the *Kyō habutae taizen* (1768) are held by the East Asian Library of the University of California, Berkeley.

18. For the *Yoshiwara hito tabane,* see Ono Susumu, ed., *Kinsei shoki yūjo hyōbankishū* (Tokyo: Koten Bunko, 1965), 1: 465–570. For additional texts, see both that series and Kinsei Bungaku Shoshi Kenkyūkai, ed., *Kinsei bungaku shiryō ruijū: Kanazōshi-hen* (Tokyo: Benseisha, 1972–79), vols. 34–36.

19. *Yarōmushi,* in Kabuki Hyōbanki Kenkyūkai, ed., *Kabuki hyōbanki shūsei* (Tokyo: Iwanami Shoten, 1972–79), 1: 15–42. For similar texts, see both this volume and the full series.

20. Ejima Kiseki, *Keisei iro jamisen,* annot. Hasegawa Tsuyoshi, in Satake Akihiro et al., eds., *Shin Nihon koten bungaku taikei* (Tokyo: Iwanami Shoten, 1989), 78: 3–248.

21. Ihara Saikaku, "The Tale of Gengobei, the Mountain of Love," in id., *Five Women Who Chose Love,* in *The Life of an Amorous Woman and Other Writings,* ed. and trans. Ivan Morris (New York: New Directions, 1963), pp. 100–118; quotation, pp. 117–18.

2. THE LIBRARY OF PUBLIC INFORMATION

1. Hitomi Hitsudai (also known as Hirano Hitsudai), *Honchō shokkan,* ed. Shimada Isao (Tokyo: Heibonsha, 1976–81). A woodblock edition (listed as *Honchō shoku kagami*) is held by the East Asian Library of the University of California, Berkeley.

2. Other monster works of the period include Kurokawa Dōyū, *Yōshū fushi,* in Shinshū Kyōto Sōsho Kankōkai, ed., *(Shinshū) Kyōto sōsho,* vol. 10, and Miyazaki Yasusada, *Nōgyō zensho,* in Yamada Tatsuo and Iiura Toku, eds., *Nihon nōsho zenshū* (Tokyo: Nō-san-gyōson Bunka Kyōkai, 1977), vols. 12–13. For a useful survey of and introduction to major works of the Edo period, see Koten no Jiten Hensan Iinkai, ed., *Koten no jiten: Seizui o yomu, Nihon-ban* (Tokyo: Kawabe Shobō Shinsha, 1986), vols. 6–11 (which cover the years 1445–1787).

3. For analysis, see Ishikawa Matsutarō, *Ōraimono no seiritsu to tenkai,* and Ishikawa, ed., *Ōraimono kaidai jiten.* For the texts, see Ishikawa, ed., *Ōraimono taikei,* and Kaigo Tokiomi, ed., *Nihon kyōkasho taikei: Kindai-hen.*

4. Basic reference works included *kinmōzui* (illustrated lexicons, usually devoted to particular subjects), *setsuyōshū* (a vast spectrum of dictionaries, often with extensive appendices of general information), and *chōhōki* (instructional manuals, ranging from encyclopedic surveys of popular knowledge to specialized coverage of particular skills). For discussion of these texts, Edo publishing, and much else, see Donald H. Shively, "Popular Culture," in *The Cambridge History of Japan,* vol. 4: *Early Modern Japan,* ed. John Whitney Hall (New York: Cambridge University Press, 1991), pp. 706–69. Also see Yokoyama Toshio, "*Setsuyōshū* and Japanese Civilization," in Jean-Pierre Lehmann and Sue Henny, eds., *Themes and Theories in Modern Japanese History: Essays in Memory of Richard Storry* (Atlantic Highlands, N.J.: Athlone Press, 1988), pp. 78–98.

5. For the categories used by early modern publishers, see the catalogues in Shidō Bunko, ed., *(Edo jidai) Shorin shuppan shoseki mokuroku shūsei.* The categories of modern scholarship are suggested by the classification system of Kinsei Bungaku Shoshi Kenkyūkai, ed., *Kinsei bungaku shiryō ruijū.* "Geographical writing" (or *chishi,* the rubric governing the great series *Kohan chishi sōsho*) is one of the most copious categories in modern bibliography, but it never stretches to include maps, primers, shogunal personnel rosters, agricultural manuals, or a great

variety of other sources with obvious geographical dimensions. The genre boundary tends to be firm and the scholarship confined by it.

6. This is a play on two of Saikaku's titles, *Nihon eitaigura* (The Eternal Storehouse of Japan) and *Seken mune sanyō* (Worldly Reckonings).

7. It is easy to develop a substantial list of exemplary "information texts" from the classical and medieval periods: notably, e.g., the *Izumo* (and *Bungo, Harima,* and *Hitachi*) *fudoki* (eighth-century gazetteers); *Shinsen shōjiroku* and *Sonpi bunmyaku* (ninth- and fourteenth-century genealogical compilations); *Wamyō ruijū* (a tenth-century dictionary); *Kuchizusami* (a tenth-century compendium of basic knowledge); *Shūgaishō* and *Nichūreki* (fourteenth- and fifteenth-century encyclopedias); *Teikin ōrai* (a fourteenth-century primer). But such texts tend to differ from their successors not only in obvious ways (their limited audience, focus on high culture, typical use of classical Chinese, and uneven reliance on empirical investigation) but in range and currency. Restricted in variety, unrevised, and rarely superseded, the texts also functioned as timeless staples, and they were thus closer to canonical knowledge than active information. For background, see Marian Ury, "Chinese Learning and Intellectual Life," in *The Cambridge History of Japan,* vol. 2: *Heian Japan,* ed. Donald H. Shively and William H. McCullough (New York: Cambridge University Press, 1999), pp. 341–89. On pre-Tokugawa "Catalogues and Bibliography," see also Kornicki, *Book in Japan,* pp. 413–27.

8. Miyazaki Yasusada, *Nōgyō zensho.* Three woodblock editions of this work (one undated, the others dated 1697 and 1815) are held by the East Asian Library of the University of California, Berkeley. For discussion, see Thomas C. Smith, *The Agrarian Origins of Modern Japan* (Stanford, Calif.: Stanford University Press, 1959), pp. 87–107. Anne Walthall has also drawn to my attention an essay by Jeff Marti, "Intellectual and Moral Foundations of Empirical Agronomy in Eighteenth-Century Japan," in *Select Papers from the Center for Far Eastern Studies,* University of Chicago, nos. 1 and 2 (1977–78) and (for a translation of the introduction to the *Nōgyō zensho*), no. 9 (1994).

9. The Kizan quotation appears in Donald Keene, "Fujimoto Kizan and *The Great Mirror of Love,*" in *Landscapes and Portraits: Appreciations of Japanese Culture* (Tokyo: Kodansha International, 1971), p. 244. For the text, Fujimoto Kizan, *Shikidō ōkagami,* ed. Noma Kōshin (Tokyo: Yagi Shoten, 1974). In addition to Keene, see, for discussion, Lawrence Rogers, "She Loves Me, She Loves Me Not: *Shinjū* and *Shikidō ōkagami,*" *Monumenta Nipponica* 49, no. 1 (Spring 1994): 31–60.

10. For promises of revision, see, e.g., *Shōkyoku Edo kagami,* in Hashimoto, ed., *Daibukan,* 1: 132. Terms for "new," "revised," and "expanded" (for example, *shinpan, shinsen, shinkai, kaisei, kaiho, kōsei, zōho, zōtei*) are most prominent in the titles of maps and Military Mirrors. See, e.g., the catalogue of the Nanbara map collection, Kōbe Shiritsu Hakubutsukan, ed., *Kanzōhin mokuroku, Chizu no bu* (Kobe: Kōbe Shiritsu Hakubutsukan, 1984–89), and the Mirror titles in Hashimoto Hiroshi, ed., *Daibukan.*

11. *Jinrin kinmōzui,* ed. Asakura Haruhiko (Tokyo: Heibonsha, 1990). For the *kujira-bune,* pp. 108–9. Facsimile in Tanaka Chitako and Tanaka Motoo, eds., *Kaseigaku bunken shūsei zokuhen, Edoki IX* (Tokyo: Watanabe Shoten, 1969).

12. The Great Mirror of Sex bears a strong resemblance—in categories of analysis, ethnographic coverage, biographical attention, and encyclopedic density—to a roughly contemporaneous masterwork on martial culture, Yamaga Sokō's *Buke jiki,* ed. Yamaga Sokō Sensei Zenshū Kankōkai (Tokyo: Nisshō Insatsu, 1921). The similarity recalls the mimicry of the Military Mirrors in the rosters of prostitutes and actors.

13. *Aizu fudoki, fūzoku-chō,* ed. Shōji Kichinosuke (Tokyo: Yoshikawa Kōbunkan, 1979–80).

14. Matsue Shigeyori, *Kefukigusa,* ed. Takeuchi Waka (Tokyo: Iwanami Shoten, 1972).

15. *Akindo sugiwai kagami,* in Takimoto Seiichi, ed., *Nihon keizai taiten* (Tokyo: Keimeisha, 1928), 13: 583–649. For discussion, Koten no Jiten Hensan Iinkai, ed., *Koten no jiten,* 11: 353–60.

16. For crustaceans (and much else), see the table of contents of Kaibara Ekiken, *Yamato honzō,* in Ekiken-kai, ed., *Ekiken zenshū* (Tokyo: Ekiken Zenshū Kankōbu, 1881), 6: 3–10. For emperors, see *Banmin chōhōki,* pp. 131–41. For *meibutsu,* see Matsue Shigenori, *Kefukigusa,* pp. 157–87.

17. For a variety of *hyōbanki* texts, see Nakano Mitsutoshi, ed., *Edo meibutsu hyōbanki shūsei* (Tokyo: Iwanami Shoten, 1987). For discussion, see Nakano Mitsutoshi, *Edo meibutsu hyōbanki annai* (Tokyo: Iwanami Shoten, 1985);

18. The dictionary is *Setsuyō taizen.* See Shively, "Popular Culture," p. 721. For the large and changing lexicon of trade, see the discussion of the *Shōbai ōrai* and its successive variants in Ishikawa Matsutarō, *Ōraimono no seiritsu to tenkai,* pp. 158–74.

19. See, e.g., the entries for these terms in the index of Oka Masahiko et al., comps., *Edo Printed Books at Berkeley.* For a thorough survey, see *Kokusho sōmokuroku* (Tokyo: Iwanami Shoten, 1989).

20. The authorship, dating, and methods of compiling the prototypical Gyōki-style map (or maps) are all matters of dispute. For analysis, see Iwahana Michiaki, "Gyōkizu, saiko no Nihonzu," in Hisatake Tetsunari and Hasegawa Kōji, eds., *(Kaitei zōho) Chizu to bunka* (Tokyo: Chijin Shobō, 1993), pp. 64–67; Kuroda Hideo, "Gyōkishiki 'Nihonzu' to wa nanika?" in Kuroda, Mary Elizabeth Berry, and Sugimoto Fumiko, eds., *Chizu to ezu no seiji bunkashi* (Tokyo: Tōkyō Daigaku Shuppankai, 2001), pp. 3–77; and Kazutaka Unno, "Cartography in Japan," in J. B. Harley and David Woodward, eds., *The History of Cartography: Cartography in the Traditional East and Southeast Asian Societies* (Chicago: University of Chicago Press, 1987), pp. 366–70.

21. For sources assessing the possibility that national mapmaking was undertaken by the medieval regimes, see chapter 3, n. 12. We have no extant surveys.

22. For the complex jurisdictional divides that impeded unitary conceptions of the city, see Kyōto-shi, ed., *Kyōto no rekishi* (Tokyo: Gakugei Shorin, 1968–76),3: 42–71, 270–304. For the paintings (*Rakuchū rakugaizu*), see Mary Elizabeth Berry, *The Culture of Civil War in Kyoto* (Berkeley: University of California Press, 1994), pp. 294–302.

23. To appreciate the differences between classical and medieval conceptions of governing structure, contrast the organizational focus of the *Ryō no gige* (nine-century commentaries on the no longer extant eighth-century *ritsuryō* codes) with the exigent concerns of the Jōei and Kenmu formularies (thirteenth and fourteenth centuries). See Richard J. Miller, *Japan's First Bureaucracy: A Study of Eighth-Century Government* (Ithaca, N.Y.: Cornell University East Asian Papers, 1979); George B. Sansom, "Early Japanese Law and Administration," *Transactions of the Asiatic Society of Japan*, 2d ser., 9 (1932): 67–109, and 11 (1934): 117–49; and Satō Shin'ichi, Ikeuchi Yoshisuke, and Momose Kesao, eds., *Chūsei hōsei shiryō-shū* (Tokyo: Iwanami Shoten, 1957–65), vol. 1 (for the Jōei code) and vol. 2 (for the Kenmu code). For the documents of everyday governance in the late medieval period, see, e.g., Imatani Akira and Takahashi Yasuo, eds., *Muromachi bakufu monjo shūsei, bugyō-nin hōsho-hen* (Kyoto: Shibunkaku Shuppan, 1986).

24. I take the liberty here and later of describing the early modern polity as "federal" or founded on a "federation," terms used in Mary Elizabeth Berry, *Hideyoshi* (Cambridge, Mass.: Harvard University Press, 1982), see esp. pp. 147–67, and in Conrad Totman, *Politics in the Tokugawa Bakufu* (Cambridge, Mass.: Harvard University Press, 1967). The terms are contested and alternatives presented in, e.g., Philip C. Brown, *Central Authority and Local Autonomy in the Formation of Early Modern Japan: The Case of Kaga Domain* (Stanford, Calif.: Stanford University Press, 1993); Mark Ravina, *Land and Lordship in Early Modern Japan* (Stanford, Calif.: Stanford University Press, 1999); and Luke S. Roberts, *Mercantilism in a Japanese Domain: The Merchant Origins of Economic Nationalism in Eighteenth-Century Tosa* (Cambridge: Cambridge University Press, 1998). Despite reservations, I continue to use the terms not to insist on a superior model, but to convey, in a conventional political vocabulary, the union under a paramount center of largely self-governing but never fully autonomous domains.

25. Kornicki, *Book in Japan*, pp. 78–99, 114–25, 278–92, 416–27.

26. See Berry, *Hideyoshi* for Hideyoshi's reforms; Toshio Tsukahira, *Feudal Control in Tokugawa Japan: the Sankin Kōtai System* (Cambridge, Mass.: Harvard East Asian Monographs, 1966) for the alternate attendance system.

27. Gilbert Rozman, *Urban Networks in Ch'ing China and Tokugawa Japan* (Princeton, N.J.: Princeton University Press, 1974), pp. 100–103. For excellent studies of Japanese urbanization, also see James L. McClain, *Kanazawa: A Seventeenth-Century Japanese Castle Town* (New Haven, Conn.: Yale University Press, 1982); Nakai Nobuhiko, "Commercial Change and Urban Growth in Early Modern Japan," in *Cambridge History of Japan*, vol. 4: *Early Modern Japan*, ed. Hall,

pp. 519–95; John Whitney Hall, "Castle Towns and Japan's Early Modern Unification," in id. and Marius B. Jansen, eds., *The Institutional History of Early Modern Japan* (Princeton, N.J.: Princeton University Press, 1968), pp. 169–81; and Yoshida Nobuyuki, ed., *Nihon no kinsei: Toshi no jidai* (Tokyo: Chūō Kōronsha, 1992).

28. For medieval trade, see Berry, *Culture of Civil War in Kyoto*, pp. 171–209. For Hideyoshi's reforms, see Kyōto-shi, ed., *Kyōto no rekishi*, 4: 361–78, and Berry, "Restoring the Past: The Documents of Hideyoshi's Magistrate in Kyoto," *Harvard Journal of Asiatic Studies* 42, no. 1 (June 1983): 479–92.

29. Kyōto-shi, ed., *Kyōto no rekishi*, 4: 105–22; 5: 19–27, 72–77.

30. Kawase Kazuma, ed., *(Zōho) Kokatsujiban no kenkyū* (Tokyo: Antiquarian Booksellers Association of Japan, 1967); Kyōto-shi, ed., *Kyōto no rekishi*, 4: 652–56; Kornicki, *Book in Japan*, pp. 125–37.

31. Kornicki, *Book in Japan*, p. 132.

32. Shively, "Popular Culture," pp. 725–27; Munemasa Isoo, *Kinsei Kyōto shuppan bunka no kenkyū* (Kyoto: Dōmeisha Shuppan, 1982), pp. 16–18, 115–17; and, for the catalogues, Shidō Bunko, ed., *(Edo jidai) Shorin shuppan shoseki mokuroku shūsei.*

33. Kornicki, *Book in Japan*, pp. 134–35, 174–75; Smith, "History of the Book in Edo and Paris," pp. 337–40.

34. Ieyasu's investment in scholarly enterprise is clearest in the editing, printing, and anthologizing efforts he undertook. See Fukui Tamotsu, *Edo bakufusen hensanbutsu* (Tokyo: Yūshōdō, 1983), pp. 63–66, and Conrad Totman, *Tokugawa Ieyasu: Shogun* (South San Francisco: Heian International, 1983), pp. 182–89.

35. Although the professional transformation of the samurai is a leitmotif in most scholarship concerning the early modern period, the only synoptic work on military men in English is Eiko Ikegami's *The Taming of the Samurai: Honorific Individualism and the Making of Modern Japan* (Cambridge, Mass.: Harvard University Press, 1995), which focuses on the control and expression of violence. Also important is Kozo Yamamura, *A Study of Samurai Income and Entrepreneurship: Quantitative Analyses of Economic and Social Aspects of the Samurai in Tokugawa and Meiji Japan* (Cambridge, Mass.: Harvard University Press, 1974), which focuses on the mobility of Tokugawa bannermen. We still need systematic research on the demography, the official and nonofficial employment, and the expectations and standards of living of a fair range of Tokugawa samurai households.

36. *Kōeki shojaku mokuroku taizen* is thick, for example, with titles concerning *rekidai narabi ni denki, gunsho, rekidai to kafu, buke yōkan, buke meimoku, isho, renga, haikai* and the like. For a general numerical breakdown, see Munemasa, *Kinsei Kyōto shuppan bunka no kenkyū*, p. 32.

37. Lexicons (*jisho*), primers (*ōraimono*), guides to calculation (*sansūsho*), and manuals for housewives (*joshisho*) were all major growth categories in booksellers' catalogues. See Munemasa, *Kinsei Kyōto shuppan bunka no kenkyū*, p. 32, and Shidō Bunko, ed., *(Edo jidai) Shorin shuppan shoseki mokuroku shūsei.*

38. For the Korean campaigns, see Kusaka Hiroshi, ed., *Hōkō ibun* (Tokyo: Hakubunkan, 1914), pp. 334–39, 569–74, and Miki Seiichirō, "Chōsen eki ni okeru gun'yaku taikei ni tsuite," in *Shigaku zasshi* 75, no. 2 (February 1966): 129–54. For the Osaka battles, see John Whitney Hall, "The *Bakuhan* System," in *Cambridge History of Japan,*, vol. 4: *Early Modern Japan*, ed. id., p. 147. If the population of Japan around 1600 was roughly 15 million, those mobilized for the offensives *and* directly affected by them (300,000 × 10 = 3 million) would have approached 20 percent of the total. If the population was as low as 12 million, the sum would have approached 25 percent. Even adjusting for exaggeration in the troop figures, they represent an unprecedented concentration of national manpower.

39. For published works, see the categories *gun, gunsho*, and *gunji* (with their listings, for example, of the *Asai sandaiki, Shingen zenshū, Shinchōki, Miyoshi gunki, Tenshōki, Taikōki, Taikō gunki, Ōsaka monogatari*), in Shidō Bunko, ed., *(Edo jidai) shorin shuppan shoseki mokuroku shūsei.* See Kornicki, *Book in Japan*, pp. 63–65 (for the broadsheets or *kawaraban*); pp. 106, 332–34 (for manuscript circulation of sensitive material); pp. 200–202 (for *jōruri* booksellers). Also see Munemasa, *Kinsei Kyōto shuppan bunka no kenkyū*, pp. 60–65, concerning publications on the theater.

40. Howard Hibbett, *The Floating World in Japanese Fiction* (New York: Oxford University Press, 1959), and Donald Keene, *World within Walls: Japanese Literature of the Pre-Modern Era, 1600–1867* (New York: Holt, Rinehart & Winston, 1976), pp. 156–215.

41. Wakita Osamu, "The *Kokudaka* System: A Device for Unification," *Journal of Japanese Studies* 1, no. 2 (Spring 1975): 297–320; Berry, *Hideyoshi*, pp. 111–26; and Akizawa Shigeru, "Taikō kenchi," in Asao Naohiro, ed., *Iwanami kōza Nihon tsūshi, Kinsei 1* (Tokyo: Iwanami Shoten, 1990), pp. 107–38. For trenchant analyses of the limitations of the *Taikō kenchi,* see Philip C. Brown, "The Mismeasure of Land: Land Surveying in the Tokugawa Period," *Monumenta Nipponica* 42, no. 1 (Spring 1987): 115–55, and *Central Authority and Local Autonomy in the Formation of Early Modern Japan: The Case of Kaga Domain* (Stanford, Calif.: Stanford University Press, 1993).

42. Kawamura Hirotada, *Edo bakufusen kuniezu no kenkyū* (Tokyo: Kokon Shoin, 1989).

43. Fukui Tamotsu, *Edo bakufu hensanbutsu*, pp. 47–62; Kuroda Hideo, "Edo bakufu kuniezu, gōchō kanken," *Rekishi chiri* 93, no. 2 (1977).

44. Like the overwhelming majority of seventeenth-century writers and cartographers, most of those featured in this book were of samurai origin, including Asai Ryōi, Hitomi Hitsudai, Kaibara Ekiken, Kurukawa Dōyū, Miyazaki Yasusada, Nishikawa Jōken, and Oshikochi Dōin.

45. For a chronological list of printed maps of Edo, see Iida Ryūichi and Tawara Motoaki, *Edozu no rekishi,* vol. 2.

46. Kornicki, *Book in Japan*, pp. 324–58; Munemasa, *Kinsei Kyōto shuppan bunka no kenkyū*, pp. 54–56. Suggestive of the "subterfuges" available to deter-

mined publishers, Henry D. Smith II notes that one "consequence of the state control of publishing was the creation of a thriving market in illegal and private printing" (especially of erotica) and the circulation of "works on current affairs known as *jitsuroku* (true accounts) in multiple manuscripts through the lending libraries that grew rapidly in number by the late Edo Period." See Smith "The Floating World in Its Edo Locale, 1750–1850," in Donald Jenkins, ed., *The Floating World Revisited* (Portland, Ore.: Portland Art Museum; Honolulu: University of Hawai'i Press, 1993), p. 40.

47. See, e.g., the entries in *Kokusho sōmokuroku* for such critics of the shogunate as Kaihō Seiryō, Ogyū Sorai, and Yamaga Sokō.

3. MAPS ARE STRANGE

1. There are two major compilations of reproductions of extant maps made (largely) before the early modern period. See Nishioka Toranosuke (with additions by Takeuchi Rizō), *Nihon shōen ezu shūsei* (Tokyo: Tōkyōdō Shuppan, 1976–77) for a total of 212 maps made between the eighth and early seventeenth centuries; and Tōkyō Daigaku Shiryō Hensanjo, ed., *Nihon shōen ezu shūei* (Tokyo: Tōkyō Daigaku Shuppankai, 1988–2002) for a total of 266 maps made between the eighth and late sixteenth centuries. The earlier compilation, though less extensive in volume, is somewhat more diverse (including, e.g., house plans). The later compilation attempts complete coverage of extant property maps (*shōen ezu*) made before the early modern surveys. Also see Takeuchi Rizō, ed., *Shōen ezu kenkyū* (Tokyo: Tōkyōdō Shuppan, 1982), pp. 392–407, for a chronological list of 225 extant maps that is based (with additions) on the earlier compilation.

2. Japanese map librarians, when pressed, estimate the number of extant early modern maps in the tens of thousands. Because of the volume, no union catalogue has ever been attempted and, indeed, many individual collections remain under only partial bibliographic control (including the collection of the National Diet Library). Cataloguing has focused on individual collections (such as the Nanba Matsutarō collection in Kobe, see Kōbe Shiritsu Hakubutsukan, ed., *Kanzōhin mokuroku, Chizu no bu*) or particular genres (see, e.g., Iida and Tawara, *Edozu no rekishi*), or particular mapmakers, notably Inō Tadataka. For discussion of cataloguing efforts, see Sasaki Junko, "Toshokan to chizu," *Libellus* 7 (December, 1992): 23–27.

3. For discussion of classical maps of Kyoto, their appearance in the tenth-century *Engi shiki*, and reproductions of later copies, see Kyōto Kokuritsu Hakubutsukan, *Koezu, tokubetsu tenrankai zuroku* (Kyoto: Kyōto Kokuritsu Hakubutsukan, 1978), p. 56 and figs. 78, 79. For discussion of a medieval "reconstitution" of the capital plan in the *Shūgaishō*, see Nicolas Fiévè, "The Urban Evolution of the City of *Heiankyō*: A Study of the Iconographic Sources, 1," *Japan Forum* 4,

no. 1 (April 1992); 91–107. The population of medieval Kyoto is unclear. While estimates approach 150,000 (see Kyōto-shi, ed., *Kyōto no rekishi*, 3: 33–41), the softness of the figures prompts my vaguer estimate.

4. Such evidence emerges most cogently in *The History of Cartography*, a massive project initiated by J. B. Harley and David Woodward and, since Harley's death, carried forward by Woodward and other editorial collaborators. For the evidence from the Ancient Near East and Greece, see vol. 1, *Cartography in Prehistoric, Ancient, and Medieval Europe and the Mediterranean* (Chicago: University of Chicago Press, 1987), esp. pp. 109, 121–24, 140–43, 177–80. Also see vol. 2, bk. 1, *Cartography in the Traditional Islamic and South Asian Societies* (1992); vol. 2, bk. 2, *Cartography in the Traditional East and Southeast Asian Societies* (1994); and vol. 2, bk. 3, *Cartography in the Traditional African, American, Arctic, Australian, and Pacific Societies* (1998).

5. See the sources mentioned in n. 1 above and, for debates concerning the meanings of individual maps, Kokuritsu Rekishi Minzoku Hakubutsukan, ed., *Shōen ezu to sono sekai* (Tokyo: Kokuritsu Rekishi Minzoku Hakubutsukan, 1993); Koyama Yasunori and Satō Kazuhiko, eds., *Ezu ni miru shōen no sekai* (Tokyo: Tōkyō Daigaku Shuppankai, 1987); Shōen Ezu Kenkyūkai, ed., *Ebiki shōen ezu* (Tokyo: Tōkyōdō Shuppan, 1991); Takeuchi Rizō, ed., *Shōen ezu no kisoteki kenkyū* (Tokyo: San'ichi Shobō, 1973); and Takahashi Masaki, ed., *Shōen ezu no rekishigaku oyobi kaidoku ni kansuru sōgōteki kenkyū* (Shiga: Shiga Daigaku Kyōiku Gakubu, 1985). Certainly there remain from the medieval period numerous views of individual temple and shrine compounds, many of them classifiable as maps. None, however, surveys more than the near environs of the immediate institutional subject. See, for illustrations, Kyōto Kokuritsu Hakubutsukan, *Koezu, tokubetsu tenrankai zuroku*. The only large-area map that survives from the medieval period (in the *Nichūreki*) is a small (152 × 255 mm) and highly schematic tracery of lines representing the main highways, which are punctuated by labels for major stations. Resembling an abbreviated subway diagram, the map lacks orientation, scale, topographical detail, and provincial markers. For a reproduction, see Akioka Takejirō, ed., *Nihon kochizu shūsei* (Tokyo: Kajima Kenkyūjo Shuppankai, 1971), pt. 2, pl. 3.

6. P. D. A. Harvey collaborated with R. A. Skelton to produce a detailed study of early British mapmaking in *Local Maps and Plans from Medieval England* (Oxford: Clarendon Press, 1986), and he summarizes this scholarship in *History of Cartography*, 1: 464–501, esp. 462–65. Discussion of other extant European maps is to be found in the same volume, pp. 283 and 464–501, passim. The Italian material, in addition to city views, includes eleven maps of northern districts and five local site maps (such as a Venetian lagoon and a Tuscan harbor). I do not include either nonlocal *mappae mundi* or Portolan charts in these counts.

7. Takeuchi Rizō, ed., *Shōen ezu kenkyū*, pp. 392–407. See n. 1 above for compilations of map reproductions.

8. Woodward and Harley, eds., *History of Cartography*, 1: 465.

9. David Woodward, for example, defines maps simply as "graphic representations that facilitate a spatial understanding of things, concepts, conditions, processes, or events in the human world." Ibid., p. xvi. Also see p. 1.

10. The following discussion relies extensively on Denis Wood's seminal book *The Power of Maps* (New York: Guilford Press, 1992), esp. chap. 5, "The Interest is Embodied in the Map in Signs and Myths." I have also been influenced by David Turnbull, *Maps Are Territories: Science Is an Atlas* (Geelong, Australia: Deakin University Press, 1989); Rolland G. Palston, ed., *Social Cartography: Mapping Ways of Seeing Social and Educational Change* (New York: Garland Pub., 1996); and Arthur S. Robinson and Barbara B. Petchenik, *The Nature of Maps* (Chicago: University of Chicago Press, 1976).

11. The ideological constructions behind mapmaking have increasingly been the focus of scholarship, largely under the influence of J. B. Harley's masterful essays, particularly "Silences and Secrecy: The Hidden Agenda of Cartography in Early Modern Europe," *Imago Mundi* 40 (1988): 57–76. Also see J. B. Harley, *The New Nature of Maps: Essays on the History of Cartography,* ed. Paul Laxton (Baltimore: Johns Hopkins University Press, 2001). There remains a tendency, however, to view the politics of mapmaking as a "problem" that somehow perverts a putatively pure cartography that can transcend bias and ideological worldviews. See, e.g., Mark Monmonier, *How to Lie with Maps* (Chicago: University of Chicago Press, 1991). Also see the statement on the margin of the *Map of the World: Peters Projection* (copyright by Akademische Verlagsanstaet, English version by Oxford Cartographers, Oxford, UK; produced with the support of the United Nations Development Programme through Friendship Press, N.Y., n.d.) to the effect that "The new map . . . provides a helpful corrective to the distortions of traditional maps. While the Peters map is superior in its portrayal of proportions and sizes, its importance goes far beyond questions of cartographic accuracy. Nothing less than our world view is at stake." The statement also declares that the Peters projection achieves "Fairness to All Peoples." As Wood and Turnbull demonstrate, however, all maps are necessarily interpretive, and notions of a transcendent cartography (fair to all peoples) are chimerical. Critics of the ideological messages miss the point, and fascination, of maps.

12. See chapter 2, n. 20, on the Gyōki map(s).

13. In connection with the *ōtabumi,* see discussion of the "Satsuma kunizu denchōan" in Tōkyō Daigaku Shiryō Hensanjo, ed., *Daisanjūkai tenrankai reppon mokuroku* (Tokyo: Tōkyō Daigaku Shiryō Hensanjo, 1992), p. 11. Imatani Akira raises the possibility of official cartography in the Muromachi period in "Shugo ryōgoku seika ni okeru kokugun shihai ni tsuite," in *Muromachi bakufu kaitai katei no kenkyū* (Tokyo: Iwanami Shoten, 1985), pp. 225–59. Unno Kazutaka discusses two maps mentioned in the *Azuma kagami* in Woodward and Harley, eds., *History of Cartography,* 2, bk. 2: 395.

14. See the sources cited in n. 5. Even efforts to classify these maps in very general categories diverge enormously. Cf., e.g., the scheme offered by Yoshida Toshi-

hiro, "Shōen ezu no bunryō o megutte," in *Shōen ezu to sono sekai,* pp. 105–11, and the organizing framework of Tōkyō Daigaku Shiryō Hensanjo, ed., *Daisanjūkai tenrankai reppon mokuroku.* The compilations cited in n. 1 above arrange maps in geographical and chronological (rather than generic) order

15. For detailed discussion of this map (one of the most widely analyzed and debated in the medieval sample), see Koyama Yasunori, "Shōen sonraku no kaihatsu to keikan," in Koyama and Satō, eds., *Ezu ni miru shōen no sekai,* pp. 85–104, and Horiuchi Hiroyasu, "Izumi no kuni Hineno-mura ezu," in Shōen Ezu Kenkyūkai, ed., *Ebiki shōen ezu,* pp. 55–62. These volumes include good "trace maps" that convert the multitude of the map's labels to modern type. For excellent trace maps of Hineno and many other medieval maps, also see Kokuritsu Rekishi Minzoku Hakubutsukan, ed., *Shōen ezu to sono sekai.*

16. For detailed discussion, see Mizuta Yoshikazu, "Kii no kuni Inoue-honshō ezu," in Shōen Ezu Kenkyūkai, ed., *Ebiki shōen ezu,* pp. 102–9. For a good trace map, see Kokuritsu Rekishi Minzoku Hakubutsukan, ed., *Shōen ezu to sono sekai,* p. 68.

17. To judge area, scale, and distortion, see the juxtaposition of the medieval material against modern topographical maps in Kokuritsu Rekishi Minzoku Hakubutsukan, ed., *Shōen ezu to sono sekai,* pp. 76, 80.

18. The other is Honedera in Mutsu province. See Koyama, "Shōen sonraku no kaihatsu to keikan," p. 85. For an excellent analysis of one medieval collectivity—its multiple and complex structures as well as its history, evolution, and nomenclature—see Hitomi Tonomura, *Community and Commerce in Late Medieval Japan: The Corporate Villages of Tokuchin-ho* (Stanford, Calif.: Stanford University Press, 1992).

19. See, e.g., the map of Fujita estate (Owari province) in Kokuritsu Rekishi Minzoku Hakubutuskan, ed., *Shōen ezu to sono sekai,* pp. 11, 58.

20. Ibid., p. 63.

21. Ibid., pp. 57, 65–66.

22. For Kyoto's medieval jurisdictions and land politics, see Kyōto-shi, ed., *Kyōto no rekishi,* 3: 42–71, 270–304.

23. Berry, *Culture of Civil War in Kyoto,* pp. 294–302.

24. Berry, "Restoring the Past," pp. 76–80.

25. For a classic treatment of the stages of daimyo development, see John Whitney Hall, "Foundations of the Modern Japanese Daimyo," in id. and Marius B. Jansen, eds., *Studies in the Institutional History of Early Modern Japan,* pp. 65–77. Also see Hall, Keiji Nagahara, and Kozo Yamamura, eds., *Japan Before Tokugawa: Political Consolidation and Economic Growth, 1500–1650* (Princeton, N.J.: Princeton University Press, 1981).

26. For details concerning the following profiles, see Berry, *Hideyoshi;* Conrad Totman, *Tokugawa Ieyasu: Shogun;* Toba Sadao, *Nihon jōkaku jiten* (Tokyo: Tōkyōdō Shuppan, 1971); Kokushi Daijiten Henshū Iinkai, ed., *Kokushi daijiten* (Tokyo: Yoshikawa Kōbunkan, 1979–97); and Yamaga Sokō, *Buke jiki.* Sokō's bi-

ographies of wartime daimyo and their major retainers are strikingly attentive to physical transfer.

27. Harold Bolitho, "The *Han*," in *Cambridge History of Japan*, vol. 4: *Early Modern Japan*, ed. Hall, pp. 191–201. The most detailed calculations of this sort appear in Fujino Tamotsu, *(Shintei) Bakuhan taiseishi no kenkyū* (Tokyo: Yoshikawa Kōbunkan, 1975).

28. For recruitment strategies for the Korean offensives, see Miki Seiichirō, "Chōsen eki ni okeru gun'yaku taikei ni tsuite," *Shigaku zasshi* 75, no. 2 (February, 1966): 129–54.

29. Philip Brown's important work *Central Authority and Local Autonomy in the Formation of Early Modern Japan* focuses attention on the limitations and failures of the Toyotomi surveys and emphasizes the critical role of local daimyo in the execution of the project. My concern here, however, is the approximation—in preliminary though workable form—of productivity figures for most of Japan by the time of Hideyoshi's death. See Kusaka Hiroshi, ed., *Hōkō ibun* (Tokyo: Hakubunkan, 1914), pp. 627–40.

30. See Kazutaka Unno, "Government Cartography in Sixteenth-Century Japan," *Imago Mundi* 43 (1991): 86–91; Kawamura Hirotada, *Edo bakufusen kuniezu no kenkyū*, pp. 22–23; and Sugimoto Fumiko, "Kuniezu," in Asao Naohiro, ed., *Iwanami kōza Nihon tsūshi, Kinsei II* (Tokyo: Iwanami Shoten, 1994), pp. 303–25.

31. The other surviving map is of Seba district, also in Echigo. Although the Kubiki map (executed in multiple sections) cannot be dated precisely, specialists agree that is was completed after 1595, when Hideyoshi's magistrates supervised cadastral surveys in Echigo, but before 1598 (when the Uesugi left Echigo for Aizu). Each label for the individual villages of Kubiki includes two productivitiy figures: one generated by the Uesugi from reports submitted by local retainers and one generated later by empirical examination. The latter figure almost certainly resulted, in each case, from Hideyoshi's surveys in 1595, although it may reflect resurveying undertaken by the Uesugi themselves in 1596–97. The Kubiki map was clearly not made immediately after Hideyoshi's 1591 order for district-level cartography. It appears to represent gradual and continuing efforts to collate village registers into both composite district accounts and district maps. The map lacks a consistent scale. It is also incomplete, for sections covering substantial parts of western Kubiki have been lost. For reproductions of both the Kubiki and Seba maps, see Tōkyō Daigaku Shiryō Hensanjo, ed., *Echigo no kuni kōri ezu* (Tokyo: Tōkyō Daigaku Shuppankai, 1983–87), which itemizes the content of the maps and provides excellent analysis (3: 159–66). Also see Kawamura Hirotada, *Edo bakufusen kuni ezu no kenkyū*, pp. 21–26.

32. The Kubiki map notes the internal boundaries of two *gō*, large administrative villages defined in the classical period. It also traces in thin lines nineteen additional divisions, though what they signify remains mysterious. The lines are unrelated to village boundaries or the land investitures of Uesugi retainers. The essential clues to village size, in addition to the productivity figures, are the picto-

rial icons for residences (typically one for a small village, two for a larger village) and the designation "small" or "medium" or "large" (*jō, chū, ge*) in the label.

33. Kawamura Hirotada, *Edo bakufusen kuniezu no kenkyū*, pp. 27–113. Because of ambiguities in the documents, some scholars use the date 1605 instead of 1604.

34. For the argument that boundary-setting became a tool of state power, see Sugimoto Fumiko, "Chiiki no kiroku," in Hamashita Takeshi and Karashima Noboru, eds., *Chiikishi to wa nani ka?* (Tokyo: Yamakawa Shuppansha, 1997), pp. 362–403. For discussion of boundary disputes and an excellent introduction to the early cartographic surveys, see Marcia Yonemoto, *Mapping Early Modern Japan: Space, Place, and Culture in the Tokugawa Period* (Berkeley: University of California Press, 2003), pp. 8–13.

35. Kawamura Hirotada, *Edo bakufusen kuniezu no kenkyū*, pp. 29–84, esp. 56–58.

36. Detailed representation of village topography did continue in small-area cartography. See, e.g., Sugimoto Fumiko, "Chiiki no kiroku," esp. pp. 381–85, and Igarashi Tsutomu, "Mura ezu ni miru kinsei sonraku no seikatsu sekai," in Katsuragawa Ezu Kenkyūkai, ed., *Ezu no kosumorojī* (Tokyo: Chijin Shobō, 1989), 2: 167–83. For discussion of Inō Tadataka and the transformation of political cartography into a land- and space-centered cartography, see Sugimoto, "Kuniezu kenkyū no ichi to kadai," esp. pp. 320–23, and "Kuniezu," esp. pp. 320–23. Sugimoto argues that Inō's work was crucial to the genuinely national cartography of an integral society (signified by national rather than internal jurisdictional boundaries) that emerged after the fall of the Tokugawa shogunate.

37. Kawamura Hirotada, *Edo bakufusen kuniezu no kenkyū*, chart following p. 68.

38. The dating and genesis of this map (known as the "Keichō map" because of an old misassociation with the earliest Tokugawa surveys) are matters of intense debate. Kawamura (*Edo bakufusen kuniezu no kenkyū*, pp. 283–301) argues that it is a product of Kan'ei-period surveys, conducted from 1633 to 1336, which were amplified in 1638–39 to collect detailed transport data. Kuroda Hideo (see "Kan'ei Edo bakufu kuniezu shōko," *Shikan*, no. 107 [October 1982]: 49–62, and "Kuniezu ni tsuite no taiwa," *Rekishi hyōron*, no. 433 [May 1986]: 27–39) regards mapmaking from the Genna through the Shōhō periods (1615–1647) as a continuous effort misrepresented as discrete cartographic episodes. For a summary of the scholarship, see Sugimoto Fumiko, "Kuniezu kenkyū no ichi to kadai: Kawamura Hirotada-shi *Kuniezu* ni yosete," *Nihon rekishi*, no. 529 (1992), esp. pp. 84–88. My own interest is not chronology but the conception of nation that emerges graphically in this map and remains consistent in official cartography.

39. Kawamura Hirotada argues this point in *Edo bakufusen kuniezu no kenkyū*, pp. 96–97, 286–308.

40. Berry, *Hideyoshi*, 193–203.

41. Yonemoto, *Mapping Early Modern Japan*, pp. 8–9, nn. 2–3 (p. 182).

42. The influence on the Japanese surveys of Ming cartography is generally as-

sumed but still only partially explored. Visual comparison reveals particularly strong similarities in icons and pictorial treatments of landscapes, but we have yet to understand how, when, and by whom the Chinese evidence was consulted in Japan. For discussion of later Qing material and its impact in Japan, see Funakoshi Akio, *Sakoku Nihon ni kita "Kōkizu" no chirigakushiteki kenkyū* (Tokyo: Hōsei Daigaku Shuppankyoku, 1986).

43. For the quotations and discussion, Berry, *Hideyoshi,* pp. 133–35, 207–17.

44. Kuroda Hideo argues in "Hidetada no godai hajime to Genna kuniezu" (unpublished paper, September 1996) that Hidetada, in addition to Ieyasu and Iemitsu, used calls for provincial maps as one of the principal exercises of accession. He also concludes that these Genna-period surveys became continuous with, and finally culminated in, the Kan'ei and Shōhō surveys. (See the sources cited in n. 36, above.)

45. Benedict Anderson, *Imagined Communities: Reflections on the Origin and Spread of Nationalism* (1983; rev ed., New York: Verso, 1991, seventh impression 1996), pp. 174–175, 181.

46. The Keichō *kuniezu* were published in 1666 as the *Nihon bunkeizu,* an atlas of sixteen regional maps. A text from the original edition is held by the East Asian Library of the University of California, Berkeley. For reproductions, see Unno et al., eds., *Nihon no kochizu taisei,* pl. 21 (six panels on pages 44 and 49). Although much official cartography remained secret (especially maps of fortifications and castle towns), the shogunate shared important material such as the Keichō maps and Hōjō Masafusa's survey of Edo with publishers. Several commercial maps of Japan that predate the atlas, moreover, indicate knowledge of official manuscripts; for they, too, locate the castle towns (with labels characteristic of state models) within the scaffold of well-delineated provinces and highway systems.

47. For discussion of Ryūsen's work and later developments in commercial cartography, see Yonemoto, *Mapping Early Modern Japan,* pp. 13–43. Also see Ronald Toby, "Kinseiki no 'Nihonzu' to 'Nihon' no kyōkai," in Kuroda, Berry, and Sugimoto, eds., *Chizu to ezu no seiji bunkashi,* pp. 79–102 . Yonemoto and Toby assign both considerable initiative and a critical role in formulating prevailing cartographic visions of Japan to commercial publishers.

48. The foundational work is by Yamori Kazuhiko: *Toshi puran no kenkyū: Hen'yō keiretsu to kūkan kōsei* (Tokyo: Ōmeidō, 1970), *Jōkamachi* (Tokyo: Gakuseisha, 1972), and *Toshizu no rekishi, Nihon-hen* (Tokyo: Kōdansha, 1974).

49. Berry, *Hideyoshi,* pp. 193–203.

4. BLOOD RIGHT AND MERIT

1. See Oka Masahiko et al., comps., *Edo Printed Books at Berkeley,* pp. 293–301, for listings of the Mirrors held by the East Asian Library, University of

California, Berkeley, and Peter Kornicki, *Book in Japan*, p. 211, for projections of annual runs.

2. See Hashimoto Hiroshi, ed., (*Kaitei zōho*) *Daibukan,* for printed versions of sixty-two Mirrors. For additional sources, see Ishii Ryōsuke, ed., *Hennen Edo bukan* (Tokyo: Kashiwa Shobō, 1981); Watanabe Ichirō, *Tokugawa bakufu daimyō hatamoto yakushoku bukan* (Tokyo: Kashiwa Shobō, 1967); and Fukai Masaumi and Fujizane Kumiko, eds., *Edo bakufu yakushoku bukan hennen shūsei* (Tokyo: Tōyō Shorin, 1996).

3. Untitled roster of Tenna 3 (1683), Hashimoto Hiroshi, ed., *Daibukan,* 1: 183–209, esp. pp. 194–209.

4. See Toshio Tsukahira, *Feudal Control in Tokugawa Japan: The Sankin Kōtai System* (Cambridge, Mass: East Asian Research Center, Harvard University, 1966) for a detailed history of the alternate attendance system.

5. Fujizane Kumiko, "Bukan no shoshigakuteki kenkyū," *Nihon rekishi* 525 (February 1992): 47–62; quotation, 48–49. An excellent study of the *bukan.*

6. See, e.g., the closing remarks of the *Shōkyoku Edo kagami* (Kanbun 12, 1672), in Hashimoto Hiroshi, ed., *Daibukan,* 1: 132.

7. The classic work in English on the foundations and development of Tokugawa rule is Totman, *Politics in the Tokugawa Bakufu.* Also see Hall, "The *Bakuhan* System"; Bolitho, "The *Han*"; and Irimoto Masuo, *Tokugawa sandai to bakufu seiritsu* (Tokyo: Shinjinbutsu Ōraisha, 2000).

8. See the *Shōkyoku Edo kagami,* Hashimoto Hiroshi, ed., *Daibukan,* 1: 120, for one compiler's remarks on methods of observation.

9. See Fujizane Kumiko, "Bukan no shoshigakuteki kenkyū," pp. 54–55, for the integration of main and collateral lines into sequential listings, a change that required close knowledge of filiation, naming, resource distribution, and precedence. For an example, see the listings for the Mōri house in the *Gorin bukan* (Hōei 2, 1705) in Hashimoto Hiroshi, ed., *Daibukan,* 1: 334.

10. See Fujizane Kumiko, "Bukan no shoshigakuteki kenkyū," pp. 56–57, for a chart indicating successive changes and additions to the *bukan* entries, and p. 58 for the Izumoji and Suwaraya totals.

11. For a modern print version, see *Gomon tsukushi* (Meireki 2, 1656) in Hashimoto Hiroshi, ed., *Daibukan,* 1: 101.

12. *Bukan* from the late eighteenth century sometimes did provide geographical lists of daimyo in indexes. In such popular works as the family encyclopedias, the listing of the daimyo in geographical order was common from the late seventeenth century. See, e.g., *Banmin chōhōki,* pp. 210–15.

13. See, e.g., the troop orders for Toyotomi Hideyoshi's first Korean invasion in Kusaka Hiroshi, comp., *Hōkō ibun* (Tokyo: Hakubunkan, 1914), pp. 334–39; the processional order for Hideyoshi's reception of the emperor at his Kyoto residence in the "Juraku gyōkōki" section of Ōmura Yūko's *Tenshōki,* ed. Kuwata Tadachika, *Taikō shiryōshū* (Tokyo: Shinjinbutsu Ōraisha, 1971), pp. 101–39; and the proces-

sional order for the ceremonies marking the seventh anniversary of Hideyoshi's death in Oze Hoan's "Toyotomi daimyōjin saireiki," ed. Hanawa Hokiichi, *(Zoku) Gunsho ruijū* (Tokyo: Zoku Gunsho Ruijū Kanseikai, 1980 [1924]), 3d ser., 63: 223–31.

14. Kodama Kōta, ed., *Shiryō ni yoru Nihon no ayumi: kinsei-hen* (Tokyo: Yoshikawa Kōbunkan, 1969), p. 71.

15. See ibid., pp. 77–88 for a collection of seminal documents, including an oath of loyalty administered to the daimyo in 1611 by Tokugawa Ieyasu and two early versions (dating from 1615 and 1635) of the *Buke shohattō* (Laws Governing the Military Households). For translations of the 1615 Laws and the oath, see David John Lu, *Sources of Japanese History* (New York: McGraw-Hill, 1974), 1: 200–204.

16. Fukui Tamotsu, *Edo bakufu hensanbutsu: Kaisetsu-hen* (Tokyo: Yūshōdō Shuppan, 1983), pp. 88–92.

17. Ibid., pp. 92–100; Zoku Gunsho Ruijū Kanseikai, ed., *Kan'ei shoka keizuden* (Tokyo: Heibonsha, 1980–97). Although this text concentrates overwhelmingly on the genealogies of the daimyo and the Tokugawa bannermen, it also traces the lineages of a number of physicians, tea masters, and artists.

18. Zoku Gunsho Ruijū Kanseikai, ed., *Kan'ei shoka keizuden,* 1: 1–2.

19. For discussion of these events and their context, see Fukui Tamotsu, *Edo bakufu hensanbutsu,* pp. 79–85; Kate Wildman Nakai, *Shogunal Politics: Arai Hakuseki and the Premises of Tokugawa Rule* (Cambridge, Mass.: Council on East Asian Studies, Harvard University, 1988), pp. 177–82; Herman Ooms, *Tokugawa Ideology: Early Constructs, 1570–1680* (Princeton, N.J.: Princeton University Press, 1985), pp. 57–62; and Karen M. Gerhart, *The Eyes of Power: Art and Early Tokugawa Authority* (Honolulu: University of Hawai'i Press, 1999), pp. 73–105.

20. Karen M. Gerhart discusses the dreams, a series of paintings based on them, and Iemitsu's psychological distress in "Visions of the Dead: Kanō Tan'yū's Paintings of Tokugawa Iemitsu's Dreams," *Monumenta Nipponica* 59, no. 1 (Spring 2004): 1–34.

21. Deathbed adoption of heirs was formally permitted in 1651. See Bolitho, "The *Han,*" p. 208.

22. For the gift and body politics of the early modern regimes, see Mary Elizabeth Berry, "Public Peace and Private Attachment: The Goals and Conduct of Power in Early Modern Japan," *Journal of Japanese Studies* 12, no. 2 (Summer 1986): 237–71.

23. See the annual ritual calendars of the military houses in Hashimoto Hiroshi, ed., *Daibukan,* 3: 1217–22.

24. *Gorin bukan* in Hashimoto Hiroshi, ed., *Daibukan,* 1: 334.

25. E.g., ibid., 1: 329–31.

26. For examples of the travel itineraries, see (surrounding the main Mōri entry in the *Gorin bukan*), the entries concerning Asano Tosa no kami, Mōri Hida no kami, Mōri Ukyō Daifu, and Mōri Suō no kami in ibid., pp. 334–35.

27. Harold Bolitho, John Whitney Hall, and Conrad Totman (see the works cited in n. 7 above) all highlight Iemitsu's reforms as critical to shogunal development. See, e.g., Totman, *Politics in the Tokugawa Bakufu*, pp. 59, 67–76, 140. These authors also see a subsequent waning in the enforcement and administration of Tokugawa authority, which is the core concern of Bolitho's important book, *Treasures among Men: The Fudai Daimyo in Tokugawa Japan* (New Haven, Conn.: Yale University Press, 1974). Kate Wildman Nakai explores continuing administrative developments in the post-Iemitsu shogunate in *Shogunal Politics*, pp. 151–72, without suggesting a narrative of decline. But let me emphasize, in any case, that my analysis of the *bukan* engages not the actual operations of the shogunate but their representation.

28. *Honchō bukei tōkan* (Genroku 4, 1691) in Hashimoto Hiroshi, ed., *Daibukan*, 1: 231–76. Totman, *Politics in the Tokugawa Bakufu*, includes an "Abbreviated Table of Tokugawa Bakufu Officials" (pp. 270–77) that roughly corresponds to the content (though not always the order) of the *yakunin* lists in the Mirrors and guides my translations of official titles. John Whitney Hall provides a chart of the mature shogunal administration in "The *Bakuhan* System," pp. 166–67, which follows scholarly analyses based on the *bukan*. Such modern charts depart significantly from their models, however, by eliminating most lesser posts, integrating Edo and provincial posts, altering the hierarchy of some offices, sorting positions by function, and establishing a unified chain of command.

29. For glosses of titles, biographies of officeholders, and administrative analysis, see Totman, *Politics in the Tokugawa Bakufu; Ishii Ryōsuke, ed., *Edo bakufu hatamoto jinmei jiten* (Tokyo: Hara Shobō, 1989); Ishii Ryōsuke, ed., *Edo bakufu shohan jinmei sōkan* (Tokyo: Kashiwa Shobō, 1983–85); and Sasama Yoshihiko, *Edo bakufu yakushoku shūsei* (Tokyo: Yūzankaku Shuppan, 1965).

30. For the transport system and its regulation, see Constantine Vaporis, *Breaking Boundaries: Travel and the State in Early Modern Japan* (Cambridge, Mass.: Council on East Asian Studies, Harvard University Press, 1994).

31. Totman, *Politics in the Tokugawa Bakufu*, pp. 187–89; Bolitho, "The *Han*," p. 195; and Nakai, *Shogunal Politics*, pp. 152–53.

32. See, e.g., the untitled *bukan* of Kyōhō 3 (1718) in Hashimoto Hiroshi, ed., *Daibukan*, 1: 516, and the untitled *bukan* of Genbun 6 (1741), ibid., 2: 579.

33. For excellent analyses of complex discourses brutally simplified here, see Ooms, *Tokugawa Ideology*, esp. pp. 63–108, and Bitō Masahide, "Thought and Religion, 1550–1700," in *Cambridge History of Japan*, vol. 4: *Early Modern Japan*, ed. Hall, esp. pp. 395–424.

34. Totman, *Politics in the Tokugawa Bakufu*, pp. 131–52.

35. See the reference to the *Shōei bukan* in the "*bukan*" entry of Kokushi Daijiten Henshū Iinkai, ed., *Kokushi daijiten* (Tokyo: Yoshikawa Kōbunkan, 1979–97), 12: 39.

36. The divisions in interest between shogunate and daimyo, and their ulti-mately enfeebling consequences for the central administration, are the focus of Bolitho's *Treasures Among Men*.

37. See, e.g., the *Shōtō bukan* (Hōei 1, 1704) in Hashimoto Hiroshi, ed., *Daibukan*, 1: 309–28. Fathers' names are omitted in the cases of both the highest-ranking officials (*tairō, rōjū*) and the lowest-ranking officials.

38. *Shōen bukan* (Shōtoku 3, 1713) in Hashimoto Hiroshi, ed., *Daibukan*, 1: 469. Also see 465–92 passim.

39. See, e.g., ibid., 465–92. Conrad Totman views the office allowances more as financial compensation for underpaid housemen than opportunities to recruit lower-ranking men of talent. See *Politics in the Tokugawa Bakufu*, pp. 149–52. Kate Wildman Nakai discusses eighteenth-century reforms to the allowance system, and Tokugawa Yoshimune's emphasis on promoting men of talent, in *Shogunal Politics*, pp. 156–58. She also discusses an increasing concern, from the time of Tokugawa Tsunayoshi, with bureaucratic performance and the mounting inci-dence of disciplinary actions for "dereliction of duty." See pp. 153–55

40. The ranges appear in Totman, *Politics in the Tokugawa Bakufu*, pp. 270–77. The *bukan* themselves indicate a greater elasticity downward than the norms of the chart indicate.

41. Cf., e.g., the listings of Confucian scholars, physicians, and gardeners in successive *bukan* from the Genroku, Shōtoku, and Kyōhō eras. Variation in the surnames is at least as common as continuity.

42. For a list approaching 400, see the *Ittō bukan* (Hōei 7, 1710) in the *Daibukan*, 1: 410–14. Here the *yoriai* are divided, as they are not in the *Honchō bukei tōkan* of 1691, into *kōtai yoriai* (assemblymen in attendance) numbering 28, and the remaining, nonattending assemblymen. Although *kōtai yoriai* are some-times described as housemen with investitures of 3,000 *koku* or more, quite a few of these 28 have smaller allowances. The pressure for hereditary officeholding, es-pecially as exerted by *fudai* daimyo, is discussed in Ooms, *Tokugawa Ideology*, pp. 55–56. Such demands are symptomatic, I think, of an ascriptive system increas-ingly influenced by criteria of merit and competition.

43. Yamaga Sokō, *Buke jiki*, ed. Yamaga Sokō Sensei Zenshū Kankōkai.

44. *Jinrin kinmōzui*, ed. Asakura Haruhiko, pp. 20–21.

45. See, e.g., the untitled *bukan* of Kyōhō 3 (1718) in Hashimoto Hiroshi, ed., *Daibukan*, 1: 519–21, and the untitled *bukan* of Kyōhō 17 (1732), ibid., 1: 552–53.

5. THE FREEDOM OF THE CITY

1. For urban administration and migration, see William B. Hauser, "Osaka: A Commercial City in Tokugawa Japan," *Urbanism Past and Present* 5 (Winter 1977–78): 23–36; Kato Takashi, "Governing Edo," in McClain et al., eds., *Edo and Paris*, pp. 41–67; Gary Leupp, *Servants, Shophands, and Laborers in the Cities of*

Tokugawa Japan (Princeton, N.J.: Princeton University Press, 1992); James L. Mc-Clain, *Kanazawa: A Seventeenth-Century Japanese Castle Town* (New Haven, Conn.: Yale University Press, 1982); and McClain and Wakita Osamu, eds., *Osaka: The Merchants' Capital of Early Modern Japan* (Ithaca, N.Y.: Cornell University Press, 1999). Other major texts in the urban literature include William B. Hauser, *Economic Institutional Change in Tokugawa Japan: Osaka and the Kinai Cotton Trade* (New York: Cambridge University Press, 1974); Jinnai Hidenobu, *Tokyo, A Spatial Anthropology,* trans. Kimiko Nishimura (Berkeley: University of California Press, 1995); William W. Kelly, "Incendiary Actions: Fires and Firefighting in the Shogun's Capital and the People's City," in McClain et al., eds., *Edo and Paris,* pp. 310–31; McClain, "Edobashi: Power, Space, and Popular Culture in Edo," in Mc-Clain et al., eds., *Edo and Paris,* pp. 105–31; Nakai Nobuhiko, "Commercial Change and Urban Growth in Early Modern Japan," in *Cambridge History of Japan,* vol. 4: *Early Modern Japan,* ed. Hall, pp. 478–518; Akira Naitō and Kazuo Hozumi, *Edo, the City That Became Tokyo: An Illustrated History,* trans. and ed. H. Mack Horton (Tokyo: Kodansha International, 2003); Nishiyama Matsuno-suke, *Edo Culture: Daily Life and Diversions in Urban Japan,* trans. and ed. Gerald Groemer (Honolulu: University of Hawai'i Press, 1997); and Gilbert Rozman, "Edo's Importance in the Changing Tokugawa Society," *Journal of Japanese Studies* 1, no. 1 (Autumn 1974): 91–112.

2. For reproductions of city maps, both manuscript and woodblock, see Harada Tomohiko and Nishikawa Kōji., eds., *Nihon no shigai kozu* (Tokyo: Kashima Kenkyūjo Shuppan, 1972–73). Representative treatments of non-castle towns include Nagasaki, where authority centers on the *oyakusho* (vol. 1, pl. 20); Hakone, also featuring the *oyakusho* (vol. 2, pl. 1); and Niigata, featuring the *go-bansho* (vol. 2, pl. 16). Also see the map of Sakai in Unno Kazutaka et al., eds., *Nihon kochizu taisei,* vol. 1, pl. 104, where authority centers on the *bugyōsho.*

3. The richest collections of such material focus individually on Kyoto, Edo, and Osaka. See Kyōto Sōsho Kankōkai, ed., *Kyōto sōsho* (Kyoto: Kyōto Sōsho Kankōkai, 1914–17); Shinshū Kyōto Kankōkai, ed. *(Shinshū) Kyōto sōsho* (Tokyo: Rinsen Shoten, 1976 [1969]); Shinsen Kyōto Sōsho Kankōkai, ed., *(Shinsen) Kyōto sōsho* (Tokyo: Rinsen Shoten, 1985–89); Edo Sōsho Kankōkai, ed., *Edo sōsho* (Tokyo: Edo Sōsho Kankōkai, 1916–17, Meichō Kankōkai, 1964); Funakoshi Ma-saichirō, ed., *Naniwa sōsho* (Osaka: Naniwa Sōsho Kankōkai, 1926–30). For varied collections without specific geographical foci, see Asakura Haruhiko, ed., *Kohan chishi sōsho*; and Kinsei Bungaku Shoshi Kenkyūkai, ed., *Kinsei bungaku shiryō ruijū: Kohan chishi-hen.* For an overview of important early texts, see Wada Man-kichi and Asakura Haruhiko, eds., *(Shintei zōho) Kohan chishi kaidai* (Tokyo: Kokusho Kankōkai, 1974). For a list of woodblock editions of geographical texts held by the East Asian Library at the University of California, Berkeley, see Oka Masahiko et al., comps., *Edo Printed Books at Berkeley,* pp. 252–87. Between 1810 and 1820, the Tokugawa shogunate compiled an extensive catalogue (meant to be exhaustive) of all geographical texts, dating from earliest times, currently extant in

Japan. The catalogue contains over 2,000 titles (although it omits maps and most ephemera). See the *Henshū chishi biyōtenseki kaidai,* in Tōkyō Daigaku Shiryō Hensanjo, ed., *Dai Nihon kinsei shiryō,* pt. 11 (Tokyo: Tōkyō Daigaku Shuppankai, 1972).

4. *Kyō habutae* in Shinshū Kyōto Sōsho Kankōkai, ed., *(Shinshū) Kyōto sōsho,* 2: 1–237. Among the holdings of the East Asian Library at the University of California, Berkeley, are a late edition of the *Kyō habutae* (1811) and two copies of the *Kyō habutae meisho taizen* (both from 1768). The Brocades are discussed in Shively, "Popular Culture," pp. 723–25, 738–40.

5. *Kyō habutae oridome* in Shinshū Kyōto Sōsho Kankōkai, ed., *(Shinshū) Kyōto sōsho,* 2: 313–539.

6. *Edo kanoko* in Asakura Haruhiko, ed., *Kohan chishi sōsho,* vol. 8, and *(Zōho) Edo sōkanoko meisho taizen* in Edo Sōsho Kankōkai, ed., *Edo sōsho,* 3: 1–88, and 4: 1–131 (individual texts in the *Edo sōsho* are paginated separately). All subsequent references in this chapter to the Dappled Fabric are to the *(Zōho) Edo sōkanoko meisho taizen.* The *Edo kanoko* is discussed in Elisonas, "Notorious Places," pp. 284–85. Although I have assigned the *Edo kanoko* to 1687, Elisonas notes that it may have appeared on one of the first days of 1688. See p. 284, n. 58.

7. See, e.g., the *Naniwa kagami* in Funakoshi Masaichirō, ed., *Naniwa sōsho,* 12: 187–342, and the *Sakai kagami* in Asakura Haruhiko, ed., *Kohan chishi sōsho,* vol. 13. Early city directories in the collection of the East Asian Library at the University of California, Berkeley, include *(Shinpen) Kamakurashi* (1685, two copies), *Sakai kagami* (1684), and *Ōsaka machikagami* (1756, three copies),

8. *Kyō habutae,* p. 1; *Edo sōkanoko meisho taizen,* 3: 1. The scolding tone tends to be conventional in prefaces to instructional texts.

9. *Kyō habutae,* p. 37 (for the *Saigyō sakura*), p. 35 (for the *Ōhashi* built by Toyotomi Hideyoshi), and p. 36 (for the *zazen ishi*).

10. See the entry for "Sakai-chō" in *Edo sōkanoko meisho taizen,* 4: 72–76.

11. Margaret Atwood, *Cat's Eye* (New York: Doubleday, 1989), p. 3.

12. *Kyō habutae,* pp. 13–14.

13. *Edo sōkanoko meisho taizen,* 3: 1–2 (page numbers repeat several times: following the preface, the list of rulers, and the table of contents). The list of military rulers includes the princes and aristocrats who served as shogun in Kamakura. It also includes Oda Nobunaga, his grandson Hidenobu, Toyotomi Hideyoshi, Hideyoshi's nephew Hidetsugu, and Hideyoshi's son Hideyori

14. Kurokawa Dōyū, *Yōshū fushi.* See the "Kaidai" by Noma Kōshin, p. 1–10, for discussion of the Ming influence on historical geography. Also see his "Kaidai" preceding the *Kyō habutae,* pp. 1–7, for discussion of the symmetries between this text and the *Yōshū fushi.* For further reference, see Tachikawa Yoshihiko, *Kyōtogaku no koten Yōshū fushi* (Tokyo: Heibonsha, 1996).

15. *Kyō habutae oridome,* pp. 319, 322–23, 326–29, 399–414.

16. *Kyō habutae,* pp. 56–62; *Kyō habutae oridome,* pp. 470–500.

17. *Kyō habutae,* pp. 62–68; *Kyō habutae oridome,* pp. 362–93.

18. *Kyō habutae,* pp. 68–70; *Kyō habutae oridome,* pp. 432–69

19. For a rich treatment of place names in the poetic tradition, see Edward Kamens, *Utamakura, Allusion, and Intertextuality in Traditional Japanese Poetry* (New Haven, Conn.: Yale University Press, 1997). Also see Baba Akiko et al., eds., *Meisho, Hare kūkan no kōzō,* special edition of *Shizen to bunka* 27 (1990); Morimoto Shigeru, *(Kochū) Utamakura taikan* (Kyoto: Daigakudō Shoten, 1979); and Katagiri Yōichi, ed., *Utamakura utakotoba jiten* (Tokyo: Kasama Shoin, 1999). Among the earliest collections are *Nōin utamakura* and *Shijō Dainagon utamakura.* Edwin A. Cranston glosses *utamakura* as a " 'song-pillow' on which the poet can share the dreams of generations past." See *A Waka Anthology,* vol. 1: *The Gem-Glistening Cup* (Stanford, Calif.: Stanford University Press, 1993), p. 263.

20. Lists appeared, e.g., in the *Shūgaishō* (under the heading *shomeisho-bu*) and the *Nichūreki.* See Baba Akiko, *Meisho, Hare kūkan no kōzō,* p. 7.

21. Nakagawa Kiun, *Kyō warabe,* in Shinshū Kyōto Sōsho Kankōkai, ed., *(Shinshū) Kyōto sōsho,* 1: 1–88; and Asai Ryōi, *Edo meishoki.* For discussion, see Shively, "Popular Culture," p. 735, and Elisonas, "Notorious Places," pp. 253–91 passim.

22. Suzuki Norio, "Meishoki ni miru Edo shūhen jisha e no kanshin to sankei," pp. 100–112. Although most *meisho* fall into the categories of temples and shrines, remarkable works of nature, and "old sites" (*kyūseki,* including graves, battlegrounds, ruins, and the like), Asai Ryōi uses the term in *Edo meishoki* to embrace Edo Castle, Nihonbashi, and the brothel quarter. Later writers extend the term to great mansions, palaces, shops, tea houses, theaters, and virtually any noteworthy site. See, e.g., *Miyako meisho zue* in Kyōto Sōsho Kankōkai, ed., *Kyōto sōsho,* vol. 1.

23. Thus, e.g., the Brocade compiler locates the origin of a mourning ritual in a grieving emperor's flight to a riverbank to pile up stones of solace for his dead son. See *Kyō habutae,* p. 71 (entry for 2/17).

24. There does appear in some pre-Edo texts (such as the sixteenth-century poetry collection *Kanginshū*) an attitude that simply seeing sights is recreation in itself. But actual guides to such activity—detached from seasonal outings, pilgrimage, and poetic travel—date from the seventeenth century. For the *Kanginshū,* see Asano Kenji, ed., *Shintei chūsei kayōshū* (Tokyo: Asahi Shinbunsha, 1973).

25. For the turtle well, *Edo sōkanoko meisho taizen,* 3: 10–11 (I have translated *susamajiki* as "awesome" or "awful"). For a full list of Edo's topographical features, see ibid., pp. 1–32; for Kyoto's, see *Kyō habutae,* pp. 31–52.

26. *Kyō habutae oridome,* 1: 317–22, 325–26, 329–41. Koshōshi borrows much of this material (and later statistics for the number of Kyoto's buildings and the size of its population, p. 325) from the *Yōshū fushi.*

27. Asai Ryōi, *Kyō suzume* in Kyōto Sōsho Kankōkai, ed., *Kyōto sōsho,* 2: 1–98; *Edo suzume* in Kokusho Kankōkai, ed., *Kinsei bungei sōsho,* 1: 1–177. For the quotation, *Kyō suzume,* p. 11.

28. *Kyō suzume,* p. 42.

29. *Edo sōganoko meisho taizen,* 4: 55.

30. Wards assumed in practice a variety of shapes that frustrate model-building, both within and across individual cities. In addition to binding neighbors who fronted a common thoroughfare, they could bind neighbors within intersecting streets. Even in the former case, residents retained complex relations with those who shared common space to the rear of their properties. For ward topography and political organization, see, e.g., Akiyama Kunizō, *Kinsei Kyōto machigumi hattatsushi* (Tokyo: Hōsei Daigaku Shuppankyoku, 1980), esp. pp. 1–43; Kyōto-shi, ed., *Kyōto no rekishi*, 5: 56–81; Yoshiwara Ken'ichirō, *Edo no machi yakunin* (Tokyo: Yoshikawa Kōbunkan, 1980), esp. pp. 14–45; Ishii Ryōsuke, ed., *Edo machikata no seido* (Tokyo: Jinbutsu Ōraisha, 1968), esp. pp. 11–27; and Miyamoto Mataji, *Ōsaka* (Tokyo: Shibundō, 1957), esp. pp. 13–28.

31. For the maps, see Yamori Kazuhiko, *Toshizu no rekishi: Nihon-hen* (Tokyo: Kōdansha, 1975), pp. 160–69, 326–44, and, for more extensive coverage, Harada Tomohiko, Yamori Kazuhiko, and Yanai Akira, *Ōsaka kochizu monogatari* (Tokyo: Mainichi Shinbunsha, 1980).

32. *Kyō habutae*, p. 14. I use the ambiguous term "dealers" when it is unclear whether a concern makes an item or sells it or both.

33. *Edo sōkanoko meisho taizen*, 4: 39. See the preceding note for my use of the term "dealers."

34. *Teikin ōrai*, ed. Ishikawa Matsutarō (Tokyo: Heibonsha, 1973).

35. Matsue Shigenori, *Kefukigusa*, pp. 157–63. Also see, for substantial notes on famous products and manufactures, the individual provincial entries throughout Kikumoto Gahō, comp., *Kokka man'yōki*.

36. Although the founding of the discipline is often associated with the encouragement of scientific learning by Tokugawa Yoshimune in the early eighteenth century, and the formation of the *Bussan-kai* by Tamura Ransui and Hiraga Gennai in the mid-eighteenth century, studies of production had strong roots in the seventeenth century. See Kokushi Daijiten Henshū Iinkai, ed., *Kokushi daijiten*, 12: 290–91. Also see Shirai Mitsutarō *(Kaitei zōho) Nihon hakubutsugaku nenpyō* (Tokyo: Okayama Shoten, 1934).

37. *Aizu fudoki, fūzoku-chō*, ed. Shōji Kichinosuke (Tokyo: Yoshikawa Kōbunkan, 1979–80), esp. 1: 1–31 (for discussion) and 38–54 (for a representative sample of the earliest entries).

38. Among the earliest and most influential texts are the *Shokoku nenjū gyōji* (1685) and Kaibara Ekiken's *Nihon saijiki* (1688). For these and other texts, see Ekiken-kai, ed., *Ekiken zenshū*, 1: 437–555, and Mori Senzō and Kitagawa Hirokuni, eds., *Minkan fūzoku nenjū gyōji* in Kokusho Kankōkai, ed., *Zoku Nihon zuihitsu taisei*, vols. 11–12 (Tokyo: Yoshikawa Kōbunkan, 1983). The East Asian Library at the University of California, Berkeley, holds a number of early printed compilations of festivals and annual ritual calendars, including Nagoya Gen'i, *Minkan saijiki* (1681); Kaibara Ekiken, *Nihon saijiki* (1688); and *Shokoku nenjū gyōji* (1717). For discussion, see Tanaka Sen'ichi, *Nenjū gyōji no kenkyū* (Tokyo:

Ōfūsha, 1992); Tanaka Sen'ichi and Miyata Noboru, eds., *(Sanseidō) Nenjū gyōji jiten* (Tokyo: Sanseidō, 1999); and Endō Motoo and Yamanaka Yutaka, *Nenjū gyōji no rekishigaku* (Tokyo: Kobundō, 1981).

39. Two important early texts, *Bussan mokuroku* (List of Products, 1692) and Kurokawa Dōyū's *Geibi kokugunshi* (Report on the Crafts and Resources of the Provinces and Districts), are cited in Kokushi Daijiten Henshū Iinkai, ed., *Kokushi daijiten*, 12: 291. For the latter text, see Kokusho Kankōkai, ed., *(Zoku zoku) Gunsho ruijū* (Tokyo: Kokusho Kankōkai, 1906–1909), 1st ser., 9: 327–79.

40. The *Banmin chōhō meibutsu ōrai* is also known as *Shokoku meisho tsukushi* and *Nihon shokoku meibutsu tsukushi*. See the entries in *Kokusho sōmokuroku* and the entry in Ishikawa Matsutarō, *Ōraimono kaidai jiten* for *Shokoku meibutsu ōrai*. Also see Ishikawa, *Ōraimono no seiritsu to tenkai*, 126–29. Among the holdings of the East Asian Library at the University of California, Berkeley, are *Shokoku meibutsu ōrai* (undated) and Chigata Nagamichi's *Meibutsu ōrai* (two copies of a late edition of 1824).

41. Matsue Shigenori, *Kefukigusa*, p. 176. This list contains two additional items—*netsufu* and *amoshitsuhei*—that I am unable to translate.

42. *Kyō habutae*, pp. 155–77. The entries for high-ranking nobles include the names of their major attendants but rarely their titles.

43. Ibid., pp. 177–96. The daimyo list includes the shogunal heir, Kōfu-sama, although without an address for a mansion. The names of the daimyo's drapers (*gofukusho*) had begun appearing in the Military Mirrors by 1673.

44. Ibid., pp. 197–200.

45. Ibid., pp. 200–209.

46. Ibid., pp. 209–35.

47. *Edo sōkanoko meisho taizen*, 4: 81–127.

48. *Kyō suzume ato-oi* in *(Shinshū) Kyōto sōsho*, 1: 271–386.

49. For Sakanoue, compare *Edo sōkanoko meisho taizen*, 4: 81, with *Honchō bukei tōkan*, in Hashimoto Hiroshi., ed., *Daibukan*, 1: 271; for Hayashi, compare the same texts on pp. 83 and 271.

50. Iwao Seiichi, ed., *Kyōto oyakusho-muki taigai oboegaki* (Osaka: Seibundō, 1973), 2: 121–44. Such lists probably existed in other cities as well, but are not extant.

51. *Kyō habutae*, pp. 235–37.

52. *Edo sōkanoko meisho taizen*, 4: 127–31.

53. *Kyō habutae oridome*, pp. 501–21. The list also includes the dealers in silk thread imported from China through Nagasaki, over fifty money changers, and a range of other enterprises (from antique dealers to sake dealers).

54. *Edo sōkanoko meisho taizen*, 4: 60–72.

55. For the agrarian revolution, see Thomas C. Smith, *The Agrarian Origins of Modern Japan;* for agrarian taxes, see Smith, "The Land Tax in the Tokugawa Period," in id., *Native Sources of Japanese Industrialization, 1750–1920* (Berkeley: Uni-

versity of California Press, 1988); for commercial organization and taxation (in the context of the Kyōhō Reforms), see Hauser, *Economic Institutional Change in Tokugawa Japan*, pp. 33–37; for consumption and standard of living, see Susan B. Hanley and Kozo Yamamura, *Economic and Demographic Change in Preindustrial Japan, 1600–1868* (Princeton, N.J.: Princeton University Press, 1977), and Hanley, *Everyday Things in Premodern Japan* (Berkeley: University of California Press, 1997), pp. 1–24. Also see, for a synoptic discussion, E. Sydney Crawcour, "The Tokugawa Period and Japan's Preparation for Modern Economic Growth," *Journal of Japanese Studies* 1, no. 1 (Autumn 1974): 113–25.

56. Donald H. Shively, "Sumptuary Regulation and Status in Early Tokugawa Japan," *Harvard Journal of Asiatic Studies* 25 (1964–65): 123–64.

57. For the economic challenges and varying policy responses of the Tokugawa regime, see Tsuji Tatsuya, "Politics in the Eighteenth Century," in *Cambridge History of Japan*, vol. 4: *Early Modern Japan*, ed. Hall, esp. pp. 445–77; Nakai, *Shogunal Politics*, pp. 95–128; and John Whitney Hall, *Tanuma Okitsugu: Forerunner of Modern Japan* (Cambridge, Mass.: Harvard University Press, 1955). A particularly powerful indictment of the later Tokugawa economy comes from Conrad Totman, who concludes *Early Modern Japan* (Berkeley: University of California Press, 1993) with two long parts titled "Struggling to Stand Still, 1710–1790" (pp. 233–395) and "The Erosion of Stability, 1790–1850" (pp. 397–539).

58. For sophisticated banking practices among the "Big Ten" money exchangers, see Susan B. Hanley and Kozo Yamamura, *Economic and Demographic Change in Preindustrial Japan*, p. 80.

59. See chapter 1, nn. 18–19, for rosters of prostitutes and actors. These evaluation books themselves became a subject of parody in the eighteenth century. See Nakano Mitsutoshi, *Edo meibutsu hyōbanki annai* (Tokyo: Iwanami Shoten, 1985).

60. For example, in the collection of the East Asian Library at the University of California, Berkeley, *Kyō meisho hitori annai*, *Naniwa meisho hitori annai*, *Edo machi hitori annai*, *Edo machimachi hitori annai iroha wake* (*Zōho*) *Noboribune hitori annai*, *Ryōkū setsu massha hitori annai*.

61. *Kyō habutae*, pp. 70–92.

62. *Edo sōkanoko meisho taizen*, 3: 42–49, 63–68.

63. This genealogy simplifies complex issues of derivation and influence. For detailed analyses of a major subject in Japanese cultural and social history, see Tanaka Sen'ichi, *Nenjū gyōji no kenkyū*, and Endō Motoo and Yamanaka Yutaka, eds., *Nenjū gyōji no rekishigaku*.

64. See n. 39 above. By the late Edo period, scholars were conducting national surveys of ritual practice by distributing exacting questionnaires to individual local communities. While yielding exceptional information, the surveys also enforced a certain convergence in ritual practice and conception by posing standard questions that encouraged standardized responses. See *Shokoku fūzoku monjō kotae* in Miyamoto Tsuneichi, Haraguchi Torao, and Higa Shunchō, eds., *Nihon shomin seikatsu shiryō shūsei* (Tokyo: San'ichi Shobō, 1968–84), 9: 453–843.

65. Nam-Lin Hur explores the manifold roles of temple and temple life in *Prayer and Play in Late Tokugawa Japan: Asakusa Sensōji and Edo Society* (Cambridge, Mass.: Harvard University Asia Center, 2000).

6. CULTURAL CUSTODY, CULTURAL LITERACY

1. Kaibara Ekiken, *Keijō shōran*, in Kyōto Sōsho Kankōkai, ed., *Kyōto sōsho*, 2: 1–39 (the third text in the volume, each paginated separately). For the quotation beginning with "Our Japan,' see pp. 1–2 of the preface. Ekiken also mentions in this section of the text that people of old had called Japan "Akitsushima." For an excellent discussion of Ekiken's travel writing, a genre distinct from the guide literature, see Yonemoto, *Mapping Early Modern Japan*, pp. 44–68 (where analysis focuses on *Jinshin kikō*).

2. The daily itineraries are so carefully planned (sometimes in circular form, always with logistical notes) that Ekiken probably meant readers to take each day's assignment in a single dose. Although it seems much less likely that he imagined readers with the leisure and perseverance to take on seventeen continuous days of touring, he probably wanted them—however long or selectively they strung out the experience—to follow his general sequence, which contains a clear geographical logic and builds on internal references that presume orderly progress. References in individual and successive entries to a variety of seasonal pleasures (autumn maples and spring cherries, for example) invite readers to initiate, resume, and repeat the tours at different times of the year.

3. *Keijō shōran*, p. 1 of the table of contents.

4. Ibid., p. 1 of the main text. As those familiar with Kyoto would expect, the instruction focuses on the use of the "four terms" (*agaru, sagaru, nishi iru, higashi iru*) that are distinctive to navigation in the imperial capital.

5. Ibid., p. 10.

6. Ibid., p. 8.

7. Ibid., p. 15.

8. Ibid., p. 28.

9. Ibid., p. 25.

10. Ibid., p. 2 of the main text.

11. Ibid., pp. 9–10, 7, 12.

12. Ibid., pp. 6–7.

13. Ibid., pp. 8–9.

14. Ekiken's major geographical text is the *Chikuzen no kuni zokufudoki*. See Ekiken-kai, ed., *Ekiken zenshū*, vol. 4. Also see ibid., vol. 7, for other travel writing, including *Azumaji no ki, Kisoji no kikō, Washū junranki, Saikoku kikō, Nanyū kikō*, and *Nikkō meishoki*.

15. *Keijō shōran*, pp. 10, 13, 14.

16. For important analyses of Ekiken's thought, see Tetsuo Najita, *Visions of*

Virtue in Tokugawa Japan: The Kaitokudō Merchant Academy of Osaka (Chicago: University of Chicago Press, 1987), esp. pp. 45–59, and Najita, "History and Nature in Eighteenth-Century Tokugawa Thought," in *Cambridge History of Japan*, vol. 4: *Early Modern Japan*, ed. Hall, pp. 621–25. Other major sources include Mary Evelyn Tucker, *Moral and Spiritual Cultivation in Japanese Neo-Confucianism: The Life and Thought of Kaibara Ekken, 1630–1714* (Albany: State University of New York Press, 1989), and Okada Takehiko, "Practical Learning in the Chu Hsi School: Yamazaki Ansai and Kaibara Ekken," in Wm. Theodore de Bary and Irene Bloom, eds., *Principle and Practicality: Essays in Neo-Confucianism and Practical Learning* (New York: Columbia University Press, 1979), esp. pp. 257–90.

17. *Banmin chōhōki*, in Kinsei Bungaku Shoshi Kenkyūkai, ed., *Kinsei bungaku shiryō ruijū: Sankō bunken-hen*, 10: 129–261.

18. For discussion, see Shively, "Popular Culture," and Yokoyama, "*Setsuyōshū* and Japanese Civilization." For classic examples, see Kataoka Osamu, ed., *Ōtani daigaku-bon setsuyōshū (Kenkyū narabini sōgō sakuin)* (Tokyo: Benseisha, 1982); and Nakada Norio and Kobayashi Shōjirō, *Gōrui setsuyōshū (Kenkyū narabini sakuin)* (Tokyo: Benseisha, 1979).

19. The seminal work in the genre, the original *Kinmōzui* by Nakamura Tekisai, appears in Kinsei Bungagku Shoshi Kenkyūkai, ed., *Kinsei bungaku shiryō ruijū: Sankō bunken-hen*, vol. 4. Also see, e.g., Asakura Haruhiko, ed., *Jinrin kinmōzui* and, for a text addressed to young women, Tanaka Chitako and Tanaka Motoo, eds., *Joyō kinmōzui* (Tokyo: Watanabe Shoten, 1969). In the latter text and elsewhere, the basic term is sometimes glossed phonetically as *kunmōzui*.

20. For a representative sample, see Kinsei Bungaku Shoshi Kenkyūkai, ed., *Kinsei bungaku shiryō ruijū: Sankō bunken-hen*, vols. 2, 5, 8, 10, 14, 15, 16. For discussion of *chōhōki* addressed to women in the Meiji period, see Yokota Fuyuhiko, "Imaging Working Women in Early Modern Japan," in Hitomi Tonomura, Anne Walthall, and Wakita Haruko, eds., *Women and Class in Japanese History* (Ann Arbor: Center for Japanese Studies, University of Michigan, 1999), pp. 153–68.

21. While most of these figures are problematic, the total number of villages is off by a considerable factor—the result, perhaps, of either scribal error or inclusion of the many subunits registered within village cadastres. The most authoritative count we have of Tokugawa villages is 63,126 in the early nineteenth century. See Kodama Kōta et al., eds., *Kinseishi no handobukku* (Tokyo: Kintō Shuppansha, 1972), pp. 215–17.

22. I am not familiar with the prototype for these calculations.

23. See *Banmin chōhōki*, pp. 206–9, for the full list of military leaders, p. 209 for Tokugawa Ieyasu.

24. See ibid., pp. 202–4 for the era names and emperors during the Nanbokuchō period (1333–92). Parallel information on the rival courts is interspersed in chronological order, although the northern or senior line (resident in Kyoto) is given pride of place. In both the opening list of emperors (item one, pp. 131–41) and the later list of era names (item 12), this text follows conventional early mod-

ern practice by associating legitimacy with the northern line. For discussion of the succession crisis, and ongoing historiographical debates, see H. Paul Varley, *Imperial Restoration in Medieval Japan* (New York: Columbia University Press, 1971).

25. These entries (which became sufficiently conventional to be reproduced in such texts as the *Kokka man'yōki*) appear to derive, directly or indirectly, from documents assembled by the office of the Kyoto magistrate. See Iwao Seiichi, ed., *Kyōto oyakusho-muki taigai oboegaki*, 1: 15–29.

26. See, e.g., the *Chōhōki taizen* in Kinsei Bungaku Shoshi Kenkyūkai, ed., *Kinsei bungaku shiryō ruijū: Sankō bunken-hen*, 10: 3–126. Although the letter-writing format was used to teach vocabulary from at least the late classical period, the Treasuries attend to the craft of correspondence itself, draft material for specific occasions, and the techniques of folding, addressing, and presenting letters. See pp. 8–43.

27. See chapter 5 for discussion of urban directories and their lists of specialized teachers and shops.

28. The Treasury list, which appears on pp. 167–68, is identical to a list in the *Kyō habutae oridome* in (Shinshū) Kyōto Sōsho Kankōkai, ed., *(Shinshū) Kyōto sōsho*, 2: 360–61.

29. The list is reproduced, e.g., in the *Edo sōganoko meisho taizen* in Edo Sōsho Kankōkai, ed., *Edo sōsho*, 3: 49–63.

30. Nishikawa Jōken, *Chōnin bukuro* and *Hyakushō bukuro*, in Takimoto Seiichi, ed., *Nihon keizai taiten*, 4: 387–490, 493–533. For discussion, see Tetsuo Najita, *Visions of Virtue in Tokugawa Japan*, pp. 48–59.

7. NATION

1. For a good introduction to Tokugawa population surveys, see Hanley and Yamamura, *Economic and Demographic Change in Preindustrial Japan*, pp. 40–45. The most detailed surviving evidence concerning administrative and commercial recordkeeping appears in the documents of the Kyoto and Nagasaki magistrates' offices. See Iwao Seiichi, ed., *Kyōto oyakusho-muki taigai oboegaki*, and (for example) Morinaga Taneo, ed., *Nagasaki bugyōsho kiroku: Oshioki ukagaishū* (Nagasaki: Hankachō Kankōkai, 1962) and *Nagasaki daikan kirokushū* (Nagasaki: Hankachō Kankōkai, 1963).

2. For a fascinating discussion of the role of advertising and promotion in the commercial literature, see David Pollack, "Marketing Desire: Advertising and Sexuality in Edo Literature, Drama, and Art," in Sumie Jones, ed., *Imaging/Reading Eros: Proceedings for the Conference, Sexuality and Edo Culture, 1750–1850* (Bloomington: East Asian Studies Center, Indiana University, 1996), pp. 47–62.

3. Exceptional efforts to explore premodern variants of the nation include Adrian Hastings, *The Construction of Nationhood: Ethnicity, Religion, and Nationalism* (Cambridge: Cambridge University Press, 1997), and Anthony D. Smith,

Nationalism: Theory, Ideology, History (Cambridge: Polity Press; Malden, Mass.: Blackwell, 2001). Smith offers a particularly trenchant review of the classic and more recent literature and its modernist bias. Although the foundational works (Ernest Renan's "What Is a Nation?"; John Stuart Mill's "Considerations on Representative Government"; and the Second International's "The National Question") specifically address the "modern nation," and hence seemingly allow the possibility of premodern variants, both their rhetoric and their comparisons effectively fuse nation-ness with modernity to frustrate as unthinkable an alternative approach. And, indeed, the vast subsequent literature focuses with rare departures on the modern experience. See, e.g., the otherwise capaciously imagined work in Homi Bhaba, ed., *Nation and Narration* (New York: Routledge, 1990).

4. Although "nation" is a pervasive and defining trope in the historiography of modern Japan, scholars also capture change (often ambivalently, in a literature of subtlety) with terms such as "modernization," "westernization," "centralization," "state-formation," and, critically, the emergence of "national consciousness" and "nationalism." Major works in a large literature include W. G. Beasely, *The Meiji Restoration* (Stanford, Calif.: Stanford University Press, 1972); Sheldon Garon, *Molding Japanese Minds: The State in Everyday Life* (Princeton, N.J.: Princeton University Press, 1997); Carol Gluck, *Japan's Modern Myths: Ideology in the Late Meiji Period* (Princeton, N.J.: Princeton University Press, 1985); Thomas R. H. Havens, *Farm and Nation in Modern Japan* (Princeton, N.J.: Princeton University Press, 1974); Kenneth Pyle, *The Making of Modern Japan* (Lexington, Mass.: D.C. Heath, 1996 [1978]); and Richard J. Samuels, *"Rich Nation, Strong Army": National Security and the Technological Transformation of Japan* (Ithaca, N.Y.: Cornell University Press, 1994). For an important (and unusual) exploration of national thought and the politicization of cultural and ethical discourse in the early modern period, see Harry Harootunian, *Toward Restoration: The Growth of Political Consciousness in Tokugawa Japan* (Berkeley: University of California Press, 1970). Most recent scholars of premodern Japan implicitly or explicitly reject national characterizations. See, e.g., Thomas LaMarre, *Uncovering Heian Japan: An Archeology of Sensation and Inscription* (Durham, N.C.: Duke University Press, 2000). Also see n. 41 below. For an early scholarly exchange on nation and nationalism, see the "Symposium on Japanese Nationalism" in the *Journal of Asian Studies* 31, no. 7 (November 1971).

5. So vexed an undertaking that scholars like Hugh Seton-Watson disavow it, definition nonetheless remains a primary concern of the literature on the nation. And, however varied their terminology and intense their debates, such leading theorists as Ernest Gellner, Eric Hobsbawm, and Benedict Anderson all ultimately stress some congruence of territory, state, and culture in their own formulations. Anderson's nation, e.g., is an "imagined community" (a *culture* of images and ideas) that is "inherently limited" (a *territory* with "boundaries, beyond which lie other nations") and "sovereign" (explicitly a "*state*"). See Anderson, *Imagined Communities*, pp. 5–7 and, quoting Seton-Watson, p. 3; Ernest Gellner, *Nations*

and Nationalism (Ithaca, N.Y.: Cornell University Press, 1985); and Eric Hobsbawm, *Nations and Nationalism since 1700: Programme, Myth, Reality* (New York: Cambridge University Press, 1992). Throughout the literature, discussions of "nation" merge with discussions of "nationalism," which, in Gellner's view, "*invents* nations where they do not exist*" (quoted by Anderson on p. 6). I separate the two notions to argue that the early modern nation of Japan was antecedent to nationalism. The definition of nation that I use here is not meant to preclude other approaches with other resolutions. Nor is my argument about the existence of nation-ness in early modernity meant to preclude arguments about the existence of nation-ness in earlier times.

6. Shinroku's tale is told in "A Feather in Daikoku's Cap," one of thirty stories in Ihara Saikaku, *The Japanese Family Storehouse, or, The Millionaire's Gospel Modernized. Nippon eitai-gura, or Daifuku shin chōja kyō (1688)*, trans. and ed. G. W. Sargent (Cambridge: Cambridge University Press, 1959), pp. 43–49. For the modern editions of the text (*Nihon eitaigura*, the reading preferred by most scholars) consulted by Sargent, see p. 148. One of the most accessible current editions appears in Asō Isoji et al., ed., *Nihon koten bungaku taikei*, vol. 48 (*Saikakushū ge*, annot. Noma Kōshin), pp. 29–189. "Saigaku o kasa ni kiru daikoku" is on pp. 67–73.

7. For the quotation, see Saikaku, *Japanese Family Storehouse*, trans. and ed. Sargent, p. 49.

8. For the encounters with the beggars, see ibid., pp. 46–48. I introduce as the second beggar the character Saikuku places third, and as the third beggar the character Saikaku places second. His treatment of the Edo native is so brief, and of the Sakai emigrant so long, that I have switched the order for narrative convenience.

9. Ibid., pp. 47–48.

10. Ibid., p. 49.

11. For the fox puns, see ibid., p. 44; for the juxtaposition of trade and Shinagawa, pp. 46, 48. In his agile introduction, translation, and notes, Sargent provides exceptional guidance to Saikaku's verbal virtuosity.

12. Ibid., pp. 22–23.

13. Ibid., p. 92.

14. Ihara Saikaku's fiction concerning samurai includes *Buke giri monogatari*, trans. Caryl Ann Callahan as *Tales of Samurai Honor: Buke giri monogatari* (Tokyo: *Monumenta Nipponica*, Sophia University, 1981); *Nanshoku ōkagami*, trans. Paul Gordon Schalow as *The Great Mirror of Male Love* (Stanford, Calif.: Stanford University Press, 1990); *Budō denraiki*; and *Shin kashōki*.

15. Saikaku, *Japanese Family Storehouse*, trans. and ed. Sargent, pp. 23–24.

16. Ibid., p. 87 for Nagasaki, and pp. 39–40 for Ōtsu.

17. Ibid., p. 101 for noh at Kitano Shichihonmatsu.

18. Ibid., p. 60 for Edo, p. 22 for Osaka, p. 30 for Nara, p. 39 for Ōtsu, p. 89 for Ise, and p. 137 for Sakai.

19. For example, in his national map of 1691 (*Nihon kaisan chōrikuzu*), the popular commercial mapmaker Ishikawa Ryūsen includes, at the margins, labels for

"Ezo," which extends (mostly beyond the picture plane) north of "Matsumae" in Hokkaido; "Ryūkyū," which extends south of Kyushu; "Chōsen," which extends north of "Tsushima"; and "Kara," which extends north of "Tango." Along the upper left margin, he also includes a distance chart to more remote foreign countries. See Unno Kazutaka et al., eds., *Nihon kochizu taisei,* vol. 1, pl. 31. For discussion of border areas, see Brett L. Walker, *The Conquest of Ainu Lands: Ecology and Culture in Japanese Expansion, 1590–1800* (Berkeley: University of California Press, 2001); David L. Howell, "Ainu Ethnicity and the Boundaries of the Early Modern Japanese State," *Past and Present* 142 (1994): 69–93; Bruce Batten, "Frontiers and Boundaries of Pre-Modern Japan," *Journal of Historical Geography* 25, no. 2 (1999): 166–82; and Tessa Morris-Suzuki, "Creating the Frontier: Border, Identity, and History in Japan's Far North," *East Asian History* 7 (1994): 1–24.

20. See Saikaku, *Japanese Family Storehouse,* trans. and ed. Sargent, p. 129 for the lotus leaves, and p. 21 for the Izumi ships.

21. Ibid., pp. 65, 87, and 106 for the imports arriving in Nagasaki.

22. Ibid., pp. 129, 65, 67, and 78 for the China references.

23. Ibid., p. 85.

24. Ibid., p. 129.

25. Ibid., p. 86.

26. Kornicki, *Book in Japan,* pp. 296–300, discusses books imported from China. Also see Emanuel Pastreich, "Grappling with Chinese Writing as a Material Language," *Harvard Journal of Asiatic Studies* 61, no. 1 (June 2001): 119–70, esp. the reference on p. 125 to the "massive importation of Chinese texts into Japan during the early eighteenth century." Early modern imports (which remain hard to count) are only one aspect of a complex transmission of knowledge that included translation, domestic publication of older as well as recent titles, Japanese scholarship based on imported texts, and the commercial repackaging and anthologizing of Chinese material. For some sense of the sources available in print, see Oka Masahiko et al., comps., *Edo Printed Books at Berkeley,* esp. the sections on "Chinese Books with Japanese Commentary," "Chinese Books Printed in Japan," "Language (*gaikokugo*)," "History (*gaikokushi*)," "Geography (*gaikoku chishi*)," "Sciences," and "Medicine." Basic texts include the family encyclopedia *Morokoshi kinmōzui* (1719); the guide to famous places, *Morokoshi meisho zue* (1805); and any number of "Japan-China" anthologies like the *Wakan shoga ichiran* (1821), which juxtaposes examples of Japanese and Chinese calligraphy and painting.

27. The texts are Nishikawa Jōken's *Ka'i tsūshō kō* (1695, rev. 1709) and Terajima Ryōan's *Wakan sansai zue* (1712, modeled on a Ming encyclopedia). For analysis, see Yonemoto, *Mapping Early Modern Japan,* pp. 103–8.

28. Korea figured prominently in Chinese and Japanese encyclopedias, gazetteers imported in the eighteenth century, and world atlases compiled in Japan after 1740. Still, the volume and impact of imported books, as well as the extent of Korean knowledge in Japan, remained limited. See Kornicki, *Book in Japan,* pp. 293–96, 299–300.

29. See ibid., pp. 300–306 and, for a good overview of "Western Learning," the entry on that subject by Frits Vos in the *Kodansha Encyclopedia of Japan* (Tokyo: Kodansha International, 1983), 8: 241–43. The East Asian Library at the University of California, Berkeley, holds woodblock editions of the original *Rangaku kaitei* (1788, by Ōtsuki Gentaku) as well as *Kōmō zatsuwa* (1787), *Bango sen* (1798), and *Rango kanriji kō* (1855).

30. For a far-reaching analysis of the Korean embassies and their representation, see Ronald P. Toby, "Carnival of the Aliens: Korean Embassies in Edo-Period Art and Popular Culture," *Monumenta Nipponica* 41, no. 4 (Winter 1986): 412–56. For representations of the embassies from Ryukyu, see, in the East Asian Library of the University of California, Berkeley, *Ryūkyūjin gyōretsu taizen* (1748), *Ryūkyūjin gyōretsuki* (1832), and *Ryūkyūjin raichō irozurizu* (undated).

31. Although they had been published in the seventeenth century, maps of Nagasaki proliferated in the eighteenth, when Nagasaki itself became a publishing center. See Yamori Kazuhiko, *Toshizu no rekishi, Nihon-hen*, pp. 176–79 and the extensive list of Nagasaki maps (most of them different editions from a variety of publishers) in Kōbe-shi Hakubutsukan, ed., *Kanzōhin mokuroku*, 3: 53–55. Yonemoto, *Mapping Early Modern Japan*, pp. 69–100, discusses the eighteenth-century travel literature concerning both Nagasaki and Ezo. I know of no published travel writing concerning Tsushima.

32. See, e.g., Yonemoto, *Mapping Early Modern Japan*, pp. 69–100, esp. pp. 74–80, 92, 94–95

33. Threats were not absent, notably the plot of Yui Shōsetsu (a samurai instructor of military science) to lead *rōnin* in a rebellion against the shogunate in 1651. The rebellion was aborted and Shōsetsu committed suicide when the plan was uncovered by the authorities.

34. This generalization is not meant to obscure two important developments: on the one hand, an expansion of various forms of illicit trade among Chinese and Japanese adventurers in southwestern ports; and, on the other, an increasing incidence in the landings of foreign ships (mainly American, British, and Russian) and demands for Japanese services. The ensuing sense of crisis in certain circles, from the late eighteenth century, is explored in Harootunian, *Toward Restoration,* and Bob Tadashi Wakabayashi, *Anti-Foreign Threat and Western Learning in Early Modern Japan* (Cambridge, Mass.: Council on East Asian Studies, Harvard University, 1986). For the general public, an awareness of the outside world may have been kept fresh (or, perhaps just as likely, routinized into oblivion) by the annual registrations *(shūmon aratame)* that continued to entail disavowals of Christian belief. It was also nurtured more dramatically by the published "castaway narratives" that described the adventures of Japanese sailors who were cast adrift by storms, recovered by foreign ships, and eventually returned home. These narratives are the subject of ongoing work by Stephen Kohl and his students at the University of Oregon.

35. For a remarkable comparison of casualties associated with the French Revolution and the Meiji Restoration, see Mikawa Hiroshi, *Meiji ishin to nashona-*

rizumu: Bakumatsu no gaikō to seiji hendō (Tokyo: Yamakawa Shuppansha, 1997), p. 320.

36. For a vivid account of the transforming impact of foreign connection on a local economy, see, e.g., Kären Wigen, *The Making of a Japanese Periphery, 1760–1920* (Berkeley: University of California Press, 1995). For the rapid integration of foreign knowledge into school primers, see Ishikawa Matsutarō, *Ōraimono no seiritsu to tenkai*, pp. 108–9. For an overview of the subject, see Hirakawa Sukehiro, "Japan's Turn to the West," in *The Cambridge History of Japan*, vol. 5: *The Nineteenth Century*, ed. Marius B. Jansen et al. (New York: Cambridge University Press, 1989), pp. 432–98.

37. See Ronald P. Toby, "Contesting the Centre: International Sources of Japanese Identity," *International History Review* 7, no. 3 (1985): 347–63, and Marius B. Jansen, *China in the Tokugawa World* (Cambridge, Mass.: Harvard University Press, 1992). Nakai, *Shogunal Politics,* pp. 327–31, discusses Arai Hakuseki's rejection of a Sino-centric worldview.

38. See, e.g., Saikaku, *Japanese Family Storehouse,* trans. and ed. Sargent, p. 19 (for licensed brothels), p. 27 (for sumptuary laws), p. 44 (for the neighborhood group), p. 48 (for the outcast guild), p. 101 (for licensed traders), p. 112 (for the calendar), and p. 133 (for currency).

39. Although censorship laws constrained mention of the shogun (see Kornicki, *Book in Japan,* pp. 331–58, esp. 334–35), a combination of ambiguity and lax enforcement resulted in fairly free reference to the Tokugawa in the Military Mirrors and other information texts. Saikaku himself refers openly to a number of potentially fraught subjects: the battle of Sekigahara (*Tales of Samurai Honor,* trans., Callahan, p. 106); the Shimabara uprising (ibid., p. 78); earlier military troublemakers such as Akechi Mitsuhide, Oda Nobunaga, Toyotomi Hideyoshi, and Ishida Mitsunari (ibid., pp. 34–38, 61–65, 97, 111); and present martial houses such as the Hachisuka (ibid., p. 52). Hence the absence of direct Tokugawa references in his texts seems hardly a result of legal coercion.

40. For the effective confinement of the shogun in Edo castle, see Totman, *Politics in the Tokugawa Bakufu,* pp. 89–109, esp. 89–90. Also see Nakai, *Shogunal Politics,* p. 152 (for the rare use of the shogunal seal), and pp. 137–41 (for Arai Hakuseki's unusual interest in projecting the shogun as the "refuge of the people" through grants of amnesty).

41. Three recent books emphasize the local autonomy of the daimyo domains and call "into question the very possibility of 'Japan' as the unit of analysis in the early modern era": Brown, *Central Authority and Local Autonomy in the Formation of Early Modern Japan;* Mark Ravina, *Land and Lordship in Early Modern Japan* (Stanford, Calif.: Stanford University Press, 1999); and Roberts, *Mercantilism in a Japanese Domain.* Ronald P. Toby (whom I quote above) undertakes a wide review of the literature on the early modern polity (focusing on Ravina and Roberts) and advances a trenchant argument that, however "rich in local and regional diversity and cross-cut by competing loyalties," Japan was nonetheless "a single protona-

tion." See "Rescuing the Nation from History: The State of the State in Early Modern Japan," *Monumenta Nipponica* 56, no. 2 (Summer 2001): 127–237. The first quotation appears on p. 199, the second on p. 230. For state-centered analyses of early modern politics, also see James W. White, *Ikki: Social Conflict and Political Protest in Early Modern Japan* (Ithaca, N.Y.: Cornell University Press, 1995) and Nakai, *Shogunal Politics,* pp. 129–50, 173–212. For discussion of the role of the court in Tokugawa Japan, see Lee Butler, *Emperor and Aristocracy in Japan: Resilience and Renewal* (Cambridge, Mass.: Harvard University Asia Center, 2002).

42. Although Hideyoshi's investment in public display is exceptional in Japanese history (see Berry, *Hideyoshi,* pp. 168–205), the "unification" period in general (c. 1575–1615) was accompanied by unusual acts of pageantry—processions, flamboyant memorial services, public festivities, massive building projects—that suggest a need to convert a general audience to some confidence in the peace and quiescent obedience to the conquerors.

43. For the moralistic flavor of Tokugawa laws, see the sample of rural and urban statutes in Lu, *Sources of Japanese History,* 1: 204–14. The absence of a controlling Neo-Confucian orthodoxy in the Tokugawa regime, and the protean virtuosity of "official" discourse, is the subject of Ooms, *Tokugawa Ideology.* For schooling and curricula, see Ronald P. Dore, *Education in Tokugawa Japan* (Berkeley: University of California Press, 1965) and Richard Rubinger, *Private Academies of Tokugawa Japan* (Princeton, N.J.: Princeton University Press, 1982). For a masterful study of a merchant academy in Osaka, see Tetsuo Najita, *Visions of Virtue.*

44. Major works on (primarily rural) protest include Herman Ooms, *Tokugawa Village Practice: Class, Status, Power, Law* (Berkeley: University of California Press, 1996); Irwin Scheiner, "Benevolent Lords and Honorable Peasants: Rebellion and Peasant Consciousness in Tokugawa Japan," in Tetsuo Najita and Scheiner, eds., *Japanese Thought in the Tokugawa Period: Methods and Metaphors* (Chicago: University of Chicago Press, 1979), pp. 39–62; Stephen Vlastos, *Peasant Uprisings and Protests in Tokugawa Japan* (Berkeley: University of California Press, 1986); Anne Walthall, "Edo Riots," in James L. McClain et al., eds., *Edo and Paris,* pp. 407–28; Walthall, *Social Protest and Popular Culture in Eighteenth-Century Japan* (Tucson: University of Arizona Press, 1986); Walthall, *Peasant Uprisings in Japan: A Critical Anthology of Peasant Histories* (Chicago: University of Chicago Press, 1991); and James W. White, *Ikki: Social Conflict and Political Protest in Early Modern Japan* (Ithaca, N.Y.: Cornell University Press, 1995). For scholarly commentary on rule, see Tetsuo Najita, *Visions of Virtue;* Ian James McMullen, *Idealism, Protest, and the Tale of Genji: The Confucianism of Kumazawa Banzan* (Oxford: Clarendon Press, 1999); J. R. McEwan, *The Political Writings of Ogyū Sorai* (Cambridge: Cambridge University Press, 1962); and Tessa Morris-Suzuki, *A History of Japanese Economic Thought* (New York: Routledge, 1989), pp. 7–43.

45. See Tetsuo Najita, "Ōshio Heihachirō (1793–1837)," in Albert M. Craig and Donald H. Shively, eds., *Personality in Japanese History* (Berkeley: University of

California Press, 1970), pp. 155–79. For the millenarian rebellions of the late Tokugawa period, see Scheiner, "Benevolent Lords and Honorable Peasants."

46. The three quotations are from the "Imperial Rescript on the Promulgation of the Constitution," which appears in the "Constitution of the Empire of Japan, 1889," in *Kodansha Encyclopedia of Japan*, 2: 7–9. See the "Imperial Rescript," p. 7, lines 11, 16, and 17. For a now classic analysis of Meiji ideology and the context of constitutional thought, see Gluck, *Japan's Modern Myths*.

47. The three quotations are from the "Preamble" to the Constitution in "Imperial Rescript," in *Kodansha Encyclopedia of Japan*, 2: 7, lines 3, 17–18, and 33–34.

48. The two quotations are from "Chapter II" of the Constitution in ibid., p. 8, articles 20 and 21.

49. "The Imperial Rescript on Education," in Ryusaku Tsunoda, Wm. Theodore de Bary, and Donald Keene, comps., *Sources of the Japanese Tradition* (New York: Columbia University Press, 1958), pp. 646–47, lines 1–2, 3, and 13–14. The novel projection of the emperor and the disciplining of commoners into a "unified and totalizing culture" is the subject of Takashi Fujitani, *Splendid Monarchy: Power and Pageantry in Modern Japan* (Berkeley: University of California Press, 1996). See, esp., the introduction, pp. 1–28 (which includes discussion of the Edo period and changes in the relations between ruler and ruled in its last decades) and, for an earlier formulation of the argument, "Inventing, Forgetting, Remembering: Toward a Historical Ethnography of the Nation-State," in Harumi Befu, ed., *Cultural Nationalism in East Asia* (Berkeley: Institute of East Asian Studies, 1993), pp. 77–106.

50. "Imperial Rescript," in *Kodansha Encyclopedia of Japan*, 2: 7, lines 19, 2, and 15–16.

51. The *Kan'ei shoka keizuden* (commissioned by the shogunate in 1641, completed in 1643, and overseen by Ōta Sukemune) is introduced in Chapter 4, pp. 113–15. It covers almost 1,500 houses.

52. For excellent treatments of early modern historical writing, see Najita, "History and Nature in Eighteenth-Century Tokugawa Thought," in *Cambridge History of Japan*, vol. 4: *Early Modern Japan*, ed. Hall; Bitō Masahide, "Thought and Religion, 1550–1700," ibid., pp. 404–12; Harry Harootunian, *Things Seen and Unseen: Discourse and Ideology in Tokugawa Nativism* (Chicago: University of Chicago Press, 1988); and Kate Wildman Nakai, "Tokugawa Confucian Historiography: The Hayashi, Early Mito School, and Arai Hakuseki," in Peter Nosco, ed., *Confucianism in Tokugawa Culture* (Princeton, N.J.: Princeton University Press, 1984), pp. 27–61.

53. The Military Mirrors invariably trace the shogun's family genealogy (see, e.g., Hashimoto Hiroshi, ed., *Dai bukan*, 1: 329–31) while broader guides and directories tend to list his predecessors in military power (see, e.g., *Edo sōkanoko meisho taizen*, 3: 1–2). Imperial and courtly genealogies appear both in general reference works (such as *Banmin chōhōki*) and palace rosters (such as *Kaisei on kuge tōkan*, 1700, in the East Asian Library of the University of California, Berkeley).

The family genealogies of daimyo and the professional genealogies of officeholders appear in most Military Mirrors from the late seventeenth century; the professional genealogies of actors and prostitutes appear in most evaluation booklets (*hyōbanki*) from the 1660s. Other widely circulated genealogical texts include, e.g., *Honchō gashi* (painters of the Kanō line); *Honchō kōsōden* (Buddhist priests); *Honchō jūsōden* (Confucian scholars); and *Shōka jinmeiroku* (merchants).

54. Friedrich Nietzsche, "On the Uses and Disadvantages of History for Life," in *Untimely Meditations*, ed. Daniel Breazeale, trans. R. J. Hollindale (Cambridge: Cambridge University Press, 1997), p. 75.

55. Ibid., p. 74.

56. See Kaibara Ekiken, *Keijō shōran*, p. 5 (for Hidetsugu's execution), p. 6 (for the retirement temple of Hideyoshi's consort), and p. 9 (for the ear mound and Hideyoshi's interment site). In general, the guide literature is replete with references to individual historical figures and their misadventures. The only sensitive historical subject I find conspicuously absent from popular texts on Kyoto is the Hokke (or Lotus) Rebellion of 1532–36 (which might well have been mentioned in conjunction with the twenty-one Lotus temples destroyed in 1536 and subsequently rebuilt). Whether the topic was uninteresting (because unassociated with any one prominent figure) or actually taboo is hard to judge.

57. "Imperial Rescript," in *Kodansha Encyclopedia of Japan*, 2: 7, lines 3, 14, and 12–13.

58. Sargent discusses the influence of the Danrin school on Saikaku's fiction in the introduction to Saikaku's *Japanese Family Storehouse*, pp. xviii–xxi, xxix–xxxix. Saikaku names the head of the Danrin school (Nishiyama Sōin) as the teacher of the Sakai aesthete in Shinroku's tale, p. 47. For a taste of the challenges in eighteenth-century fiction, see Robert W. Leutner, *Shikitei Sanba and the Comic Tradition in Edo Fiction* (Cambridge, Mass.: Council on East Asian Studies, Harvard University, 1985), particularly the annotation to the translation of *Ukiyoburo*, pp. 193–204.

59. For a wonderful study of early modern and modern humor, see Howard Hibbett, *The Chrysanthemum and the Fish: Japanese Humor since the Age of the Shoguns* (Tokyo: Kodansha International, 2002). Saikaku is the subject of chap. 2, pp. 43–86.

60. Ihara Saikaku, "The Tale of Gengobei, the Mountain of Love," in id., *Five Women Who Chose Love*, in *The Life of an Amorous Woman and Other Writings*, ed. and trans. Ivan Morris (New York: New Directions, 1963), p. 117.

61. The quotation appears in Saikaku, *Japanese Family Storehouse*, trans. and ed. Sargent, p. 242. Also see, in the same volume, Sargent's translations of "The Millionaire's Gospel," pp. 239–44, and "The Seventeen Injunctions of Shimai Sōshitsu," pp. 245–50. For discussion and translation of other merchant house codes, see J. Mark Ramseyer, "Thrift and Diligence: House Codes of Tokugawa Merchant Families," *Monumenta Nipponica* 34, no. 2 (Summer 1979): 209–30.

62. Ihara Saikaku, *Life of an Amorous Woman*, ed. and trans. Morris, pp. 121–208. See p. 207 for the count.

63. See the classic article by John Whitney Hall, "Rule by Status in Tokugawa Japan," *Journal of Japanese Studies* 1, no. 1 (Autumn 1974): 39–49, and David L. Howell, "Territoriality and Collective Identity in Tokugawa Japan," *Daedalus* 127, no. 3 (Summer 1998): 105–32. The "complexity" and "flexibility" that necessarily attended so durable an ascriptive system also made room for a performance ethic that is the subject of Thomas C. Smith's article, " 'Merit' as Ideology in the Tokugawa Period," in id., *Native Sources of Japanese Industrialization*, pp. 156–72.

64. Many of the themes I explore in this chapter—concepts of society, sociability, and the social; the culture of play; the lightness of history—are compellingly developed in a later context, and with different emphases, by Harry Harootunian in "Late Tokugawa Culture and Thought," in *Cambridge History of Japan*, vol. 5: *The Nineteenth Century*, ed. Jansen et al., pp. 168–258.

65. The scholarly literature on what we might broadly call the "public sphere" in the Meiji period is large. For an authoritative survey of critical developments in the early years, see Stephen Vlastos, "Opposition Movements in Early Meiji, 1868–1885," in *Cambridge History of Japan*, vol. 5: *The Nineteenth Century*, ed. Jansen et al., pp. 367–431. Also see Michael Lewis, *Rioters and Citizens: Mass Protest in Imperial Japan* (Berkeley: University of California Press, 1990), and Irokawa Daikichi, *The Culture of the Meiji Period*, translation ed. Marius B. Jansen (Princeton, N.J.: Princeton University Press, 1985).

66. Ryusaku Tsunoda et al., comps., *Sources of the Japanese Tradition*, p. 644, article 1.

67. For scholarship on the academy and popular protest, see n. 44, above.

68. The classic and still standard analysis of early modern literacy in Japan appears in Dore, *Education in Tokugawa Japan*. Also see Herbert Passin, *Society and Education in Japan* (New York: Teachers College Press, 1965), and, for continuing debate, Richard Rubinger, "Who Can't Read and Write? Illiteracy in Meiji Japan," *Monumenta Nipponica* 55, no. 2 (Summer 2000): 163–98, and Peter Kornicki, "Literacy Revisited: Some Reflections on Richard Rubinger's Findings," ibid., 56, no. 3 (Autumn 2001): 381–94. Correlations between reading ability and cultural literacy are necessarily weak, I believe, since the latter is variously expanded through exposure to readers, compliance with state disciplines, participation in rituals and other social performances, travel, and oral transmission.

BIBLIOGRAPHY

Aizu fudoki, fūzoku-chō. Edited by Shōji Kichinosuke. 3 vols. Tokyo: Yoshikawa Kōbunkan, 1979–80.

Akindo sugiwai kagami. In vol. 13 of *Nihon keizai taiten*, ed. Takimoto Seiichi, 583–649.

Akioka Takejirō, ed. *Nihon kochizu shūsei*. 5 parts. Tokyo: Kajima Kenkyūjo Shuppankai, 1971.

Akiyama Kunizō. *Kinsei Kyōto machigumi hattatsushi*. Tokyo: Hōsei Daigaku Shuppankyoku, 1980.

Akizato Ritō. Illus. Shunchōsai Takehara Nobushige. *Miyako meisho zue*. 6 fascicles. Kyoto: Yoshinoya Tamehachi, 1787. East Asian Library, University of California, Berkeley.

————. Illus. Shunchōsai Takehara Nobushige. *Miyako meisho zue*. In vol. 1 of *Kyōto sōsho*, ed. Kyōto Sōsho Kankōkai.

Akizawa Shigeru. "Taikō kenchi." In *Kinsei 1*, vol. 11 of *Iwanami kōza Nihon tsūshi*, ed. Asao Naohiro, 107–38.

Anderson, Benedict. *Imagined Communities: Reflections on the Origin and Spread of Nationalism*. 1983. Rev. ed., New York: Verso, 1991, seventh impression, 1996.

Asai Ryōi. *Edo meishoki*. In vol. 2 of *Edo sōsho*, ed. Edo Sōsho Kankōkai, 1–160.

————. *Edo meishoki*. Facsimile in vol. 8 of *Kinsei bungaku shiryō ruijū: Kohan chishi-hen*, ed. Asakura Haruhiko.

————. *Kyō suzume*. In vol. 2 of *Kyōto sōsho*, ed. Kyōto Sōsho Kankōkai, 1–98.

————. *Tōkaidō meishoki*. Edited by Asakura Haruhiko. 2 vols. Tokyo: Heibonsha, 1979.

————. *Tōkaidō meishoki*. Facsimile in vol. 8 of *Kinsei bungaku shiryō ruijū: Kohan chishi-hen*, ed. Kinsei Bungaku Shoshi Kenkyūkai.

Asakura Haruhiko, ed. *Kohan chishi sōsho*. 15 vols. Tokyo: Sumiya Shobō, 1969–71.

Asao Naohiro, ed. *Kinsei 1–5*. Vols. 11–15 of *Iwanami kōza Nihon tsūshi*. Tokyo: Iwanami Shoten, 1993–95.

Atwood, Margaret. *Cat's Eye*. New York: Doubleday, 1989.

Baba Akiko et al., eds. *Meisho, Hare kūkan no kōzō*. Special edition of *Shizen to bunka* 27 (1990).

Banmin chōhōki. Facsimile in vol. 10 of *Kinsei bungaku shiryō ruijū: Sankō bunken-hen,* ed. Kinsei Bungaku Shoshi Kenkyūkai, 129–261.

Batten, Bruce. "Frontiers and Boundaries of Pre-Modern Japan." *Journal of Historical Geography* 25, no. 2 (1999): 166–82.

Beasely, W. G. *The Meiji Restoration.* Stanford, Calif.: Stanford University Press, 1972.

Befu, Harumi. *Cultural Nationalism in East Asia.* Berkeley: Institute of East Asian Studies, 1993.

Berry, Mary Elizabeth. *The Culture of Civil War in Kyoto.* Berkeley: University of California Press, 1994.

———. *Hideyoshi.* Cambridge, Mass.: Harvard University Press, 1982.

———. "Public Peace and Private Attachment: The Goals and Conduct of Power in Early Modern Japan." *Journal of Japanese Studies* 12, no. 2 (Summer 1986): 237–71.

———. "Restoring the Past: The Documents of Hideyoshi's Magistrate in Kyoto." *Harvard Journal of Asiatic Studies* 42, no. 1 (June 1983): 479–92.

Bhaba, Homi, ed. *Nation and Narration.* New York: Routledge, 1990.

Bitō Masahide. "Thought and Religion, 1550–1700." In *The Cambridge History of Japan,* vol. 4: *Early Modern Japan,* ed. John Whitney Hall, 373–424.

Bolitho, Harold. "The Han." In *The Cambridge History of Japan,* vol. 4: *Early Modern Japan,* ed. John Whitney Hall, 183–234.

———. *Treasures among Men: The Fudai Daimyo in Tokugawa Japan.* New Haven: Yale University Press, 1974.

Brown, Philip C. *Central Authority and Local Autonomy in the Formation of Early Modern Japan: The Case of Kaga Domain.* Stanford, Calif.: Stanford University Press, 1993.

———. "The Mismeasure of Land: Land Surveying in the Tokugawa Period." *Monumenta Nipponica* 42, no. 1 (Spring 1987): 115–55.

Butler, Lee. *Emperor and Aristocracy in Japan: Resilience and Renewal.* Cambridge, Mass.: Harvard University Asia Center, 2002.

Chibbett, David. *The History of Japanese Printing and Book Illustration.* Tokyo: Kodansha International, 1977.

Chihōshi Kenkyū Kyōgikai, ed. *Toshi shūhen no chihōshi.* Tokyo: Yūzankaku Shuppan, 1990.

Chōhōki taizen. Facsimile in vol. 10 of *Kinsei bungaku shiryō ruijū: Sankō bunken-hen,* ed. Kinsei Bungaku Shoshi Kenkyūkai, 3–126.

Cortazzi, Hugh. *Isles of Gold: Antique Maps of Japan.* New York: John Weatherhill, 1983.

Cranston, Edwin A. *A Waka Anthology,* vol. 1: *The Gem-Glistening Cup.* Stanford, Calif.: Stanford University Press, 1993.

Crawcour, Sydney E. "The Tokugawa Period and Japan's Preparation for Modern Economic Growth." *Journal of Japanese Studies* 1, no. 1 (Autumn 1974): 113–25.

Dore, Ronald P. *Education in Tokugawa Japan.* Berkeley: University of California Press, 1965.

Edo kagami. Publishing information worn away. East Asian Library, University of California, Berkeley.

Edo kanoko. Facsimile in vol. 8 of *Kohan chishi sōsho,* ed. Asakura Haruhiko.

(Zōho) Edo sōkanoko meisho taizen. In *Edo sōsho,* ed. Edo Sōsho Kankōkai, 3: 1–88; 4: 1–131.

Edo Sōsho Kankōkai, ed. *Edo sōsho.* 12 vols. Tokyo: Edo Sōsho Kankōkai, 1916–17. Reprint, Tokyo: Meichōkai, 1964.

Edo suzume. In vol. 1 of *Kinsei bungei sōsho,* ed. Kokusho Kankōkai, 1–177 of 1910 edition.

Ejima Kiseki. *Keisei iro jamisen.* Annot. Hasegawa Tsuyoshi. In vol. 78 of *Shin Nihon koten bungaku taikei,* ed. Satake Akihiro et al., 3–248. Tokyo: Iwanami Shoten, 1989.

Elisonas, Jurgis. "Notorious Places: A Brief Excursion in the Narrative Topography of Early Edo." In *Edo and Paris: Urban Life and the State in the Early Modern Era,* ed. James L. McClain, John M. Merriman, and Ugawa Kaoru, 253–91.

Endō Motoo and Yamanaka Yutaka. *Nenjū gyōji no rekishigaku.* Tokyo: Kōbundō, 1981.

Fiévè, Nicolas. "The Urban Evolution of the City of *Heiankyō:* A Study of the Iconographic Sources, 1." *Japan Forum* 4, no. 1 (April 1992): 91–107.

Fujimoto Kizan. *Shikidō ōkagami.* Edited by Noma Kōshin. 3 vols. Tokyo: Yagi Shoten, 1974.

Fujino Tamotsu. *(Shintei) Bakuhan taiseishi no kenkyū.* Tokyo: Yoshikawa Kōbunkan, 1975.

Fujitani, Takashi. "Inventing, Forgetting, Remembering: Toward a Historical Ethnography of the Nation-State." In *Cultural Nationalism in East Asia,* ed. Harumi Befu, 77–106.

———. *Splendid Monarchy: Power and Pageantry in Modern Japan.* Berkeley: University of California Press, 1996.

Fujizane Kumiko. "Bukan no shoshigakuteki kenkyū." *Nihon rekishi* 525 (February 1992): 47–62.

Fukai Masaumi and Fujizane Kumiko, eds. *Edo bakufu yakushoku bukan hennen shūsei.* 35 vols. Tokyo: Tōyō Shorin, 1996.

Fukui Tamotsu. *Edo bakufu hensanbutsu: Kaisetsu-hen.* Tokyo: Yūshōdō Shuppan, 1983.

Funakoshi Akio. *Sakoku Nihon ni kita "Kōkizu" no chirigakushiteki kenkyū.* Tokyo: Hōsei Daigaku Shuppankyoku, 1986.

Funakoshi Masaichirō, ed. *Naniwa sōsho.* 17 vols. Osaka: Naniwa Sōsho Kankōkai, 1926–30.

Garon, Sheldon. *Molding Japanese Minds: The State in Everyday Life.* Princeton, N.J.: Princeton University Press, 1997.

Gellner, Ernest. *Nations and Nationalism.* Ithaca, N.Y.: Cornell University Press, 1985.

Gerhart, Karen M. *The Eyes of Power: Art and Early Tokugawa Authority.* Honolulu: University of Hawai'i Press, 1999.

————. "Visions of the Dead: Kanō Tan'yū's Paintings of Tokugawa Iemitsu's Dreams." *Monumenta Nipponica* 59, no. 1 (Spring 2004): 1–34.

Gluck, Carol. *Japan's Modern Myths: Ideology in the Late Meiji Period.* Princeton, N.J.: Princeton University Press, 1985.

Gomon tsukushi. In vol. 1 of *(Kaitei zōho) Daibukan,* ed. Hashimoto Hiroshi, 100–103.

Gorin bukan. 1 fascicle. Edo: Suwaraya Mobei, 1701. East Asian Library, University of California, Berkeley.

Gorin bukan. In vol. 1 of *(Kaitei zōho) Daibukan,* ed. Hashimoto Hiroshi, 329–63.

Hall, John Whitney. "The *Bakuhan* System." In *The Cambridge History of Japan,* vol. 4: *Early Modern Japan,* ed. John Whitney Hall, 128–82.

————. "Castle Towns and Japan's Early Modern Unification." In *Studies in the Institutional History of Early Modern Japan,* ed. John Whitney Hall and Marius B. Jansen, 169–81.

————. "Foundations of the Modern Japanese Daimyo." In *Studies in the Institutional History of Early Modern Japan,* ed. John Whitney Hall and Marius B. Jansen, 65–77.

————. "Rule by Status in Tokugawa Japan." *Journal of Japanese Studies* 1, no. 1 (Autumn 1974): 39–49.

————. *Tanuma Okitsugu: Forerunner of Modern Japan.* Cambridge, Mass.: Harvard University Press, 1955.

————, ed. *Early Modern Japan.* Vol. 4 of *The Cambridge History of Japan.* New York: Cambridge University Press, 1991.

Hall, John Whitney, and Marius B. Jansen, eds. *Studies in the Institutional History of Early Modern Japan.* Princeton, N.J.: Princeton University Press, 1968.

Hall, John Whitney, Keiji Nagahara, and Kozo Yamamura, eds. *Japan before Tokugawa: Political Consolidation and Economic Growth, 1500–1650.* Princeton, N.J.: Princeton University Press, 1981.

Hamashita Takeshi and Karashima Noboru, eds. *Chiikishi to wa nani ka?* Tokyo: Yamakawa Shuppansha, 1997.

Hanley, Susan B. *Everyday Things in Premodern Japan.* Berkeley: University of California Press, 1997.

Hanley, Susan B., and Kozo Yamamura. *Economic and Demographic Change in Preindustrial Japan, 1600–1868.* Princeton, N.J.: Princeton University Press, 1977.

Harada Tomohiko and Nishikawa Kōji, eds. *Nihon no shigai kozu.* 2 vols. Tokyo: Kashima Kenkyūjo Shuppan, 1972–73.

Harada Tomohiko, Yamori Kazuhiko, and Yanai Akira. *Ōsaka kochizu monogatari.* Tokyo: Mainichi Shinbunsha, 1980.

Harley, J. B. *The New Nature of Maps: Essays on the History of Cartography.* Edited by Paul Laxton. Baltimore: Johns Hopkins University Press, 2001.

———."Silences and Secrecy: The Hidden Agenda of Cartography in Early Modern Europe." Paper read at the XIIth International Conference on the History of Cartography, Paris, September 1987. Revised for publication in *Imago Mundi* 40 (1988): 57–76.

Harley, J. B., and David Woodward, eds. *Cartography in Prehistoric, Ancient, and Medieval Europe and the Mediterranean.* Vol. 1 of *The History of Cartography.* Chicago: University of Chicago Press, 1987.

———, eds. *Cartography in the Traditional East and Southeast Asian Societies.* Vol. 2, bk. 2 of *The History of Cartography.* Chicago: University of Chicago Press, 1994.

———, eds. *Cartography in the Traditional Islamic and South Asian Societies.* Vol. 2, bk. 1 of *The History of Cartography.* Chicago: University of Chicago Press, 1992.

Harootunian, Harry. "Late Tokugawa Culture and Thought." In *The Cambridge History of Japan,* vol. 5: *The Nineteenth Century,* ed. Marius B. Jansen et al., 168–258.

———. *Things Seen and Unseen: Discourse and Ideology in Tokugawa Nativism.* Chicago: University of Chicago Press, 1988.

———. *Toward Restoration: The Growth of Political Consciousness in Tokugawa Japan.* Berkeley: University of California Press, 1970.

Harvey, P. D. A., and R. A. Skelton. *Local Maps and Plans from Medieval England.* Oxford: Clarendon Press, 1986.

Hasegawa, Koji. "Road Atlases in Early Modern Japan and Britain." In *Geographical Studies and Japan,* ed. John Sargent and Richard Wilshire, 15–24.

Hashimoto Hiroshi, ed. *(Kaitei zōho) Daibukan.* 3 vols. Tokyo: Meichō Kankōkai, 1966.

Hastings, Adrian. *The Construction of Nationhood: Ethnicity, Religion, and Nationalism.* Cambridge: Cambridge University Press, 1997.

Hauser, William B. "Osaka: A Commercial City in Tokugawa Japan." *Urbanism Past and Present* 5 (Winter 1977–78): 23–36.

———. *Economic Institutional Change in Tokugawa Japan: Osaka and the Kinai Cotton Trade.* New York: Cambridge University Press, 1974.

Havens, Thomas R. H. *Farm and Nation in Modern Japan.* Princeton, N.J.: Princeton University Press, 1974.

Henny, Sue, and Jean-Pierre Lehmann. *Themes and Theories in Modern Japanese History: Essays in Memory of Richard Storry.* Atlantic Highlands, N.J.: Athlone Press, 1988.

Henshū chishi biyō tenseki kaidai. In part 11, vols. 1–6 of *Dai Nihon kinsei shiryō,* ed. Tōkyō Daigaku Shiryō Hensanjo.

Hibbett, Howard. *The Chrysanthemum and the Fish: Japanese Humor since the Age of the Shoguns.* Tokyo: Kodansha International, 2002.

————. *The Floating World in Japanese Fiction*. New York: Oxford University Press, 1959.

Hirakawa Sukehiro. "Japan's Turn to the West." In *The Cambridge History of Japan*, vol. 5: *The Nineteenth Century*, ed. Marius B. Jansen et al., 432–98.

Hisatake Tetsunari and Hasegawa Kōji, eds. *(Kaitei zōho) Chizu to bunka.* Tokyo: Chijin Shobō, 1993.

Hitomi Hitsudai [Hirano Hitsudai]. *Honchō shokkan.* Edited by Shimada Isao. 5 vols. Tokyo: Heibonsha, 1976–81.

Hobsbawm, Eric. *Nations and Nationalism since 1700: Programme, Myth, Reality.* New York: Cambridge University Press, 1992.

Honchō bukei tōkan. In vol. 1 of *(Kaitei zōho) Daibukan,* ed. Hashimoto Hiroshi, 231–76.

Horiuchi Hiroyasu. "Izumi no kuni Hineno-mura ezu." In *Ebiki shōen ezu,* ed. Shōen Ezu Kenkyūkai, 55–62.

Howell, David L. "Ainu Ethnicity and the Boundaries of the Early Modern Japanese State." *Past and Present* 142 (1994): 69–93.

————. "Territoriality and Collective Identity in Tokugawa Japan." *Daedalus* 127, no. 3 (Summer 1998): 105–32.

Hur, Nam-Lin. *Prayer and Play in Late Tokugawa Japan: Asakusa Sensōji and Edo Society.* Cambridge Mass.: Harvard University Asia Center, 2000.

Igarashi Tsutomu. "Mura ezu ni miru kinsei sonraku no seikatsu sekai." In vol. 2. of *Ezu no kosumorojī,* ed. Katsuragawa Ezu Kenkyūkai, 167–83.

Ihara Saikaku. *The Great Mirror of Male Love.* Translated by Paul Gordon Schalow. Stanford, Calif.: Stanford University Press, 1990.

————. *The Japanese Family Storehouse, or, The Millionaire's Gospel Modernised. Nippon eitai-gura, or Daifuku shin chōja kyō (1688).* Translated and edited by G. W. Sargent. Cambridge: Cambridge University Press, 1959.

————. *The Life of an Amorous Woman and Other Writings.* Edited and translated by Ivan Morris. New York: New Directions, 1963.

————. *Nihon eitaigura.* Annot. Noma Kōshin. In *Saikakushū ge,* vol. 48 of *Nihon koten bungagu taikei,* ed. Asō Isoji et al., 29–189.

————. *Saikakushū jō, ge.* Vols. 47–48 of *Nihon koten bungaku taikei,* ed. Asō Isoji et al.. Tokyo: Iwanami Shoten, 1957–60.

————. *Tales of Samurai Honor: Buke giri monogatari.* Translated by Caryl Ann Callahan. Tokyo: *Monumenta Nipponica,* Sophia University, 1981.

Iida Ryūichi and Tawara Motoaki. *Edozu no rekishi.* 2 vols. Tokyo: Tsukiji Shokan, 1988.

Ikegami, Eiko. *The Taming of the Samurai: Honorific Individualism and the Making of Modern Japan.* Cambridge, Mass.: Harvard University Press, 1995.

Imatani Akira. *Muromachi bakufu kaitai katei no kenkyū.* Tokyo: Iwanami Shoten, 1985.

————. "Shugo ryōgoku seika ni okeru kokugun shihai ni tsuite." In *Muromachi bakufu kaitai katei no kenkyū,* 225–59.

Imatani Akira and Takahashi Yasuo, eds. *Muromachi bakufu monjo shūsei, bugyōnin hōsho-hen.* 2 vols. Kyoto: Shibunkaku Shuppan, 1986.

Irimoto Masuo. *Tokugawa sandai to bakufu seiritsu.* Tokyo: Shinjinbutsu Ōraisha, 2000.

Irokawa Daikichi. *The Culture of the Meiji Period.* Translation edited by Marius B. Jansen. Princeton, N.J.: Princeton University Press, 1985.

Ishii Ryōsuke, ed. *Edo bakufu hatamoto jinmei jiten.* 4 vols. Tokyo: Hara Shobō, 1989.

———, ed. *Edo bakufu shohan jinmei sōkan.* 2 vols. Tokyo: Kashiwa Shobō, 1983–85.

———, ed. *Edo machikata no seido.* Tokyo: Jinbutsu Ōraisha, 1968.

———, ed. *Hennen Edo bukan.* 9 vols. Tokyo: Kashiwa Shobō, 1981.

Ishikawa Matsutarō. *Ōraimono no seiritsu to tenkai.* Tokyo: Yūshōdō Shuppan, 1988.

———, ed. *Ōraimono kaidai jiten.* 2 vols. Tokyo: Ōzorasha, 2001.

———, ed. *Ōraimono taikei.* 100 vols. Tokyo: Ōzorasha, 1992–94.

Ishikawa Ryūsen. *Bundo Edo ōezu.* Edo: Sudō Gonbei, 1710. East Asian Library, University of California, Berkeley.

———. *Nihon kaisan chōrikuzu.* Edo: Sagamiya Tahei, 1694. East Asian Library, University of California, Berkeley.

———. *Nihon kaisan chōrikuzu.* Reproduced as pl. 31 in vol. 1 of *Nihon kochizu taisei,* ed. Unno Kazutaka, Oda Takao, and Muroga Nobuo.

Ittō bukan. In vol. 1 of *(Kaitei zōho) Daibukan,* ed. Hashimoto Hiroshi, 364–425.

Iwahana Michiaki. "Gyōkizu, saiko no Nihonzu." In *(Kaitei zōho) Chizu to bunka,* ed. Hisatake Tetsunari and Hasegawa Kōji, 64–67.

Iwao Seiichi, ed. *Kyōto oyakusho-muki taigai oboegaki.* 2 vols. Osaka: Seibundō, 1973.

Jansen, Marius B. *China in the Tokugawa World.* Cambridge, Mass.: Harvard University Press, 1992.

Jansen, Marius B., John Whitney Hall, Madoka Kanai, and Denis Twitchett, eds. *The Nineteenth Century.* Vol. 5 of *The Cambridge History of Japan.* New York: Cambridge University Press, 1989.

Jinnai Hidenobu. *Tokyo, A Spatial Anthropology.* Translated by Kimiko Nishimura. Berkeley: University of California Press, 1995.

Jinrin kinmōzui. Edited by Asakura Haruhiko. Tokyo: Heibonsha, 1990.

———. Facsimile in *Kaseigaku bunken shūsei zokuhen, Edoki IX,* ed. Tanaka Chitako and Tanaka Motoo. Tokyo: Watanabe Shoten, 1969.

Jones, Sumie, ed. *Imaging/Reading Eros: Proceedings for the Conference, Sexuality and Edo Culture, 1750–1850.* Bloomington: East Asian Studies Center, Indiana University, 1996.

Joyō kinmōzui. Facsimile in *Kaseigaku bunken shūsei zokuhen, Edoki VIII,* ed. Tanaka Chitako and Tanaka Motoo. Tokyo: Watanabe Shoten, 1969.

Kabuki Hyōbanki Kenkyūkai, ed. *Kabuki hyōbanki shūsei.* 10 vols. Tokyo: Iwanami Shoten, 1972–79.

Kaibara Ekiken. *Ekiken zenshū.* Edited by Ekiken-kai. 8 vols. Tokyo: Ekiken Zenshū Kankōbu, 1881.

———. *Keijō shōran.* 2 fascicles. Kyoto: Ogawa Tazaemon, 1718. East Asian Library, University of California, Berkeley.

———. *Keijō shōran.* In vol. 2 of *Kyōto sōsho,* ed. Kyōto Sōsho Kankōkai, 1–39.

———. *Yamato honzō.* In vol. 6 of *Ekiken zenshū,* ed. Ekiken-kai.

Kaigo Tokiomi, ed. *Nihon kyōkasho taikei: Kindai-hen.* 27 vols. Tokyo: Kōdansha, 1961–67.

Kamens, Edward. *Utamakura, Allusion, and Intertextuality in Traditional Japanese Poetry.* New Haven, Conn.: Yale University Press, 1997.

Kanginshū. In *Shintei chūsei kayōshū,* ed. Asano Kenji. Tokyo: Asahi Shinbunsha, 1973.

Kansei bukan. 4 fascicles. Edo: Suwaraya Mobei, 1789.

Katagiri Yōichi, ed. *Utamakura utakotoba jiten.* Tokyo: Kasama Shoin, 1999.

Kataoka Osamu, ed. *Ōtani daigaku-bon setsuyōshū (Kenkyū narabini sōgō sakuin).* Tokyo: Benseisha, 1982.

Kato Takashi. "Governing Edo." In *Edo and Paris: Urban Life and the State in the Early Modern Era,* ed. James L. McClain, John M. Merriman, and Ugawa Kaoru, 41–67.

Katsuragawa Ezu Kenkyūkai, ed. *Ezu no kosumoroji.* 2 vols. Tokyo: Chijin Shobō, 1989.

Kawamura Hirotada. *Edo bakufusen kuniezu no kenkyū.* Tokyo: Kokon Shoin, 1989.

Kawase Kazuma, ed. *(Zōho) Kokatsujiban no kenkyū.* 2 vols. Tokyo: Antiquarian Booksellers Association of Japan, 1967.

Keene, Donald. "Fujimoto Kizan and *The Great Mirror of Love.*" In *Landscapes and Portraits: Appreciations of Japanese Culture,* 242–49.

———. *Landscapes and Portraits: Appreciations of Japanese Culture.* Tokyo: Kodansha International, 1971.

———. *World within Walls: Japanese Literature of the Pre-Modern Era, 1600–1867.* New York: Holt, Rinehart & Winston, 1976.

Kelly, William W. "Incendiary Actions: Fires and Firefighting in the Shogun's Capital and the People's City." In *Edo and Paris: Urban Life and the State in the Early Modern Era,* ed. James L. McClain, John M. Merriman, and Ugawa Kaoru, 310–31.

Kikumoto Gahō, comp. *Kokka man'yōki.* 21 fascicles. Naniwa: Kariganeya Shōbei, 1697. East Asian Library, University of California, Berkeley.

———, comp. *Kokka man'yōki.* Facsimile in vols. 1–4 of *Kohan chishi sōsho,* ed. Asakura Haruhiko.

Kinsei Bungaku Shoshi Kenkyūkai, ed. *Kinsei bungaku shiryō ruijū: Kanazōshi-hen.* 38 vols. Tokyo: Benseisha, 1972–79.

————, ed. *Kinsei bungaku shiryō ruijū: Kohan chishi-hen.* 22 vols. Tokyo: Benseisha, 1975–81.

————, ed. *Kinsei bungaku shiryō ruijū: Sankō bunken-hen.* 18 vols. Tokyo: Benseisha, 1975–81.

Kōbe Shiritsu Hakubutsukan, ed. *Kanzōhin mokuroku, Chizu no bu.* 6 vols. Kobe: Kōbe Shiritsu Hakubutsukan, 1984–89.

Kodama Kōta, ed. *Shiryō ni yoru Nihon no ayumi: Kinsei-hen.* Tokyo: Yoshikawa Kōbunkan, 1969.

Kodama Kōta et al., eds. *Kinseishi no handobukku.* Tokyo: Kintō Shuppansha, 1972.

Kodansha Encyclopedia of Japan. 9 vols. Tokyo: Kodansha International, 1983.

Kōeki shojaku mokuroku. In vol. 1 of *(Edo jidai) Shorin shuppan shoseki mokuroku shūsei,* ed. Shidō Bunko, 223–317.

Kōeki shojaku mokuroku taizen. 5 fascicles. Kyoto: Yao Ichibei, 1692. East Asian Library, University of California, Berkeley.

Kokuritsu Rekishi Minzoku Hakubutsukan, ed. *Shōen ezu to sono sekai.* Tokyo: Kokuritsu Rekishi Minzoku Hakubutsukan, 1993.

Kokushi Daijiten Henshū Iinkai, ed. *Kokushi daijiten.* 15 vols. Tokyo: Yoshikawa Kōbunkan, 1979–97.

Kokusho Kankōkai, ed. *(Zoku zoku) Gunsho ruijū.* 16 vols. Tokyo: Kokusho Kankōkai. 1906–9.

————, ed. *Kinsei bungei sōsho.* 12 vols. 1910–12. Reprint, Tokyo: Kokusho Kankōkai, 1976.

Kokusho sōmokuroku. 8 vols. Tokyo: Iwanami Shoten, 1989.

Kornicki, Peter. *The Book in Japan: A Cultural History from the Beginnings to the Nineteenth Century.* Boston: Brill, 1998.

————. "Literacy Revisited: Some Reflections on Richard Rubinger's Findings." *Monumenta Nipponica* 56, no. 3 (Autumn 2001): 381–94.

————. "Obiya Ihei: A Japanese Provincial Publisher." *British Library Journal* 11 (1985): 131–42.

Koten no Jiten Hensan Iinkai, ed. *Koten no jiten: Seizui o yomu, Nihon-ban.* 15 vols. Tokyo: Kawabe Shobō Shinsha, 1986.

Koyama Yasunori. "Shōen sonraku no kaihatsu to keikan." In *Ezu ni miru shōen no sekai,* ed. Koyama Yasunori and Satō Kazuhiko, 85–104.

Koyama Yasunori and Satō Kazuhiko, eds. *Ezu ni miru shōen no sekai.* Tokyo: Tōkyō Daigaku Shuppankai, 1987.

Kuroda Hideo. "Edo bakufu kuniezu, gōchō kanken." *Rekishi chiri* 93, no. 2 (1977).

————. "Gyōkishiki 'Nihonzu' to wa nanika?" In *Chizu to ezu no seiji bunkashi,* ed. Kuroda Hideo, Mary Elizabeth Berry, and Sugimoto Fumiko, 3–77.

————. "Hidetada no godai hajime to Genna kuniezu." MS. September, 1996.

————. "Kan'ei Edo bakufu kuniezu shōko." *Shikan* 107 (October 1982): 49–62.

————. "Kuniezu ni tsuite no taiwa." *Rekishi hyōron* 433 (May 1986): 27–39.

Kuroda Hideo, Mary Elizabeth Berry, and Sugimoto Fumiko, eds. *Chizu to ezu no seiji bunkashi*. Tokyo: Tōkyō Daigaku Shuppankai, 2001.

Kurokawa Dōyū. *Geibi kokugun-shi*. In ser. 1, vol. 9 of *(Zoku zoku) Gunsho ruijū*, ed. Kokusho Kankōkai, 327–79.

———. *Yōshū fushi*. In vol. 10 of *(Shinshū) Kyōto sōsho*, ed. Shinshū Kyōto Sōsho Kankōkai.

Kusaka Hiroshi, comp. *Hōkō ibun*. Tokyo: Hakubunkan, 1914.

Kyō habutae. In vol. 2 of *(Shinshū) Kyōto sōsho*, ed. Shinshū Kyōto Sōsho Kankōkai, 1–237.

Kyō habutae oridome. In vol. 2 of *(Shinshū) Kyōto sōsho*, ed. Shinshū Kyōto Sōsho Kankōkai, 313–539.

Kyō habutae taizen. 8 fascicles. Kyoto: Hakushōdō Mukadeya Jirōbei, 1768. East Asian Library, University of California, Berkeley.

Kyō suzume ato-oi. In vol. 1 of *(Shinshū) Kyōto sōsho*, ed. Shinshū Kyōto Sōsho Kankōkai, 271–386.

Kyōto kaimono hitori annai. 1 fascicle. Edo: Yamashiroya Sahei, 1831.

Kyōto Kokuritsu Hakubutsukan. *Koezu, tokubetsu tenrankai zuroku*. Kyoto: Kyōto Kokuritsu Hakubutsukan, 1978.

Kyōto Sōsho Kankōkai, ed. *Kyōto sōsho*. 15 vols. Kyoto: Kyōto Sōsho Kankōkai, 1914–17.

Kyōto-shi, ed. *Kyōto no rekishi*. 10 vols. Tokyo: Gakugei Shorin, 1968–76.

LaMarre, Thomas. *Uncovering Heian Japan: An Archeology of Sensation and Inscription*. Durham, N.C.: Duke University Press, 2000.

Leupp, Gary. *Servants, Shophands, and Laborers in the Cities of Tokugawa Japan*. Princeton, N.J.: Princeton University Press, 1992.

Leutner, Robert W. *Shikitei Sanba and the Comic Tradition in Edo Fiction*. Cambridge, Mass.: Council on East Asian Studies, Harvard University, 1985.

Lewis, Michael. *Rioters and Citizens: Mass Protest in Imperial Japan*. Berkeley: University of California Press, 1990.

Lu, David John. *Sources of Japanese History*. 2 vols. New York: McGraw-Hill, 1974.

Map of the World: Peters Projection. © Akademische Verlagsanstaet. English version by Oxford Cartographers, Oxford, UK; produced with the support of the United Nations Development Programme through Friendship Press, N.Y., n.d.

Marti, Jeff. "Intellectual and Moral Foundations of Empirical Agronomy in Eighteenth-Century Japan." In *Select Papers from the Center for Far Eastern Studies 1 and 2*. Chicago: University of Chicago, 1977–78.

———, trans. "Introduction" to *Nōgyō zensho*. In *Select Papers from the Center for Far Eastern Studies 9*. Chicago: University of Chicago, 1994.

Matsue Shigeyori. *Kefukigusa*. Edited by Takeuchi Waka. Tokyo: Iwanami Shoten, 1972.

McClain, James L. "Edobashi: Power, Space, and Popular Culture in Edo." In *Edo and Paris: Urban Life and the State in the Early Modern Era*, ed. James L. McClain, John M. Merriman, and Ugawa Kaoru, 105–31.

―――. *Kanazawa: A Seventeenth-Century Japanese Castle Town.* New Haven, Conn.: Yale University Press, 1982.

McClain, James L., John M. Merriman, and Ugawa Kaoru, eds. *Edo and Paris: Urban Life and the State in the Early Modern Era.* Ithaca, N.Y.: Cornell University Press, 1994.

McClain, James L., and Wakita Osamu, eds. *Osaka: The Merchants' Capital of Early Modern Japan.* Ithaca, N.Y.: Cornell University Press, 1999.

McEwan, J. R. *The Political Writings of Ogyū Sorai.* Cambridge: Cambridge University Press, 1962.

McMullen, Ian James. *Idealism, Protest, and the Tale of Genji: The Confucianism of Kumazawa Banzan.* Oxford: Clarendon Press, 1999.

Mikawa Hiroshi. *Meiji ishin to nashonarizumu: Bakumatsu no gaikō to seiji hendō.* Tokyo: Yamakawa Shuppansha, 1997.

Miki Seiichirō. "Chōsen eki ni okeru gun'yaku taikei ni tsuite." *Shigaku zasshi* 75, no. 2 (February 1966): 129–54.

Miller, Richard J. *Japan's First Bureaucracy: A Study of Eighth-Century Government.* Ithaca, N.Y.: Cornell University East Asian Papers, 1979.

Miyamoto Mataji. *Ōsaka.* Tokyo: Shibundō, 1957.

Miyazaki Yasusada. *Nōgyō zensho.* In vols. 12–13 of *Nihon nōsho zenshū,* ed. Yamada Tatsuo and Iiura Toku.

Mizuta Yoshikazu. "Kii no kuni Inoue-honshō ezu." In *Ebiki shōen ezu,* ed. Shōen Ezu Kenkyūkai, 102–9.

Monmonier, Mark. *How to Lie with Maps.* Chicago: University of Chicago Press, 1991.

Mori Fusae. *Bunken Edo ōezu.* Edo: Suwaraya Mohei, 1858.

Mori Senzō and Kitagawa Hirokuni, eds. *Minkan fūzoku nenjū gyōji.* In vols. 11–12 of *(Zoku) Nihon zuihitsu taisei,* ed. Kokusho Kankōkai. Tokyo: Yoshikawa Kōbunkan, 1983.

Morimoto Shigeru. *(Kochū) Utamakura taikan.* Kyoto: Daigakudō Shoten, 1979.

Morinaga Taneo. *Nagasaki bugyōsho kiroku: Oshioki ukagaishū.* 2 vols. Nagasaki: Hankachō Kankōkai, 1962.

―――, ed. *Nagasaki daikan kirokushū.* 3 vols. Nagasaki: Hankachō Kankōkai, 1963.

Morris-Suzuki, Tessa. "Creating the Frontier: Border, Identity, and History in Japan's Far North." *East Asian History* 7 (1994): 1–24.

―――. *A History of Japanese Economic Thought.* New York: Routledge, 1989.

Munemasa Isoo. *Kinsei Kyōto shuppan bunka no kenkyū.* Kyoto: Dōmeisha Shuppan, 1982.

Naitō, Akira, and Kazuo Hozumi. *Edo, the City That Became Tokyo: An Illustrated History.* Translated and edited by H. Mack Horton. Tokyo: Kodansha International, 2003.

Najita, Tetsuo. "History and Nature in Eighteenth-Century Tokugawa Thought."

In *The Cambridge History of Japan,* vol. 4: *Early Modern Japan,* ed. John Whitney Hall, 596–659.

———. "Ōshio Heihachirō (1793–1837)." In *Personality in Japanese History,* ed. Albert M. Craig and Donald H. Shively, 155–79. Berkeley: University of California Press, 1970.

———. *Visions of Virtue in Tokugawa Japan, The Kaitokudō Merchant Academy of Osaka.* Chicago: University of Chicago Press, 1987.

Najita, Tetsuo, and Irwin Scheiner, eds. *Japanese Thought in the Tokugawa Period: Methods and Metaphors.* Chicago: University of Chicago Press, 1979.

Nakada Norio and Kobayashi Shōjirō. *Gōrui setsuyōshū (Kenkyū narabini sakuin).* Tokyo: Benseisha, 1979.

Nakagawa Kiun. *Kyō warabe.* 6 fascicles. Kyoto: Hiranoya Sahei, 1658. East Asian Library, University of California, Berkeley.

———. *Kyō warabe.* In vol. 1 of *(Shinshū) Kyōto sōsho,* ed. Shinshū Kyōtō Sōsho Kankōkai, 1–88.

Nakai, Kate Wildman. *Shogunal Politics: Arai Hakuseki and the Premises of Tokugawa Rule.* Cambridge, Mass.: Council on East Asian Studies, Harvard University, 1988.

———. "Tokugawa Confucian Historiography: The Hayashi, Early Mito School, and Arai Hakuseki." In *Confucianism in Tokugawa Culture,* ed. Peter Nosco, 27–61.

Nakai Nobuhiko. "Commercial Change and Urban Growth in Early Modern Japan." In *The Cambridge History of Japan,* vol. 4: *Early Modern Japan,* ed. John Whitney Hall, 519–95.

Nakamura Tekisai. *Kinmōzui.* Facsimile in vol. 4 of *Kinsei bungaku shiryō ruijū: Sankō bunken-hen,* ed. Kinsei Bungaku Shoshi Kenkyūkai.

Nakano Mitsutoshi. *Edo meibutsu hyōbanki annai.* Tokyo: Iwanami Shoten, 1985.

———, ed. *Edo meibutsu hyōbanki shūsei.* Tokyo: Iwanami Shoten, 1987.

Naniwa kagami. In vol. 12 of *Naniwa sōsho,* ed. Funakoshi Masaichirō, 187–342.

Nietzsche, Friedrich. "On the Uses and Disadvantages of History for Life." Translated by R. J. Hollindale. In *Untimely Meditations,* ed. Daniel Breazeale. Cambridge: Cambridge University Press, 1997.

Nihon ōrai. In *Ōrai-hen,* vol. 9 of *Nihon kyōkasho taikei: Kindai-hen,* ed. Kaigo Tokiomi.

Nishikawa Jōken. *Chōnin bukuro.* In vol. 4 of *Nihon keizai taiten,* ed. Takimoto Seiichi, 387–490.

———. *Hyakusho bukuro.* In vol. 4 of *Nihon keizai taiten,* ed. Takimoto Seiichi, 493–533.

Nishioka Toranosuke (with additions by Takeuchi Rizō). *Nihon shōen ezu shūsei.* 2 vols. Tokyo: Tōkyōdō Shuppan, 1976–77.

Nishiyama Matsunosuke. *Edo Culture: Daily Life and Diversions in Urban Japan.* Translated and edited by Gerald Groemer. Honolulu: University of Hawai'i Press, 1997.

Nosco, Peter. *Confucianism in Tokugawa Culture.* Princeton, N.J.: Princeton University Press, 1984.

Ochikochi Dōin and Hishikawa Moronobu. *Tōkaidō bunken ezu.* Facsimile in vol. 12 of *Kohan chishi sōsho,* ed. Asakura Haruhiko.

————. *Tōkaidō bunken ezu,* ed. Kohan Edozu Shūsei Kankōkai. 2 vols. Tokyo: Kohan Edozu Shūsei Kankōkai, 1970.

Oka Masahiko, Kodama Fumiko, Tozawa Ikuko, and Ishimatsu Hisayuki, comps. *Edo Printed Books at Berkeley, Formerly of the Mitsui Library in the Collection of the University of California at Berkeley.* Tokyo: Yumani Shobō, 1990.

Okada Takehiko. "Practical Learning in the Chu Hsi School: Yamazaki Ansai and Kaibara Ekken." In *Principle and Practicality: Essays in Neo-Confucianism and Practical Learning,* ed. Wm. Theodore de Bary and Irene Bloom, 231–305. New York: Columbia University Press, 1979.

Omura Yūko. "Juraku gyōkōki." From *Tenshōki,* in *Taikō shiryōshū,* ed. Kuwata Tadachika, 101–39. Tokyo: Shinjinbutsu Ōraisha, 1971.

Ono Susumu, ed. *Kinsei shoki yūjo hyōbankishū.* 2 vols. Tokyo: Koten Bunko, 1965.

Ooms, Herman. *Tokugawa Ideology: Early Constructs, 1570–1680.* Princeton, N.J.: Princeton University Press, 1985.

————. *Tokugawa Village Practice: Class, Status, Power, Law.* Berkeley: University of California Press, 1996.

Oze Hoan. "Toyotomi daimyōjin saireiki." In. ser. 3, vol. 63 of *Zoku gunsho ruijū,* ed. Hanawa Hokiichi, 223–31. 1924. Reprint, Tokyo: Zoku Gunsho Ruijū Kanseikai, 1980.

Palston, Rolland G., ed. *Social Cartography: Mapping Ways of Seeing Social and Educational Change.* New York: Garland Pub., 1996.

Passin, Herbert. *Society and Education in Japan.* New York: Teachers College Press, 1965.

Pastreich, Emanuel. "Grappling with Chinese Writing as a Material Language." *Harvard Journal of Asiatic Studies* 61, no. 1 (June 2001): 119–70.

Pollack, David. "Marketing Desire: Advertising and Sexuality in Edo Literature, Drama, and Art." In *Imaging/Reading Eros: Proceedings for the Conference, Sexuality and Edo Culture, 1750–1850,* ed. Sumie Jones, 47–62. Bloomington: East Asian Studies Center, Indiana University, 1996.

Pyle, Kenneth. *The Making of Modern Japan.* 1978. Lexington, Mass.: D.C. Heath, 1996.

Ramseyer, J. Mark. "Thrift and Diligence: House Codes of Tokugawa Merchant Families." *Monumenta Nipponica* 34, no. 2 (Summer 1979): 209–30.

Ravina, Mark. *Land and Lordship in Early Modern Japan.* Stanford, Calif.: Stanford University Press, 1999.

Roberts, Luke S. *Mercantilism in a Japanese Domain: The Merchant Origins of Economic Nationalism in Eighteenth-Century Tosa.* Cambridge: Cambridge University Press, 1998.

Robinson, Arthur S., and Barbara B. Petchenik. *The Nature of Maps.* Chicago: University of Chicago Press, 1976.

Rogers, Lawrence. "She Loves Me, She Loves Me Not: *Shinjū* and *Shikidō ōkagami.*" *Monumenta Nipponica* 49, no. 1 (Spring 1994): 31–60.

Rozman, Gilbert. "Edo's Importance in the Changing Tokugawa Society." *Journal of Japanese Studies* 1, no. 1 (Autumn 1974): 91–112.

———. *Urban Networks in Ch'ing China and Tokugawa Japan.* Princeton, N.J.: Princeton University Press, 1974.

Rubinger, Richard. *Private Academies of Tokugawa Japan.* Princeton, N.J.: Princeton University Press, 1982.

———. "Who Can't Read and Write? Illiteracy in Meiji Japan." *Monumenta Nipponica* 55, no. 2 (Summer 2000): 163–98.

Sakai kagami. Facsimile in vol. 13 of *Kohan chishi sōsho,* ed. Kohan Chishi Kenkyūkai.

Samuels, Richard J. *"Rich Nation, Strong Army": National Security and the Technological Transformation of Japan.* Ithaca, N.Y.: Cornell University Press, 1994.

Sansom, George B. "Early Japanese Law and Administration." In *Transactions of the Asiatic Society of Japan* 9, 2d ser. (1932): 67–109, and 11, 2d ser. (1934): 117–49.

Sargent, John, and Richard Wilshire, eds. *Geographical Studies and Japan.* Sandgate, Folkestone, Kent: Japan Library, 1993.

Sasaki Junko. "Toshokan to chizu.*" Libellus* 7 (December 1992): 23–27.

Sasama Yoshihiko. *Edo bakufu yakushoku shūsei.* Tokyo: Yūzankaku Shuppan, 1965.

Satō Shin'ichi, Ikeuchi Yoshisuke, and Momose Kesao, eds. *Chūsei hōsei shiryōshū.* 3 vols. Tokyo: Iwanami Shoten, 1957–65.

Scheiner, Irwin. "Benevolent Lords and Honorable Peasants: Rebellion and Peasant Consciousness in Tokugawa Japan." In *Japanese Thought in the Tokugawa Period: Methods and Metaphors,* ed. Tetsuo Najita and Irwin Scheiner, 39–62.

Shidō Bunko, ed. *(Edo jidai) Shorin shuppan shoseki mokuroku shūsei.* 3 vols. Tokyo: Inoue Shobō, 1962–64.

Shinsen Kyōto Sōsho Kankōkai, ed. *(Shinsen) Kyōto sōsho.* 12 vols. Kyoto: Rinsen Shoten, 1985–89.

———, ed. *(Shinshū) Kyōto sōsho.* 23 vols. 1969. Reprint, Kyoto: Rinsen Shoten, 1976.

Shirai Mitsutarō. *(Kaitei zōho) Nihon hakubutsugaku nenpyō.* Tokyo: Okayama Shoten, 1934.

Shively, Donald H. "Popular Culture." In *The Cambridge History of Japan,* vol. 4: *Early Modern Japan,* ed. John Whitney Hall, 706–69.

———. "Sumptuary Regulation and Status in Early Tokugawa Japan." *Harvard Journal of Asiatic Studies* 25 (1964–65): 123–64.

Shively, Donald H., and William H. McCullough, eds. *Heian Japan.* Vol. 2 of *The Cambridge History of Japan.* New York: Cambridge University Press, 1999.

Shōen bukan. In vol. 1 of *(Kaitei zōho) Daibukan,* ed. Hashimoto Hiroshi, 426–92.

Shōen Ezu Kenkyūkai, ed. *Ebiki shōen ezu.* Tokyo: Tōkyōdō Shuppan, 1991.

Shokoku annai tabi suzume. Facsimile in vol. 9 of *Kohan chishi sōsho,* ed. Asakura Haruhiko.

Shokoku fūzoku monjō kotae. In vol. 9 of *Nihon shomin seikatsu shiryō shūsei,* ed. Miyamoto Tsuneichi, Haraguchi Torao, and Higa Shunchō, 453–843.

Shōkyoku Edo kagami. In vol. 1 of *(Kaitei zōho) Daibukan,* ed. Hashimoto Hiroshi, 120–32.

Shōtō bukan. In vol. 1 of *(Kaitei zōho) Daibukan,* ed. Hashimoto Hiroshi, 309–28.

Smith, Anthony D. *Nationalism: Theory, Ideology, History.* Cambridge: Polity Press; Malden, Mass.: Blackwell, 2001.

Smith, Henry D., II. "The Floating World in Its Edo Locale, 1750–1850." In *The Floating World Revisited,* ed. Donald Jenkins, 25–45. Portland, Ore.: Portland Art Museum; Honolulu: University of Hawai'i Press, 1993.

———. "The History of the Book in Edo and Paris." In *Edo and Paris: Urban Life and the State in the Early Modern Era,* ed. James L. McClain, John M. Merriman, and Ugawa Kaoru, 332–52.

———. "Japaneseness and the History of the Book." Review of *The Book in Japan: A Cultural History from the Beginnings to the Nineteenth Century,* by Peter Kornicki. *Monumenta Nipponica* 53, no. 4 (Winter 1998): 499–515.

Smith, Thomas C. *The Agrarian Origins of Modern Japan.* Stanford, Calif.: Stanford University Press, 1959.

———. "The Land Tax in the Tokugawa Period." In id., *Native Sources of Japanese Industrialization, 1750–1920,* 50–70. Reprinted from *Journal of Asian Studies* 18, no. 1 (November 1958).

———. " 'Merit' as Ideology in the Tokugawa Period." In id., *Native Sources of Japanese Industrialization, 1750–1920,* 156–72. Reprinted from *Aspects of Social Change in Modern Japan,* ed. Ronald P. Dore (Princeton, N.J.: Princeton University Press, 1967).

———. *Native Sources of Japanese Industrialization, 1750–1920.* Berkeley: University of California Press, 1988.

Sugimoto Fumiko. "Chiiki no kiroku." In *Chiikishi to wa nani ka?* ed. Hamashita Takeshi and Karashima Noboru, 362–403.

———. "Kuniezu." In *Kinsei 2,* vol. 12 of *Iwanami kōza Nihon tsūshi,* ed. Asao Naohiro, 303–25.

———. "Kuniezu kenkyū no ichi to kadai: Kawamura Hirotada-shi *Kuniezu* ni yosete." *Nihon rekishi* 529 (June 1992): 84–94.

Suzuki Norio. "Meishoki ni miru Edo shūhen jisha e no kanshin to sankei." In *Toshi shūhen no chihōshi,* ed. Chihōshi Kenkyū Kyōgikai, 108–26.

"Symposium on Japanese Nationalism." *Journal of Asian Studies* 31, no. 7 (November 1971).

Tachikawa Yoshihiko. *Kyōtogaku no koten Yōshū fushi.* Tokyo: Heibonsha, 1996.

Takahashi Masaaki, ed. *Shōen ezu no rekishigaku oyobi kaidoku ni kansuru sōgōteki kenkyū.* Shiga: Shiga Daigaku Kyōiku Gakubu, 1985.

Takeuchi Rizō, ed. *Shōen ezu kenkyū.* Tokyo: Tōkyōdō Shuppan, 1982.

———, ed. *Shōen ezu no kisoteki kenkyū.* Tokyo: San'ichi Shobō, 1973.

Takeuchi Rizō, Harada Tomohiko, and Hirayama Toshijirō, eds. *Nihon shomin seikatsu shiryō shūsei.* 31 vols. Tokyo: San'ichi Shobō, 1968–84.

Takimoto Seiichi, ed. *Nihon keizai taiten.* 54 vols. Tokyo: Keimeisha, 1928–30.

Tanaka Sen'ichi. *Nenjū gyōji no kenkyū.* Tokyo: Ōfūsha, 1992.

Tanaka Sen'ichi and Miyata Noboru, eds. *(Sanseidō) Nenjū gyōji jiten.* Tokyo: Sanseidō, 1999.

Teikin ōrai. Edited by Ishikawa Matsutarō. Tokyo: Heibonsha, 1973.

Toba Sadao. *Nihon jōkaku jiten.* Tokyo: Tōkyōdō Shuppan, 1971.

Toby, Ronald P. "Carnival of the Aliens: Korean Embassies in Edo-Period Art and Popular Culture." *Monumenta Nipponica* 41, no. 4 (Winter 1986): 412–56.

———. "Contesting the Centre: International Sources of Japanese Identity." *International History Review* 7, no. 3 (1985): 347–63.

———. "Kinseiki no 'Nihonzu' to 'Nihon' no kyōkai." In *Chizu to ezu no seiji bunkashi,* ed. Kuroda Hideo, Mary Elizabeth Berry, and Sugimoto Fumiko, 79–102.

———. "Rescuing the Nation from History: The State of the State in Early Modern Japan." *Monumenta Nipponica* 56, no. 2 (Summer 2001): 127–237.

Tōkyō Daigaku Shiryō Hensanjo, ed. *Dai Nihon kinsei shiryō.* 13 pts., 121 vols. Tokyo: Tōkyō Daigaku Shuppankai, 1953–2001.

———, ed. *Daisanjūkai tenrankai reppon mokuroku.* Tokyo: Tōkyō Daigaku Shiryō Hensanjo, 1992.

———, ed. *Echigo no kuni kōri ezu.* 3 vols. Tokyo: Tōkyō Daigaku Shuppankai, 1983–87.

———, ed. *Nihon shōen ezu shūei.* 5 vols., 7 bks. Tokyo: Tōkyō Daigaku Shuppankai, 1988–2002.

Tonomura, Hitomi. *Community and Commerce in Late Medieval Japan: The Corporate Villages of Tokuchin-ho.* Stanford, Calif.: Stanford University Press, 1992.

Tonomura, Hitomi, Anne Walthall, and Wakita Haruko, eds. *Women and Class in Japanese History.* Ann Arbor: Center for Japanese Studies, University of Michigan, 1999.

Totman, Conrad. *Early Modern Japan.* Berkeley: University of California Press, 1993.

———. *Politics in the Tokugawa Bakufu.* Cambridge, Mass.: Harvard University Press, 1967.

———. *Tokugawa Ieyasu: Shogun.* South San Francisco: Heian International, 1983.

Tsuji Tatsuya. "Politics in the Eighteenth Century." In *The Cambridge History of Japan,* vol. 4: *Early Modern Japan,* ed. John Whitney Hall, 425–77.

Tsukahira, Toshio. *Feudal Control in Tokugawa Japan: The Sankin Kōtai System.* Cambridge, Mass.: Harvard East Asian Monographs, 1966.

Tsunoda, Ryusaku, Wm. Theodore de Bary, and Donald Keene, comps. *Sources of Japanese Tradition.* 2 vols. New York: Columbia University Press, 1958–64.

Tucker, Mary Evelyn. *Moral and Spiritual Cultivation in Japanese Neo-Confucianism: The Life and Thought of Kaibara Ekken, 1630–1714.* Albany: State University of New York Press, 1989.

Turnbull, David. *Maps Are Territories: Science Is an Atlas.* Geelong, Australia: Deakin University Press, 1989.

Unno, Kazutaka. "Cartography in Japan." In *Cartography in the Traditional East and Southeast Asian Societies,* vol. 2, bk. 2 of *The History of Cartography,* ed. J. B. Harley and David Woodward, 346–477.

———. "Government Cartography in Sixteenth-Century Japan." *Imago Mundi* 43 (1991): 86–91.

Unno Kazutaka, Oda Takao, and Muroga Nobuo, eds. *Nihon kochizu taisei.* 3 vols. Tokyo: Kōdansha, 1972–75.

Ury, Marian. "Chinese Learning and Intellectual Life." In *The Cambridge History of Japan,* vol. 2: *Heian Japan,* ed. Donald H. Shively and William H. McCullough, 341–89.

Vaporis, Constantine. *Breaking Boundaries: Travel and the State in Early Modern Japan.* Cambridge, Mass.: Council on East Asian Studies, Harvard University Press, 1994.

Varley, H. Paul. *Imperial Restoration in Medieval Japan.* New York: Columbia University Press, 1971.

Vlastos, Stephen. "Opposition Movements in Early Meiji, 1868–1885." In *The Cambridge History of Japan,* vol. 5: *The Nineteenth Century,* ed. Marius B. Jansen et al., 367–431.

———. *Peasant Uprisings and Protests in Tokugawa Japan.* Berkeley: University of California Press, 1986.

Wada Mankichi and Asakura Haruhiko. *(Shintei zōho) Kohan chishi kaidai.* Tokyo: Kokusho Kankōkai, 1974.

Wakabayashi, Bob Tadashi. *Anti-Foreign Threat and Western Learning in Early Modern Japan.* Cambridge, Mass.: Council on East Asian Studies, Harvard University, 1986.

Wakita, Osamu. "The *Kokudaka* System: A Device for Unification." *Journal of Japanese Studies* 1, no. 2 (Spring 1975): 297–320.

Walker, Brett L. *The Conquest of Ainu Lands: Ecology and Culture in Japanese Expansion, 1590–1800.* Berkeley: University of California Press, 2001.

Walthall, Anne. "Edo Riots." In *Edo and Paris: Urban Life and the State in the Early Modern Era,* ed. James L. McClain, John M. Merriman, and Ugawa Kaoru, 407–28.

———. *Peasant Uprisings in Japan: A Critical Anthology of Peasant Histories.* Chicago: University of Chicago Press, 1991.

———. *Social Protest and Popular Culture in Eighteenth-Century Japan.* Tucson: University of Arizona Press, 1986.

Watanabe Ichirō. *Tokugawa bakufu daimyō hatamoto yakushoku bukan.* 5 vols. Tokyo: Kashiwa Shobō, 1967.

White, James W. *Ikki: Social Conflict and Political Protest in Early Modern Japan.* Ithaca, N.Y.: Cornell University Press, 1995.

Wigen, Kären. *The Making of a Japanese Periphery, 1760–1920.* Berkeley: University of California Press, 1995.

Wood, Denis. *The Power of Maps.* New York: Guilford Press, 1992.

Woodward, David, and G. Malcolm Lewis, eds. *Cartography in the Traditional African, American, Arctic, Australian, and Pacific Societies.* Vol. 2, bk. 3 of *The History of Cartography.* Chicago: University of Chicago Press, 1998.

Yamada Tatsuo and Iiura Toku. *Nihon nōsho zenshū.* 35 vols. Tokyo: Nō-sangyōson Bunka Kyōkai, 1977.

Yamaga Sokō. *Buke jiki.* Edited by Yamaga Sokō Sensei Zenshū Kankōkai. 3 vols. Tokyo: Nisshō Insatsu, 1921.

Yamamura, Kozo. *A Study of Samurai Income and Entrepreneurship: Quantitative Analyses of Economic and Social Aspects of the Samurai in Tokugawa and Meiji Japan.* Cambridge, Mass.: Harvard University Press, 1974.

Yamori Kazuhiko. *Jōkamachi.* Tokyo: Gakuseisha, 1972.

———. *Toshi puran no kenkyū: hen'yō keiretsu to kūkan kōsei.* Tokyo: Ōmeidō, 1970.

———. *Toshizu no rekishi, Nihon-hen.* Tokyo: Kōdansha, 1974.

Yarōmushi. In vol. 1 of *Kabuki hyōbanki shūsei,* ed. Kabuki Hyōbanki Kenkyūkai, 15–42.

Yokota Fuyuhiko. "Imagining Working Women in Early Modern Japan." In *Women and Class in Japanese History,* ed. Hitomi Tonomura, Anne Walthall, and Wakita Haruko, 153–68.

Yokoyama Toshio. "*Setsuyōshū* and Japanese Civilization." In *Themes and Theories in Modern Japanese History: Essays in Memory of Richard Storry,* ed. Sue Henny and Jean-Pierre Lehmann, 78–98.

Yonemoto, Marcia. *Mapping Early Modern Japan: Space, Place, and Culture in the Tokugawa Period (1603–1868).* Berkeley: University of California Press, 2003.

Yoshida Nobuyuki, ed. *Nihon no kinsei: Toshi no jidai.* Tokyo: Chūō Kōronsha, 1992.

Yoshida Toshihiro. "Shōen ezu no bunryō o megutte." In *Shōen ezu to sono sekai,* ed. Kokuritsu Rekishi Minzoku Hakubutsukan, 105–11.

Yoshiwara hito tabane. In vol. 1 of *Kinsei shoki yūjo hyōbankishū,* ed. Ono Susumu, 465–570.

Yoshiwara Ken'ichirō. *Edo no machi yakunin.* Tokyo: Yoshikawa Kōbunkan, 1980.

Zoku Gunsho Ruijū Kanseikai, ed. *Kan'ei shoka keizuden.* 17 vols. Tokyo: Heibonsha, 1980–97.

INDEX

Page numbers in *italics* indicate figures.

80; panoramic paintings, 22; population growth, 28

Kyoto Brocade (*Kyō habutae;* also called Brocade 1): "Annual Ritual Calendar," 174, 176–77; authorial tone in preface, 144; entries on aristocrats and daimyo, 160; entries on shogunal officeholders, 160; excerpt from preface, 144; "Great Summary of the Trades of This Street and Its Wards" (Kyōgoku Avenue), 156; historical references, 146–53; job categories, 163; mortuary monuments, 147–48; old places, 148; old things, 148; selective listing of emperors, 145; six overlapping cityscapes, 143; street index, 153; topographic categories, 150–51; "Various Masters and Artists," 160–62; "Various Traders and Craftsmen," 162–63; urban membership and ritual life, 176–78. *See also* Rewoven Brocade of Kyoto

Kyoto Brocade Omnibus (*Kyō habutae taizen*), *161*

Kyōto kaimono hitori annai (Self-Guided Tour to Kyoto Shopping), *167*

Kyoto Sparrow (*Kyō suzume*), 153–54

Kyō warabe (Child of Kyoto), *36*

land, unreclaimed or "wild" (*arano*), 71
land registers, provincial (*ōtabumi*), 69
lexicons (*kinmōzui,* "illustrated lexicons for the ignorant"), 136, 196, 256n4
library of public information, 15; accounts of urban life, 140; alternate version of social entanglement, 244–45, 246; attitude of texts, 16–17; authorial motives, 44; city as inventory challenge, 141; classical precedents, 18; classification, 23–24; collective experiences of upheaval, 33–38; comparison of medieval and early modern texts, 26, 257n7; concern with mundane experience, 19–20; concern with timeliness, 19; conflation of cultural literacy with membership in collectivity, 211; conservatism and conformity, 44–45; conventionality, 48–49; conversion of public into a subject of service, 210;

creation of new reading public, 22, 32–33; disruption of convention, 50–51, 52; emergence of, 26–27; factors in emergence of publishing industry, 21–22; guises of history, 235–39; imagined audience, 208; importance of differences, 241–42; imported books, 224; influence of commercial publishing, 20–21; influence of state-making, 44–45; investigative style, 18–19; lexicon of unification, 39–40; limits, 51–53; medieval information texts, 257n7; new notions of "public," 35, 37; personal authentication, 19; public (*kō*) versus private (*shi*), 49–50, 52, 250–51; publication genres, 13–14, 15; repackaging of information, 48; samurai authors, 43–44; scope, 22–23; state-centered orientation, 210; stratification, 207; urban migration, 27–29. *See also* history in information texts; publishing, commercial

Life of an Amorous Woman, 246

linked verse, 198, 214

machibugyō, machi onbugyō (city magistrates), 126, *130*
machikata (city people), 140
Maeda Toshiie, daimyo, 80
manufacture, traditional crafts, 172
manufactures, famous (*meisan*), 157. *See* famous products
map, Angelica College, *62–63, 64–67*
mapmaking: basic challenge of, 60; cartographic communication, 67; classification, 67–68; codification types, 61; comparison with other media, 67; conventions of social geography, 40–41; contribution to creation of a public, 209–10; difference between medieval and early modern mapmaking, 60; findings of cognitive scientists, 55; findings of historians, 55; general definition of a map, 61, 64; iconic code, 61, 64–65, 66; influence on urban directories, 43; linguistic code, 65, 66; Map of Japan, *41;*

settlements, small, 74–75
Sex Music (*Keisei iro jamisen*), 11
Shakyamuni, 176
shi (master) suffix, 168
shi (private), 49–50, 52
Shiba Shinmei festival, 179
Shikidō ōkagami (Great Mirror of Sex),
 18–19, 20, 21, 258n12
Shimabara Rebellion (1637–38), 115, 231
Shimazu house, 80
shinnō gomonzeki (princely abbots), 188
Shinpan Heian-jō narabi ni Rakugai no zu
 (Newly Published Map of the Citadel
 of Heian and Its Surroundings), *102*
Shinran Shōnin, religious leader, 176, 178
Shinroku. *See* Eternal Storehouse of Japan
 (*Nihon eitaigura*)
Shively, Donald Howard, xv
Shōgoin temple, 192
shogunate, Ashikaga, 55, 76; tenures of titleholders, 75–76, 78
shogunate, Kamakura, 69
shogunate, Tokugawa: alternate attendance
 system, 28; early modern revival of
 Gyōki-style image, 98; effect of bureaucratic rosters, 123; Map of Japan
 (*Nihonzu*), 92–95, *93;* and meaning of
 "daimyo," 112–13; mortuary temples
 Kan'eiji and Zōjōji, 116; national maps
 of Keichō period (*Keichō kuniezu*),
 286n46; recreation of image through
 Military Mirrors, 136–37; release of
 national map to commercial publishers, 98, 286n46; restriction of daimyo
 to one headquarters each, 84; role in
 compiling Military Mirrors, 110–11;
 shogun's household administration,
 124; surveying legacies of, 209–10;
 willingness to publicize personnel rosters, 122–23. *See also* state, Tokugawa
Shōichi Kokushi Enni, Zen priest, 188
Shokoku annai tabi suzume (Traveling Sparrow's Guide to the Provinces), 4–5
Shokoku meibutsu kanoko (Dappled Fabric
 of Our Famous Things), 159
Shōmu, Emperor, 148
Shōren'in temple, 190
shrines, 152; Benzaiten, 176; Hie, 179;
 Imagumano, 193; Ima Miya, *177;*

Inari, 190, 191; Ise, 95; Kamigamo,
 190; Kamo, 176, 191; Kanda Myōjin,
 178; Mukō no Myōjin, 193; Nikkō,
 175; Oiso, 213; Shimogamo, 178;
 Wakamiya Hachiman, 176; Yasaka,
 179; Yoshida, 192, 193
Shūgaishō, 25, 257n7, 262n3
Shunchōsai Takehara Nobushige, illustra-
 tor, *164–65, 177, 180–81, 182–83, 186*
Silver Pavilion (Ginkakuji), 148, 192,
 188
Sōchō, linked-verse poet, 148
social contracts. *See* contracts, social
state, Meiji: centralized authority, 233;
 compulsory schooling, 233; context of
 imperialism, 227; dissolution of status
 order, 249; foundation myth, 234;
 Japaneseness, 240–41; notions of collective attachment, 248; rich coun-
 try/strong army (*fukoku kyōhei*),
 227
state, Tokugawa: construction of public
 sphere, 248–50; foreign contact,
 225–26; foreign relations, 223–27;
 foundation myth, 234–35; internal
 consolidation versus external tension,
 227, 241; invisibility of authority,
 229–30; isolation of the ruler, 231–32;
 public as subject of rule, 250; relationship to daimyo confederates, 232–33;
 relationship of ruler and ruled, 230–
 31; remoteness of authority, 229–33,
 241; role in the information library,
 232; significance of status distinctions,
 249; society connected by social commerce, 251. *See also* myths, state foundation; shogunate, Tokugawa
stone of Benkei, 152
Storehouse of Worldly Reckonings, 15,
 257n6
Sugawara no Michizane, minister and
 scholar, 176
Suminokura Ryōi, merchant and civil engineer, 191
Suminokura Sōan, merchant, 30
sumptuary laws, 170–71
surveying, cadastral. *See* cadastral surveying
 and registration
surveying, cartographic. *See* mapmaking

Compositor: Sheridan Books, Inc.
Text: 11/13.5 Adobe Garamond
Display: Adobe Garamond
Map designer: Deborah Reade
Printer and binder: Sheridan Books, Inc.

Printed in the USA
CPSIA information can be obtained
at www.ICGtesting.com
JSHW021339041224
74776JS00010B/35